The Preferential Liberalization of Trade in Services

Comparative Regionalism

Edited by

Pierre Sauvé

Director, External Programs and Academic Partnerships, World Trade Institute, University of Bern, Switzerland

Anirudh Shingal

Senior Research Fellow, World Trade Institute, University of Bern, Switzerland

Edward Elgar

Cheltenham, UK • Northampton, MA, USA

Published by
Edward Elgar Publishing Limited
The Lypiatts
15 Lansdown Road
Cheltenham
Glos GL50 2JA
UK

Edward Elgar Publishing, Inc.
William Pratt House
9 Dewey Court
Northampton
Massachusetts 01060
USA

A catalogue record for this book
is available from the British Library

Library of Congress Control Number: 2013954379

This book is available electronically in the ElgarOnline.com
Law Subject Collection, E-ISBN 978 1 78254 896 6

MIX
Paper from
responsible sources
FSC® C013056

ISBN 978 1 78254 895 9

Typeset by Servis Filmsetting Ltd, Stockport, Cheshire
Printed and bound in Great Britain by T.J. International Ltd, Padstow

Contents

About the editors

Pierre Sauvé is Director of Studies, External Programs and Academic Partnerships at the World Trade Institute, University of Bern, Switzerland, whose faculty he also serves on.

He holds Visiting Professor appointments at the College of Europe in Bruges, Belgium and at the University of Barcelona, whose LLM programme in international economic law and policy (IELPO) he advises.

He was a Visiting Professor at the Institut d'Etudes Politiques (Sciences-Po) in Paris, France in 2003–04 and at the London School of Economics in 2007–08. He served as a senior economist in the Organisation for the Economic Co-operation and Development (OECD) Trade Directorate from 1993 to 2002, a period during which he also taught at the John F. Kennedy School of Government at Harvard University and was appointed Non-resident Senior Fellow at the Brookings Institution in Washington, DC (1998–2000).

Prior to joining the OECD, he served as services negotiator within the Canadian Department of Foreign Affairs and International Trade's Office of North American Free Trade Negotiations (1991–3). He was previously a staff member of the GATT in Geneva, Switzerland (1988–91) as well as the Bank for International Settlements in Basel, Switzerland (1987–8).

Mr Sauvé was educated in economics and international relations at the Université du Québec à Montreal and Carleton University in Canada as well as at Cambridge and Oxford Universities in the United Kingdom. He has advised the governments of a number of OECD and developing countries and served as a consultant to leading regional and multilateral agencies involved in trade, finance and development. He serves on the Editorial Board of the *Journal of International Economic Law* and the *Journal of World Trade* and is a Member of the Review Committee of the United Nations Conference on Trade and Development (UNCTAD)'s Series on International Investment and Development. He served as a member of the Warwick Commission on the Future of the Multilateral Trading System in 2007. He is a member of the Scientifc Committee of the Swiss Network for International Studies and serves on the Advisory Board of the Academic Chairs program of the World Trade Organization.

Anirudh Shingal is a Senior Research Fellow at the WTI, where he serves as co-leader of the NCCR Trade work program on the impact assessment of trade. He is also a member of the faculty of the WTI's flagship Masters of International Law and Economics (MILE) program.

A PhD in Economics from the University of Sussex, Anirudh specializes in International Economics, Econometrics and Development. Anirudh has worked in international trade for close to eight years, including at the WTO and the World Bank and has conducted specific research on trade in services, government procurement, preferential trade agreements, LDC market access, trade defence, trade facilitation, competition policy, trade in agriculture and SPS issues. He has also published in these areas in refereed journals, as well as for the World Bank, the WTO, the European Commission, UNCTAD and the Commonwealth Secretariat. Anirudh is also Research Affiliate at the Centre for the Analysis of Regional Integration at Sussex (CARIS) and has co-authored several reports on the impact of preferential trade agreements on partner and excluded countries.

Anirudh graduated *summa cum laude* on the MILE Program at the WTI and also holds a Master's degree in Economics from the Delhi School of Economics. His undergraduate degree was in Economics (Honors) from St. Stephen's College, Delhi University.

Contributors

A.P.C. Subhashini Abeysinghe, The Ceylon Chamber of Commerce, Colombo, Sri Lanka

Malcolm Bosworth, Visiting Economist, ANU Enterprise, Australia

Rupa Chanda, Indian Institute of Management, Bangalore, India

Aaditya Mattoo, World Bank, Washington, DC, USA

Maryse Robert, Chief of the Office of Trade in the Department of Economic Development, Trade and Tourism, General Secretariat of the Organization of American States (OAS), Washington, DC, USA

Martin Roy, Counsellor, Trade in Services Division, World Trade Organization, Geneva, Switzerland

Sherry Stephenson, Head of Institutional Relations within the Department of International Affairs, General Secretariat of the Organization of American States (OAS), Washington, DC, USA

Imola Streho, Professor of Law at the Institut d'Etudes Politiques (Sciences-Po), Paris, France

Ray Trewin, Visiting Professor, Crawford School, Australia National University (Canberra), Australia

Natasha Ward, Trade in Services Advisor, USAID Southern Africa Trade Hub project in Gaborone, Botswana

Introduction and overview

Pierre Sauvé and Anirudh Shingal

One of the striking features of trade diplomacy over the past two decades has been the seemingly unstoppable march of preferential trade liberalization and rule-making. Such a trend routinely extends to trade in services. Of the 81 preferential trade agreements (PTAs) in force before 2000, 70 (representing 86.4% of the total) featured provisions dealing exclusively with trade in goods. During the ensuing decade, more than a third of PTAs that have been notified to the World Trade Organization (WTO) and remain in force include provisions on services. To date, 118 PTAs covering services have been notified to the WTO. Such a trend signals both the heightened importance of services trade in general and the fact that, since the advent of the General Agreement on Trade in Services (GATS) at the end of the Uruguay Round, services trade forms a central part of modern trade craft.

If all trade agreements can be described as "incomplete contracts", then market opening and rule-making in the services field is undoubtedly the most incomplete of all areas subject to multilateral governance. Indeed, close to two decades after the completion of the Uruguay Round, trade diplomats are still struggling with a complex set of unfinished issues. These include issues as diverse as the development of emergency safeguard provisions for services trade, to disciplines on trade and investment distorting subsidy practices in services markets, the trade-inhibiting effects of disproportionate or unduly burdensome domestic regulation of a non-discriminatory kind, as well as rules governing public procurement in services markets. Despite the rising salience of PTAs and a burgeoning literature devoted to its driving forces and main incarnations, there is surprisingly little literature on the services dimension of the phenomenon.

Rooted in research carried out at the World Trade Institute by several of the world's leading services experts in the context of the NCCR-Trade Regulation project funded by the Swiss National Science Foundation (SNF), this volume addresses a range of novel issues arising from the theory and practice of preferential liberalization and rule-making in services trade. It notably explores the political economy of preferences and of preference erosion in services trade. The two main research questions it addresses are: (i) just how "preferential" is the preferential liberalization of services trade? and (ii) what can be done to multilateralize preferential access and rule-making in services trade? The research on offer documents the nature, modal and sectoral incidence of the trade and investment preferences spawned by PTAs in services based on the most recent WTO data.

The novelty and analytical value-added of this edited volume derives from its focus on the most recent generation of service sector PTAs through the lens of comparative regionalism, exploring the forces which, across different geographical, institutional and developmental settings, have weighed on the advent of trade and investment disciplines in services and shaped the nature of market opening bargains struck under such agreements.

The volume explores to what extent, and in what way, PTAs have helped to fill the multilateral rule-making void in services trade, the degree to which PTAs have served as laboratories in which to experiment with novel rules and negotiating architectures for services and the extent of market opening that such agreements have generated. It does so by exploring meta-trends in services PTAs and in detailing observed advances across regional settings spanning Africa, the Americas, South and South-East Asia. Among the key research questions addressed in this volume's various contributions are the following:

- How can developments in services PTAs inform approaches to market opening and rule-making and help complete the GATS contract?
- How do PTAs in services differ from the GATS?
- Do PTAs in services afford member countries space in which to explore new rule-making configurations and thus complete the "Unfinished Agenda" of GATS?
- How much further than the GATS have PTAs gone (i.e. GATS+ and GATS–X) in both rule-making and market opening terms and what are the key factors that have shaped such advances?
- What has been the trade effect of negotiated services PTAs?
- Do differences in negotiating architectures across PTAs matter and can they inform the WTO's post-Doha architecture?
- What do we know and what can we say about preference erosion in services trade?
- Can PTAs in services be likened to optimal regulatory convergence areas?
- How great are cross-regional differences in services PTAs and what explains the differences observed in market opening and rule-making terms?

SKETCHING THE BROAD LANDSCAPE

Part I of the volume provides a broad-brush portrait of the services landscape through chapters that explore the GATS+ and DDA+ nature of the recently negotiated services accords, consider the policy implications of this recent wave of services preferentialism and use advanced econometric techniques to estimate the trade effects of negotiated services PTAs.

Chapter 1 by Martin Roy presents the expansion of the dataset initially developed in Marchetti and Roy (2009).[1] The data allow an assessment of the extent to which market access commitments undertaken by WTO Members in recent PTAs go beyond those made under the GATS and, more interestingly, the latest offers tabled in the context of the Doha Development Agenda.

While the dataset in Marchetti and Roy (2009) covered 37 Members in 40 PTAs, the one presented in this volume covers 53 Members in a much broader sample of 67 agreements. Roy's dataset does not purport to represent the quality of commitments nor to determine their level of trade restrictiveness. Rather, his chapter's focus is on the extent to which PTA commitments go beyond GATS commitments and services offers in the Doha Development Agenda.

Overall, Roy's dataset highlights the fact that, on average, commitments undertaken in PTAs far outweigh those contained in WTO Members' GATS schedules but also those offered in the current round of negotiations. Such results straddle both Modes 1 (cross-border supply) and 3 (commercial presence), and different levels of development, although, as may be expected, the level of GATS+ commitments varies significantly across Members. The analysis of an additional 16 new Members and 27 new PTAs has provided further evidence of such trends. Indeed, more recent agreements have matched or exceeded levels of commitments achieved by parties in earlier preferential agreements. Recent PTAs have also involved significant GATS+ commitments from a number of WTO Members that had previously not taken part in services PTAs (i.e. Pakistan and 12 CARIFORUM countries).

Figure I.1, reproduced from Chapter 1 in this volume, underscores that services commitments in PTAs far outweigh GATS commitments and offers for both Modes 1 and 3. It also shows that GATS+ commitments in PTAs have, on average, been more important in developing economies,

[1] Marchetti, Juan and Martin Roy (eds.) (2009), *Opening Markets for Trade in Services; Countries and Sectors in Bilateral and WTO Negotiations*, Cambridge: Cambridge University Press.

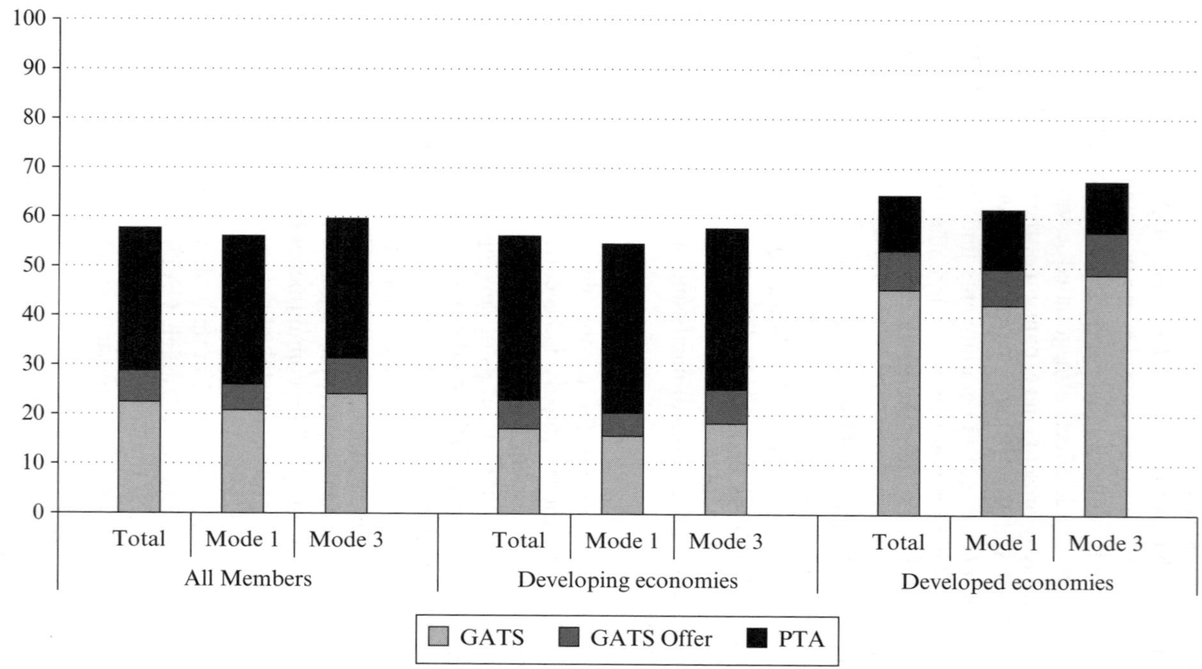

Note: The data reflect each Member's "best" PTA commitment among all the PTAs to which it is a party. The index is brought onto a 0–100 scale, with 100 representing full commitments in all subsectors and relevant modes.

Source: Updated from Marchetti and Roy (2009) on the basis of the expanded dataset.

Figure I.1 Comparing services commitments across members and agreements

which is partly explained by the different levels of GATS commitments undertaken by these two groups of Members. In fact, through their PTA commitments, developing country Members have significantly reduced the gap with the levels of bindings attained by developed country Members. Figure I.1 also reveals that, on average, PTA advances have taken place in similar fashion for both Modes 1 and 3, irrespective of Members' level of development.

Regional differences, which the chapters in Part II of this volume explore and document in considerable detail, are also found to be centrally important. Only a handful of countries in Africa and the Middle East have so far concluded services PTAs. Most agreements involve developed countries and developing countries from Asia as well as Latin America and the Caribbean. Comparing commitments undertaken by governments in Asia and Latin America shows that the latter have, on average, been significantly more ambitious.

Chapter 2 by Mattoo and Sauvé explores the economics of preferences in services and asks whether services trade differs sufficiently from trade in goods so as to require different policy instruments and approaches in the context of preferential liberalization. The chapter discusses whether and how PTAs in services allow for deeper forms of regulatory cooperation and highlights the importance for third countries of multilateral disciplines on PTAs and the criteria suggested by economic theory to minimize adverse effects on non-members.

Chapter 3 by Shingal is one of the first attempts in this literature to empirically explore the extent to which negotiated reciprocity, particularly in PTAs, is trade creating in the services field. The chapter endogenizes the impact of services preferentialism in estimating the trade effect of PTAs and also considers the "anticipation effects" of such agreements by using the OECD's bilateral trade in services data during 1999–2003. The chapter further enriches the literature by distilling the trade effects of PTAs into those emanating from services and "goods only" agreements. In so doing, Shingal confirms the strong complementarities between the two types of trade. The chapter further studies the above relationships disaggregated by the economic status of partner countries (North–North; North–South and South–South) and by the level of reciprocity of commitments.

The early empirical literature on gravity model estimation of bilateral services trade exhibits neither consensus nor conformity to economic theory in estimating the impact of the determinants of such trade. The role of bilateral goods trade in determining bilateral services trade has also not been explored in detail, nor has the separate impact of "goods only" and services accords on bilateral services trade ever been studied. Methodologically, only recent empirical work accounts for the influence of heterogeneity in trading country pairs in determining bilateral services trade, but even this work fails to recognize the endogeneity of agreements in model estimation.

Chapter 3 by Shingal marks an improvement on all the above fronts. His results suggest a trade effect of 15% from having a services accord alone. This effect rises to 32.3% for intra-EU trading partners in the sample data. The total incremental impact of a "goods only" PTA is found to be 7.6% (with services PTAs accounting for one-third of this and "goods only" PTAs for the rest). Both North–North and North–South services agreements are found to generate positive trade effects, suggesting that the associated pattern of trade is both intra- and inter-industry. Moreover, within North–South agreements, and irrespective of the type of agreement, asymmetric accords always exert the largest observed trade effects, and these are always positive. The services trade effect rises to 59.7% once the anticipation effects of services accords are included in the analysis. These results also suggest that the maximum impact of a services accord is felt the farthest in time from actual entry into force. This would appear to imply that services agreements seem to have a significant "announcement effect".

LESSONS FROM COMPARATIVE REGIONALISM

The broad overview of recent developments in services preferentialism suggests that this wave does travel beyond borders. Part II of the book provides a rich series of case studies of services PTAs across the globe, including two regions – Sub-Saharan Africa and South Asia – which have remained relatively under-studied to date.

In Chapter 4, chronicling the treatment of services liberalization in PTAs concluded in the Americas, Robert and Stephenson recall that the Western Hemisphere was the first of the world's regions to embrace preferentialism wholeheartedly. The region has remained at the forefront in developing innovative approaches to the treatment of services trade. The authors note that the region has produced a major alternative to the multilateral liberalization of services trade in the form of the North American Free Trade Agreement (NAFTA) template. A subsequent generation of NAFTA-type agreements has further improved and refined the original template, incorporating key features of the GATS for both cross-border trade and investment in services. The NAFTA template has also been exported in numerous PTAs negotiated between countries of the Americas and extra-regional partners. Chapter 4 by Robert and Stephenson also shows that, although assessing the impact of PTAs remains a complex issue, for those

PTAs with an adequate dataset to merit an examination of trends, services trade has increased more between PTA partners than it has with the rest of the world after the entry into force of the agreements. Finally, Stephenson and Robert note that the increasing number of NAFTA-type agreements in the Americas has also given rise to a movement toward convergence and a rationalization of overlapping substantive trade disciplines and market access opportunities.

Chapter 5 by Streho chronicles the richness of the European journey on services trade, retracing the historical origins and jurisprudence-led evolution of the internal market rules governing services trade among an expanding group of advanced nations and identifying how the experience gained in building the internal market both influenced and paralleled the EU's engagement with the rest of the world in services and notably how the EU experiment helped shape the nascent multilateral body of rules governing services trade in the WTO.

The depth and range of legal instruments and institutions deployed in the EU in pursuit of market integration objectives knows no equivalent. Such uniqueness needs to be borne in mind in pondering whether, how and to what extent lessons from the EU's ongoing experiment at market integration are replicable in other regional settings and policy contexts. In most instances, the EU model is not easily transposable, resting as it does on a degree of pooling of regulatory sovereignty that few regional groupings appear capable of or even aspire to. It also bears noting that EU advances relate in no small measure to the Union's first-mover advantages, with progress rooted in more than 60 years of policy- and rule-making experimentation on the internal front and close to three decades of external experimentation. Such a path has afforded all EU stakeholders – Member States, the European Commission, regulatory agencies, the European Court of Justice (ECJ) as well as private actors, considerable space in which to learn by doing, make mistakes, learn from them and fine-tune an evolving governance regime for services production, trade and investment.

Meanwhile, while its aims have in essence been more modest on the global stage, the EU has nonetheless engaged with the world through all possible negotiating means at its disposal – multilaterally in the WTO-GATS, and preferentially through a series of bilateral, regional, plurilateral and bloc to bloc agreements aimed at affording EU services and service providers wider and progressively freer markets in which to operate, whilst also harnessing the gains to be had from the reciprocal opening of the EU's internal market to efficient third country services and service suppliers.

Chapter 6 by Sauvé and Ward takes stock of the nascent state of play of preferential trade negotiations in services in Africa. It explores the factors that lie behind the general reluctance of African governments to bind service sector policy under international treaties. The chapter chronicles several ongoing initiatives aimed at deepening intra-regional trade and investment among the eight regional economic cooperation areas found on the continent. It also describes external liberalization efforts engaging Africa with the rest of the world in services trade, devoting particular attention to negotiations under way with the European Community (EC) with a view to concluding WTO-compatible Economic Partnership Agreements (EPAs). In so doing, the chapter draws attention to several novel features of the EC-CARIFORUM EPA in the services field and discusses its possible implications for Africa's ongoing processes of integration in services markets at both the intra- and extra-regional levels.

On the whole, the chapter highlights the considerable policy precaution that African governments continue to profess in the field of services trade and investment, preferring instead to experiment with reversible autonomous policy change. The authors question how governments in the region will meaningfully tackle the imperative of economic diversification, support the insertion of African producers into regional and global supply chains in manufacturing, take advantage of a new international division of labour in remotely supplied services, meaningfully improve the transparency and efficiency of domestic and regional regulatory regimes and live up to the lofty aims embedded in the numerous integration schemes under negotiation without a deeper commitment to the progressive liberalization of services trade and investment throughout the continent.

In Chapter 7, devoted to services PTAs in Asia, Chanda analyses the relationship and dynamics between multilateral and preferential trade rules and commitments. She does so using a sample of eight PTAs involving Asian countries. Her chapter examines the evolving universe of rules and negotiating architectures in services and the extent to which PTAs have gone beyond the GATS. The analysis reveals that although countries tend to commit more sectors and subsectors under PTAs than under the GATS, these commitments are not deeper within subsectors or modes and are typically less liberal than existing policies. Where PTAs most improve upon the GATS is in terms of their overall architecture by including additional chapters and annexes which go into considerable detail on a variety of cross-cutting, sector-specific and emerging issues. The analysis suggests that North–North agreements tend to cover some of the more difficult issues, such as government procurement, while North–South agreements have a predominant focus on issues such as the recognition of qualifications which relate to the importance of Mode 4 in North–South services trade. South–South agreements further tend to focus on institutional cooperation, reflecting the need for strengthening capacity and institution building in these countries. However, overall, there is considerable diversity among PTAs. These do not follow a uniform pattern, indicating that the negotiating dynamics vary by partner countries and across PTAs.

In Chapter 8, devoted to the India-Sri Lanka Closer Economic Partnership Agreement (CEPA), Abeysinghe explores how India, an emerging global power in services trade, approaches negotiations in the sector. The India–Sri Lanka CEPA is the first trade agreement negotiated by Sri Lanka to include services. This agreement, together with the South Asian Association for Regional Cooperation (SAARC) Agreement on Trade in Services, will form the basis of future services agreements in South Asia. The chapter analyses the CEPA's architecture and content and the degree to which it goes beyond the GATS in promoting transparency, credibility and the actual liberalization of trade in services. Complementing the chapter by Chanda, the chapter also compares CEPA with other services agreements in the region to identify key features that will determine the future regional trade policy of India and Sri Lanka in services. The chapter suggests that the CEPA has made little progress beyond GATS in terms of its architecture. In liberalization terms, although both India and Sri Lanka have moved beyond GATS, this still largely reflects the status quo and at times even falls significantly short of it, a trend that obtains more broadly throughout the region. The chapter concludes that liberalization of the services sector and the expansion of services trade in South Asia is likely to result more from the "silent" forces of market dynamics in the region as well as from unilateral reform efforts than from negotiated reciprocal liberalization efforts. The best that reciprocal liberalization can achieve is to enhance transparency and policy credibility by offering means of harvesting autonomous liberalization and by compelling countries to share information on non-conforming measures. Yet given the flexibility of the GATS-type architecture adopted in the region, even the latter good governance-promoting outcome cannot be guaranteed.

Moving next to Australia, Chapter 9 by Bosworth and Trewin argues critically that Australian PTAs have delivered little significant actual services trade liberalization, and may have even obstructed its pursuit. Moreover, on the few occasions where such agreements have changed regulatory measures, Bosworth and Trewin are of the view that their economic value is questionable at best, since they entail discriminatory measures and/or policy changes that have not been adequately assessed economically, instead being touted as "negotiated outcomes". Their chapter also explains recent trade policy developments in Australia, and outlines the authors' belief that the Australian Government's planned return to unilateralism offers greater liberalization potential than the pursuit of PTAs.

FINAL AND FORWARD THOUGHTS

Despite the many arguments for and against it, preferentialism in goods and services trade is here to stay. The chapters in this volume both provide a broad overview of recent developments in services preferentialism and document regional experiences across five different continents. The volume's two final chapters, by Sauvé and Shingal[2] and by Sauvé, synthesize many of the key findings emanating from the volume and ponder the scope for forward movement likely to emanate from ongoing efforts to craft a plurilateral (and most likely preferential) Trade in Services Agreement (TISA) that would co-exist alongside the GATS and some of the systemic challenges that such rule-making and market-opening parallelism could entail.

Chapter 10 by Sauvé and Shingal takes stock of the forces that lie behind the recent rise of preferential agreements in services trade. Drawing on the findings reported in Chapter 2 by Mattoo and Sauvé, such a rise is seen as lying in a number of distinguishing features of services trade that set it apart from trade in goods and which has shaped trade liberalization and rule-making approaches in the services field. Much like Roy in Chapter 1, the authors probe more deeply into the nature, modal and sectoral incidence of trade and investment preferences spawned by services PTAs.

In light of the issues taken up in this volume, the chapter also addresses the critical question of just how "preferential" is the preferential treatment of services trade. The short answer holds in two words: not very. Sauvé and Shingal cite examples where *de jure* preferential liberalization becomes *de facto* MFN liberalization and highlights the case of Article V.6 of the GATS that requires North–North and North–South commitments to adopt the most liberal rule of origin via a "denial of benefits" provision of particular salience to commercial presence – the most important mode of contesting services markets. As the authors point out, this is far from trivial – Mode 3 trade accounts for close to two-thirds of services trade and, most importantly, is that against which the greatest share of commitments are typically scheduled in all negotiating settings (generally in excess of 60% of commitments).

While there is generally little debate over whether services PTAs offer economic welfare gains relative to the status quo ex ante, still one cannot deny that the gains from multilateral liberalization are likely to be larger

2 This chapter first appeared as Sauvé, P. and A. Shingal (2011), "Reflections on the Preferential Liberalization of Services Trade", *Journal of World Trade*, 45(5), 953–63.

as most favoured nation (MFN)-based competition is not only unbiased but also thwarts the first-mover advantages of possibly second-best service providers. Chapter 10 concludes by advancing a number of suggestions on how best to multilateralize preferential access and rule-making in services trade.

The volume's closing chapter by Sauvé explores a number of considerations arising from ongoing attempts to craft a plurilateral Trade in Services Agreement (TISA) among the so-called "Really Good Friends of Services" coalition of WTO Members. The chapter suggests that considerable scope exists to move forward a multilateral negotiating agenda on services that both the digital revolution and a continued surge of preferential rule-making has rendered increasingly obsolete. As the most significant attempt to date to craft a GATS Article V-compatible PTA in services, TISA offers considerable promise. The chapter, however, cautions that the case for embedding TISA in the architecture of WTO rules alongside the General Agreement on Trade in Services or in its place is weak on both procedural and substantive grounds. This is so to the extent that the ongoing talks take place behind doors that remain closed even to the WTO Secretariat, let alone to many of the world's leading developing country suppliers of services, and involve potentially significant departures from GATS rules liable to complicate any hoped-for multilateral migratory journey.

PART I

Overall trends

1. Services commitments in preferential trade agreements: surveying the empirical landscape

Martin Roy[1]

1.1 INTRODUCTION

From being a marginal phenomenon before 2000, preferential trade agreements (PTAs) on services have now become a central aspect of bilateral and regional trade agreements being negotiated outside the multilateral system. While only 5 services agreements involving 11 Members had been notified to the WTO before 2000, over 100 additional agreements have been notified since then, and various others are under negotiation and remain to be notified.[2] As a result, most WTO Members are nowadays involved in at least one services PTA. Overall, while about two-thirds of the PTAs in force do not cover services, the majority of PTAs between developed and developing economies do contain services commitments. Moreover, since 2010, about half of all notifications under GATS Article V concern agreements involving solely developing Members.

The purpose of this chapter is to briefly present the latest trends regarding the services market access commitments that Members have undertaken in PTAs. It is based on an expansion of the dataset developed in Marchetti and Roy (2008). Much of this new data was

1 All views expressed are those of the author and should not be attributed to the WTO Secretariat or WTO Members. Deep appreciation is expressed to Weiwei Zhang for her work in reviewing several recent PTA commitments. Thanks are also due to Rudolf Adlung, Juan Marchetti, Gianluca Orefice, Roberta Piermartini, Nadia Rocha and Pierre Sauvé for comments and discussions. The author is also grateful to Clémence Moreau for her work on the figures. Errors remain the author's.

2 The number of notifications does not include EU enlargements or agreements that are no longer in force. The number of notifications is as of 15 December 2013. The European Union is here counted as 1 Member.

also used for the World Trade Report 2011: *The WTO and Preferential Trade Agreements: From Co-existence to Coherence*. While the dataset in Marchetti and Roy (2008) covered 37 Members in 40 PTAs, the one presented here covers 53 Members in 67 agreements.[3] The dataset does not attempt to represent the quality of commitments or to determine their level of trade restrictiveness, but focuses on the extent to which RTA commitments go beyond GATS commitments and services offers in the Doha Development Agenda. Like its initial version, this expanded dataset is available at: http://www.wto.org/english/tratop_e/serv_e/dataset_e/dataset_e.htm.

This chapter refrains from discussing the implications or motivations of services PTAs, as this has been done in earlier discussions of the dataset, as well as in other chapters of this volume.[4] It is rather meant as a factual piece to accompany other chapters by providing an overall picture of GATS+ commitments in PTAs.

1.2 OVERVIEW

While various aspects of services PTAs have been discussed in the literature, a fundamental starting point in the study of PTAs relates to the content of liberalization commitments.[5] Liberalization commitments refer to the level of treatment bound under 'market access' and 'national treatment', which are the two obligations of services agreements that guarantee a certain level of openness to foreign competition.[6]

As examined in Roy, Marchetti and Lim (2007) and Marchetti and Roy (2008), PTA commitments on services generally go well beyond those undertaken by the same governments under the GATS, and even well beyond the services offers that have so far been submitted by the same governments in the Doha Development Round (DDA) negotiations. The expanded dataset presented here allows to further explore this phenom-

---

[3] This expanded dataset covers 2 additional PTAs from the dataset used for the WTR 2011.

[4] For a fuller depiction of services PTAs and their motivations, see Roy, Marchetti and Lim (2007); Roy, Marchetti and Lim (2008); Marchetti and Roy (2008). See also: WTO (2011); Miroudot, Sauvage and Sudreau (2010); Mattoo and Sauvé (2011); Fink and Molinuevo (2008a); Fink and Molinuevo (2008b); and Sauvé and Shingal (2011).

[5] Liberalization commitments are also central to determining whether services PTAs comply with Article V of the GATS.

[6] In the GATS, the market access obligation is found in Article XVI and national treatment in Article XVII.

enon by providing information on GATS+ commitments by Member, by mode of supply, by agreement, as well as by sector. Such an expanded dataset covers the PTA commitments of an additional 16 WTO Members. It includes most of the services PTAs have notified to the WTO since 2000, as well as a few additional ones that have been signed, but have not yet entered into force. The lists of Members and PTAs covered are found in Tables 1A.1 and 1A.2 in the appendix to this chapter.

Like its earlier version, the expanded dataset limits its assessment of services commitments to mode 1 (cross-border trade) and mode 3 (commercial presence), which represent the overwhelming share of total world services trade. While a similar assessment with respect to mode 4 (movement of natural persons) would be valuable, commitments under this mode are essentially horizontal in nature, and would therefore best be captured by a different approach than the one used here. Indeed, rather than looking at 'improvements' sub-sector by sub-sector, assessing mode 4 commitments would need to qualitatively assess the value of each Member's horizontal commitments, and then examine the sub-sectors to which such horizontal undertakings would apply. In contrast, mode 2 (consumption abroad) is largely unrestricted, and comparing GATS and PTA commitments in this area may provide limited value-added.

The expanded dataset still factors in GATS offers that have been submitted by WTO Members during the Doha Round. Looking at PTA commitments that go beyond these offers provides a better understanding of their value-added, as opposed to comparing them to GATS commitments that are, for the most part, more than 15 years old. Doing so also permits getting a glance at the extent to which DDA offers may be improved if preferential commitments were to be multilateralized. Finally, the dataset only looks at PTA commitments that go beyond the GATS offer, not at areas where PTAs may provide for less. For additional details on the methodology used to produce the dataset, see Marchetti and Roy (2008) and Box 1A.1 in the appendix.

1.3 MEASURING GATS+ COMMITMENTS IN SERVICES PTAS: PROPORTION OF SUB-SECTORS WHERE PTA COMMITMENTS GO BEYOND GATS COMMITMENTS AND DDA OFFERS

A first level of analysis consists of looking at the proportion of services sub-sectors where a party to a PTA undertakes commitments that go beyond its DDA services offer (as per Roy et al. 2007). These improvements take the form of either 'new bindings' or 'improved bindings'. The former consists of sub-sectors that were not subject to commitments under the GATS (nor included in GATS offers) and that have been committed in PTAs. The latter means sub-sectors that benefit from a certain guarantee of access under the GATS (or proposed in GATS offers) and that are granted better terms of access in a PTA (e.g. moving from a 40 to a 51 per cent foreign equity limit, or from a 40 per cent equity cap to full openness).

Such an approach makes no attempt to assess the precise type of improvements or levels of commitment, including whether new bindings are 'full' or 'partial' commitments. On the other hand, it permits a straightforward assessment, revealing in how many and in which sectors PTA commitments go beyond multilateral undertakings. On that basis, Figure 1.1 provides a picture of GATS+ commitments under modes 1 and 3 for each Member, on the basis of the 'best' commitment undertaken across all the PTAs to which it is party.[7]

Figure 1.2 provides an overall picture for all Members reviewed by looking at the average proportion of sub-sectors subject to GATS commitments, GATS offers, and PTA commitments. Figures 1.1 and 1.2 both highlight that relevant Members have, in general, undertaken more and better commitments in a much greater proportion of services sub-sectors than they have under the GATS, or even than they had so far proposed to do in GATS offers. This broad picture holds for both of the modes of supply examined, as well for developed and developing Members. At the same time, as shown in Figure 1.1, variations also exist between Members: while GATS+ commitments in PTAs have been spectacular in the case of certain Members, advances in PTAs have been more modest for others.

1.4 MEASURING GATS+ COMMITMENTS IN SERVICES PTAS: INDEX OF GATS + COMMITMENTS IN PTAS

The dataset made available at http://www.wto.org/english/tratop_e/serv_e/dataset_e/dataset_e.htm also updates information collected on the basis of an index of GATS+ commitments in PTAs as developed in Marchetti and Roy (2008). Rather than simply indicating the proportion of sub-sectors

[7] In the dataset as well as in all figures presented in this chapter, commitments of the European Union are analysed as those of the EU-15.

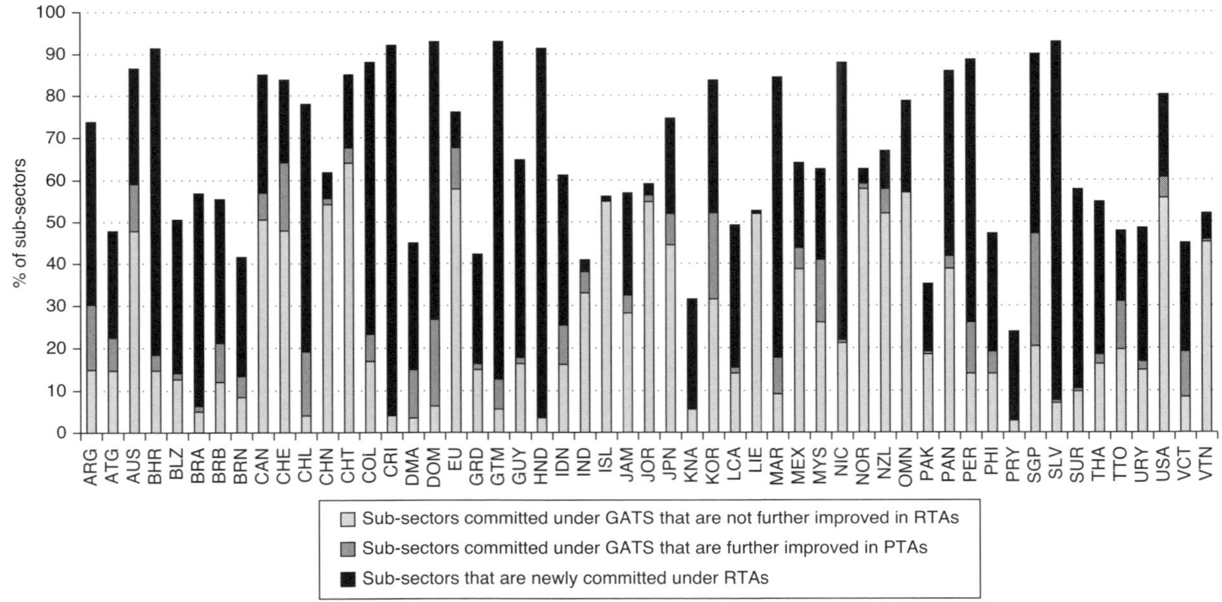

Note: GATS stands here for GATS commitments and DDA offers. The legend of the acronyms for the Members is provided in the appendix. The data reflect each Member's 'best' PTA commitment among all the PTAs to which it is a party.

Source: Updated from Roy et al. (2007) on the basis of the expanded dataset.

Figure 1.1 Proportion of services sub-sectors subject to new or improved commitments in PTAs, compared to GATS (by Member)

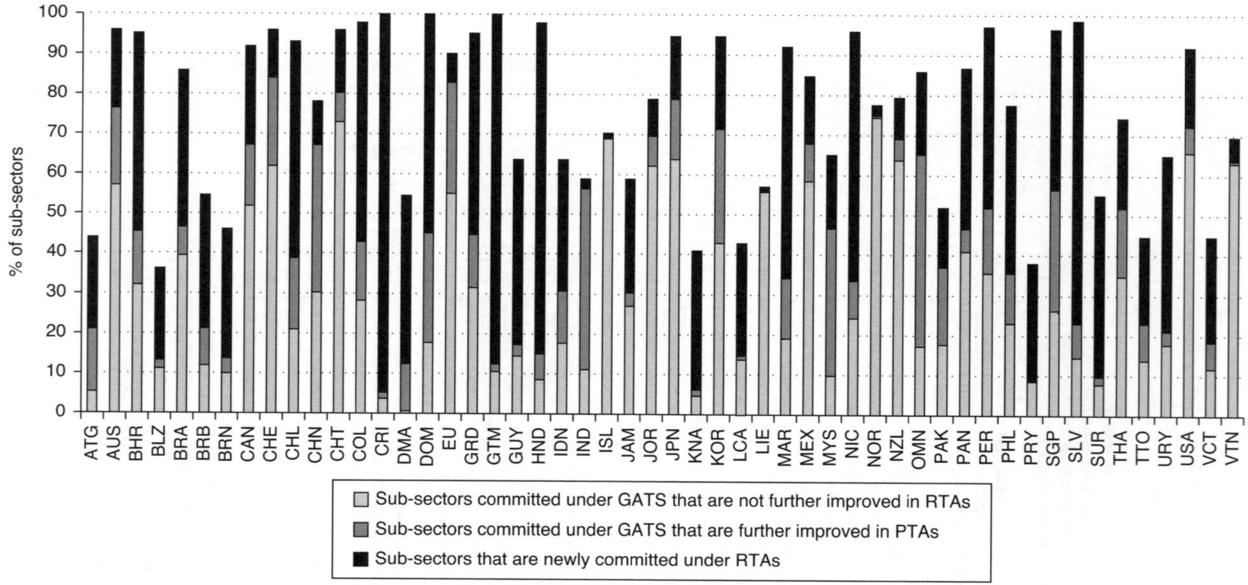

Figure 1.1 (continued)

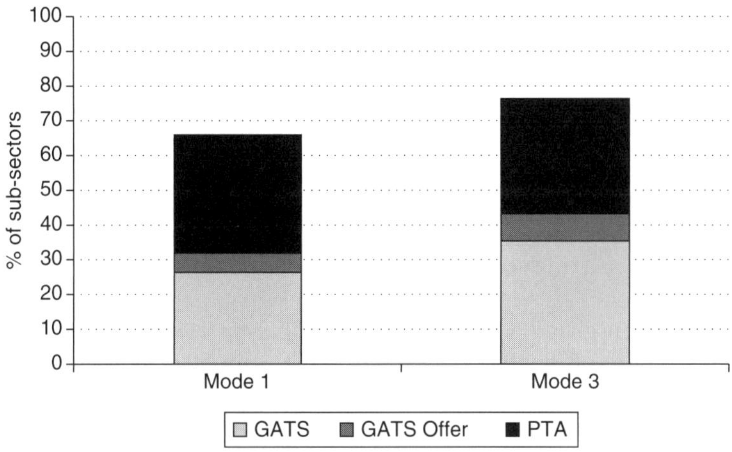

Note: The data reflect each Member's 'best' PTA commitment among all the PTAs to which it is a party.

Source: Updated from Roy et al. (2008) on the basis of the expanded dataset.

Figure 1.2 Sector coverage in PTAs in comparison with GATS commitments and DDA offers

in which PTAs provide for better commitments than under GATS and GATS offers, the index takes into account, in a basic and straightforward manner, the level of commitments undertaken. Such information permits, in particular, comparison of a Member's commitments across its different PTAs.

Fully assessing the depth and quality of commitments is a complicated matter. The approach taken in Marchetti and Roy (2008) builds upon the one initially used by Hoekman (1996) to assess the content of GATS schedules emerging from the Uruguay Round where, for each sub-sector and mode of supply, a score of 1 is given for full commitment (without limitations), 0.5 for partial commitments, and 0 for the absence of commitments.

Naturally, such an approach has its limitations, the most obvious being that it only captures in a general manner the restrictiveness/openness of commitments. Among all the partial commitments with a score of 0.5, some could be subject to limitations heavily restricting trade, while others only contain limitations that only marginally affect trade. Still, such an index provides a general overview of differences in levels of commitments across Members, modes of supply, and sectors. Further, capturing the restrictiveness of commitments would be fraught with difficulties given the wide variety of non-tariff measures being used, and also because of the lack of clarity with which schedules are sometimes drafted.[8]

In Marchetti and Roy (2008), the Hoekman index is adapted so as to allow the comparison of a Member's partial commitments in different PTAs. Comparison is easy when, for example, a partial commitment (score of 0.5) in a given sub-sector becomes a full commitment in another PTA (score of 1). However, differences between a Member's commitments in the GATS and in its various PTAs often consists of removing or relaxing some, but not all, limitations in a given sub-sector and mode.

Rather than giving a score of 0.5 to all partial commitments without taking account of greater concessions made from one negotiation to the other, the index gives a higher score for each improvement in a Member's partial commitments: for each step, half the difference between the score for a full commitment (1) and the score for a partial commitment being improved is added. For example, a partial commitment being improved by way of a foreign equity limit moving from 49 to 51 per cent would obtain a score of 0.75. A further improvement by the Member in the same sub-sector and mode would get a score of 0.875 (e.g. moving up to 60 per cent).[9] Such an approach naturally has its limitations. Principally, it does not pretend to capture the relative restrictiveness of commitments; for this, only a case-by-case qualitative analysis would be satisfactory.

Figure 1.3 uses the index to highlight variations in the levels of commitments granted by certain Members to their different PTA partners. It shows that, for a number of Members, the level of services concessions granted vary significantly across agreements. Singapore's services commitments, for example, vary notably in its agreements with the United States, Japan, and ASEAN countries. Important variations are also observed in the PTA commitments of Chile and Korea. Commitments by the United States, in contrast, do not vary significantly among PTAs, except for its agreement with Jordan, which was based on GATS. The figure also suggests that the larger trading powers tend to receive more concessions. For example, the United States got comparatively high levels of concessions from Chile, Korea, and Singapore.

The index can also be used to provide an overall picture of GATS+ commitments undertaken in PTAs. Unlike Figure 1.1, using the index has the advantage of taking account of the level of commitment undertaken, albeit in a limited manner. Figure 1.4 provides the overall score for the

---

8 See Adlung et al. (2011).

9 See Marchetti and Roy (2008), pp. 78–81.

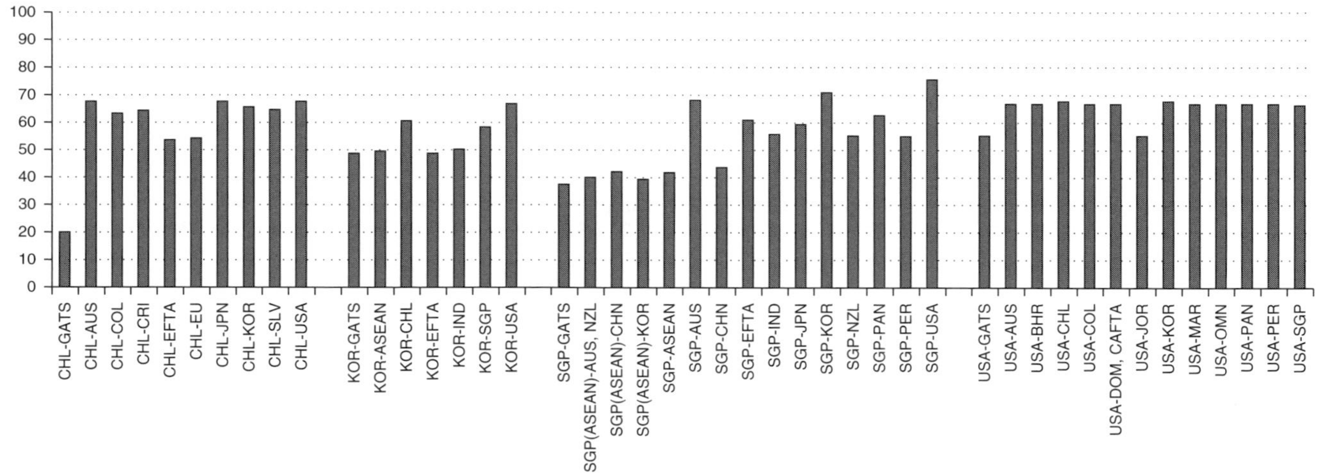

Note: GATS stands here for GATS commitments and DDA offers. The index is brought onto a 0–100 scale, with 100 representing full commitments in all sub-sectors and relevant modes. Index scores are for both modes 1 and 3. On the horizontal axis, the first Member listed is the one whose commitments are reviewed; the second Member listed is the one to which these concessions have been granted.

Source: From updated data, see Marchetti and Roy (2008).

Figure 1.3 Variations in the level of commitments offered in different PTAs: Chile, Korea, Singapore, and United States

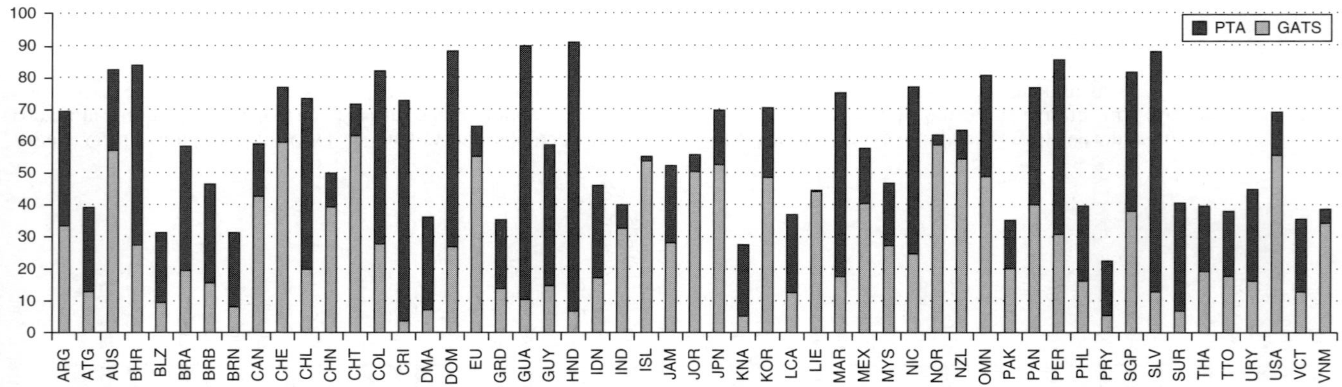

Note: GATS stands here for GATS commitments and DDA offers. The data reflect each Member's 'best' PTA commitment among all the PTAs to which it is a party. The index is brought onto a 0–100 scale, with 100 representing full commitments in all sub-sectors and relevant modes. Index scores are for both modes 1 and 3.

Source: Updated from Marchetti and Roy (2008) on the basis of the expanded dataset.

Figure 1.4 Index scores per Member reviewed

'best' level of commitment undertaken by each Member reviewed in the dataset, across all PTAs to which it is party.[10] The general trends are similar to those presented in Figure 1.1. Accordingly, the 16 new Members added in this expanded dataset, most of which are developing – and in many cases small – economies, have undertaken PTA commitments well beyond their GATS commitments and/or GATS offers.

This is notably the case for the 12 CARIFORUM Members. While their PTA commitments do not reach high index scores compared with the other Members reviewed, they far exceed these countries' GATS commitments/offers, which, on average, are relatively limited. Brunei Darussalam, Canada, and Pakistan, although from very different starting points under the GATS, have all undertaken various commitments providing for greater openness in their respective PTAs. Viet Nam's GATS+ commitments in PTAs are more limited. This is likely due to the fact that, as an acceding Member, it undertook more commitments than other Members at the same level of development.

The greater number of agreements in this expanded dataset also translated into higher levels of PTA commitments by a number of Members covered in the initial assessments done in Roy et al. (2007) and in Marchetti and Roy (2008). This is notably the case for Switzerland (as a result of its PTA with Japan), as well as such ASEAN Members as Indonesia, Malaysia, the Philippines or Thailand (as a result, in part, of the 7th package of commitments under the ASEAN Framework Agreement on Services).

A more general picture is captured through Figure 1.5, which presents average scores for all Members reviewed. Like Figure 1.2, it underscores that services commitments in PTAs far outweigh GATS commitments and offers, in both modes 1 and 3. This overall picture differs only slightly from the one presented in 2008 on the basis of a smaller sample of Members and PTAs. While the overall PTA score for Members reviewed is lower in the expanded dataset, so are the overall scores for GATS commitments and DDA offers. This results from adding to the dataset a good number of Members with relatively limited GATS commitments.

---

10 Care should be exercised in comparing Members' commitments with one another by means of the index. Just as the Hoekman index assumes that all partial commitments are equivalent, the index assumes that all commitments coded 0.5 are equivalent, or, similarly, that all those coded 0.75 are equivalent. This is obviously a simplification and cannot substitute for a qualitative analysis of the depth and value of commitments undertaken. The index is best used to compare each Member's commitments across different agreements, whether multilateral or preferential.

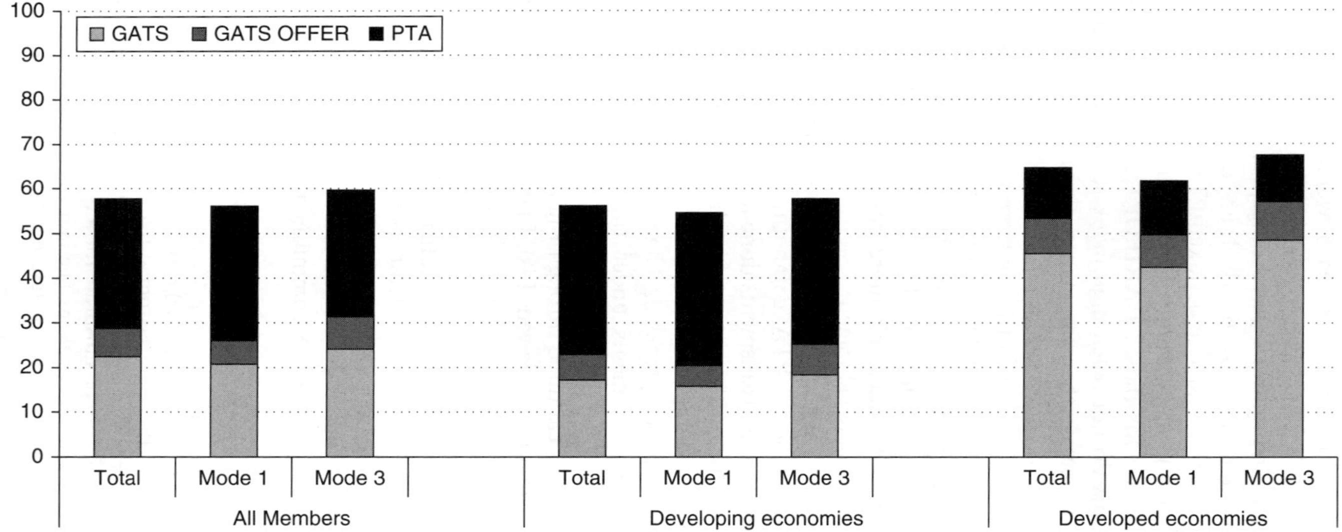

Note: The data reflect each Member's 'best' PTA commitment among all the PTAs to which it is a party. The index is brought onto a 0–100 scale, with 100 representing full commitments in all sub-sectors and relevant modes.

Source: Updated from Marchetti and Roy (2008) on the basis of the expanded dataset.

Figure 1.5 Average index score across Members reviewed

Figure 1.5 also shows that GATS+ commitments in PTAs have, on average, been more important in developing economies, which is partly explained by the different levels of GATS commitments undertaken by these two groups of Members. In fact, through PTA commitments, developing-country Members significantly reduce the gap with the levels of bindings attained by developed-country Members. The figure also shows that, on average, PTA advances have taken place in similar fashion for both modes 1 and 3, irrespective of Members' level of development.

The index also provides a sectoral picture of advances in PTAs. Figure 1.6 shows the average index value for GATS and 'best' PTA commitments, per selected sectors. As noted in the World Trade Report 2011 and in Marchetti and Roy (2008), advances in PTAs have occurred across all major sectors. While certain sectors that had proved more difficult in multilateral negotiations still attracted fewer commitments in PTAs (e.g. audiovisual, health), advances have nevertheless been important there too when compared with GATS commitments/offers.[11]

Finally, the data sheds light on a number of regional features. Although the number of Members now involved in services PTAs has increased significantly over the last decade, most countries in Africa (except Morocco) and the Middle East (except Jordan, Oman, Bahrain) have not so far concluded such preferential agreements. Latin America and Asia-Pacific are the regions where most countries have signed services PTAs. Among the agreements reviewed in the dataset (see the appendix), about half involve at least one Latin American country as a party, and almost two-thirds involve a Member from Asia-Pacific.

Asia-Pacific is also the region where most intra-regional agreements have been concluded: about a third of agreements reviewed in this chapter. In comparison, 15 per cent of all these PTAs are signed between Latin American countries. Overall, about half of services PTAs are intra-regional.

Figure 1.7 presents information on services commitments undertaken by Members from Latin America and Asia.[12] It shows that, on average, Latin American countries have tended to undertake much more significant GATS+ commitments in services PTAs than Members from

---

[11] It can be observed that levels of PTA commitments appear particularly limited in financial services. As noted in Marchetti and Roy (2008), this results largely from limited overall PTA advances on mode 1 in this sector.

[12] Given the limited number of countries involved in services PTAs, data for other regions are not presented here.

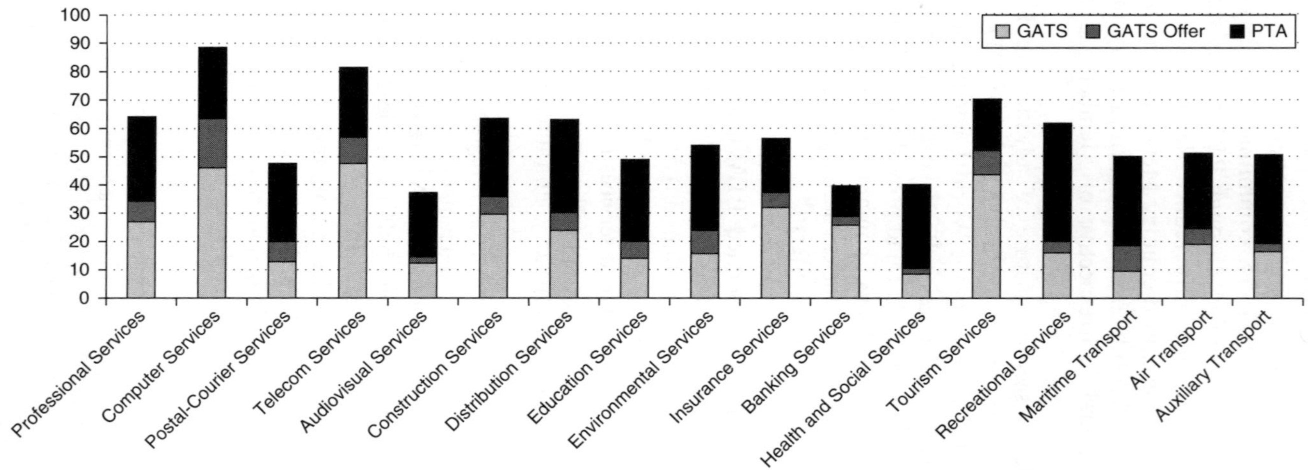

Note: The data reflect each Member's 'best' PTA commitment among all the PTAs to which it is a party. The index is brought onto a 0–100 scale, with 100 representing full commitments in all sub-sectors and relevant modes of the sector grouping. Index scores are for both modes 1 and 3.

Source: Updated from Marchetti and Roy (2008) on the basis of the expanded dataset.

Figure 1.6 Average index scores for GATS commitments, GATS offers, and 'best' PTA commitments, per selected sectors

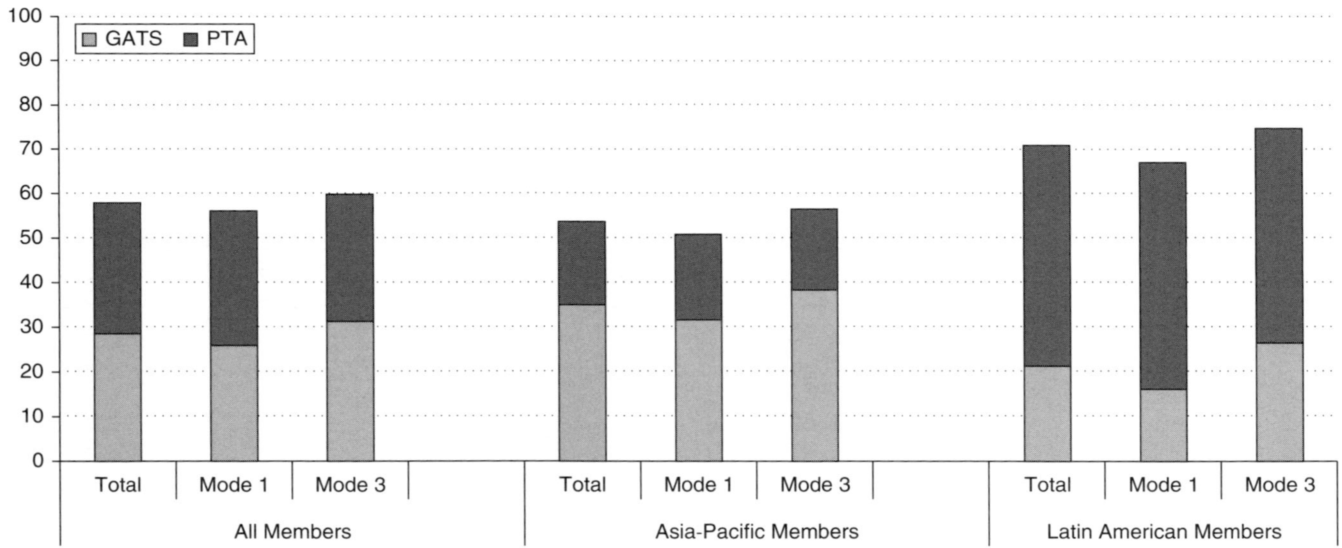

Note: The data reflect each Member's 'best' PTA commitment among all the PTAs to which it is a party. The index is brought onto a 0–100 scale, with 100 representing full commitments in all sub-sectors and relevant modes. GATS stands here for GATS commitments and DDA offers.

Figure 1.7 Average index score across Members reviewed, by region

Asia-Pacific.[13] A first explanation for such results is that the involvement of many Asian countries in services PTAs (e.g. India, China, Japan) is more recent than in Latin America. A second reason relates to the different liberalization modalities used in PTAs. While most Latin American countries typically sign PTAs based on negative-list modalities, many in Asia-Pacific have only concluded PTAs using positive-list modalities for the scheduling of commitments. Indeed, China, India, Pakistan, and most ASEAN Members have not concluded negative-list type agreements.[14]

A third and connected reason relates to the differing involvement so far of the United States in both regions. Earlier studies of services PTAs underscored that the United States typically extracts the most significant concessions from its trading partners.[15] While the US has signed services PTAs with various Latin American countries, it has only done so with Singapore, Korea, and Australia in Asia-Pacific. Even though developed economies like Japan and Australia have signed services PTAs with many Asian countries, they have not managed to obtain the type of concessions that the United States has obtained in its agreements within the hemisphere, nor have they imposed the use of a negative-list approach in the same way the United States have.

1.5 CONCLUDING REMARKS

Overall, the dataset highlights that, on average, commitments undertaken in PTAs far outweigh those contained in GATS schedules, but also those offered in the current round of negotiations. This goes for both modes 1 and 3, and different levels of development, although, naturally, the level of GATS+ commitments varies significantly across Members. The analysis of an additional 16 new Members and 27 new PTAs has provided further evidence of these trends. Indeed, more recent agreements have matched or exceeded levels of commitments achieved by parties in earlier preferential agreements. Recent PTAs have also involved significant GATS+ commitments from a number of WTO Members

13 The 'Asia-Pacific' and 'Latin America' groups are each composed of 15 WTO Members that are parties to services PTAs. Excluding developed countries from the 'Asia-Pacific' group did not significantly modify the group's average GATS+ commitments. 'Latin America' does not include Caribbean countries.

14 Overall, GATS+ commitments have been more important in 'negative-list' agreements than in 'positive-list' ones: Roy, Marchetti and Lim (2008), p. 82.

15 See Marchetti and Roy (2008).

that had previously not taken part in services PTAs (i.e. Pakistan and 12 CARIFORUM countries). The detailed dataset on the WTO website allows further analysis, either to compare Members' commitments in different PTAs or to assess what different PTAs achieved. Ongoing research being conducted on the basis of this data includes work on reciprocity in services PTAs as well as on the impact of services commitments on trade flows.

Regional differences are also important. Only a handful of countries in Africa and the Middle East have so far concluded services PTAs. Most agreements involve developed countries and developing countries from Asia as well as Latin America and the Caribbean. Comparing commitments undertaken by governments in Asia and Latin America shows that the latter's have, on average, been significantly more ambitious.

BIBLIOGRAPHY

Adlung, Rudolf, Peter Morrison, Martin Roy and Weiwei Zhang (2011), 'Fog in GATS Commitments – Boon or Bane?', WTO Staff Working Paper ERSD-2011-04, 31 March 2011.

Fink, Carsten and Martin Molinuevo (2008a), 'East Asian Free Trade Agreements in Services: Key Architectural Elements', *Journal of International Economic Law*, 11(2): 263–311.

Fink, Carsten and Martin Molinuevo (2008b), 'East Asian Preferential Trade Agreements in Services: Liberalization Content and WTO Rules', *World Trade Review*, 7(4): 641–73.

Hoekman, Bernard (1996), 'Assessing the General Agreement on Trade in Services', in W. Martin and L.A. Winters (eds.), *The Uruguay Round and Developing Countries*, Cambridge: Cambridge University Press.

Marchetti, Juan and Martin Roy (2008), 'Services Liberalization in the WTO and in PTAs', in J. Marchetti and M. Roy (eds.), *Opening Markets for Trade in Services: Countries and Sectors in Bilateral and WTO Negotiations*, Cambridge: Cambridge University Press and WTO.

Mattoo, Aaditya and Pierre Sauvé (2011), 'Services', in Jean-Pierre Chauffour and Jean-Christophe Maur (eds.), *Preferential Trade Agreement Policies for Development: A Handbook*, Washington, DC: The World Bank, pp. 235–74.

Miroudot, Sébastien, Jehan Sauvage and Marie Sudreau (2010), 'Multilateralising Regionalism: How Preferential Are Services Commitments in Regional Trade Agreements?', OECD Trade Policy Working Papers No. 106.

Roy, Martin, Juan Marchetti and Hoe Lim (2007), 'Services Liberalization in the New Generation of Preferential Trade Agreements: How Much Further than the GATS?', *World Trade Review*, 6(2): 155–92.

Roy, Martin, Juan Marchetti and Hoe Lim (2008), 'The Race Towards Preferential Trade Agreements in Services: How Much Market Access Is Really Achieved?', in Marion Panizzon, Nicole Pohl and Pierre Sauvé (eds.), *GATS and the*

Regulation of International Trade in Services, Cambridge: Cambridge University Press.
Sauvé, Pierre and Anirudh Shingal (2011), 'Reflections on the Preferential Liberalization of Services Trade', *Journal of World Trade*, 45(5): 953–63.
WTO (2011), *World Trade Report 2011; The WTO and Preferential Trade Agreements: From Coexistence to Coherence*, Geneva.

APPENDIX

Table 1A.1 List of services agreements in the dataset

Korea (Rep.)-India	Pakistan-China	EFTA-Chile
ASEAN-Korea (Rep.)	Japan-Thailand	Korea (Rep.)-Chile
ASEAN-Australia-New Zealand	Chile-Japan	EU-Chile
Honduras-El Salvador-China Taipei	Chile-China	Chile-El Salvador
Peru-China	India-Singapore	China-Macao, China
Japan-Vietnam	Panama-Singapore	China-Hong Kong, China
Japan-Switzerland	US-Bahrain	US-Singapore
Chile-Colombia	EFTA-Korea (Rep.)	US-Chile
Canada-Peru	Costa Rica-Mexico	Singapore-Australia
Panama-Chinese Taipei	Japan-Malaysia	EFTA-Singapore
Nicaragua-Chinese Taipei	Mexico-Honduras	Japan-Singapore
China-New Zealand	Jordan-Singapore	Chile-Costa Rica
Australia-Chile	Mexico-Guatemala	US-Jordan
China-Singapore	Mexico-El Salvador	New Zealand-Singapore
US-Peru	Dominican Rep.-Cent. America-US	EFTA-Mexico
US-Oman	Korea (Rep.)-Singapore	China-Peru
Japan-Philippines	US-Morocco	EU-Mexico
EU-CARIFORUM	Peru-Singapore	US-Korea (Rep.)
Brunei Darussalam-Japan	US-Australia	Mercosur (6th negotiated round)
Japan-Indonesia	ASEAN-China	ASEAN (7th package)
Panama-Chile	Japan-Mexico	US-Colombia
Pakistan-Malaysia	Panama-El Salvador	US-Panama
	Thailand-Australia	

Note: All these agreement were reviewed for creating the dataset, although some parties' commitments were not coded. For example, Hong Kong China and Macao China do not have detailed lists of commitments in their agreements with China. For ASEN's Framework Agreement on Services, the commitments reviewed are those of the 7th package.

Source: WTO Secretariat.

Table 1A.2 Members covered and acronyms

Acronyms	Member	Acronyms	Member
ARG	Argentina	KNA	Saint Kitts and Nevis
ATG	Antigua and Barbuda	KOR	Rep. of Korea
AUS	Australia	LCA	St. Lucia
BHR	Bahrain	LIE	Liechtenstein
BLZ	Belize	MAC	Macao, China
BRA	Brazil	MAR	Morocco
BRB	Barbados	MEX	Mexico
BRN	Brunei Darussalam	MYS	Malaysia
CAN	Canada	NIC	Nicaragua
CHE	Switzerland	NOR	Norway
CHL	Chile	NZL	New Zealand
CHN	China	OMN	Oman
COL	Colombia	PAK	Pakistan
CRI	Costa Rica	PAN	Panama
DMA	Dominica	PER	Peru
DOM	Dominican Rep.	PHL	Philippines
EU	European Union	PRY	Paraguay
GRD	Grenada	SGP	Singapore
GTM	Guatemala	SLV	El Salvador
GUY	Guyana	SUR	Suriname
HKG	Hong Kong, China	CHT	Chinese Taipei
HND	Honduras	THA	Thailand
IDN	Indonesia	TTO	Trinidad and Tobago
IND	India	URY	Uruguay
ISL	Iceland	USA	USA
JAM	Jamaica	VCT	Saint Vincent and the Grenadines
JOR	Jordan		
JPN	Japan	VNM	Viet Nam

Source: WTO Secretariat.

BOX 1A.1 ADDITIONAL DETAILS ABOUT THE METHODOLOGY

- In producing estimates for each country, commitments undertaken in all services sub-sectors have been compared on the basis of the Services Sectoral Classification List (MTN.GNS/W/120), as well as the GATS Annex on Financial Services, the maritime model schedule for maritime auxiliary services, and the GATS Annex on Air Transport Services.
- The universe of services sectors has been split up so as to permit the most precise assessment: 152 sub-sectors for mode 3 and 142 for mode 1. Some sub-sectors were excluded from our comparison of commitments under mode 1 because they appear of quite limited relevance or are simply not technically feasible, e.g. building cleaning, storage warehousing. This aimed to ensure that results did not overestimate the improvements made in negative-list agreements, where all sectors are liberalized unless provided otherwise.
- In computing scores for PTA commitments, situations where PTA commitments fell short of GATS schedules/offers were not factored in.
- A score was provided for a country's commitments in each agreement, for each sub-sector and each mode of supply (i.e. modes 1 and 3). A different score was not given for market access on the one hand and national treatment on the other hand. To get the maximum score of 1 for a given sub-sector and mode of supply, full commitments need to be undertaken under both the national treatment and market access obligations. Since, as noted above, 152 sub-sectors are reviewed for mode 3 and 142 for mode 1, the maximum score that can be obtained is 294. In the chapter, we have presented this score on a scale of 0 to 100. The scoring does not factor in improvements with regard to additional commitments (Article XVIII of the GATS). MFN provisions and exceptions were similarly not reviewed.
- Horizontal limitations, which applying to all scheduled sectors, were also assessed. However, so as not to overestimate the number of sectors where bindings were improved,

we only factored into the scoring the more stringent types of horizontal limitations (and improvements to them), in particular foreign equity restrictions, limitations on the number of suppliers, including through economic needs tests, joint-venture requirements, and nationality requirements.

- A number of agreements using a negative-list approach do not include in their List of existing non-conforming measures those applied by sub-central entities, either at the state/provincial level or local level. Even if these measures are not listed, the existing level of access is nevertheless bound and cannot be made more restrictive. Given the importance of state/provincial entities in federal states, we considered as 'partial commitments' – as opposed to 'full commitments' with a score of 1 – situations where a country had no limitations in a given sector but where state/provincial level measures were not listed. These were only scored as 'full commitments' in view of information suggesting that non-conforming measures were applied (for example where a commitment in another negotiating context revealed that no such measures were in existence).
- Assessing the extent to which PTAs provide for new and improved bindings necessarily involves a degree of value judgement, especially when comparing commitments framed under a positive-list approach and others under a negative-list one. Therefore, the overview does not in any way amount to a legal evaluation of commitments.

Source: Reproduced from Marchetti and Roy (2008), pp.109–10.

2. The preferential liberalization of services trade: economic insights*

Aaditya Mattoo and Pierre Sauvé

INTRODUCTION

While there is a large literature on the costs and benefits of integration agreements on trade in goods, there is hardly any analysis of the implications of such agreements in services. Such a gap is surprising given the strong growth witnessed since the mid-1990s in the number of preferential trade agreements (PTAs) featuring detailed disciplines on trade and investment in services.

If all trade agreements can of essence be likened to "incomplete contracts", then the incipient multilateral regime for services is arguably the most incomplete of all. This greatly heightens the salience of studying the relationship between preferential and multilateral regimes for services trade. This chapter takes up this challenge by considering a number of questions – both theoretical and policy-related – arising from the study of the PTA-WTO divide in services trade. The chapter questions whether the tools of economic analysis developed for studying the effects of preference in goods trade yield meaningful insights in the services field.

Regional and bilateral attempts at developing trade rules for services continue to parallel efforts at framing similar disciplines in the WTO, under the aegis of the GATS. For this reason, regional and multilateral efforts at services rule-making are closely – indeed increasingly – intertwined processes, with much iterative learning by doing, imitation, and reverse engineering. Experience gained in developing the services provisions of PTAs has built up negotiating capacity in participating countries, providing expertise available for deployment in a multilateral setting. Since the GATS itself remains incomplete, with negotiations pending in a number of

* This chapter draws in part on: Mattoo, Aaditya and Pierre Sauvé (2011), "Services", in Chauffour, J.-P. and J.-C. Maur, eds., Preferential Trade Agreement Policies for Development: A Handbook, Washington, D.C.: The World Bank, pp. 235–74.

key areas (e.g. emergency safeguards, subsidies, government procurement, domestic regulation), regional and bilateral experimentations have generated a number of useful policy lessons in comparative negotiating and rule-making dynamics. As well, developments in WTO jurisprudence in the services field have begun to be reflected in patterns of market opening commitments found in PTAs, a trend that one may well expect to deepen as judicial activism under the GATS rises.[1]

The efforts that countries devote to developing rules governing the process of services-trade liberalization at the regional level typically come in the wake of the far-reaching changes in many countries' services and investment policy frameworks that have taken hold in the post-Uruguay Round period. For many countries, PTA negotiations offer the opportunity to pursue, deepen or lock in some (or much) of the policy reforms put in place domestically in recent years and to reap the benefits, notably in terms of improved investment climates, likely to flow from such policy consolidation.

This chapter takes stock of the more recent wave of PTAs with a view to informing some of the policy choices developing countries will typically confront in negotiating regional regimes for services trade and investment. While a country's choice of integration strategy will in most instances be dictated by political considerations, there remains a need for a careful assessment of the economic benefits and costs of alternative approaches to services liberalization.

The chapter considers the economics of preferential integration in services, asking whether services trade differs sufficiently from trade in goods as to require different policy instruments and approaches. Also discussed is whether and how PTAs may allow deeper forms of regulatory cooperation to occur. It highlights the importance for third countries of multilateral disciplines on PTAs and the criteria for PTAs not to be detrimental to non-members.

2.1 THE ECONOMICS OF SERVICES TRADE IN PTAS

While the economic effects of preferential tariff arrangements are generally well understood and form the core of conventional trade theory, such is hardly the case for services. The analysis of preferential agreements in

---

[1] Evidence of such causality can be found in recent PTAs involving the United States, notably in respect of reservations made in regard to trade in on-line gambling services (Baptista Neto, 2009). It may further be expected in the aftermath of the most recent WTO ruling in the dispute brought by the United States against China in the area of publications and audio-visual products (Shi and Chen, 2011).

services trade requires an extension of conventional trade theory in two ways, both of which relate to core distinguishing features of services: first, the manner in which trade in services occurs and, second, the form that trade protection takes in the sector.

Since services trade often requires proximity between the supplier and the consumer, one needs to consider preferences extended not just to cross-border trade, but also to foreign direct investment (FDI) and foreign individual service providers. Moreover, preferential treatment in services is granted not through tariffs but through discriminatory restrictions on the movement of labor and capital (e.g. in terms of the quantity or share of foreign ownership), and a variety of domestic regulations, such as technical standards, licensing and qualification requirements.

Given such differences, can one say that trade in services differs enough from trade in goods so as to modify the conclusions reached so far as regards the economic effects of preferential liberalization? In particular, what would happen if a country liberalized services trade faster in a regional or bilateral context than at the multilateral level? To answer such questions, the rest of this section will (1) review the various costs and benefits of trade preferences arising in services trade; and (2) discuss the scope for regional or bilateral regulatory cooperation in services trade.

2.1.1 Costs and Benefits of Preferential Treatment in Services Trade

The manner in which privileged access can be granted in services markets depends on the instrument of protection in use. By imposing a quantitative restriction on services output or on the number of service providers, a country can allocate a larger proportion of the quota to a preferred source. Examples of the former abound in air, land and maritime transport, where countries often allocate freight and passenger quotas on a preferential basis, and in audiovisual services, where preferential quotas exist on airtime allocated to foreign broadcasts. Examples of the latter include restrictions on the number of telecommunications operators, banks or professionals that may be allowed to operate.

Another common means of restricting access to service markets that lends itself to preferential treatment concerns limitations on foreign ownership, on the type of allowed legal entity or on branching rights. While most host country governments provide foreign investors with post-establishment national treatment, such treatment rarely applies in the pre-establishment phase. This allows host countries to impose a range of performance requirements on foreign services providers, for instance in terms of training or employment in managerial level positions. These can easily be waived for members of a preferential arrangement.

Preferences can also be granted through taxes and subsidies. Foreign providers can be subject to different taxes and may be denied access to certain subsidy programs. Again, these forms of discrimination can be waived selectively, as is the case, for example, in co-production agreements in audiovisual services.

Another much practiced form of preferential treatment occurs through domestic regulations pertaining to technical regulations, licensing and qualification requirements. Countries can and do impose qualification and licensing requirements on foreign providers that may be more burdensome than necessary to satisfy otherwise legitimate public policy objectives. Where these are waived selectively in favor of members of a PTA, and denied to others who would otherwise qualify for the benefits, de facto preferences result. While regulatory preferences may arise in all sectors, they are especially prevalent in professional and financial services, where domestic regulatory requirements and licensing regimes respond to information asymmetries.

2.1.2 Measures Affecting Variable Costs

A common effect of many restrictive measures in services trade is to increase the variable costs of operation faced by foreign providers without necessarily generating equivalent rents. In such cases, the analysis of discriminatory regulation can proceed in a manner analogous to tariffs. When tariffs are the instruments of protection, the costs of trade diversion can be an important disincentive to concluding preferential liberalization agreements. Despite the increase in consumer surplus from any liberalization, there may still be an aversion to such agreements because the displacement of high tariff imports from third countries by low or zero-tariff imports from preferential sources implies lost revenue.

The situation may differ when the protectionist instrument is a regulatory barrier that imposes a cost on the exporter without necessarily yielding a corresponding revenue for the government or any other domestic entity. Under such circumstances, which characterize much of services trade (given the regulatory nature of impediments), there may be little or no cost to granting preferential access because there is little or no revenue to lose. In such circumstances, preferential liberalization will necessarily be welfare-enhancing.

However, countries outside the preferential arrangement may lose. Exemption from a needlessly burdensome regulation implies reduced costs for a class of suppliers and hence a decline in prices in the importing countries. This decline in prices may hurt third-country suppliers who may suffer reduced sales and a decline in producer surplus.

The analysis of discriminatory regulation is also relevant to quantitative restrictions on the sale of services. In the case of goods, the quota rents can be appropriated by domestic intermediaries like the importer rather than the foreign exporter. However, in many services, intermediation is difficult because the service is not always storable and directly supplied by producers to consumers. Rents are, therefore, usually appropriated by exporters rather than domestic importers. As in the case of frictional measures that increase variable costs, there is typically no cost of trade diversion to the preference-granting country.

The main policy implication one can draw from the above discussion is that where a country maintains regulations that impose a cost on foreign providers without generating any benefit (such as improved quality) or revenue for the government or other domestic entities, welfare would necessarily be enhanced by preferential liberalization. However, it bears noting that non-preferential liberalization would yield an even greater increase in welfare, both nationally and globally, because the service would then be supplied by the most efficient providers.

2.1.3 Measures Affecting Fixed Costs

A number of measures that countries maintain can have the effect of increasing the fixed costs of entry or establishment in services markets. Examples include requirements to establish a local presence, license fees for entry into the market, or the need to re-qualify for purposes of providing professional services. As with measures affecting variable costs, a country is likely to benefit from eliminating, even on a preferential basis, any excessive fixed costs of entry by removing unnecessary burdensome qualification, licensing and local establishment requirements in professional and financial services.

Regardless of the chosen partners, the presumption that a country will benefit from such initiatives is greater if agreements are not exclusionary but rather open to all parties able to satisfy the regulatory requirements maintained within the integrating area. The greatest benefits arise if recognition agreements include all countries that have comparable regulation. The benefits in such instances come from both increased competition and greater diversity of services.

2.1.4 Measures Restricting the Number of Service Providers

The norm in many service industries is for the quantum (level) of competition to be restricted by government regulation. There may be legitimate reasons to do so, such as the existence of significant economies of scale or in industry segments characterized by natural monopoly features (the case of a number of network-based industries in energy, water distribution or transportation/railways). In such circumstances, the question of the manner in which entry is allowed – by mergers and acquisitions or through greenfield (i.e. *de novo*) investments – can assume considerable significance.

Interestingly, allowing limited new entry by foreign firms, irrespective of whether this is done preferentially or on a most-favored-nation (MFN) treatment basis, may not be welfare-enhancing. The main reason is that even though consumers may benefit from the increased level of competition, such a gain may be offset by the transfer of rents from domestic to foreign oligopolists.

Restrictions on *de novo* entry are often imposed with a view to channeling new foreign capital into weak or undercapitalized domestic institutions (a common occurrence in financial services for example) to help the restructuring process in the context of progressive liberalization. The above considerations may affect the preferred mode of entry: entry through acquisition implies less competition than greenfield entry, but it allows domestic firms to extract some rents through the disposal of their assets.

Liberalization tends to generate gains when all barriers to entry are removed. But if only limited entry is allowed, then open, non-discriminatory access – for instance through the global auctioning of licenses – would predominate over preferential access, which cannot guarantee that preferential (i.e. insider) investors will be the most efficient ones. Absent liberal rules of origin on investment, the establishment of preferences may indeed result in entry by inferior suppliers. Because the most efficient suppliers (in terms of costs and/or quality) may also generate the greatest positive externalities (including the dynamic learning properties associated with knowledge flows and the associated rise of total factor productivity), the downside risks of preferential liberalization may be greater (Mattoo and Fink, 2002). The ability of non-preferential liberalization to more readily secure access to the most efficient suppliers of services is a matter of some importance given the crucial infrastructural role many services perform and the strong influence such intermediate inputs can exert on economy-wide performance.

Preferential liberalization of entry barriers may also bring higher prices for consumers, lower takeover prices for domestic assets or lower license fees for the government (by limiting the pool of potential buyers). These concerns are likely to be compounded in concentrated markets, a common occurrence in many service industries in the developing world.

2.1.5 Sunk Costs and the Sequence of Liberalization

Sunk costs are important in goods and services industries alike. However, location-specific sunk costs – those incurred in supplying a particular market – are arguably higher in a number of service sectors to the extent that their provision requires proximity between suppliers and consumers. One consequence (which is closely related to the above discussion on barriers to new entrants) is that preferential liberalization may exert more durable effects on the nature of competition than in the case of goods. For instance, concluding an agreement that allows inferior providers to establish may mean that a country could be stuck with such providers even if it subsequently liberalizes on an MFN basis.

Sunk costs matter because they have commitment value and can be used strategically by first movers to deter new entrants (Tirole, 1998). A firm that establishes a telecommunications or transport network signals that it will be around tomorrow if it cannot easily dispose of its assets. The commitment value is stronger the more slowly capital depreciates and the more firm-specific it is.

Firms allowed early entry into such types of markets may accumulate a quantity of capital sufficient to limit the entry of new rivals. Such incumbency effects may be stronger in services with network externalities, such as telecommunications, where new entrants must match the technical standards of the incumbent (standards that the latter may have also played a large part in defining). The incumbent may also succeed in assuring itself of the services of the best franchisees by selecting them early on and imposing exclusivity arrangements on them. Each of these forms of capital accumulation enhances first-mover advantages and allows the established firm(s) to prevent, restrict or retard competition.

Because of the importance of sunk costs in many service industries, sequential entry (which preferential liberalization with restrictive rules of origin may entail) can produce very different results from simultaneous entry. If entry is costly, an incumbent may be able to completely deter entry, leading to greater market concentration. Furthermore, the first-mover advantage may be conferred on an inferior supplier. The latter may naturally use such advantages to establish a position of market dominance, insulated from more efficient third-country competitors. How durable such a position may be in practice will depend on the importance of sunk costs relative to differences in price and quality.

Two important qualifications to the above reasoning can nonetheless be made. First, subsequent entry by a more efficient firm can take place through the acquisition route, thus circumventing some of the problems linked to first-mover advantages. This has notably been the experience of a number of countries in the financial sector, especially those where first movers may have overbid or sunk excessive costs in setting up their operations in the early stages of liberalization. Second, in certain service sectors, firms could learn by doing: the experience acquired by established operators during a previous period may reduce their current costs, enhancing their profitability and discouraging others from entering. Caveats aside, a country needs to carefully evaluate not just the static costs of granting preferential access to a particular partner country, but also how the eventual benefits from multilateral liberalization are likely to be affected.

2.1.6 Static and Dynamic Economies of Scale

Enlargement of services markets through a regional integration agreement can lead to gains arising from a combination of scale effects and changes in the intensity of competition. In a market of a given size, there is a trade-off between scale economies and competition: if firms are larger, there are fewer of them and the market is less competitive. Enlarging the market shifts this trade-off, as it becomes possible to have both larger firms and more competition (World Bank, 2000).

Regional liberalization can also act as an inducement to FDI. Apart from changing the organization of local industry, if PTAs create large markets and do not impose stringent ownership-related rules of origin, they may also assist in attracting foreign investment when economies of scale matter. For example, a foreign transport service provider might not find it worthwhile to establish in Latin America if each country market were segmented, but might find Latin America attractive with a continent-wide integrated market.

One rationale for PTAs covering services is a variant of dynamic economies of scale or the infant-industry argument. "South-South" PTAs, in particular, are seen as a form of gradual liberalization. Exposure to competition first in the more sheltered confines of a regional market may help firms prepare for global competition. This approach improves on traditional infant-industry protection because some degree of international competition is fostered as a result of the integration process. There is also the possibility that firms that have gained competitiveness at the regional level are less likely to resist broader-based liberalization. They may even champion subsequent MFN liberalization as they begin to reap the benefits of open markets and run up against the constraints of a regional market. In this sense, PTAs can be seen as "building blocks" towards multilateral liberalization (Bhagwati, 1990; Lawrence, 1991). The risk does exist, however, that regional liberalization might create a new constellation of vested interests that could resist further market opening, raising the concern that regionalism can become a "stumbling block" to further multilateral liberalization. The GATS offers a way out of this dilemma by allowing member countries to pre-commit to future multilateral liberalization, signaling a time frame over which regional preferences may be progressively eroded and/or eliminated.

2.2 REGIONALISM AND REGULATORY COOPERATION

The gains from PTAs are likely to be significant in areas where there is scope for reaping economies of scale, as in certain international transport and financial services, and for securing increased competition, as in business or professional services. In principle, these gains can also be reaped through MFN liberalization, but in practice the integration of markets often requires a convergence of regulatory regimes. Such convergence might well be more feasible in a bilateral or regional context, for instance when "proximity" (be it geographic or in terms of income levels or legal traditions) implies closer institutional and regulatory ties. The regulatory intensity of services trade makes it necessary to consider whether and how PTAs can be conduits for trade- and investment-facilitating convergence in domestic regulatory practices. Simply put, under what circumstances is a country more likely to benefit from cooperation in a plurilateral or regional forum than in a multilateral one?

2.2.1 Addressing the Regulatory Intensity of Services Trade

The economic case for regulation in services arises essentially from market failure attributable to three kinds of problems: (1) asymmetric information (especially in knowledge-intensive industries, such as financial or professional services); (2) externalities (tourism, transport, water distribution); and (3) natural monopoly/oligopolies (especially in network-based services where access to essential facilities is a critical ingredient).

In the first two cases, national remedies can themselves become impediments to trade if domestic regulatory requirements are needlessly burdensome or framed with a view to tilt competitive conditions in favor of domestic suppliers. The institution of some variant of a necessity test in services agreements (the purpose of which, as in goods trade, is to ensure some broad measure of proportionality between regulatory objectives and the means of pursuing them), together with strengthened disciplines on transparency, would enable exporters to challenge the appropriateness of regulatory regimes abroad. Doing so would help ensure that domestic regulations serve legitimate objectives rather than mask protectionist interests, and hence create benefits for domestic consumers and users of services.

In the third case (natural monopoly/oligopoly), it is the absence of regulation (typically pro-competitive regulation) that can lead to trade problems and directly inhibit and/or nullify negotiated market access. As negotiations in basic telecommunications services have shown already, international rules on access to essential facilities, and on means of ensuring that dominant suppliers do not abuse their market advantages to deter entry and stifle competition, can provide significant benefits to consumers and users of telecommunications services.

In order to ensure that domestic regulations at home and abroad support trade, a country must decide on the appropriate level of coordination (i.e. multilateral, regional or bilateral), the appropriate mechanism (i.e. international rules or standards), and the appropriate approach (i.e. mutual recognition or harmonization) to pursue in individual service sectors. International rules can do little to address impediments to trade arising from fundamental differences across countries in regulatory standards. In such circumstances, two approaches can be envisaged: harmonization and mutual recognition. Even though these approaches are often presented as alternatives, the former tends to be either a precondition or a result of the latter. Where differences in mandatory quality standards matter, mutual recognition may be feasible only when there is a certain degree of prior harmonization of mutually acceptable minimum standards. A similar logic applies to compatibility standards, though there may be no alternative to full harmonization if differences matter, as for instance in the case of road-safety standards, railway gauges or legal procedures.

Regulatory cooperation may be more desirable – and likely more feasible – among a subset of countries than if pursued on a global scale. However, there is little, if any, empirical guidance on the payoffs to regulatory cooperation. What are the costs and benefits of deeper harmonization of regulatory standards and/or the establishment of mutual recognition agreements? The lack of empirical evidence complicates the task of deciding on the scope and depth, as well as the geographical reach and the optimal institutional forms, of regulatory cooperation.

If national standards are not optimal or insufficiently developed, then regional and/or international harmonization or standardization can be a way of improving such standards, as has happened in the financial services field with the Basle accord on capital adequacy. In such situations, the best partners for regulatory cooperation are likely to be those with the soundest regulatory frameworks. Such partners may not always be found within regional compacts. Moreover, the standard-setting process can at times be captured by protectionist interests, in which case convergence around "best" regulatory practice can serve a useful liberalizing purpose.

Another consideration is that there are gains from regulatory cooperation but also costs. The former will dominate where national regulation can be improved. The aggregate adjustment cost of regulatory convergence depends on the level of differences between the policy-related standards of the countries involved in an integration area. The costs are likely to be smallest when foreign regulatory preferences are similar and regulatory institutions are broadly compatible. The benefits of eliminating policy differences through harmonization depend on the prospects of creating a truly integrated market, which depends on the "natural distance" between countries, and that in turn depends on factors such as levels of development, physical distance, legal systems, and language.

If national standards optimally serve national objectives, there is a trade-off between the gains from integrated markets and the costs of transition and of departing from optimal domestic standards. For instance, a poor country may prefer to maintain a low mandatory standard for certain services because that reflects the socially optimal trade-off between price, quality and implementation capacities, whereas the socially optimal trade-off in a rich country may lead to the adoption of – and a preference for – a higher standard. Under such circumstances, a harmonization of standards could create benefits in terms of increased competition in integrated markets, but would necessarily impose a social cost in at least one country. This matter may be non-trivial in the growing number of integration agreements concluded along "North-South" lines.

2.2.2 PTAs as Optimum Regulatory Areas for Services

"Optimum regulatory areas" can be thought of as defining the set of countries for which aggregate welfare would be maximized by regulatory convergence. Such an area would balance the benefits and costs of participation. The benefits of eliminating policy differences through harmonization depend on the prospects of creating truly integrated markets, which depends on natural ties between countries and factors such as geographic and linguistic proximity. The costs depend on the ex ante similarity of regulatory preferences and compatibility of regulatory institutions.

In the definition of an optimal regulatory area, it must also be recognized that cooperation can be a vehicle to exchange information on different experiences with regulatory reform and to identify good regulatory practices. This form of cooperation can be especially useful for regulating new services in sectors characterized by continuous technical change. Developing countries may have a particular interest in cooperating with advanced industrial countries that have the longest experience with regulatory reform and where the newest technologies and their regulatory implications are often first introduced.

However, whether an individual country benefits from regulatory convergence or harmonization, its willingness to participate in such an area may depend on where the standard is set, the level at which it is set, and the regulatory environment to which such a standard responds. The latter factors will in turn determine who will bear the costs of transition towards the adoption of such a standard. The incentive to make regulations converge may depend on the relative size of markets, with small countries often having more to gain. This may explain why small countries acceding to the European Union (EU) agree to bear the full cost of transition.

It should be noted that the process of regulatory convergence can itself involve sunk costs of transition. The sequence in which a country chooses to harmonize (or progressively converge) its regulations with different trading partners is thus a relevant consideration. One reason is that the sequence of harmonization may influence the bargaining power of different country groupings in the negotiation over the level at which the harmonized standard should be set. For example, the countries in Eastern Europe that acceded to the EU on an individual basis could arguably have had a greater say in the EU-wide standard in specific areas if they had either been original members, negotiated collectively, or both. Similarly, harmonization first conducted at the MERCOSUR level, and then at the Free Trade Area of the Americas (FTAA) or WTO level, could imply different costs and produce a different outcome from direct harmonization at the broader level.

A final consideration to note in regard to preferential regulatory convergence relates to the possible administrative burden implied by the maintenance – and administration – of distinct regulatory requirements and procedures as between members and non-members of a PTA. Such costs may be sufficiently acute for a number of developing countries as to tilt negotiating incentives in favor of multilateral undertakings. It may also encourage the multilateralization of norms first brokered at the regional level or incite countries to simply extend to all third countries treatment similar to that afforded to PTA members, bearing in mind the limits of MFN-based outcomes on regulatory issues.

2.3 THIRD-COUNTRY EFFECTS

PTAs between countries that are WTO members or accessing the WTO can be potentially harmful to non-member countries as they imply preferential liberalization in favor of certain member states. Such discrimination violates one of the central obligations imposed by both the GATT and the GATS – the MFN treatment rule. The GATS is similar to the GATT in permitting signatories to pursue preferential liberalization arrangements, subject however to a number of conditions that are intended to minimize potential adverse effects on non-members as well as on the multilateral trading system as a whole.

In the context of agreements liberalizing trade in goods, a sufficient condition for preferential liberalization to be deemed multilaterally acceptable is that it not have detrimental impacts on third countries. That is, the volume of imports by member countries from the rest of the world should not decline on a product-by-product basis after the implementation of the agreement (Kemp and Wan, 1976; McMillan, 1993). While in principle a simple enough criterion, it is not straightforward to implement in practice given that the focus is on trade flows at the individual product level.

The liberalization of services trade implies not only that measures restricting the ability of foreign suppliers to engage in cross-border trade are reduced or eliminated, but also that factor mobility (and especially the establishment of a commercial presence) is allowed.

In determining the welfare implications for third parties of regional integration agreements covering services, account therefore needs to be taken of the impact on trade *and* factor flows. Both of these flows are endogenous and interdependent. Simple prescriptions or criteria along Kemp-Wan lines therefore can no longer be applied. If, for example, trade and factor flows are substitutes, a decline in trade in products need not necessarily be detrimental to an outside country, as greater factor flows substitute for trade. This is the standard case in neoclassical trade theory assuming constant-returns-to-scale technology. If, conversely, there are increasing returns, the relationship between factor movements and product-trade flows may well be complementary, i.e. an increase in one may be associated with an increase in the other. Although the presumption is that, by liberalizing both product and factor markets, the aggregate benefits for participants will increase, and this in turn will be beneficial to the rest of the world as a whole (partly through induced growth and investment effects), straightforward criteria with which to evaluate such integration effects ex ante do not exist. These problems are compounded by the difficulty of establishing clear-cut criteria of product likeness in services, given the far greater degree of product differentiation and customer tailoring arising in services markets.

2.3.1 Rules of Origin/Denial of Benefits

A final area of rule-making deserving attention in a discussion of PTAs and services trade concerns the issue of rules of origin. Such rules condition who ultimately qualifies for preferential treatment under PTAs. In services agreements, this matter is generally addressed under provisions dealing with denial of benefits.[2]

The literature on rules of origin has focused almost exclusively on merchandise trade flows and hence on policies for determining the origin or nationality of tangible *products*. Much less attention has been devoted to the increasingly important issue of how to determine the origin of *producers*, which is primarily what the study of rules of origin in services trade and investment is concerned with. Since contesting service markets often requires the physical presence of suppliers in the territory of consumers, either in the form of individual service providers performing cross-border transactions on a temporary (i.e. contract) basis or as entities servicing a foreign market on the basis of a commercial presence in that market, governments that are signatories of trade and investment agreements may need to ascertain whether suppliers originate in other countries, with a view to extending or denying the benefits foreseen under such agreements.

Experience shows that rules of origin for services and investment can play a significant role in determining the degree to which regional trading arrangements discriminate against non-member countries, and hence the extent of potentially costly trade and investment diversion. When levels of protection differ between participating countries, the effective preference granted to a trading partner will depend on how restrictive the applied rule of origin is. In the extreme, if one participant has a fully liberalized market, the adoption of a liberal rule of origin by the other participants can be likened to MFN liberalization, as services and service suppliers can enter or establish themselves in the liberal jurisdiction and from there move to – or service – the other partner countries.

From an efficiency perspective, the policy on origin rules for services should be to allow for third-country service suppliers, particularly those operating through a commercial presence (e.g. via Mode 3 entry) to take advantage of – and contribute to – the benefits of an integrating area. Under a liberal rule of origin for services and investment[3] aimed at ensuring that established foreign operators are not mere shell companies

---

[2] For a fuller discussion of rules of origin in services trade, see Beviglia-Zampetti and Sauvé (2006).

[3] More restrictive rules of origin conditioning the receipt of preferences may relate to various factors, such as local incorporation (such that benefits are denied to branches of third-country invested entities), place of incorporation or location of headquarters or ownership and control tests aimed at limiting PTA benefits to local juridical persons. Examples of the latter can be found under MERCOSUL or the Andean Pact.

but conduct substantial business operations in the host country market, third-country investors and service providers can take full advantage of the expanded market opportunities afforded by the creation of a PTA by establishing a commercial presence within the integration area. Not surprisingly, participants who seek to benefit from preferential access to a protected market and deny benefits to third-country competitors are likely to argue for the adoption of restrictive rules of origin. This could be the attitude, in particular, of regionally dominant but non-globally competitive service providers towards third-country competition within a regionally integrating area.

The adoption of restrictive rules of origin are permissible under GATS Article V:3, which allows PTAs concluded *between* developing countries (i.e. South-South PTAs) to restrict the benefits of integration to service suppliers that are owned and controlled by citizens of the integrating area. It is not clear whether such flexibility serves the development interests of those that use them. Several South-South PTAs, notably ASEAN, MERCOSUL, the Andean Pact, the China-Hong Kong or the China-Macau FTAs, have opted for a restrictive policy stance in this area.

The policy stance taken with regard to rules of origin for services and investment in a PTA can play an important role in promoting or inhibiting access to the most efficient suppliers of services. In many service sectors, the most efficient (or globally competitive) suppliers will tend to be either developed country firms or firms originating outside an integrating area. Accordingly, the adoption of rules of origin that restrict benefits to nationals of member states can exert detrimental effects by potentially locking in integrating partners into sub-optimal patterns of production and consumption. The above problem may be compounded, and generate longer-term deadweight losses, to the extent that many services, particularly network-based services, involve significant location-specific sunk costs, such that first movers (even if relatively inefficient) can exert long-term dominance and extract monopolistic rents. As discussed earlier, the problem with location-specific sunk costs is that a country may be stuck with inferior suppliers for a long time even if it subsequently liberalizes on an MFN basis. Indeed, because of the importance of sunk costs in many service industries, sequential entry (which preferential liberalization with restrictive rules of origin can easily promote) can produce very different results from simultaneous entry. If entry is costly, an incumbent may indeed be able to fully deter entry, leading to greater market concentration and a reduction in consumer welfare.[4]

---

4 For a fuller discussion, see Mattoo and Fink (2002).

Some measure of solace can therefore be taken from the observation that the vast majority of preferential agreements have to date adopted the most liberal rule of origin for Mode 3 suppliers, whereby any juridical person incorporated in any party to an integration agreement and conducting substantial business operations therein receives full treaty benefits.

2.3.2 Sequencing

The sequence of preferential market opening in services rarely, if ever, predates preferential talks in goods trade. Countries that engage in services-related PTAs either pursue such negotiations alongside merchandise trade negotiations in a manner analogous to the WTO's "Single Undertaking" approach or pursue services talks sequentially once a PTA in goods trade has been agreed. The latter approach is more common among South-South PTAs, whereas agreements involving OECD countries typically espouse the Single Undertaking route.

Countries preferring sequential liberalization may wish to test the waters in goods trade first, raising comfort levels with new trading partners. They may also wish to limit the scope for bargaining across several policy areas that come from WTO-type negotiations, though such a choice may well constrain negotiations given the greater narrowness of the negotiating remit. Sequential liberalization may also allow partners to identify key services inputs and address potential service sector bottlenecks holding back trade in manufactured products or primary commodities. The greater degree of liberalization achieved to date under North-South PTAs, particularly those based on a negative list approach, helps explain why PTAs predicated on a Single Undertaking approach have tended to entail greater levels of market opening.

The fact that PTAs have achieved significant progress in market opening terms when compared to the GATS should come as no surprise when one considers that the WTO commitments under GATS are those brokered in the early 1990s and, in the case of telecommunications and financial services (where most progress was made), in 1997. The vast majority of services-related PTAs were concluded after the entry into force of the GATS. Such agreements have taken advantage both of rising comfort levels afforded by the pedagogical journey undertaken during the Uruguay Round, from the rising level of services-specific trade-related technical assistance dispensed at both the multilateral and PTA levels in the post-Uruguay Round period as well as the far-reaching degree of unilateral liberalization in services markets that characterized the period and which the WTO-GATS has yet been able to catch up with and consolidate.

A more analytically meaningful comparison is thus the one that can be made between the level and nature of PTA commitments and that of negotiating offers made by WTO members in the ongoing Doha Development Agenda (despite the tactical considerations that may well hold back services offers in a round that has placed agriculture and NAMA (non-agricultural market access) squarely at the center of discussions).

CONCLUDING REMARKS

The analysis of PTAs in services trade on offer in this chapter suggests the need for an extension of conventional trade theory in two ways, both of which relate to core-distinguishing features of services: first, the manner in which trade in services occurs (i.e. the typical need for proximity between the supplier and the consumer) and, second, the form that trade protection takes in the sector (i.e. restrictions on the movement of labor and capital, and stringent domestic regulations, such as technical standards, licensing and qualification requirements).

A common effect of many restrictive measures in services trade (given their regulatory nature) is to increase the costs of operation faced by foreign providers without necessarily generating equivalent domestic rents. There is therefore little or no cost to granting preferential access because there is little or no revenue to lose. In such circumstances, preferential liberalization will necessarily be welfare-enhancing. However, countries outside the preferential arrangement may lose.

A country is likely to benefit from eliminating, even on a preferential basis, any excessive fixed costs of entry by removing unnecessarily burdensome qualification, licensing and local establishment requirements. The presumption that a country will benefit from such initiatives is greater if agreements are not exclusionary but rather open to all parties able to satisfy the regulatory requirements maintained within the integrating area. The greatest benefits arise if recognition agreements include all countries that have comparable regulation.

Absent liberal rules of origin on investment that confer the full benefits of an integration scheme to third-country investors, the establishment of preferences may result in entry by inferior suppliers. Because the most efficient suppliers may also generate the greatest positive externalities, the downside risks of preferential liberalization may be greater – especially in crucial infrastructural services. This is particularly the case in service sectors with high location-specific sunk costs requiring the establishment of a presence close to consumers. Preferential liberalization may then exert more durable effects on the nature of competition than in the case of trade in goods. For instance, concluding an agreement that allows second-best providers to obtain a first-mover advantage may imply that a country could be stuck with such providers even if it subsequently liberalizes on an MFN basis.

The gains from preferential agreements are likely to be significant in areas where there is scope for more fully reaping economies of scale. In principle, these gains can also be reaped through MFN liberalization, but in practice the full integration of markets may require a deeper convergence of regulatory regimes. Regulatory cooperation may be more desirable – and likely more feasible – among a subset of countries than if pursued on a global scale.

Regional and/or international harmonization or standardization can be an important and cost-effective way of improving national standards. In such situations, the best partners for regulatory cooperation are likely to be those with the soundest regulatory frameworks. Such partners may not always be found within regional compacts.

There are gains from regulatory cooperation but also costs. The former will dominate where national regulation can be improved and where the process of regulatory convergence or harmonization can take place, taking into account local circumstances. The costs are likely to be smallest when foreign regulatory preferences are similar and regulatory institutions are broadly compatible.

"South-South" PTAs covering services can be looked at as a variant of the infant-industry argument. Exposure to competition first in the more sheltered confines of a regional market may help firms prepare for global competition. Firms that have gained competitiveness at the regional level may also be less likely to resist broader-based liberalization. The risk does exist, however, that regional liberalization might create a new constellation of vested interests that could resist further market opening. The GATS offers a way out of this dilemma by allowing member countries to pre-commit to future multilateral liberalization, signaling a time frame over which regional preferences may be progressively eroded and/or eliminated.

The sequence of preferential market opening in services rarely, if ever, predates preferential talks in goods trade. Countries that engage in services-related PTAs either pursue such negotiations alongside merchandise trade negotiations in a manner analogous to the WTO's "Single Undertaking" approach or pursue services talks sequentially once a PTA in goods trade has been agreed.

The relationship between PTAs and the WTO is not unidirectional in character but involves iterative, two-way, interaction between the two layers of trade governance in ways that can inform subsequent patterns of rule-making and market opening at both the PTA and WTO levels. Examples of such interaction can notably be found in areas where WTO jurisprudence has clarified or interpreted the scope of key provisions governing services trade that are typically found both in the WTO-GATS and in the services and investment chapters of PTAs.

REFERENCES AND SUGGESTED READING

Abugattas, L. and S. Stephenson (2002), "Liberalization of Trade in Services: Options and Implications for Latin American and Caribbean Countries", in D. Tussie (ed.), *The Promise and Problems of Trade Negotiations in Latin America*, Basingstoke: Palgrave.

Adlung, R. (2007), "Negotiations on Safeguards and Subsidies in Services: A Never-Ending Story?", *Journal of International Economic Law*, 10(2): 235–65.

Baier, S.L. and J.H. Bergstrand (2001), "International Trade in Services, Free Trade Agreements, and the WTO", in R.M. Stern (ed.), *Services in the International Economy*, Michigan: University of Michigan Press, chapter 7.

Bhagwati, Jagdish (1990), "Multilateralism at Risk: The GATT is Dead, Long Live the GATT", *The World Economy*, 13(2): 149–69.

Baldwin, R. (2000), "Regulatory Protectionism, Developing Nations and a Two-tier World Trade System", Centre For Economic Policy Research (CEPR) Discussion Paper Series (October) 2574: 1–39. London: CEPR.

Baldwin, Richard E. (2006), "Multilateralising Regionalism: Spaghetti Bowls as Building Blocs on the Path to Global Free Trade", Paper presented at the 2006 World Economy Annual Lecture, Nottingham, 22 June 2006.

Baldwin, R., S. Evenett and P. Low (2009), "Beyond Tariffs: Multilateralizing Non-tariff RTA Commitments", in R. Baldwin and P. Low (eds.), *Multilateralizing Regionalism: Challenges for the Global Trade System*, Cambridge, UK: Cambridge University Press.

Baptista Neto, J.A. (2009), "United States Preferential Trade Agreements in Services: How Far Beyond the NAFTA?", Thesis submitted in partial fulfillment of the Masters of International Law and Economics (MILE), World Trade Institute, University of Bern, Bern (30 October).

Beviglia-Zampetti, A. (2000), "Market Access through Mutual Recognition: The Promise and Limits of *GATS* Article VII", in P. Sauvé and R.M. Stern (eds.), *GATS 2000: New Directions in Services Trade Liberalization*, Washington, DC: The Brookings Institution, pp. 283–306.

Beviglia-Zampetti, A. and P. Sauvé (2006), "Rules of Origin for Services: Economic and Legal Considerations", in O. Cadot, A. Estevadeordal, A. Suwa-Eisenmann and T. Verdier (eds.), *The Origin of Goods: Rules of Origin in Regional Trade Agreements*, Oxford: Oxford University Press and CEPR, pp. 114–45.

Beviglia-Zampetti, A. and P. Sauvé (2007), "International Investment", in Alan O. Sykes and Andrew Guzman (eds.), *Research Handbook in International Economic Law*, Cheltenham, UK and Northampton, MA, USA: Edward Elgar, pp. 211–70.

Bureau of Economic Analysis (2008), "US International Services: Cross Border Trade in 2007 and Services Supplied through Affiliates in 2006", in BEA's Survey of Current Business. Available at: http://www.bea.gov/scb/pdf/2008/10%20 October/services_text.pdf.

Coe, D.T., E. Helpman and A.W. Hoffmaister (1997), "North-South R&D Spillovers", *The Economic Journal*, 107: 134–49.

Commission of the European Communities (2002), *The State of the Internal Market for Services – Report from the Commission to the Council and the European Parliament, presented under the first stage of the Internal Market Strategy for Services*, COM(2002)41 Final, Brussels (30 July).

Copeland, B.R. (2001), "Benefits and Costs of Trade and Investment Liberalization in Services: Implications from Trade Theory", Paper prepared for the Department of Foreign Affairs and International Trade, Government of Canada.

Curzon, G. (1965), *Multilateral Commercial Diplomacy*, London: Michael-Joseph.

Dam, Kenneth W. (1970), *The GATT: Law and International Economic Organization*, Chicago: University of Chicago Press.

Delimatsis, P. (2008), "Towards a Horizontal Necessity Test for Services: Completing the GATS Article VI:4 Mandate", in M. Panizzon, N. Pohl and P. Sauvé (eds.), *Trade in Services: New Perspectives on Liberalization, Regulation and Development*, Cambridge: Cambridge University Press, pp. 370–96.

Doove, S., O. Gaabitas, D. Nguyen-Hong, and J. Owen (2001), "Price Effects of Regulation: Telecommunication, Air Transport and Electricity Supply", Productivity Commission Staff Research Paper, AusInfo, Canberra (October).

Ethier, W. (1982), "National and International Returns to Scale in the Modern Theory of International Trade", *American Economic Review*, 72 (June): 492–506.

Evenett, S.J. (2005), "A Competitive Liberalization: A Tournament Theory-based Interpretation". Available at: http://www.alexandria.unisg.ch/publications/22172.

Evenett, S.J. and M. Meier (2007), "An Interim Assessment of the U.S. Trade Policy of 'Competitive Liberalization'", St. Gallen University Discussion Paper, No. 2007–18. Available at: http://ssrn.com/abstract=985521.

Feketekuty, Geza (1998), "Setting the Agenda for Services 2000: The Next Round of Negotiations on Trade in Services", Paper presented at "The Future of Services Trade liberalization – Services 2000," a conference sponsored by the Coalitions of Service Industries. Ditchley Park, England, April.

Feketekuty, G. (2000a), "Regulatory Reform and Trade Liberalization", in P. Sauvé and R.M. Stern (eds.), *GATS 2000: New Directions in Services Trade Liberalization*, Washington, DC: Brookings Institution Press.

Feketekuty, Geza (2000b), "Assessing the WTO General Agreement on Trade and Improving the GATS", in P. Sauvé and R.M. Stern (eds.), *GATS 2000: New Directions in Services Trade Liberalization*, Washington, DC: Brookings Institution Press.

Findlay, C. and T. Warren (2000), *Impediments to Trade in Services: Measurement and Policy Implications*, London and New York: Routledge.

Finger, J. Michael (1992), "GATT's Influence on PTAs", Paper presented at a World Bank/CEPR conference on New Dimensions in Regional Integration, 2–3 April 1992, Washington, DC.

Fink, C. (2008a), "Liberalizing Services Trade in the ASEAN Region", in Aaditya Matto, Robert M. Stern, and Gianni Zanini (eds.), *International Trade in Services: A Handbook*, Washington, DC: The World Bank and Oxford University Press.

Fink, C. (2008b), "PTAs in Services: Friends or Foes of the Multilateral Trading System?", in J. Marchetti and M. Roy (eds.), *Opening Markets for Trade in Services: Countries and Sectors in Bilateral and WTO Negotiations*, Cambridge: Cambridge University Press, pp. 113–47.

Fink, C. and M. Molinuevo (2007), "East Asian FTAs in Services: Roaring Tigers or Timid Pandas", East Asia and Pacific Region, Report No. 40175, The World Bank.

Fink, C. and M. Jansen (2009), "Services Provisions in Regional Trade Agreements: Stumbling Blocks or Building Blocks for Multilateral Liberalization", in R. Baldwin and P. Low (eds.), *Multilateralizing Regionalism: Challenges for the Global Trade System*, Cambridge, UK: Cambridge University Press.

Frankel, J., E. Stein and S. Wei (1995), "Trading Blocs and the Americas: The Natural, the Unnatural and the Supernatural", *Journal of Development Economics*, 47: 61–96.

Glassman, C.A. (2000), "Customer Benefits from Current Information Sharing by Financial Services Companies", Study for the Financial Services Roundtable, December.

Greenaway, D. (1993), "Study on Regional Integration: Third Country Responses", Paper prepared as a background document for the OECD Trade Directorate project on Regional Integration, mimeo, Paris: Organisation for Economic Co-operation and Development.

Hamilton, B. and J. Whalley (1984), "Efficiency and Distributional Implications of Global Restrictions on Labor Mobility: Calculations and Policy Implications", *Journal of Development Economics*, 14: 61–75.

Hardin, I. and P. Holmes (1997), "Services Trade and Foreign Direct Investment", Staff Research Paper, Industry Commission. Canberra: Australia Government Publishing Services.

Hart, M. and P. Sauvé (1997), "Does Size Matter? Canadian Perspectives on the Development of Government Procurement Disciplines in North America", in Bernard Hoekman and Petros Mavroidis (eds.), *Law and Policy in Public Purchasing*, Ann Arbor: University of Michigan Press, pp. 203–21.

Hoekman, B. (1995), "Tentative First Steps – An Assessment of the Uruguay Round Agreement on Services", The Uruguay Round and the Developing Economies. World Bank Discussion Paper Series No. 307, Washington, DC.

Hoekman, B. (1996), "Assessing the General Agreement on Trade in Services", in Will Martin and L. Alan Winters (eds.), *The Uruguay Round and the Developing Countries*, Cambridge and New York: Cambridge University Press.

Hoekman, B. and C.A. Primo Braga (1997), "Protection and Trade in Services: A Survey", *Open Economies Review*, 8: 285–308.

Hoekman, B.M. and P. Sauvé (1994), "Liberalizing Trade in Services", World Bank Discussion Paper 243, Washington, DC: The World Bank.

Holmes, P. and I. Hardin (2000), "Assessing Barriers to Services Sector Investment", in C. Findlay and T. Warren (eds.), *Impediments to Trade in Services: Measurement and Policy Implications*, London and New York: Routledge.

Horn, H., P. Mavroidis and A. Sapir (2009), *Beyond the WTO? An Anatomy of US and EC Preferential Trade Agreements*, Bruegel Blueprint Series, Volume VII (January). Brussels: Bruegel. Available at: http://www.bruegel.org/uploads/tx_btbbreugel/bp_trade_jan09.pdf.

IADB (2002), *Beyond Borders: The New Regionalism in Latin America*, Economic

and Social Progress in Latin America, 2002 Report, Washington, DC: Inter-American Development Bank.
Iida, Keyia and Julia Nielson (2003), "Strengthening Regulatory Transparency", in A. Mattoo and P. Sauvé (eds.), *Domestic Regulation and Service Trade Liberalization*, Washington, DC: Oxford University Press for the World Bank, pp. 7–26.
IMF (2009), "Balance of Payments Manual", 6th edition, New York: IMF. Available at: http://www.imf.org/external/pubs/ft/bop/2007/bopman6.htm.
Kalirajan, K. (2000), "Restrictions on Trade and Distribution Services", Productivity Commission Staff Research Paper, AusInfo, Canberra (August).
Kelton, M. (2003), "The AUSFTA and the Current Alignment of US Trade and Security Strategy", Refereed paper presented to the Australasian Political Studies Association Conference. Available at: http://www.utas.edu.au/government/APSA/MKeltonfinal.pdf.
Kemp, S. (2000), "Trade in Education Services and the Impacts of Barriers on Trade", in C. Findlay and T. Warren (eds.), *Impediments to Trade in Services: Measurement and Policy Implications*, London and New York: Routledge.
Kemp, Murray and H. Wan (1976), "An Elementary Proposition Concerning the Formation of Customs Unions", *Journal of International Economics*, 6: 95–7.
Kessides, Ioannis N., Roger G. Noll and Nancy C. Benjamin (2009), "Regionalizing Telecommunications Reform in West Africa", Policy Research Working Paper 5126, Washington: The World Bank (November). Available at: http://www-wds.worldbank.org/external/default/WDSContentServer/IW3P/IB/2009/11/11/000158349_20091111153540/Rendered/PDF/WPS5126.pdf.
Kowalczyk, Carsten (1990), "Welfare and Customs Unions", NBER Working Paper No. 3476, October.
Lawrence, Robert Z. (1991), "Regional Trade Agreements: Building Blocks or Stumbling Blocks?", in R. O'Brien (ed.), *Finance and the International Economy: 5*, Oxford: Oxford University Press.
Leebron, David (2003), "Regulatory Discrimination in Domestic United States Law: A Model for the GATS?", in A. Mattoo and P. Sauvé (eds.), *Domestic Regulation and Service Trade Liberalization*, Washington, DC: Oxford University Press for the World Bank, pp. 43–56.
Leroux, Eric (1995), *Le libre-échange nord-américain et les services financiers*, Collection Minerve, Montréal: Editions Yvon Blais.
Low, P. and A. Mattoo (2000), "Is There a Better Way? Alternative Approaches to Liberalization under GATS", in P. Sauvé and R.M. Stern (eds.), *GATS 2000: New Directions in Services Liberalization*, Washington, DC: Brookings Institution Press.
Lumengo-Neso, O., M. Olarreaga and M. Schiff (2001), "On Indirect Trade-Related Research and Development Spillovers", World Bank Policy Research Working Paper No. 2580, Washington, DC: The World Bank.
Marconni, Mario (2005), "Emergency Safeguard Measures in the GATS: Beyond Feasible and Desirable", UNCTAD/DITC/TNCD/2005/4, Geneva: UNCTAD.
Marchetti, J. (2004), "Developing Countries in the WTO Services Negotiations", WTO Economic Research and Statistics Division, Staff Working Paper ERSD-2004–06.
Marchetti, J. and M. Roy (2008), "Services Liberalization in the WTO and in PTAs", in J. Marchetti and M. Roy (eds.), *Opening Markets for Trade in Services: Countries and Sectors in Bilateral and WTO Negotiations*, Cambridge: Cambridge University Press, pp. 61–112.

Markusen, James (1983), "Factor Movements and Commodity Trade as Complements", *Journal of International Economics*, 14: 341–56.
Mattoo, A. (1998), "Financial Services and the WTO: Liberalization in the Developing and Transitional Economies", Paper for presentation in the Workshop, "Measuring Impediments to Trade in Services", Productivity Commission, Canberra, 30 April–1 May 1998.
Mattoo, A., R. Rathindran and A. Subramanian (2001), "Measuring Services Trade Liberalization and its Impact on Economic Growth: An Illustration", World Bank Policy Research Working Paper No. 2380, Washington, DC: World Bank.
Mattoo, Aaditya and Carsten Fink (2002), "Regional Agreements and Trade in Services: Policy Issues", World Bank Policy Research Working Paper No. 2852 (June), Washington, DC: The World Bank.
Mattoo, A. and P. Sauvé (2002), "Regionalism and Trade in Services in the Western Hemisphere: A Policy Agenda", Paper prepared for "FTAA and Beyond: Prospects for Integration in the Americas", a Forum organized by the Inter-American Development Bank and Harvard University, Punta del Este, (15–16 December).
Mattoo, A. and P. Sauvé (2003), "Domestic Regulation and the GATS: Looking Ahead", in Mattoo, A. and P. Sauvé (eds.), *Domestic Regulation and Service Trade Liberalization*, Washington, DC: Oxford University Press for the World Bank.
Mattoo, A. and P. Sauvé (2008), "Regionalism in Services Trade", in A. Mattoo, R. Stern and G. Zanini (eds.), *A Handbook in International Trade in Services*, New York: Oxford University Press.
McGuire, G. and M. Schuele (2000), "Restrictiveness of International Trade in Banking Services", in C. Findlay and T. Warren (eds.), *Impediments to Trade in Services: Measurement and Policy Implications*, London and New York: Routledge.
McGuire, G., M. Schuele and T. Smith (2000), "Restrictiveness of International Trade in Maritime Services", in C. Findlay and T. Warren (eds.), *Impediments to Trade in Services: Measurement and Policy Implications*, London and New York: Routledge.
McLaren, J. (1997), "Size, Sunk Costs, and Judge Bowker's Objection to Free Trade", *American Economic Review*, 87 (June): 400–20.
McLaren, J. (1999), "A Theory of Insidious Regionalism", mimeo, Department of Economics, Columbia University (June).
McMillan, John (1993), "Does Regional Integration Foster Open Trade? Economic Theory and GATT's Article XXIV", in Kym Anderson and Richard Blackhurst (eds.), *Regional Integration and the Global Trading System*, London: Harvester-Wheatsheaf.
Mengozzi, Paolo (1993), "Trade in Services and Commercial Policy", in Marc Maresceau (ed.), *The European Community's Commercial Policy After 1992: The Legal Dimension*, Dordrecht: Martinus Nijhoff.
Messerlin, Patrick (2009), "Economic Partnership Agreements: How to Rebound?", in Emily Jones and Darlan F. Marti (2009), *Updating Economic Partnership Agreements to Today's Global Challenges*, Economic Policy Paper Series 09, Washington, DC and Brussels: The German Marshall Fund of the United States, pp. 22–7. Available at: http://www.gmfus.org/publications/index.cfm.

Monge-Narango, Alexander (2003), "Lessons from the NAFTA for Latin America and the Caribbean", mimeo, Washington, DC: The World Bank.
Nguyen-Hong, D. (2000), "Restrictions on Trade in Professional Services", Productivity Commission, Staff Research Paper, AusInfo, Canberra (August).
Nicolaidis, K. and J.P. Trachtman (2000), "From Policed National Treatment to Managed Recognition: Mapping the Boundary in GATS", in P. Sauvé and R.M. Stern (eds.), *GATS 2000: New Directions in Services Trade Liberalization*, Washington, DC: Brookings Institution Press, pp. 241–82.
Nielson, J. and D. Taglioni (2004), "Services Trade Liberalisation: Identifying Opportunities and Gains", OECD Trade Policy Working Papers, No. 1.
Organization of American States (1998), "Sectoral Agreements on Services in the Western Hemisphere", Washington, DC.
Organization of American States (1999), "Provisions on Trade in Services in the Trade and Integration Agreements of the Western Hemisphere", Washington, DC.
OECD (2002a), *GATS: The Case for Open Services Markets*, Paris: OECD.
OECD (2002b), "The Relationship Between the Multilateral Trade System and Regional Trade Agreements: Government Procurement", TD/TC/WP(2002)24 (15 April).
OECD (2002c), "The Relationship Between Regional Trade Agreements and the Multilateral Trading System: Investment", TD/TC/WP(2002)18.
OECD (2002d), "Labor Mobility in PTAs", TD/TC/WP(2002)16.
OECD (2002e), "Service Providers on the Move: Taking a Closer Look at Labor Mobility and the GATS", Paris: OECD Trade Directorate.
OECD (2002f), "The Relationship Between Regional Trade Agreements and the Multilateral Trading System: Services", TD/TC/WP(2002)21.
OECD (2003), "Quantifying the Benefits of Liberalising Trade in Services", Paris: OECD.
OECD (2007), "The Services Trade Restrictiveness Index: Issues and Challenges in its Design", Meeting of the Experts on the STRI. OECD Document TAD/TC/SXM(2007)2.
OECD (2009), "Assessing Barriers to Trade in Services in the MENA Region", OECD Trade Policy Working Paper No. 84. OECD document TAD/TC/WP(2008)25/FINAL.
Patterson, G. (1966), *Discrimination in International Trade: The Policy Issues, 1945–1965*, Princeton: Princeton University Press.
Panagariya, Arvind (2000), "Preferential Trade Liberalization: The Traditional Theory and New Developments", *Journal of Economic Literature*, 38(2): 287–331.
PECC (Pacific Economic Cooperation Council) (1995), "Survey of the Impediments to Trade and Investment in the APEC Region", Singapore: PECC.
Pena, Maria-Angelica (2000), "Services in MERCOSUR: The Protocol of Montevideo", in Sherry M. Stephenson (ed.), *Services Trade in the Western Hemisphere: Liberalization, Integration and Reform*, Washington, DC: Trade Unit of the Organization of American States and Brookings Institution Press, pp. 154–68.
Pierola, Fernando (2008), "A Safeguards Regime for Services", in M. Panizzon, N. Pohl and P. Sauvé (eds.), *Trade in Services: New Perspectives on Liberalization, Regulation and Development*, Cambridge: Cambridge University Press, pp. 434–65.
Poretti, Pietro (2008), "Waiting for Godot? Subsidy Disciplines in Services

Trade", in M. Panizzon, N. Pohl and P. Sauvé (eds.), *Trade in Services: New Perspectives on Liberalization, Regulation and Development*, Cambridge: Cambridge University Press, pp. 466–88.

Prieto, F. (2000), "The GATS, Sub-PTAs and the FTAA: How Much is Left to be Done", in S. Stephenson (ed.), *Services Trade in the Western Hemisphere: Liberalization, Integration and Reform*, Washington, DC: Brookings Institution Press.

Primo-Braga, Carlos (1992), "NAFTA and the Rest of the World", in N. Lustig, B. Bosworth and R. Lawrence (eds.), *North American Free Trade: Assessing the Impact*. Washington, DC: Brookings Institution.

Qian, Y. (2000), "Analysis of the Commitments under the GATS and the World Trade Organization", mimeo, 8 February.

Robert, Maryse, Pierre Sauvé and Karsten Steinfatt (2001), "Negotiating Investment Rules: Possible Scenarios for an EU-MERCOSUL Agreement", mimeo, Paris: Institut d'Etudes Politiques.

Robinson, S., Z. Wang and W. Martin (1999), "Capturing the Implications of Services Trade Liberalization", Paper presented at the Second Annual Conference on Global Economic Analysis, GL Avernaes Conference Center, Ebberup, Denmark, 20–22 June.

Roy, M., J. Marchetti and H. Lim (2006), "Services Liberalization in the New Generation of Preferential Trade Agreements: How Much Further than the GATS?", WTO Staff Working Paper ERSD-2006–07.

Roy, M., J. Marchetti and H. Lim (2008), "The Race towards Preferential Trade Agreements in Services: How Much Further than the GATS?", in M. Panizzon, N. Pohl and P. Sauvé (eds.), *Trade in Services: New Perspectives on Liberalization, Regulation and Development*, Cambridge: Cambridge University Press, pp. 77–110.

Salazar-Xirinachs, J.M. and M. Robert (2001), *Toward Free Trade in the Americas*, Washington, DC: Organization of American States and Brookings Institution Press.

Sapir, Andre (1998), "GATS 1994–2000", *Journal of World Trade*, 33: 51–66.

Sauvé, Pierre (1996), "Services and the International Contestability of Markets", *Transnational Corporations*, 5(1) (April): 37–56.

Sauvé, Pierre (1997), "Preparing for Services 2000", CSI Occasional Paper No. 4, Washington, DC: Coalition of Services Industries.

Sauvé, Pierre (2000), "Making Progress on Trade and Investment: Multilateral vs. Regional Perspectives", in Sherry M. Stephenson (ed.), *Services Trade in the Western Hemisphere: Liberalization, Integration and Reform*, Washington, DC: Trade Unit of the Organization of American States and Brookings Institution Press, pp. 72–85.

Sauvé, Pierre (2002), "Completing the GATS Framework: Safeguards, Subsidies and Government Procurement", in Bernard Hoekman, Aaditya Mattoo and Philip English (eds.), *Development, Trade and the WTO: A Handbook*, Washington, DC: The World Bank, pp. 326–35.

Sauvé, P. (2003), "Assessing the General Agreement on Trade in Services: Half-full or Half-empty?", in Pierre Sauvé, *Trade Rules Behind Borders: Essays on Services, Investment and the New Trade Agenda*, London: Cameron May.

Sauvé, P. (2009), "Trade and Investment in Services: A Training Module for the Greater Mekong Sub-Region", Bangkok and Manila: Asian Development Bank with the International Institute for Trade and Development (October 2009).

Available at: http://www.adb.org/Documents/Guidelines/Trade-Investment-Services/default.asp.

Sauvé, P. (forthcoming), "Conducting a Trade-Related Regulatory Audit in Financial Services", in M. Haddad and C. Stephanou (eds.), *Financial Services and Preferential Trading Arrangements*, Washington, DC: The World Bank.

Sauvé, P. and D. Audet (2009), "The Treatment of Trade in Services in Economic Partnership Agreements: Implications for Prospective EPA Partners", in E. Jones and D.F. Marti (eds.), *Updating Economic Partnership Agreements to Today's Global Economic Challenges*, Economic Policy Paper Series 09, Washington, DC: German Marshall Fund of the United States, pp. 85–91. Available online at: http://www.gmfus.org//doc/GMF7257_Final_Ebook.pdf.

Sauvé, Pierre and Brenda Gonzalez-Hermosillo (1993), "Implications of the NAFTA for Canadian Financial Institutions", *C.D. Howe Commentary*, No. 44, Toronto: C.D. Howe Institute (April).

Sauvé, P. and M. Marconini (2009), "Negotiating Trade in Services: A Practical Guide for Developing Countries", International Trade Department, PREM, Washington, DC: The World Bank (May).

Sauvé, Pierre and Karsten Steinfatt (2001), "Financial Services and the WTO: What Next?", in Robert E. Litan, Paul Masson and Michael Pomerleano (eds.), *Open Doors: Foreign Participation in Financial Systems in Developing Countries*, Washington, DC: The World Bank Group, the International Monetary Fund and the Brookings Institution Press, pp. 351–86.

Sauvé, Pierre and Natasha Ward (2009a), "Services and Investment in the EC-CARIFORUM Economic Partnership Agreement: Innovation in Rule-design and Implications for Africa", in G. Faber and J. Orbie (eds.), *Beyond Market Access for Economic Development: EU-Africa Relations in Transition*, London: Routledge, pp. 137–72.

Sauvé, Pierre and Natasha Ward (2009b), "Tourism_Services Liberalization: The Role of Business Advocacy in the Caribbean-European Union Economic Partnership Agreement", Business and Trade Policy Case Study, Geneva: International Trade Centre, available at http://www.intracen.org/btp/business_advocacy/publications/tourism_services_liberalization..pdf.

Sauvé, Pierre and Christopher Wilkie (2000), "Investment Liberalization in GATS", in Pierre Sauvé and Robert M. Stern (eds.), *GATS 2000: New Directions in Services Trade Liberalization*, Washington, DC: Center for Business and Government, Harvard University and the Brookings Institution Press, pp. 331–63.

Schiff, M. and W. Chang (2003), "Market Presence, Contestability, and the Terms-of-Trade Effects of Regional Integration", *Journal of International Economics*, 60(1) (May): 161–75.

Schott, Jeffrey (ed.) (1989), *Free Trade Areas and U.S. Trade Policy*, Washington DC: Institute for International Economics.

Shi, Jingxia and Weidong Chen (2011), "How Far Can the Specificity of Cultural Products Go? Reflecting on 'China – Publications and Audiovisual Products', *Journal of World Trade*, 45(1) (February): 159–86.

Silver, Sara (2002), "US under Pressure over Mexican Trucking", *Financial Times*, 4 November.

Snape, Richard (1993), "History and Economics of GATT's Article XXIV", in Kym Anderson and Richard Blackhurst (eds.), *Regional Integration and the Global Trading System*, London: Harvester-Wheatsheaf.

Snape, Richard, Jan Adams and David Morgan (1993), *Regional Trading Arrangements: Implications and Options for Australia*, Canberra: Australian Government Publishing Service.
Snape, Richard and Malcolm Bosworth (1996), "Advancing Services Negotiations", in Jeffrey Schott (ed.), *The World Trading System: Challenges Ahead*, Washington, DC: Institute for International Economics, pp. 185–203.
Stephenson, Sherry M. (1999), "PTAs on Services within APEC and Disciplines of the Multilateral Trading System", Paper presented to the meeting of the APEC Group on Services, Wellington, New Zealand (February).
Stephenson, S. (2000), "PTAs on Services and Multilateral Disciplines: Interpreting and Applying GATS Article V", in P. Sauvé and R.M. Stern (eds.), *GATS 2000: New Directions in Services Trade Liberalization*, Washington, DC: The Brookings Institution Press.
Stephenson, S. (2001a), "Multilateral and Regional Services Liberalization by Latin America and the Caribbean", *OAS Trade Unit Studies*, OEA/Ser.D/XXII, SG/TU/TUS-9 (March).
Stephenson, S.M. (2001b), "Services", in Jose-Manuel Salazar-Xirinachs and Maryse Robert (eds.), *Toward Free Trade in the Americas*, Washington, DC: Trade Unit of the Organization of American States and Brookings Institution Press, pp. 163–85.
Stephenson, S.M. (2001c), "Deepening Disciplines for Trade in Services", *OAS Trade Unit Studies: Analyses on Trade and Integration in the Americas*, Washington, DC: Organization of American States (March).
Stephenson, S. (2001d), "Deepening Disciplines for Trade in Services", *OAS Trade Unit Studies: Analyses on Trade and Integration in the Americas*, Washington, DC: Organization of American States (March).
Stephenson, S. (2002), "Regional versus Multilateral Liberalization of Services", *World Trade Review*, 1(2): 187–209.
Stephenson, S. and S. Yi (2002), "Transparency in Regulation of Services", Paper prepared for the meeting of the APEC Group on Services, Mexico City, February, as part of the project on the Menu of Options for Voluntary Liberalization, Facilitation and Economic and Technical Cooperation in Services Trade and Investment.
Thompson, Rachel (2000), "Formula Approaches to Improving GATS Commitments", in Pierre Sauvé and Robert M. Stern (eds.), *GATS 2000: New Directions in Services Trade Liberalization*, Washington, DC: Center for Business and Government, Harvard University and the Brookings Institution Press, pp. 473–86.
Tirole, Jean (1998), *The Theory of Industrial Organization*, Cambridge, MA: MIT Press.
Trachtman, Joel P. (2003), "Lessons for the GATS from Existing WTO Rules on Domestic Regulation", in A. Mattoo and P. Sauvé (eds.), *Domestic Regulation and Service Trade Liberalization*, Washington, DC: Oxford University Press for the World Bank.
United Nations and World Bank (1993), *Liberalizing International Transactions in Services: A Handbook*, Geneva: UNCTAD.
United States Coalition of Service Industries (2003), Reports of ISAC 13 on the US-Chile and US-Singapore Free Trade Agreements. Available at www.uscsi.org.
United Nations (2002), "Manual on Statistics of International Trade in Services",

Geneva, Luxembourg, New York, Paris, Washington, DC. Available at: http://unstats.un.org/unsd/tradeserv/TFSITS/manual.htm.

Viner, Jacob (1950), *The Customs Union Issue*, New York: Carnegie Endowment for International Peace.

Walmsley, T. and L.A. Winters (2002), "Relaxing the Restrictions on the Temporary Movement of Natural Persons: A Simulation Analysis", mimeo, University of Sussex.

Warren, T. (2000), "The Identification of Impediments to Trade and Investment in Telecommunications and Financial Services", in C. Findlay and T. Warren (eds.), *Impediments to Trade in Services: Measurement and Policy Implications*, London and New York: Routledge.

Winters, L.A. (1996), "Regionalism versus Multilateralism", World Bank Policy Research Working Paper, 1687, Washington, DC: World Bank.

Winters, L.A. (2001), "Harnessing Trade for Development", mimeo, University of Sussex.

Wonnacott, P. and R. Wonnacott (1981), "Is Unilateral Tariff Reduction Preferable to a Customs Union? The Curious Case of the Missing Foreign Tariffs", *The American Economic Review*, 71(4) (September): 704–14.

World Bank (2000), *Trade Blocs*, New York: Oxford University Press.

World Bank (2002), *Global Economic Prospects and the Developing Countries 2002: Making Trade Work for the Poor*, Washington, DC: The World Bank.

World Bank (2003), *Global Economic Prospects and the Developing Countries 2003: Investing to Unlock Global Opportunities*, Washington, DC: The World Bank.

World Bank (2004), *Global Economic Prospects and the Developing Countries 2004: Realizing the Promise of the Doha Round*, Washington, DC: The World Bank.

World Trade Organization (1995), *Regionalism and the World Trading System*, Geneva: World Trade Organization.

World Trade Organization (1999), "The Fundamental WTO Principles of National Treatment, Most-Favored-Nation Treatment and Transparency", WT/GTCP/W/114.

World Trade Organization (2001), *Market Access: Unfinished Business – Post Uruguay Round Issues*, Special Study No. 6, Geneva: World Trade Organization.

World Trade Organization (2003), *Regional Trade Agreements*, Geneva: World Trade Organization, available at www.wto.org.

World Trade Organization (2010), "RTA Database", available online from http://rtais.wto.org/UI/PublicMaintainRTAHome.aspx.

Wunsch-Vincent, Sacha (2003), "The Digital Trade Agenda of the U.S.: Parallel Tracks of Bilateral, Regional and Multilateral Liberalization", *Aussenwirtschaft*, No. 58, pp. 7–46.

Wunsch-Vincent, S. (2006), *The WTO, the Internet and Digital Products: EC and US Perspectives*, Oxford: Hart Publishing.

Wunsch-Vincent, S. (2008), "Trade Rules for the Digital Age", in M. Panizzon, N. Pohl and P. Sauvé (eds.) (2008), *GATS and the Regulation of International Trade in Services*, Cambridge: Cambridge University Press, pp. 497–529.

Zoellick, R.B. (2001), "Free Trade and the Hemispheric Hope", Prepared Remarks of Robert B. Zoellick, US Trade Representative, Council of the Americas, Washington, DC, 7 May 2001.

APPENDIX

Table 2A.1 List of Preferential Trade Agreements (PTAs) featuring provisions on trade in services

PTA Name	Date of entry into force
ASEAN–Australia–New Zealand	01 Jan 2010
ASEAN–China	01 Jan 2005(G) / 01 Jul 2007(S)
ASEAN–Korea, Republic of	01 Jan 2010(G) / 01 May 2009(S)
Australia–Chile	06 Mar 2009
Australia–New Zealand (ANZCERTA)	01 Jan 1983(G) / 01 Jan 1989(S)
Brunei Darussalam–Japan	31 Jul 2008
Canada–Chile	05 Jul 1997
Canada–Colombia	15 Aug 2011
Canada–Panama	01 Apr 2013
Canada–Peru	01 Aug 2009
Caribbean Community and Common Market (CARICOM)	01 Aug 1973(G) / 04 Jul 2002(S)
Chile–China	01 Oct 2006(G) / 01 Aug 2010(S)
Chile–Colombia	08 May 2009
Chile–Costa Rica (Chile–Central America)	15 Feb 2002
Chile–El Salvador (Chile–Central America)	01 Jun 2002
Chile–Guatemala (Chile–Central America)	23 Mar 2010
Chile–Honduras (Chile–Central America)	19 Jul 2008
Chile–Japan	03 Sep 2007
Chile – Mexico	01 Aug 1999
Chile–Nicaragua (Chile–Central America)	19 Oct 2012
China–Costa Rica	01 Aug 2011
China–Hong Kong, China	29 Jun 2003
China–Macao, China	17 Oct 2003
China–New Zealand	01 Oct 2008
China–Singapore	01 Jan 2009
Colombia – Mexico	01 Jan 1995
Colombia–Northern Triangle (El Salvador, Guatemala, Honduras)	12 Nov 2009
Costa Rica–Mexico	01 Jan 1995
Costa Rica–Peru	01 Jun 2013
Dominican Republic–Central America	04 Oct 2001
Dominican Republic–Central America–United States Free Trade Agreement (CAFTA-DR)	01 Mar 2006
East African Community (EAC)	07 Jul 2000(G) / 01 Jul 2010(S)
EC (15) Enlargement	01 Jan 1995
EC (25) Enlargement	01 May 2004
EC (27) Enlargement	01 Jan 2007
EC Treaty	01 Jan 1958
EFTA–Chile	01 Dec 2004
EFTA–Colombia	01 Jul 2011
EFTA–Hong Kong, China	01 Oct 2012

Table 2A.1 (continued)

PTA Name	Date of entry into force
EFTA–Korea, Republic of	01 Sep 2006
EFTA–Mexico	01 Jul 2001
EFTA–Singapore	01 Jan 2003
EFTA–Ukraine	01 Jun 2012
El Salvador–Honduras and the Separate Customs Territory of Taiwan, Penghu, Kinmen and Matsu	01 Mar 2008
EU–Albania	01 Dec 2006(G) / 01 Apr 2009(S)
EU–CARIFORUM States EPA	01 Nov 2008
EU–Central America	01 Aug 2013
EU–Chile	01 Feb 2003(G) / 01 Mar 2005(S)
EU–Colombia and Peru	01 Mar 2013
EU–Former Yugoslav Republic of Macedonia	01 Jun 2001(G) / 01 Apr 2004(S)
EU–Korea, Republic of	01 Jul 2011
EU–Mexico	01 Jul 2000(G) / 01 Oct 2000(S)
EU–Montenegro	01 Jan 2008(G) / 01 May 2010(S)
EU (28) Enlargement	01 Jul 2013
European Economic Area (EEA)	01 Jan 1994
European Free Trade Association (EFTA)	03 May 1960(G) / 01 Jun 2002(S)
Guatemala–the Separate Customs Territory of Taiwan, Penghu, Kinmen and Matsu	01 Jul 2006
Hong Kong, China–New Zealand	01 Jan 2011
Iceland–Faroe Islands	01 Nov 2006
India–Japan	01 Aug 2011
India–Malaysia	01 Jul 2011
India–Singapore	01 Aug 2005
Japan–Indonesia	01 Jul 2008
Japan–Malaysia	13 Jul 2006
Japan–Mexico	01 Apr 2005
Japan–Peru	01 Mar 2012
Japan–Philippines	11 Dec 2008
Japan–Singapore	30 Nov 2002
Japan–Switzerland	01 Sep 2009
Japan–Thailand	01 Nov 2007
Japan–Viet Nam	01 Oct 2009
Jordan–Singapore	22 Aug 2005
Korea, Republic of–Chile	01 Apr 2004
Korea, Republic of–India	01 Jan 2010
Korea, Republic of–Singapore	02 Mar 2006
Korea, Republic of–US	15 Mar 2012
Malaysia–Australia	01 Jan 2013
Mexico–El Salvador (Mexico–Northern Triangle)	15 Mar 2001
Mexico–Guatemala (Mexico– Northern Triangle)	15 Mar 2001
Mexico–Honduras (Mexico–Northern Triangle)	01 Jun 2001
Mexico–Nicaragua	01 Jul 1998
Mexico–Uruguay	15 Jul 2004
New Zealand–Malaysia	01 Aug 2010

Table 2A.1 (continued)

PTA Name	Date of entry into force
New Zealand–Singapore	01 Jan 2001
Nicaragua and the Separate Customs Territory of Taiwan, Penghu, Kinmen and Matsu	01 Jan 2008
North American Free Trade Agreement (NAFTA)	01 Jan 1994
Pakistan–China	01 Jul 2007(G) / 10 Oct 2009(S)
Pakistan–Malaysia	01 Jan 2008
Panama–Chile	07 Mar 2008
Panama–Costa Rica (Panama–Central America)	23 Nov 2008
Panama–El Salvador (Panama–Central America)	11 Apr 2003
Panama–Guatemala (Panama–Central America)	20 Jun 2009
Panama–Honduras (Panama–Central America)	09 Jan 2009
Panama–Nicaragua (Panama–Central America)	21 Nov 2009
Panama–Peru	01 May 2012
Panama–Singapore	24 Jul 2006
Panama and the Separate Customs Territory of Taiwan, Penghu, Kinmen and Matsu	01 Jan 2004
Peru–Chile	01 Mar 2009
Peru–China	01 Mar 2010
Peru–Korea, Republic of	01 Aug 2011
Peru–Mexico	01 Feb 2012
Peru–Singapore	01 Aug 2009
Singapore–Australia	28 Jul 2003
Southern Common Market (MERCOSUR)	29 Nov 1991(G) / 07 Dec 2005(S)
Thailand–Australia	01 Jan 2005
Thailand–New Zealand	01 Jul 2005
Trans-Pacific Strategic Economic Partnership	28 May 2006
Ukraine–Montenegro	01 Jan 2013
US–Australia	01 Jan 2005
US–Bahrain	01 Aug 2006
US–Chile	01 Jan 2004
US–Colombia	15 May 2012
US–Jordan	17 Dec 2001
US–Morocco	01 Jan 2006
US–Oman	01 Jan 2009
US–Panama	31 Oct 2012
US–Peru	01 Feb 2009
US–Singapore	01 Jan 2004
Total number of services PTAs	118
Total number of PTAs in force	379
Share of services PTAs in total PTAs in force	31.1%

Source: World Trade Organization, RTAs Database. Available online at http://www.wto.org/english/tratop_e/region_e/region_e.htm.

3. Do negotiated agreements foster trade in services? Evidence from PTAs

Anirudh Shingal

3.1 INTRODUCTION

Of the 83 Preferential Trade Agreements (PTAs) notified to the WTO in the period before 2000, only ten (12%) were notified to the WTO as services agreements. In the years since 2000 on the other hand, 60% of the additional 176 notified-PTAs have covered trade in services. Clearly then, more and more trading partners are negotiating services provisions in PTAs which suggests both the growing importance of services trade in general and the need to institutionalize such trade between countries. The obvious question then is how effective these agreements have been in fostering services trade.

Economic literature is replete with theoretical models and empirical analyses documenting the impact of PTAs on trade between partner countries. Most of this work, however, has looked at trade in merchandise goods only. An important reason for this has been the lack of availability of bilateral services trade data. This lacuna has, however, been filled with the publication of the OECD's database on bilateral services trade;[1] since its publication Grünfeld and Moxnes (2003), Kimura (2003), Kimura and Lee (2004, 2006), Lejour and Verheijden (2004), Mirza and Nicoletti (2004), Kox and Lejour (2005), Lennon (2006) and Walsh (2006) have used this dataset to assess determinants of bilateral services trade using the gravity framework.

However, there is a general lack of consensus and conformity to economic theory in these authors' key findings. Grünfeld and Moxnes (2003), for instance, find the impact of PTAs to be insignificant. Kimura and Lee (2004) find distance to be more important for services trade, while Lejour

[1] In 2002, the OECD Secretariat presented data on total trade in services, broken down by partner country, for 26 OECD member countries over 1999–2002.

and Verheijden (2004) and Lennon (2006) report the converse to be true. Walsh (2006), on the other hand, finds the impact of distance to be insignificant. Similarly, Kimura and Lee (2004) find the impact of common language to be insignificant, which is refuted by Lennon (2006) and Walsh (2006).

In this chapter, we base the gravity model on an intuitive understanding of the determinants of bilateral services trade by sector and mode of delivery and thereby generate results that are better validated by economic theory. We add to the literature in this area by distilling the trade effects of PTAs into those emanating from services and "goods only" agreements and further confirm complementarities between the two. We also study the impact of bilateral trade in goods on bilateral services trade more directly than has hitherto been explored in the empirical literature. Our analysis also explores the PTA-services trade relationship disaggregated by the economic status of the partner countries and by the reciprocity (or lack thereof) of commitments. To the best of our knowledge, this is also the first attempt in the literature on gravity model estimation of services trade to endogenize the impact of preferentialism in estimating the trade effect using advanced estimation techniques and also to look at the anticipation effects of services accords.

On the whole, our results suggest a trade effect of 15% from having a services accord alone. This effect rises to 32.3% for the intra-EU trading partners in our sample. The total incremental impact of a "goods only" PTA is found to be 7.6% (services PTAs accounting for one-third of this and "goods only" PTAs the rest). We also find both North-North and North-South services agreements to generate positive trade effects, which suggests that the associated pattern of trade is both intra- and inter-industry. Moreover, within North-South agreements and irrespective of the type of the agreement, asymmetric accords always have the larger trade effect and this is always positive. Finally, the services trade effect is accentuated to 59.7% once anticipation effects of services accords are included in the analysis. Our results also suggest that the maximum impact of a services accord is felt the farthest in time from actual accession; thus services agreements seem to have a significant "announcement effect".

The rest of the chapter is structured as follows. In the next section, we look at the determinants of services trade by sector and mode of delivery based on their classification in the GATS to arrive at the common set of factors that may have a bearing on bilateral services trade. Section 3.3 introduces the empirical model used while Section 3.4 looks at the dummy variables used in the analysis to capture the trade effects of different types and forms of PTAs. Section 3.5 describes the data and conducts a preliminary examination of it. The next two sections discuss the basic results from the empirical model as well as the results disaggregated by type of agreement and nature of relationship. Section 3.8 concludes.

3.2 DETERMINANTS OF BILATERAL SERVICES TRADE

We consider the set of major services sub-sectors (listed in the Central Products Classification of the GATS) for trade between any two possible trading partners and, for each of them, suggest possible modes of services delivery[2] and the most important likely determinants of such trade, based on our intuitive understanding of the latter. This is reported in Table 3.1. The purpose of this exercise is to distil the common set of factors that may affect trade in services between partners and to use them as explanatory variables in a gravity model for bilateral services trade. Thus, if we look at Table 3.1 for computer and related services, we see that these are delivered cross-border, through commercial presence and the movement of professionals (Modes 1, 3 and 4, respectively) and the likely determinants of such trade between partners include infrastructure and human capital resources as well as the presence of a common business language and an open policy regime.

Replicating this analysis for the other sub-sectors listed in Table 3.1, we find that the common set of factors that emerges as important determinants of bilateral services trade is market size (economic), trade in goods, the presence of a common business language (where we consider English), quality infrastructure, open policy regime (i.e. few restrictions on the various modes of services delivery), low cost human capital and common laws/legal systems. These are the variables that we use in a gravity model as determinants of bilateral services trade. We also use geographical distance to proxy the costs involved in transportation between countries. Finally, to estimate the trade effect of a services agreement, we include a PTA dummy that takes the value 1 for countries that are members of a PTA that has an element of services liberalization in it.

---

[2] The WTO's General Agreement on Trade in Services (GATS) classifies four "modes" of services delivery (these are the different ways in which services can be traded across borders): Mode One, which is the cross-border supply of services. An illustration of this is business process outsourcing units in India doing online medical transcriptions. Mode Two is consumption of services abroad for e.g. Indian tourists going to the EU. Mode Three is commercial presence, such as Deutsche Bank setting up operations in Mumbai. Finally, Mode Four is the movement of natural persons across borders to deliver services. An illustration of this is Indian software professionals working on-site on IT projects in the UK.

Table 3.1 Determinants of services trade by sector and mode of delivery

Sector	Mode of Delivery	Determinants of Trade
Computer & related services	1,3,4	Infrastructure, human capital, English language, open policy regime
Telecom	3	Market, infrastructure, open policy regime
Insurance	1,3	Infrastructure, English language, open policy regime, market size
Banking	1,3	Infrastructure, English language, open policy regime, market size
Construction	3,4	Infrastructure, open policy regime, trade in goods
Distribution	3	Market size, open policy regime, trade in goods
Health	1,2,3,4	Infrastructure, human capital, open policy regime
Architectural services	1,3,4	Infrastructure, human capital, open policy regime
Legal services	1,3,4	Infrastructure, human capital, open policy regime, common legal system
Accountancy services	1,3,4	Infrastructure, human capital, open policy regime, common laws
Hotels, restaurant and tourism services	2,3	Market size, cultural ties/ hospitality, English language, infrastructure,
Transport services	3	Market size, infrastructure, open policy regime, trade in goods

3.3 THE EMPIRICAL MODEL

Using the determinants identified above, we estimate our model in a log-linerarized form, setting bilateral services trade data in a panel for 25 exporting and 53 importing countries for five years over 1999–2003, available from the OECD's database. The baseline specification is as follows:

$$svsx_{ijt} = \alpha_{ij} + \beta_1 gdp_{it} + \beta_2 gdp_{jt} + \beta_3 pcgdp_{it} + \beta_4 pcgdp_{jt} + \beta_5 dist_{ij} + \beta_6 gdsx_{ijt} + \beta_7 ENG_{ij} + \beta_8 teleden_{it} + \beta_9 teleden_{jt} + \beta_{10} rest_i + \beta_{11} rest_j + \beta_{12} hk_{it} + \beta_{13} hk_{jt} + \beta_{14} LAW_{ij} + \beta_{15} PTA\_SVS_{ijt} + \varepsilon_{ijt} \quad (3.1)$$

All variables in lower case are in log levels; the sub-script 'i' refers to the exporter, 'j' to the importer, 't' is the sub-script on variables that vary over time. All continuous variables are in log form with the exception of the dummy variables. The variables, their description and data sources are reported in Table 3.2.

A priori, we expect the estimates of β_1 through β_4, β_6 through β_9, and β_{12} through β_{15} to be positive and those of β_5, β_{10} and β_{11} to be negative.

3.4 MORE ABOUT THE PTA DUMMIES

The crucial explanatory variable in our model is the dummy on participation in PTAs involving elements of services liberalization. We refer to WTO-notified PTAs for country-specific information in this regard. The estimated coefficient on the PTA_SVS dummy provides the direction and magnitude of the impact of a services agreement on the bilateral services trade between the trading partners in our sample[3].

At the outset it is important to note that for the period of our analysis (1999–2003), 22.3% of the observations in our sample have a services accord (PTA_SVS), while 27.8% of them have a goods agreement (PTA_GDS). All trading partners that have a services agreement also have a goods agreement. Thus, the impact of a services accord also carries with it the impact of goods agreements and, in that, the two cannot be separated from each other. This also implies, however, that about 5.5% of our observations have a "goods only" agreement (GOPTA) and we can thus study the independent and joint impacts of having a "goods only" agreement and the "pseudo-incremental" impact of having a services agreement.

We also classify agreements (both services and any) as North-North (NN), South-South (SS) and North-South (NS) depending on the economic status of the partner countries.[4] Following Gasiorek et al. (2007), we also break down NS accords into symmetric and asymmetric depending on the

---

[3] A lacuna in this analysis, however, is the homogeneity of the PTA_SVS dummy, i.e. the use of the same dummy for all trading pairs in our sample. Ideally, the PTA dummies should be calibrated according to the extent of liberalization achieved/expected to be attained in each of the agreements, which would then yield more precise estimates of the trade effects.

[4] We follow the WTO definitions here. Thus, while Mexico is an OECD country, we classify it as a South country. All EU-15 Members are classified as "North" countries, while the new EU Members are classified as "South" countries since they had not acceded to the EU for the sample period (1999–2003) in our analysis.

Table 3.2 List of variables, their description and data source

Variable Name	Description	Data Source
$SVSX_{ijt}$	Services exports from country i (reporter) to country j (partner)	OECD bilateral trade in services database
GDP_{kt}	GDP of country k (k = i,j)	World Bank's World Development Indicators (WDI)
$PCGDP_{kt}$	Per capita income of country k (k = i,j)	World Bank's WDI
$DIST_{ij}$	Geographical distance between the two countries' economic centres (capital cities for simplicity)	Vulcansoft (http://www.vulconsoft.com/html97) Indocom (http://www.indocom.com/distance)
$GDSX_{ijt}$	Goods exports from country i (reporter) to country j (partner)	IMF's Direction of Trade Statistics
ENG_{ij}	A dummy variable that takes the value 1 if English is the official language in the trading partners	CIA's Factbook about languages in the countries of the world
$REST_{k}$	Extent of restrictiveness to services trade in country k (k = i,j) measured by trade restrictiveness indices	Developed by Australian Productivity Commission; compiled by Dee (2005). Appendix Table 3A.2 shows the countries, sectors and years for which this information is available $REST_{k}$ is an unweighted average of the restrictiveness indices for each of these services sub-sectors
$TELEDEN_{kt}$	Index of telecom density measured by fixed line and mobile phone subscribers (per 1000 people) (proxy for infrastructure development in country k (k = i,j))	World Bank WDI
HK_{kt}	Measure of human capital in country k (k = i,j) proxied by gross tertiary school enrolment[26] (%)	World Bank WDI
LAW_{ij}	A dummy variable that takes the value 1 if the trading partners have a common legal system	CIA's Factbook about legal systems in the countries of the world
PTA_SVS_{ijt}	A dummy variable that takes the value 1 if the trading partners are a member of the same services accord	WTO's Committee on Regional Trade Agreements

extent of reciprocity of commitments and their implementation between the partner countries.[5] We also found our sample of symmetric pairings to include former Central and Eastern European Countries[6] (CEEC) that were signing and implementing Association Agreements with the EU. It is therefore possible that services trade flows towards the CEEC may have also been influenced by other factors such as the likelihood of future accession to the EU. Our analysis, therefore, also includes a division of the North-South symmetric dummy into two parts, one, which looks at flows from the North to the South countries such as Israel and South Africa and two, which covers flows from the EU to CEEC to control for the impact of trade agreements between the EU and CEEC, especially if, as expected, trade flows to the latter have been affected more by non-trade-related reasons.

We thus have:

- the South-South PTA dummy that takes value 1 if the two countries are both developing and in the same preferential agreement, 0 otherwise;
- the symmetric North-South PTA dummy that takes value 1 if one country partner is developed, the other is developing and both countries are in the same agreement characterized by a perfectly reciprocal implementation, 0 otherwise;
- the EUCEEC dummy that takes value 1 if one partner country is from EU-15 and the other is one of the CEEC;
- the asymmetric North-South PTA dummy that takes value 1 if one country partner is developed, the other is developing and both countries are in the same agreement characterized by a less than reciprocal implementation, 0 otherwise;
- the North-North PTA dummy that takes value 1 if the two countries are both developed and in the same preferential agreement, 0 otherwise.

Since our data covers the period 1999–2003, if an agreement was reached before 1999, the associated dummy variable takes a value 1 over 1999–2003. On the other hand, if the agreement came into effect after 1999, then the dummy takes a value 1 in the year of accession and every year after that and a value 0 otherwise.[7]

---

[5] USA-Singapore would be an example of a symmetric NS PTA, while USA-Chile would be an example of an asymmetric NS PTA.

[6] These included Bulgaria, the Czech Republic, Hungary, Slovakia and Poland in our sample, all of which have now acceded to the EU.

[7] This treatment also renders our PTA dummies time-variant, which, from the

3.5 DATA DESCRIPTION AND PRELIMINARY ANALYSIS

There are more than 6600 observations on the variables in our model for the 25 exporting and 53 importing countries in our sample (the list of these countries is included in Appendix Table 3A.1). Preliminary diagnosis of the data revealed that four trading partners had reported negative services exports.[8] These observations were excluded from the sample. In addition, data on services exports was found to be missing for over 2000 observations over 1999–2003, which effectively reduces the sample size by that number. Table 3.3 shows the mean value for our sample variables, along with the minimum, maximum and the standard deviation. Wherever required, the nominal values have been converted into real terms, using the US GDP implicit price deflator.

Figure 3.1 shows trading partner pairs in our sample which had bilateral services exports in excess of USD 10 bn over 1999–2003. Looking at these cross-section averages over 1999–2003, we find that 17 trading pairs (1.7% of the entire sample) had bilateral services exports in excess of USD 10 bn and, interestingly, half of these had a services agreement with each other.

The data has also been tabulated by decile distribution of bilateral services exports averaged over 1999–2003 and the existence of PTAs (see Table 3.4). About 17% of all trading pairs in the sample had a value exceeding USD 1 bn (and more than half of these had a services accord with each other), which points towards a highly skewed distribution (bilateral services exports of the top decile is 526 times that of the last decile in Table 3.4). Also, as expected, both larger bilateral goods and services exports are associated with a PTA or a services PTA between trading partners. Bilateral services exports are 2.3 (2.0) times higher and bilateral goods exports 3.7 (3.1) times higher in the presence of a services (any) PTA than otherwise (see Table 3.4).

Bivariate relationships between bilateral services exports and each of the independent variables are evident from Table 3.5 on cross-correlation (column 2) and suggest that these relationships validate the empirical model that we use. Table 3.5 also shows that the data suffer from multicollinearity; per capita income in particular was found to be strongly correlated with human capital, teledensity and the restrictiveness measures

perspective of empirical analysis, means that they can be retrieved in fixed-effects specifications.

[8] These were: France-Norway, France-Philippines, Ireland-Brazil and Czech Republic-Colombia.

Table 3.3 Description of data for variables used in the model

Variable	Obs	Mean	Std. Dev.	Min	Max
svsx (real USD bn)	4327	1.0	3.1	0.0	38.0
gdsx (real USD bn)	6363	3.1	11.6	0.0	250.0
gdpi (real USD bn)	6603	1040.0	2130.0	19.5	11700.0
gdpj (real USD bn)	6603	604.0	1530.0	7.8	11700.0
popi (mn)	6603	37.0	59.0	0.4	291.0
popj (mn)	6603	90.5	219.0	0.3	1290.0
pcgdpi (USD, cur intl PPP)	5544	26397.8	9218.4	10800.0	65349.0
pcgdpj (USD, cur intl PPP)	6603	16805.2	10384.9	795.0	37501.0
hki	6180	55.2	17.2	9.0	87.0
hkj	5781	44.7	20.0	3.0	87.0
teledeni	6603	1194.2	262.5	430.0	1998.0
teledenj	6603	796.8	491.3	4.0	1750.0
engij (dummy for common language)	6603	0.1	0.3	0.0	1.0
lawij (dummy for common legal system)	6603	0.3	0.5	0.0	1.0
resti	6603	0.2	0.1	0.1	0.5
restj	6228	0.3	0.2	0.1	0.7
distij	6478	6196.3	4755.8	66.0	19845.0
Documents for import (year 2005)	6603	8.2	3.4	3.0	16.0
Time for import (year 2005)	6603	22.0	12.3	3.0	53.0
Cost of import (year 2005)	6603	999.7	448.0	333.0	2260.0
Simple avg. appd. Tariff	6353	8.6	1.3	2.0	9.6
Import-wted. MFN tariff	6353	7.8	1.1	2.4	8.6
Simple avg. MFN tariff	6353	10.4	1.2	5.3	11.9
Import-wted. MFN tariff	6353	9.6	1.0	4.6	10.5
PTA_GDS (dummy for goods PTAs)	6603	0.28	0.45	0.00	1.00
PTA_SVS (dummy for services PTAs)	6603	0.22	0.42	0.00	1.00
PTA_ANY (dummy for any PTA)	6603	0.28	0.45	0.00	1.00
GOPTA (dummy for "goods only" PTAs)	6603	0.05	0.23	0.00	1.00
nngopta	6603	0.01	0.11	0.00	1.00
ssgopta	6603	0.00	0.00	0.00	0.00
nsgopta	6603	0.04	0.20	0.00	1.00
asymnsgopta	6603	0.00	0.07	0.00	1.00
symngopta	6603	0.04	0.19	0.00	1.00
euceecgopta	6603	0.02	0.13	0.00	1.00

Table 3.3 (continued)

Variable	Obs	Mean	Std. Dev.	Min	Max
nn_pta_svs	6603	0.20	0.40	0.00	1.00
ss_pta_svs	6603	0.00	0.00	0.00	0.00
ns_pta_svs	6603	0.02	0.15	0.00	1.00
asymns_pta_svs	6603	0.01	0.10	0.00	1.00
symns_pta_svs	6603	0.01	0.11	0.00	1.00
euceec_pta_svs	6603	0.01	0.11	0.00	1.00
nn_pta_any	6603	0.21	0.41	0.00	1.00
ss_pta_any	6603	0.00	0.00	0.00	1.00
ns_pta_any	6603	0.06	0.24	0.00	1.00
asymns_pta_any	6603	0.01	0.12	0.00	1.00
symns_pta_any	6603	0.05	0.22	0.00	1.00
euceec_pta_any	6603	0.03	0.16	0.00	1.00

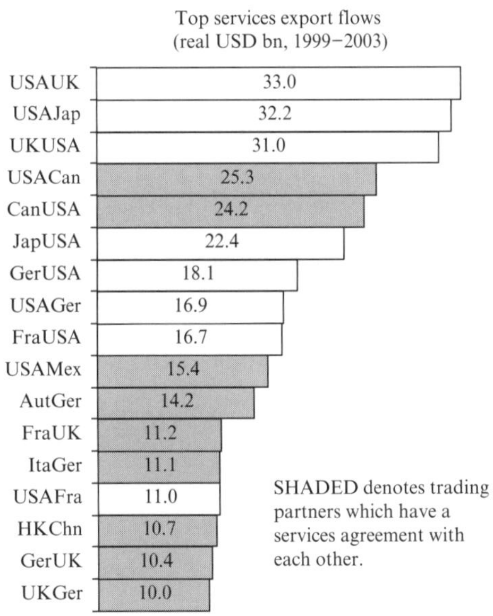

Figure 3.1 Top services export flows (real USD bn, 1999–2003)

(correlation coefficient exceeding absolute 0.45 in each case). We addressed this problem by using the difference in the levels of per capita gross domestic product (PCGDP) as an explanatory variable instead of the log levels, which also served to test Linder's hypothesis, which states that countries at similar levels of per capita income (PCY) trade more intensively with

Table 3.4 *Averages by groups – top services exporters and PTAs*

Deciles	SvsX (real USD mn)	GdsX (real USD bn)	GDPi (real USD bn)	GDPj (real USD bn)	PCGDPi	PCGDPj	POPi (mn)	POPj (mn)	HKi	HKj	TELE-DENi	TELE-DENj	RESTi	RESTj	CULTi	CULTj	DISTij (km)
D1	2300.0	6.0	2130.0	1370.0	29563.6	29393.2	82.3	146.0	75.2	70.8	1445.0	1392.2	0.4	0.5	32	30	12110
D2	719.0	2.6	1510.0	533.0	29208.2	26670.6	59.3	82.3	72.0	60.1	1392.2	1205.2	0.2	0.4	28	17	9839
D3	397.0	1.4	693.0	317.0	27816.4	26157.8	40.9	62.0	60.6	54.8	1281.2	1160.2	0.2	0.3	16	13	8833
D4	230.0	0.8	430.0	216.0	26670.6	23018.4	19.4	44.6	59.5	52.8	1239.6	1102.2	0.2	0.3	13	9	7660
D5	130.0	0.5	257.0	179.0	26549.8	17329.0	10.3	31.1	58.2	48.8	1182.8	985.4	0.2	0.2	13	8	5702
D6	70.6	0.3	186.0	129.0	26239.2	10827.2	10.2	15.6	52.8	36.6	1138.6	567.0	0.2	0.2	8	7	3209
D7	41.7	0.2	136.0	105.0	26034.4	8929.4	8.1	10.2	50.6	30.3	1102.2	360.8	0.2	0.2	7	6	2019
D8	15.0	0.1	123.0	74.0	18544.8	6412.2	5.4	6.7	48.8	23.4	1083.8	273.8	0.2	0.2	7	5	1329
D9	4.4	0.0	60.9	47.2	16303.8	4074.0	4.5	4.5	30.3	15.0	984.0	192.6	0.1	0.2	4	3	892
D1/D9	525.9	222.8	35.0	29.0	1.8	7.2	18.2	32.3	2.5	4.7	1.5	7.2	3.1	3.5	8.0	10.0	13.6

Agreements	SvsX (real USD mn)	GdsX (real USD bn)	GDPi (real USD bn)	GDPj (real USD bn)	PCGDPi	PCGDPj	POPi (mn)	POPj (mn)	HKi	HKj	TELE DENi	TELE DENj	RE STi	RESTj	DIST ij (km)
PTA_SVS=0	766.8	2.0	1152.0	616.1	25913.5	14607.9	40.3	109.0	54.9	41.1	1168.4	683.2	0.2	0.3	7491.7
PTA_SVS=1	1727.0	7.3	631.1	560.5	28475.5	24450.8	25.2	26.1	56.4	56.3	1284.2	1192.0	0.2	0.2	1759.6
(1/0)	**2.3**	**3.7**	**0.5**	**0.9**	**1.1**	**1.7**	**0.6**	**0.2**	**1.0**	**1.4**	**1.1**	**1.7**	**0.8**	**0.8**	**0.2**
PTA_ANY=0	768.7	2.0	1185.0	649.4	25664.2	14448.7	41.3	115.0	54.6	41.7	1157.2	666.1	0.2	0.3	7752.5
PTA_ANY=1	1522.0	6.1	649.2	485.0	28616.0	22918.9	25.7	27.0	56.6	51.7	1290.4	1136.0	0.2	0.2	2234.6
(1/0)	**2.0**	**3.1**	**0.5**	**0.7**	**1.1**	**1.6**	**0.6**	**0.2**	**1.0**	**1.2**	**1.1**	**1.7**	**0.8**	**0.8**	**0.3**

Table 3.5 Correlation between variables (panel 1999–2003)

(n = 3123)	lsvsx	lgdsx	lgdpi	lgdpj	lpcgdpi	lpcgdpj	lteledeni	lteledenj	lhki	lhkj	engij	lawij	lresti	lrestj	pta_svs	pta_gds	ldist
lsvsx	1.00																
lgdsx	**0.85**	1.00															
lgspi	**0.55**	**0.58**	1.00														
lgdpj	**0.49**	**0.47**	0.03	1.00													
lpcgdpi	0.30	0.18	0.28	−0.01	1.00												
lpcgdpj	0.36	0.28	−0.06	0.25	−0.03	1.00											
lteledeni	0.11	0.03	0.06	−0.03	**0.68**	−0.04	1.00										
lteledenj	0.26	0.22	−0.09	0.10	−0.02	**0.91**	0.04	1.00									
lhki	0.22	0.29	**0.47**	0.03	−0.02	0.01	0.07	0.00	1.00								
lhkj	0.20	0.14	−0.07	0.07	−0.03	**0.76**	0.00	**0.77**	−0.01	1.00							
engij	0.17	0.09	0.12	−0.02	0.13	−0.01	0.04	−0.06	0.07	0.00	1.00						
lawij	0.17	0.21	−0.03	0.07	0.00	0.18	−0.02	0.20	−0.05	0.06	0.14	1.00					
lresti	−0.22	−0.18	−0.28	0.03	**−0.66**	0.04	**−0.58**	0.05	−0.32	0.04	−0.19	0.00	1.00				
lrestj	−0.21	0.12	0.00	−0.18	0.01	**−0.46**	0.05	−0.36	−0.01	**−0.46**	−0.06	−0.03	−0.03	1.00			
pta_svs	0.21	0.20	0.00	−0.09	0.15	0.35	0.19	0.37	0.11	0.31	−0.12	0.20	−0.14	−0.17	1.00		
pta_gds	0.22	0.20	0.01	−0.13	0.17	0.32	0.22	0.38	0.14	0.21	−0.12	0.23	−0.18	−0.14	**−0.83**	1.00	
ldist	−0.19	−0.27	0.18	0.21	0.11	−0.25	0.05	−0.32	0.06	−0.23	0.19	−0.28	−0.10	−0.06	**−0.51**	**−0.51**	1.00

each other. The correlation between goods exports and GDP is addressed in Appendix A1 to this chapter, which discusses the treatment of bilateral goods trade as an explanatory variable in our model. The other variables found to be correlated included GDP and human capital of the exporting country; teledensity and restrictiveness in the exporting country; teledensity and human capital in the importing country; goods and services PTA dummies; and PTA dummies and distance.

The first set of regressions was carried out using ordinary least squares (OLS) on the complete model with all the explanatory variables. It was found that GDP_{kt}, $PCGDP_{kt}$, $GDSX_{ijt}$, $TELEDEN_{it}$, $REST_j$, $DIST_{ij}$ and the dummies for ENG_{ij}, RTA_{ij} and PTA_SVS were all statistically significant and of the "right" sign. The coefficient on HK_{kt} was negative and statistically significant, which was due to its correlation with GDP_{kt}. We addressed this problem by regressing GDP_{kt} on HK_{kt} in separate estimations for the exporting and importing countries and using the residuals from these equations in lieu of HK_{kt}. The counter-intuitive estimates of $TELEDEN_{jt}$ and $REST_i$ were due to multicollinearity as well; this was addressed by excluding these variables one by one from the complete model. The coefficient for LAW_{ijt}, however, was found to be negative and statistically significant throughout specifications, a perverse result, which we could not account for. It was thus decided to leave this variable out of the estimation.

The final baseline specification was as follows:

$$svsx_{ijt} = \alpha_{ij} + \beta_1 gdp_{it} + \beta_2 gdp_{jt} + \beta_3 DPCGDP^9{}_{ijt} + \beta_4 dist_{ij} + \beta_5 gdsx_{ijt} + \beta_6 ENG_{ij} + \beta_7 teleden_{it} + \beta_8 teleden_{jt} + \beta_9 rest_i + \beta_{10} rest_j + \beta_{11} hk_{it} + \beta_{12} hk_{jt} + \beta_{13} PTA\_SVS_{ijt} + \varepsilon_{ijt} \quad (3.2)$$

Initial empirical diagnosis also showed Luxembourg and the Slovak Republic to be outliers amongst our services exporters and Iceland, Nigeria and Pakistan to be outliers amongst our list of importers. We found that the outliers biased the estimates of the coefficients on some of our explanatory variables (such as goods exports, exporter GDP, importer human capital, importer teledensity, common language and services PTA[10]) upwards and others (such as importer GDP, restric-

[9] Since the difference in PCY can be negative, if we used the log of this difference, we would lose observations; hence, we use the level of the difference. Statistically, we can still derive the elasticity by multiplying the mean of the difference in PCY by the coefficient on this variable.

[10] Evenett (2002) came up with an identical direction of the bias in his analysis

tiveness and distance[11]) downwards. However, in view of the fact that the magnitude of the bias on the variable of our interest, the estimated trade effect, was only 1.2 percentage points,[12] while the exclusion of the outliers from the sample decreased the potential size of the sample by 19%, we decided to continue with the entire sample in our empirical investigations.

3.6 EMPIRICAL STRATEGY AND ESTIMATION RESULTS

The choice of empirical strategy is governed by the underlying theory, data and its characteristics, recent developments in estimation methodology and any other objective(s) that the researcher may have. In our case, the main econometric problems were to correct for biases emanating from (i) the unobserved heterogeneity characterizing trading partner samples; (ii) the incidence of "export zeroes";[13] and (iii) treating the PTA explanatory variable(s) as exogenous. Given that less than 5% of our dependent variable observations reported "zero" exports, we focussed on addressing problems (i) and (iii) by using the bilateral fixed-effects model (FEM) with country-and-time effects as suggested by Baier and Bergstrand (2007). More details on the methodological issues that governed the final choice of estimation technique for our empirical model and various robustness checks based on recent developments in the literature on gravity model estimation are included in Appendix A2.

For purposes of comparison, we provide the results from using different estimation techniques in Table 3.6. However, for the reasons outlined in Appendix A2, we focus on the results from Baier and Bergstrand (B&B, 2007), both for this section and for the remainder of the analysis in this chapter.

The estimation results validate the choice of determinants in our empirical model. Since our preferred B&B (2007) estimation involves

---

of the estimated trade effect (but an opposite direction in the case of distance). "My econometric findings suggest that the presence of outliers tends to substantially increase the absolute value of the estimated distance parameter and the estimated dummy variable." (Evenett, 2002, p. 558).

[11] i.e the absolute values of the estimated restrictiveness and distance parameters increased in the absence of outliers.

[12] The estimated coefficient went up from 0.11 to 0.12.

[13] For instance see Helpman et al. (2008), Baldwin and Harrigan (2008) and Shepherd (2008).

Table 3.6 Results from multivariate analysis

Variables/ Estimation	Dependent variable: Bilateral services exports								
	OLS	OLS	PPML	PPML	HTM	FEM	FEM	B&B (2007)	DID
GDSXijt	0.4***	0.396***	0.43***	0.43***	0.17***	0.075*	0.034	0.17***	
GDPit	0.67***	0.7***	0.8***	0.8***	0.58***	0.59***	0.78***		
GDPjt	0.54***	0.5*	0.84***	0.85***	0.49***	0.66*	1.3***		
HKit	0.34***	0.31***	−0.12	−0.06	0.84***	0.28***	0.2***		
HKjt	0.33	0.37#	−0.23**	−0.26***	0.089	0.18	−0.3		
TELEDENit	0.8***	1.6***	0.6***	1.5***	0.17	0.5***	0.96***		
TELEDENjt	0.26***	0.3***	0.3***	0.37***	0.38***	0.0	0.12#		
DPCGDPijt					very small				
ENGij	1.3***	1.3***	0.6***	0.64***	0.87				
RESTi	−0.5***	−0.2*	−0.58***	−0.37***	−1.7	−.24	0.33	−19.9	
RESTj	−0.37***	−0.36***	−0.56***	−0.55***	−1.4	−.42*	−0.33#	−261*	
SVS_PTAijt	0.126*	0.11*	−0.44***	−0.45***	0.11*	−0.03	−0.044	0.14*	0.19***
DISTij	−0.76***	−0.76***	−0.64***	−0.64***	−0.68**				
Year2000		−0.26***		−0.26***	−0.003		−0.05		
Year2001		−0.4***		−0.36***	−0.094		−0.17***		
Year2002		−0.5***		−0.4***	−0.16***		−0.26***		
Year2003		−0.7***		−0.5***	−0.18**		−0.43***		
Constant	−16.2**	−21.5***	−25.6***	−32.5***	−16.4***	−19*	−42.7***	−696*	−0.09
Observations	3123	3123	3296	3296	3123	3123	3123	3262	3069
R-squared	0.8	0.8	0.9	0.9	*Within*	0.3	0.3	0.5	0.09
					Between	0.56	0.57	0.1	
					Overall	0.56	0.57	0.1	

Note: "OLS" is Ordinary Least Squares; "PPML" is Poisson Pseudo-Maximum Likelihood; "HTM" is Hausman-Taylor Method; "B&B" is Baier and Bergstrand (2007). Estimations based on PPML, B&B & HTM used log levels of HKi and HKj as independent variables; the other methods used their respective residuals from separate regressions on the log levels of GDPi and GDPj to account for multicollinearity.

Levels of significance: #10%; *5%; **1%; ***0.1%.

using bilateral fixed and country-and-time effects, the coefficients of the time-invariant pairwise and time-varying country-specific explanatory variables cannot be retrieved. So we focus on the results for the remaining explanatory variables.

- Goods exports have an estimated coefficient of 0.17, thereby suggesting that a 10% rise in bilateral goods exports would, *ceteris paribus* and on average, lead to a 1.7% rise in bilateral services exports in this model.
- The coefficient on the difference in PCGDP between the exporting and importing countries was found to be negative, which therefore confirmed Linder's hypothesis, but this result was statistically insignificant.
- Our restrictiveness measures of services trade show huge symmetric negative effects on bilateral services export, with elasticities of −19.9 and −261 for the exporter and importer, respectively. The much larger magnitude of these estimates using B&B (2007) compared to other estimation methods in Table 6 reflects their endogenous treatment.
- Finally, the PTA_SVS dummy had a positive and significant coefficient of 0.14, which translates into a trade effect of 15%,[14] *ceteris paribus and on average*.

Baier and Bergstrand (2007) have accounted for the phasing-in of PTAs by introducing the lagged effects of PTA on trade. Given that every PTA has a phase-in period, typically of over ten years,[15] the entire treatment effect on trade cannot be captured in the concurrent year. They therefore use one or two lagged levels of the PTA dummy in their estimation ($PTA_{ij,t-1}$ and $PTA_{ij,t-2}$), which accentuates the average treatment effect (ATE). Since they use a panel of cross-section time series data at five-year intervals from 1960 to 2000, they thus include ten years preceding accession to study the lagged effects of PTA on trade.

Since our data range from 1999 to 2003, we could only include up to five years preceding accession but, like Baier and Bergstrand (2007), we too found the ATE to be accentuated to 59.7% by including such anticipation effects. The trade effects in the three years preceding accession were negative (and statistically significant only in the second year)

14 Calculated as [exp(0.14)-1]*100.

15 For instance, both the original EEC agreement of 1958 and the NAFTA had a ten-year phase-in provision.

but significantly positive in the fourth and fifth year preceding accession (15% and 55.3%, respectively). However, the services trade effect in the actual year of accession reduced to 13.9% if we included such anticipation effects, and also became statistically insignificant. This suggested that the maximum impact of a services accord was felt the farthest in time from actual accession and that services agreements seem to have a significant "announcement effect".

3.7 DISAGGREGATING THE IMPACT OF PREFERENTIAL TRADE AGREEMENTS

In what follows, we use the B&B (2007) estimation to study the impact of PTAs in detail, breaking these down by the economic status of the trading partners and by the reciprocity (or the lack thereof) of commitments. The trade effect by type of PTA in each case is shown in Table 3.7. The empirical estimates of the other variables in the estimation have not been shown in this table as our focus is on detailing the impact of PTAs as opposed to discussing the entire estimation output.

Looking at services agreements (columns I–II, Table 3.7), we found the trade effect of NN_PTA_SVS to be both statistically and economically significant (16.2% increase in bilateral services exports), while that of NS_PTA_SVS to be statistically insignificant (but with a trade effect of 5.3%). We found the result for NS_PTA_SVS to be driven by asymmetric agreements (statistically insignificant but with a trade effect of 5.3%). SS_PTA_SVS and symmetric NS_PTA_SVS dummies dropped out of the estimation.

Replicating the analysis for "any agreement" (columns III–IV, Table 3.7), we found the trade effect of NN_PTA_ANY to be both economically and statistically significant as well (20.9% increase in bilateral services exports), while that of NS_PTA_ANY to be statistically insignificant (but with a trade effect of 4.1%). SS_PTA_ANY dropped out of the estimation. A la services accords, the result for NS_PTA_ANY was largely due to asymmetric agreements (statistically insignificant but with a trade effect of 13.1%). Symmetric NS_PTA_ANY, on the other hand, reported a statistically insignificant trade effect of -6.1%.

Finally, looking at "goods only" agreements (columns V–VI, Table 3.7), we found NN accords to have the largest services trade effect (105.4% increase in bilateral services exports). The result for NS_GOPTA, however, lacked statistical significance and was also small in magnitude (trade effect of 1.8%) but was again driven by asymmetric agreements (statistically insignificant but with a trade effect of 6.9%). Symmetric NS_GOPTA

Table 3.7 Trade effect by type of PTA

Type of PTA/Trade effect (%)	I	II	III	IV	V	VI
NN_PTA_SVS	16.2*	16.2*				
NS_PTA_SVS	5.3					
ASYM_NS_PTA_SVS		5.3				
SYM_NS_PTA_SVS						
EUCEEC_PTA_SVS						
NN_PTA_ANY			20.9***	20.9***		
NS_PTA_ ANY			4.1			
ASYM_NS_PTA_ ANY				13.1		
SYM_NS_PTA_ ANY				−6.1		
EUCEEC_PTA_ ANY						
NN_GOPTA					105.4**	105.4**
NS_GOPTA					1.8	
ASYM_NS_GOPTA						6.9
SYM_NS_GOPTA						−5.6
EUCEEC_GOPTA						Huge

Significance levels: *5%, **1%, ***0.1%.

Table 3.8 Summarizing impact of PTAs on bilateral services exports

Code	Type of agreement	Any PTA	PTA_SVS	"Goods Only" PTA
I	North-North	20.9%***	16.2%*	105.4%**
II	South-South	Dropped	Dropped	Dropped
III	North-South	4.1% *(Insignificant)*	**5.3%** *(Insignificant)*	1.8% *(Insignificant)*
III. A	Asymmetric North-South	**13.1%** *(Insignificant)*	**5.3%** *(Insignificant)*	6.9% *(Insignificant)*
III. B	Symmetric North-South	−6.1% *(Insignificant)*	Dropped	−5.6% *(Insignificant)*

Significance levels: *5%, **1%, ***0.1%.

reported a statistically insignificant trade effect of -5.6%. SS_GOPTA again dropped out of the estimation.[16]

Table 3.8 summarizes these results.

Thus, only North-North agreements (services or any) report both a positive and statistically significant trade effect between partners, which

[16] There are no South-South agreements in our sample of countries over 1999–2003 which is why the associated PTAs drop out of all of these estimations.

points to the predominance of increasing returns to scale (IRS) and intra-industry services trade in our sample. Empirically, this emanates from the fact that our data are dominated[17] by North-North accords and there are comparatively fewer observations in our sample on North-South agreements and none at all on South-South accords, which therefore drop out of the estimation.

The lack of statistical significance in the other results suggests that these should be interpreted with caution. However, as Schafer (1993) points out, "the event of nonsignificance suggests only that the data are not sufficient to estimate a parameter. This does not mean the data estimate the parameter to be zero!"[18] In further defence, our point estimates are not small in magnitude and there is no a priori reason for assuming the trade effect to be zero; therefore in the absence of a Bayesian prior, the estimated coefficient is thus perhaps our best measure of the trade effect.

Schafer (1993) also recommends that "nonsignificant results be accompanied by an evaluation of statistical power"[19] wherein his decision rule rules out results with too low or too high a statistical power.[20] Our evaluation of statistical power revealed that only three of the ten estimates that reported statistical non-significance in Table 3.8 had a statistical power[21] that was neither too low, nor too high and these have been highlighted in bold in that table.[22]

These are the results that we focus on while comparing the magnitudes of the statistically insignificant trade effects and find that North-South services agreements also report *positive* trade effects. This finding suggests that services trade between countries in our sample may be driven by differences in factor endowments as well and, in that, such trade may be inter-industry. Further, within North-South agreements and irrespective of the form the agreement takes, asymmetric accords always have the larger trade effect and this is always positive. These findings thus suggest greater alliance between the North and the South in a bid to boost bilateral services trade and, more importantly, suggest that this

---

17 21% of all observations in our sample are NN, while only 6% are NS and there are no observations on SS accords during the period covering our analysis.

18 Schafer (1993), pp. 384–5.

19 Schafer (1993), pp. 386–7.

20 "Should it turn out that the power of the study was low against even a reasonably large effect size, then we are forced to the conclusion that nothing much has been learned. On the other hand, when the power is large, then we can infer that if an effect exists it seems too small to be of much value." Schafer (1993), p. 386.

21 This ranged from 0.37 to 0.58 at the 5 and 10% levels of significance.

22 The statistical power was less than 0.2 in all other cases.

relationship can be less than perfectly reciprocal to be net trade-creating. Such agreements could thus attempt to capitalize on cost differences between trading partners based on differences in factor endowments and regulatory requirements and generate more inter-industry trade. Finally, North-North "goods only" agreements report the largest positive trade effect on bilateral services exports, confirming complementarities between provisions in such agreements and bilateral services trade. And this is what we discuss next.

Table 3.9 summarizes the trade effects from multivariate analyses conducted to study the sequential impacts of services and "goods only" agreements for different trading partner samples using the B&B (2007) estimation. As this table shows, services accords by themselves report a positive and statistically significant trade effect (except for the non-EU trading partners in our sample). "Goods only" agreements do not report a statistically significant[23] (services) trade effect in our sample of countries[24] but they do report a positive (services) trade effect. However, when such accords are paired with services agreements in non-EU countries or in

Table 3.9 Sequential and incremental impact of PTAs on bilateral services exports

Serial no.	PTA_SVS		"Goods only" PTA		Sample coverage
	Trade effect	Statistical significance	Trade effect	Statistical significance	
1	15.0%	Yes*			All
2			9.8%	No	All
3	17.4%	Yes*	15.0%	No	All
4	32.3%	Yes***			Intra-EU
5			Dropped	Dropped	Intra-EU
6	32.3%	Yes***	Dropped	Dropped	Intra-EU
7	−10.8%	No			Non-EU
8			13.9%	No	Non-EU
9	−0.8%	No	13.9%	No	Non-EU

Significance levels: *5%, ***0.1%.

23 None of the results in Table 3.9 that show statistical non-significance passed Schafer's (1993) decision rule in an evaluation of statistical power. They should thus be interpreted with caution.

24 Once again, this may be the result of the sample size since "goods only" accords comprise only 5% of all observations in our sample.

the entire sample, the (services) trade effect of each set of agreements is enhanced, thereby confirming complementarities between the two. The magnitude of the incremental (services) trade effect was found to be 7.6%, with the trade effect of services agreements going up by 2.4% and that of "goods only" accords rising by 5.2%, *ceteris paribus* and on average. This also suggests that trading partners would benefit more from negotiating goods and services agreements in tandem, as opposed to sequentially.

3.8 CONCLUSION

The empirical literature on gravity model estimation of bilateral services trade exhibits neither consensus nor conformity to economic theory in estimating the impact of the determinants of such trade. The role of bilateral goods trade in determining bilateral services trade has not been explored in detail; nor has the separate impact of "goods only" and services accords on bilateral services trade ever been studied. Methodologically, only recent empirical work accounts for the influence of heterogeneity in trading country pairs in determining bilateral services trade, but even this fails to recognize the endogeneity of agreements in model estimation.

This chapter is an improvement on all these fronts. Our analysis explicitly accounts for the existence of alternative modes of supply and their relationships, which is needed not just for better understanding of the determinants and pattern of services trade, but also for the effects of policies as can be seen from the results of our analyses.

A caveat in the analysis undertaken here is the homogeneity of the PTA dummies, the calibration of which does not take into account the varying extents of liberalization in different agreements. This could therefore be an agenda for further research in this area. In addition, the chapter does not look into the political economy of bilateral services trade nor at issues of regulatory harmonization, both of which could be candidates for further research and analysis.

BIBLIOGRAPHY

Anderson, James E. (1979), "A Theoretical Foundation for the Gravity Equation", *American Economic Review*, 69(1), 106–116.

Anderson, J. and E. van Wincoop (2003), "Gravity with Gravitas: A Solution to the Border Puzzle", *American Economic Review*, 93(1), 170–92.

Baier, Scott L. and Jeffrey H. Bergstrand (2002), "On the Endogeneity of International Trade Flows and Free Trade Agreements", Manuscript, August 2002, http://www.nd.edu/~jbergstr/Working_Papers/EndogeneityAug2002.pdf.

Baier, Scott L. and Jeffrey H. Bergstrand (2004), "Economic Determinants of Free Trade Agreements', *Journal of International Economics*, 64(1), 29–63 (October).

Baier, S.L. and Jeffrey H. Bergstrand (2007), "Do Free Trade Agreements Actually Increase Members' International Trade?", *Journal of International Economics*, 71 (2007), 72–95.

Baldwin, Richard and James Harrigan (2008), "Zeroes, Quality and Space: Trade Theory and Trade Evidence", NBER Working Paper 13214, March.

Carrere, Celine (2006), "Revisiting the Effects of Preferential Trade Agreements on Trade Flows with Proper Specification of the Gravity Model", *European Economic Review*, 50 (2006), 223–47.

Cheng, I.-H. and H. Wall (2005), "Controlling for Heterogeneity in Gravity Models of Trade and Integration", *Federal Reserve Bank of St. Louis Review*, 87(1), 49–63.

Dee, Philippa (2005), "A Compendium of Barriers to Trade in Services", Australian National University, Canberra.

Egger, P. (2000), "A Note on the Proper Econometric Specification of the Gravity Equation", *Economics Letters*, 66, 25–31.

Egger, P. (2002), "An Econometric View on the Estimation of Gravity Models and the Calculation of Trade Potentials", *The World Economy*, 25, 297–312.

Egger, P. (2005), "Alternative Techniques for Estimation of Cross-section Gravity Models", *Review of International Economics*, 13(5), 881–91.

Egger, H., Egger, P. and David Greenaway (2008), "The Trade Structure Effects of Endogenous Preferential Trade Agreements", *Journal of International Economics*, 74 (2008), 278–98.

Evenett, Simon J. (2002), "The Impact of Economic Sanctions on South African Exports", *Scottish Journal of Political Economy*, 49(5), 557–73.

Feenstra, R. (2004), *Advanced International Trade: Theory and Evidence*, Princeton: Princeton University Press.

Feenstra, R.C., J.R. Markusen and A.K. Rose (2001), "Using the Gravity Equation to Differentiate among Alternative Theories of Trade", *Canadian Journal of Economics*, 34(2), 430–47.

Frankel, J.A. (1997). *Preferential Trading Blocs*, Washington, DC: Institute for International Economics.

Gasiorek, Michael, Peter Holmes, Sherman Robinson, Jim Rollo and Anirudh Shingal (2007), "Qualitative Analysis of a Potential Free Trade Agreement between the European Union and India", the European Commission and CARIS, Department of Economics, University of Sussex, UK, February, http://trade.ec.europa.eu/doclib/docs/2007/june/tradoc_135101.pdf.

Grünfeld, Leo A. and Andres Moxnes (2003), "The Intangible Globalization: Explaining the Patterns of International Trade in Services", Discussion Paper No. 657, Norwegian Institute of International Affairs.

Hausman, A. and E. Taylor (1981), "Panel Data and Unobservable Individual Effects", *Econometrica*, 49, 1377–98.

Helpman, Elhanan, Marc Melitz and Yona Rubinstein (2008), "Estimating Trade Flows: Trading Partners and Trading Volumes", *Quarterly Journal of Economics*, 123(2), 441–87.

Karsenty, G. (2000), "Assessing Trade in Services by Mode of Supply", in P. Sauvé and R.M. Stern (eds.), *GATS 2000: New Directions in Services Trade Liberalisation*, Brookings Institution, Washington DC, pp. 33–56.

Kimura, Fukunari (2003), "Economic Analysis on Japan-Korea FTA: Services Trade", manuscript, Keio University.
Kimura, F. and H. Lee (2004), "The Gravity Equation in International Trade in Services", European Trade Study Group Conference, University of Nottingham, 9–11 September.
Kimura, F. and H. Lee (2006), "How does Economic Freedom Affect International Trade in Services?", May.
Kox, H. and A. Lejour (2005), "Regulatory Heterogeneity as Obstacle for International Services Trade", CPB Discussion Paper No. 49.
Lejour, A. and J. de P. Verheijden (2004), "Services Trade with Canada and the European Union", CPB Discussion Paper No.42, CPB Netherlands Bureau for Economic Policy Analysis.
Lennon, C. (2006), "Trade in Services and Trade in Goods: Differences and Complementarities", Paper presented at the 8th Annual Conference of the European Trade Study Group, 7–9 September, Vienna.
Magee, Chris (2003), "Endogenous Preferential Trade Agreements: An Empirical Analysis", *Contributions to Economic Analysis and Policy*, 2(1), Berkeley Electronic Press.
Mirza, Daniel and Giuseppe Nicoletti (2004), "What is so Special about Trade in Services?", Research Paper 2004/02, Leverhulme Centre for Research on Globalisation and Economic Policy.
OECD (2002), "OECD Statistics on International Trade in Services, Detailed Tables by Partner Country 1999–2002".
Santos Silva, J.M.C. and S. Tenreyro (2006), "The Log of Gravity", *The Review of Economics and Statistics*, 88(4), 641–58.
Schafer, William D. (1993), "Interpreting Statistical Significance and Nonsignificance", *Journal of Experimental Education*, 61(4), 383–7.
Schumacher, D. and B. Siliverstovs (2007), "Estimating Gravity Equations: To Log or Not to Log?", Discussion Paper 739, German Institute for Economic Research, DIW Berlin, October.
Shepherd, Ben (2008), "Notes on the 'Theoretical' Gravity Model of International Trade", background paper for ARTNeT.
Soloaga, I. and L.A. Winters (2001), "Regionalism in the Nineties: What Effect on Trade?", *The North American Journal of Economics and Finance*, 12(1), 1–29.
Walsh, Keith (2006), "Trade in Services: Does Gravity Hold? A Gravity Model Approach to Estimating Barriers to Services Trade", IIIS Discussion Paper, No. 183, October 2006.

APPENDIX

A1. Treatment of Bilateral Goods Trade as an Explanatory Variable

The inclusion of bilateral goods export ($GDSX_{ijt}$) in our estimation suffers from the obvious problem of endogeneity as there are several common factors that have an impact on both goods and services trade such as GDP for instance and, hence, it is not easy to distinguish the impact of goods trade (on services trade) from that of these other factors.

We thought of four different ways of tackling these problems:

(1) Treat bilateral services and bilateral goods trade as a system of simultaneous equations where the bilateral trade variable in each case is the endogenous variable and the exogenous variables in the system are the other explanatory variables common to both as discussed above.[25]
(2) Use instrumental variable (IV) estimation, where instrumental variables such as tariffs, costs of importing, etc. could be used as instruments for bilateral goods trade in our model for bilateral services trade.
(3) Estimate bilateral goods trade using the explanatory variables in our model that are common determinants for services trade as well and to use the residual obtained from this as an additional explanatory variable in our bilateral services trade model in lieu of GDSX as this residual would be stripped off the effect of all the common factors.
(4) Use the predicted value of goods trade in (3) or its lagged values as an explanatory variable in our model for bilateral services trade.

We tried out these alternatives in turn with the following results:

(1) Our simultaneous equation system predicted both bilateral goods and bilateral services trade very well (R-squared of 99% in each case). The estimation however inflated the coefficient on GDSX and deflated those on GDP_k in predicting bilateral services trade. The latter were in fact returned with negative and significant signs! The results remained equally unsound if the model was run separately for intra-EU and all other trading partners in our sample. Given that 75% of global trade is merchandise trade, the estimation of goods

[25] The only difference was to use applied weighted tariffs instead of RESTj in the determination of bilateral goods trade and replace PTA_SVS with PTA_GDS as the PTA dummy.

trade thus seems to swamp that of services trade in a simultaneous equation system, which therefore seems to account for such a result.

(2) For our IV model, we used time taken to import goods as an instrument for bilateral goods trade. We also tried other instruments like tariffs and costs of an import container but found these to be less correlated with bilateral goods trade than time taken to import.[26] In this IV estimation, bilateral goods trade had an elasticity of 2.7 but was insignificant. GDP_k also had insignificant but large negative elasticities.[27] These results are possibly on account of our choice of the instrument, which may be not as independent of our dependent variable as one would want. At least 25% of all bilateral services trade flows are transportation services and import time would therefore be negatively related with these.[28 29]

(4) The predicted value of goods trade from the bilateral goods trade estimation had a coefficient of -0.276 as an explanatory variable for bilateral services trade. Lagged values of goods trade, even as far back as ten years, were strongly correlated with current values of bilateral services trade. Thus, using them as an explanatory variable would lead to the same endogeneity problems that we were trying to account for in the first place.

(3) But the residual from the bilateral goods trade estimation had a coefficient of 0.4 and was also significant at 1%, which suggests that the marginal impact of bilateral goods exports on bilateral services exports is 40%, *ceteris paribus* and on average. This residual is what we thus used in our final empirical estimations.

A2. Recent Developments in Gravity Model Estimation and Methodological Issues

In this appendix, we provide more details on the methodological issues that governed the final choice of estimation technique for our empirical

---

26 Even this had a low statistical correlation of −0.257 with bilateral goods trade.

27 For intra-EU trading partners in our sample, the coefficient on goods export remained negative and insignificant. For the other remaining trading partners, the coefficient on goods export remained insignificant but became positive (0.46).

28 Data in fact confirmed this. The correlation coefficient between time taken to import and bilateral services exports was −0.2276.

29 Lennon (2006), however, used tariffs as an instrument for goods trade and got results in the right direction, but she included only "other commercial services" (OCS) in her analysis.

model and also discuss robustness checks based on recent developments in the literature on gravity model estimation.

The earliest applications of the gravity equation to international trade flows were not grounded in formal theory. It was only with Anderson (1979) that formal theoretical economic foundations to the gravity model surfaced. One of the salient features of the latter has been the inclusion of multilateral price measures in estimating the gravity model, which *ipso facto* takes care of the omitted variable bias that existed in the earlier models owing to the absence of such variables.[30] Following Anderson and van Wincoop (2003) and Feenstra (2004), this has been achieved in the literature by including country-specific effects in the model, which is a computationally easier route for the inclusion of multilateral price measures. Cheng and Wall (2005) further showed that the best estimates came from estimating a pair-wise bilateral fixed effects model (FEM), while Baier & Bergstrand (2007) have recently added country-and-time effects to the pairwise bilateral FEM, wherein the former account explicitly for the time-varying multilateral price terms in a panel setting.

The other recent change in gravity model estimation has been scaling the dependent variable by the product of the real GDPs of the trading partners (i.e. svsx/gdpi.gdpj), which amounts to imposing unitary income elastic restrictions on the gravity model. While Baier and Bergstrand (2007) found this to have no impact on the coefficient of the PTA dummy if the model was estimated with country-and-time effects, in our case, the services trade effect actually became negative (-5.3%). We further found that the explanatory power was significantly reduced in this specification.[31] For both these reasons, we did not impose any unitary income elastic restrictions on our empirical specification.

Finally, in a significant departure from earlier work, researchers (Magee, 2003; Baier and Bergstrand, 2002, 2004, 2007; Egger et al., 2008) have begun to treat the PTA dummy as an endogenous (as opposed to hitherto exogenous) independent variable. While we document the results from both approaches in this chapter, our results focus on the treatment of the PTA dummy as an endogenous variable in line with Baier and Bergstrand (2007).

---

30 It is now fairly well established in gravity model literature that a simple OLS estimation tends to bias the results as there are likely to be effects common to the trading countries that are not included in the estimation (Cheng and Wall, 2005). In other words, heterogeneity is not allowed for. These effects could be due to "historical, cultural, ethnic, political, or geographic factors that affect the level of trade and correlated with the gravity variables (GDP, population, distance)" (Cheng and Wall, 2005, p. 54).

31 The within-R-squared was reduced to 0.3 from 0.5.

We began our estimation of the gravity model with the PTA dummy as an exogenous variable and, in that, report results from four different techniques by way of comparison: ordinary least squares (OLS), pairwise fixed-effects (FEM), Hausman-Taylor (HTM) and Poisson Pseudo-Maximum Likelihood (PPML) (see Table 3.6).

Both FEM and HTM, as opposed to OLS, account for the heterogeneity in the data stemming from the unobservables common to the trading partner pairs and in that are superior to OLS, which *ipso facto* suffers from an omitted variable bias. The HTM also has the added advantage of retrieving the coefficients of time-invariant variables like distance and common language in the results, which is not possible using FEM, which also consumes too many degrees of freedom. Moreover, unlike FEM, HTM also empirically enables the treatment of the FTA dummy as an endogenous (as opposed to exogenous) variable in estimating the trade effect of an accord.[32] While Egger (2002, 2005) and Carrere (2006, pp. 231–2) advocate the use of HTM over FEM in cross-section and panel settings, respectively, Egger (2000) and Baier and Bergstrand (2007) advocate the use of the FEM over random effects (REM) in a panel setting for both theoretical and empirical reasons and the HTM is a REM. In fact, the use of the Hausman test also provided evidence for estimating our empirical model using fixed as opposed to random effects.

PPML, on the other hand, neither accounts for the unobserved heterogeneity in the data nor enables endogenous treatment of the PTA dummy. Rather, it advocates the use of a simple Poisson Pseudo-Maximum Likelihood because in the presence of heteroskedasticity in the data, the standard log-linearized gravity model yields inconsistent estimates[33] (Santos Silva and Tenreyro, 2006; Schumacher and Siliverstovs, 2007). "An additional problem of log-linearization is that it is incompatible with the existence of zeroes in trade data, which led to several unsatisfactory solutions, including truncation of the sample and further non-linear transformations of the dependent variable." (Santos Silva and Tenreyro,

[32] Using the Hausman over-identification test, we identified some of our independent variables as endogenous (these included GDP, human capital, teledensity, and the PTA dummies) and others as exogenous (distance, common language and restrictiveness variables in our specification) and used the mean of the exogenous independent variables as instruments for the time-variant or endogenous independent variables correlated with (specific) bilateral effects to account for the unobservables, à la Hausman and Taylor (1981).

[33] "This is because the expected value of the logarithm of a random variable depends on higher-order moments of its distribution. Therefore, if the errors are heteroskedastic, the transformed errors will be generally correlated with the covariates" (Santos Silva and Tenreyro, 2006, p. 653).

2006, p.653). The PPML, therefore, corrects for all these problems. However, these problems were found not to be as important for our data as the biases emanating from unobserved heterogeneity and the exogenous treatment of the PTA dummy, for which reason the bilateral FEM with country-and-time effects was our preferred estimation.

The recent acknowledgement of endogeneity of the PTA dummy in the empirical trade literature is based on the intuition that, if there is a tendency for countries to "self-select"[34] themselves into an accord, then treating the PTA dummy as exogenous would under-estimate the magnitude of the trade effect.[35] The treatment of endogeneity in cross-section data has been done through the use of instrumental variables and Heckman control functions (Magee, 2003; Baier and Bergstrand, 2002, 2004, 2007), but this has been said to be unsatisfactory (see e.g. Baier and Bergstrand, 2007) largely on account of the choice of instruments and the instruments not being exogenous of the error term. On the other hand, Baier and Bergstrand (2007) have claimed that the use of a bilateral pairwise FEM with country-and-time effects or alternatively, the use of OLS in a difference-in-difference model, both using panel data, leads to a more satisfactory treatment of the endogeneity problem. A la Baier and Bergstrand (2002, 2007), we thus also estimated a bilateral pairwise FEM with country-and-time effects as well as a difference-in-difference (DID) model to endogenize the effects of the PTA dummy in our panel. The latter resulted in an even larger and more statistically significant services trade effect of 20.9%. To the best of our knowledge, this is the first attempt in the literature on gravity model estimation of bilateral services trade to endogenize the trade effect.

Other recent changes in gravity model estimation have involved decomposing the total trade effect of a PTA into the Vinerian effects of trade creation and trade diversion (see e.g. Frankel, 1997; Soloaga and Winters, 2001; Santos Silva and Tenreyro, 2006; Carrere, 2006). This essentially involves introducing a new dummy variable in the equation (say OPENNESS) that takes the value 1 when any or both trading partners have a trade agreement with the rest of the world (ROW). The net trade creation effect of a PTA is then the difference between the estimated coefficients on the PTA and the OPENNESS dummies.[36] In our sample, all

---

[34] i.e. countries that enter into an agreement are already those that trade significantly with each other and vice versa.

[35] For instance, Baier and Bergstrand (2007) find the trade effect from goods agreements to quintuple once the PTA variable's endogeneity is accounted for econometrically.

[36] Logically, the functioning of these dummies is relative to none of the countries in the sample having any agreement with ROW.

Table 3A.1 List of exporters and importers

Exporters: Australia, Austria, Belgium, Canada, Czech Republic, Denmark, Finland, France, Germany, Greece, Hong Kong, Hungary, Ireland, Italy, Japan, Republic of Korea, Luxembourg, the Netherlands, Norway, Portugal, Slovak Republic, Spain, Sweden, the United Kingdom and USA.
Importers: Argentina, Australia, Austria, Benelux, Brazil, Bulgaria, Canada, Chile, China, Colombia, Croatia, Czech Republic, Denmark, Egypt, Finland, France, Germany, Greece, Hong Kong, Hungary, Iceland, India, Indonesia, Islamic Republic of Iran, Ireland, Israel, Italy, Japan, Republic of Korea, Malaysia, Mexico, the Netherlands, New Zealand, Nigeria, Norway, Pakistan, the Philippines, Poland, Portugal, Russia, Saudi Arabia, Singapore, Slovak Republic, South Africa, Spain, Sweden, Switzerland, Thailand, Turkey, the United Kingdom, Ukraine, USA and Venezuela.

trading partners have some form of an agreement with ROW such that the OPENNESS variable takes the value 1 throughout and, hence, is dropped out of our estimation due to collinearity. We therefore estimate our model without this dummy. Our PTA dummies therefore denote the *gross*, as opposed to the *net*, trade creation effect of an agreement.

Table 3A.2 Snapshot of services restrictiveness indices across countries and sub-sectors

Country	Air transport	Banking	Distribution	Electricity generation	Maritime	Professional	Telecom
Argentina	1995	1997	1999	1999	2001	1999 (AArE)	1997
Australia	1995	1997, 2005	1999, 2005	1999	2001	1999 (AArEL)	1997, 2005
Austria	1995	1997	1999	1999	n.a.	1999 (AArEL)	1997
Belgium	1995	1997	1999	1999	2001	1999 (AArEL)	1997
Brazil	1995	1997, 2004	1999, 2004	1999	2001	1999 (AArE)	1997, 2004
Canada	1995	1997	1999	1999	2001	1999 (AArEL)	1997
Chile	1995	1997, 2004	1999	1999	2001	1999 (AArE)	1997, 2004
Hong Kong	1995	1997	1999	1999	2001	1999 (AArEL)	1997
Colombia	1995	1997	1999	1999	2001	1999 (A)	1997
Denmark	1995	1997	1999	1999	2001	1999 (AArEL)	1997
Finland	1995	1997	1999	1999	2001	1999 (AArEL)	1997
France	1995	1997	1999	1999	2001	1999 (AArEL)	1997
Germany	1995	1997	1999	1999	2001	1999 (AArEL)	1997
Greece	1995	1997	1999	1999	2001	1999 (AArEL)	1997
India	1995	1997	1999	1999	2001	1999 (AArEL)	1997
Indonesia	1995	1997	1999	1999	2001	1999 (AArEL)	1997
Ireland	1995	1997	1999	1999	2001	1999 (AArEL)	1997
Italy	1995	1997	1999	1999	2001	1999 (AArEL)	1997
Japan	1995	1997, 2005	1997, 2005	1999	2001	1999 (AArEL)	1997, 2005
Korea	1995	1997	1999	1999	2001	1999 (AArEL)	1997
Luxemburg	1995	1997	1999	1999	n.a.	1999 (AArEL)	1997
Malaysia	1995	1997, 2003	1999	1999	2001	1999 (AArEL)	1997, 2002

Table 3A.2 (continued)

Country	Air transport	Banking	Distribution	Electricity generation	Maritime	Professional	Telecom
Mexico	1995	1997	1999	1999	2001	1999 (AArEL)	1997
Netherlands	1995	1997	1999	1999	2001	1999 (AArEL)	1997
New Zealand	1995	1997	1999	1999	2001	1999 (AArEL)	1997
Peru	1995	1997	1999	1999	2001	1999 (A)	1997
Philippines	1995	1997	1999	1999	2001	1999 (AArEL)	1997
Portugal	1995	1997	1999	1999	2001	1999 (AArEL)	1997
Russia	1995	2004	2004	1999	2001	2004 (E)	1997
Singapore	1995	1997	1999	1999	2001	1999 (AArEL)	1997
South Africa	1995	1997	1999	1999	2001	1999 (AArE)	1997
Spain	1995	1997	1999	1999	n.a.	1999 (AArEL)	1997
Sweden	1995	1997	1999	1999	2001	1999 (AArEL)	1997
Switzerland	1995	1997	1999	1999	n.a.	1999 (AArEL)	1997
Thailand	1995	1997, 2004	1999, 2002	1999, 2002	2001	1999 (AArEL)	1997, 2004
Turkey	1995	1997	1999	1999	2001	1999 (AArEL)	1997
USA	1995	1997	1999	1999	2001	1999 (AArEL)	1997
UK	1995	1997	1999	1999	2001	1999 (AArEL)	1997
Vietnam	1995	2004	2004	1999, 2004	2001	2004 (AArEL)	1997, 2004

Note: A = Accountancy; Ar = Architectural; E = Engineering; and L = Legal Services.

Source: Dee (2005).

PART II

Comparative regionalism

4. Innovating regionalism: the Americas

Sherry Stephenson and Maryse Robert[1]

4.1 INTRODUCTION

More than any other region in the world, the Americas was the first to embrace regionalism wholeheartedly and has remained at the forefront in developing innovative approaches to the treatment of services trade. In the mid-1980s and early 1990s, numerous countries in the Americas undertook reforms aimed at dismantling protectionist measures in their own markets and at promoting a more open and dynamic pattern of integration into the world economy. In several countries, trade in services and investment rulemaking were at the forefront of the reforms being undertaken. It was felt that easing restrictions on foreign investment could foster economic growth and that removing barriers to trade in services could lead to lower prices, improved quality and greater variety of both goods and services, as well as stimulate exports.

Since 1994, numerous free trade agreements (FTAs) have been signed by countries of the Americas. To expand their trade opportunities,

---

[1] Sherry Stephenson is Senior Fellow at the International Centre for Trade and Sustainable Development (ITCSD) in Geneva and Maryse Robert is Director of the Department of Economic and Social Development in the Executive Secretariat for Integral Development at the General Secretariat of the Organization of American States (OAS). The views expressed in this chapter are personal and should not be attributed to any OAS Member State or the General Secretariat of the OAS. The authors would like to recognize with gratitude the contributions of Alicia Nicholls, a research consultant at the Shridath Ramphal Centre for International Trade Law, Policy & Services at the University of the West Indies, Cave Hill Campus in Barbados, and Thibaud Delourme, a graduate student at the Institut de Sciences Politiques in Strasbourg, France, who both provided helpful research assistance for the chapter. The authors also wish to thank Gary C. Hufbauer for his comments on an earlier draft of this chapter. Questions or comments on the chapter may be addressed to sstephenson@ictsd.ch or mrobert@oas.org.

they have signed FTAs among themselves and have also reached out to partners beyond their own borders such as the European Union (EU), China, Japan, Singapore and South Korea, among others.

While the Canada-U.S. FTA (CUSFTA), which entered into force in 1989, was the first trade agreement to cover trade in services in the Americas, it is the North American Free Trade Agreement (NAFTA) negotiated a few years later which set a model for other FTAs to follow in the region. The path-breaking influence of NAFTA cannot, in fact, be overstated in the services and investment area, as it set an alternative course to the treatment of these important issues from that negotiated in the General Agreement on Trade and Services (GATS) of the World Trade Organization (WTO). In so doing, it inspired a generation of regional agreements that has pushed the envelope in the services and investment areas well beyond that at the multilateral level.

This chapter focuses on the innovations of regionalism in services that have been developed by countries in the Americas. It discusses the new approach that NAFTA brought to the structure of a services agreement, highlighting the design of rules in general and those for the key sector of financial services in particular, as well as for the temporary movement of labor. It compares and contrasts the similarities and differences between the NAFTA-type FTAs negotiated within the Americas and FTAs negotiated between countries of the Americas and those in other regions. The chapter reviews in a very preliminary manner, based on available data, the results produced by the first generation of FTAs in the Americas, examining the extent to which these agreements have stimulated greater output in services as well as greater cross-border trade and investment in services for their members. It discusses the possibilities for convergence of those FTAs with similar structure in the Americas. And lastly, it touches upon the governance problem created for the multilateral system by the widening gap between FTAs and the WTO GATS.

4.2 DEVELOPMENT OF A NEW FRAMEWORK FOR SERVICES TRADE IN THE AMERICAS

The crafters of NAFTA in the early 1990s took a different path from the negotiators of the WTO GATS, though both agreements were being negotiated simultaneously. While political caution on the part of developing countries dictated a very timid approach to the structure of the GATS as well as the adoption of a "positive list" or gradual approach to the undertaking of market access commitments, the NAFTA negotiators took the opposite track of high ambition. Spurred by the active participation of the business community, they abandoned the CUSFTA model, which applied only to a list of covered services where services that were not covered were not subject to the obligations of the agreement, to famously adopt the alternative "negative list" approach to market opening. Although often mistakenly understood as meaning a complete liberalization of service restrictions, in reality the "negative list" translated into an across-the-board legal assurance of access for service providers and investors at the level of existing regulations.

The greatest achievement of this alternative approach developed in the Americas in terms of services and investment was to bring the main virtues of the GATT for trade in goods, namely transparency and the predictability of a rules-based system, to bear on services in a way that the WTO GATS structure and rules failed to do. This proved to be of great importance because over time, as countries began to perceive the numerous shortcomings of the GATS and its rigidities, the alternative offered by the NAFTA structure became increasingly attractive and its adherents increasingly numerous.

Since the mid-1990s the countries of the Americas have been at the vanguard of the negotiation of NAFTA-type free trade agreements, whose salient characteristics are their ambitious nature and their objective of carrying out trade liberalization and integration not only for goods but also for services, as well as other key issues such as intellectual property and government procurement. Since the entry into force of the NAFTA on January 1, 1994 no fewer than 29 sub-regional arrangements[2] containing disciplines on trade in services, either in the form of new FTAs or as part of an effort to deepen already existing regional economic integration groupings have been signed or have entered into force among countries in the Western Hemisphere.

Most countries in the Americas have embraced the comprehensive, "negative list" approach of the NAFTA for services in their FTAs negotiated with other partners in the region. Twelve countries stretching from Canada to Chile along the Pacific Coast, and the Dominican Republic, have negotiated similar-type FTAs using this approach. Moreover, the members of the Central American Common Market (CACM)[3] also chose the same approach in their services and investment agreement, whereas the members of the Andean Community[4]

---

[2] As of February 1, 2012.

[3] The CACM members are: Costa Rica, El Salvador, Guatemala, Honduras, and Nicaragua.

[4] The current members of the Andean Community are: Bolivia, Colombia, Ecuador, and Peru. The liberalization of trade in services has been suspended

and those of CARICOM[5] each opted for a "negative list" services agreement within their own separate integration process, though with a slightly different structure from that of NAFTA. In South America the members of the Common Market of the South (MERCOSUR)[6] chose a different model than the NAFTA and adopted the Protocol of Montevideo on Trade in Services in 1997, with the objective of achieving full liberalization of trade in services and an open regional market for services through periodic rounds of negotiations. Seven such rounds have already taken place. The Protocol of Montevideo, which entered into force on December 7, 2005, establishes a program for the liberalization of intra-trade in services within an overall implementation period of ten years from the date of entry into force, i.e. by December 2015. Although modeled after the "positive list" approach of the GATS, MERCOSUR countries have also innovated with respect to the WTO by agreeing in 2001 to a transparency exercise consisting of the listing of all existing restrictions in services trade with a view to their progressive removal. This transparency exercise is complemented by a "*standstill*" provision prohibiting the adoption of new restrictions.[7] It is worth

in the Plurinational State of Bolivia since December 2006, in accordance with Decision No. 659 of the Commission of the Andean Community ("Service Sectors Subject to Further Liberalization or Regulatory Harmonization") of December 14, 2006. Decision No. 659 also provides that financial services and the further liberalization of the minimum percentages of nationally produced programming on national free-to-air television will be subject to special treatment and will continue to be regulated by sectoral decisions on which, to date, the members of the Andean Community have not yet agreed. For more information, see http://www.comunidadandina.org/normativa/dec/D659.htm.

[5] The members of CARICOM are: Antigua and Barbuda, the Bahamas, Barbados, Belize, Dominica, Grenada, Guyana, Haiti, Jamaica, Montserrat, Saint Lucia, St. Kitts and Nevis, St. Vincent and the Grenadines, Suriname, and Trinidad and Tobago.

[6] The members of MERCOSUR are: Argentina, Brazil, Paraguay, and Uruguay. On July 4, 2006, MERCOSUR members approved the Protocol of Adhesion of the Bolivarian Republic of Venezuela to MERCOSUR. The entry into force of the Protocol must be ratified by the parliaments of the five countries involved. As of December 2011, the approval of the Congress of Paraguay was still pending.

[7] In December 2008 MERCOSUR adopted a Plan of Action to Further the Program for the Liberalization of Trade in Services. This Plan of Action has a four-stage timeline, the target being to complete the liberalization program in 2015. By 2009: each Member had to analyze the current situation in order to define the least sensitive sectors (whose liberalization would not pose serious problems), as well as those of intermediate and high sensitivity, and those whose regulatory frameworks could be harmonized or complemented. By 2010: each Member com-

noting though that Uruguay, a MERCOSUR member, has also elected the NAFTA-type approach in its free trade agreement with Mexico, which entered into force on July 15, 2004, albeit the "negative list" has yet to be completed.[8]

Although there is no doubt that the Americas is in fact the region that has most wholeheartedly moved beyond the multilateral system toward deeper and more comprehensive services disciplines, and for this reason among others, it is noteworthy of distinction and of study, two countries have in recent years gone back on the NAFTA model. In 2006, the Bolivarian Republic of Venezuela withdrew from the Group of Three (G3) FTA,[9] between Colombia, Mexico and Venezuela, which had entered into force on January 1, 1995. And Bolivia withdrew from the Bolivia-Mexico FTA, in force since January 1, 1995, and replaced it with an Economic Complementarity Agreement (No. 66) with Mexico, which came into force on June 7, 2010. The Plurinational State of Bolivia considered "the chapters on investment, services, intellectual property and government procurement incompatible with the country's new Constitution, which had entered into force in February 2009."[10] The scope of the new agreement is strictly limited to trade in goods and does not include any service-related provisions.

Several countries of the Americas have in turn taken the NAFTA-type approach beyond the borders of the region to "export" this model around the world. They have negotiated similar agreements with trading partners in Asia, Northern Africa and the Middle East. As of February 2012, 23

---

mitted to consolidate the regulatory status quo of sectors where no commitments yet exist; to eliminate restrictions on market access and national treatment in the least sensitive sectors; and to take steps to harmonize or complement regulatory frameworks in sectors where this is deemed necessary. By 2012: each Member committed to eliminate restrictions on market access and national treatment in sectors of intermediate sensitivity. By 2015: each Member committed to eliminate restrictions on market access and national treatment in the most sensitive sectors and to eliminate domestic regulatory measures that have been identified as bureaucratic obstacles to intra-zone trade. For more information, see http://www.sice.oas.org/Trade/MRCSRS/Decisions/DEC4908_s.pdf. On December 16, 2010 the MERCOSUR Common Market Council reiterated to MERCOSUR members the need to implement the December 2008 decision. For more information, see http://www.sice.oas.org/Trade/MRCSRS/Decisions/DEC5410_s.pdf.

8 The agreement does not cover financial services, air transport services or government procurement. For more information, see http://www.sice.oas.org/TPD/MEX_URY/Negotiations/Texto_s.pdf.

9 For more information, see http://www.sice.oas.org/Trade/go3/G3INDICE.ASP.

10 See ECLAC (2010).

NAFTA-type agreements have been negotiated over the past 15 years between countries of the Americas and those outside the region, most of these with countries in East Asia. At present, the largest experiment in regional integration involving services is being carried out under the Trans-Pacific Partnership (TPP) negotiations, begun in March 2010. The TPP (discussed later in this chapter in more detail) is slated to become the nucleus of a possible APEC-wide future Free Trade Area of the Asia-Pacific (FTAAP). Of the current nine participants in the TPP negotiations, seven have previously negotiated NAFTA-type agreements that include services and investment, and this is the basic model that is being followed.

The following section discusses the innovations of the NAFTA approach and in what ways it has provided a new framework for services trade, including a discussion of how the earlier NAFTA-type agreements have been deepened since 2002.

4.2.1 Innovations in Structure and Rules

The structure of the NAFTA-type agreements reflects recognition of modal neutrality which has been codified through a more or less equal treatment of the modes of supply within the agreement. This structure is set out in Figure 4.1. The Cross-Border Services chapter covers modes 1, 2 and 4 (the latter to a limited extent) and often contains an Annex on Professional Services. The chapter on Investment covers investment in both goods and services (mode 3 plus additional types of investment). The chapter on Temporary Entry for Business Persons contains a set of provisions to facilitate administrative and legal procedures for temporary entry for a limited number of categories under mode 4. Separate chapters deal with Financial Services and Telecommunications in a more in-depth manner.

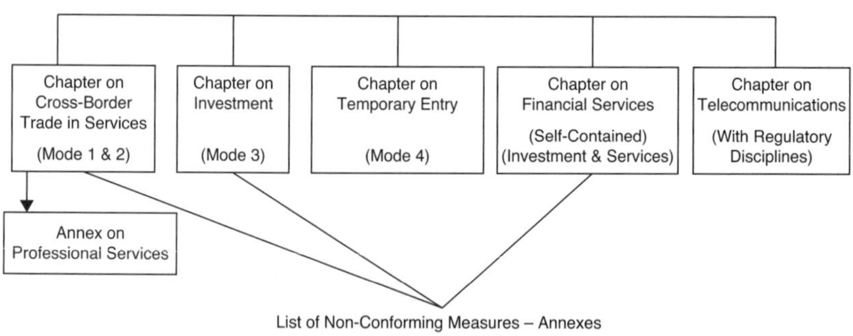

Figure 4.1 Structure of most FTAs for services in the Americas

Other chapters in the agreements that apply to both goods and services in a comprehensive manner include those on: intellectual property rights; government procurement; electronic commerce; and, in the more recent agreements, a chapter on transparency. Finally, NAFTA-type agreements in the Americas provide for measures that violate the basic disciplines of the agreement to be recorded in lists of Existing and Future Non-Conforming Measures that are set out in Annexes. The main features of each chapter are discussed below.

Cross-border trade in services The chapter on Cross-Border Trade in Services in these regional trade agreements (RTAs) recognizes and captures the importance of open cross-border trade in services and provides the legal certainty for service exporters to choose which mode of supply best suits their comparative advantage and is most cost effective. This is assured in the agreements through a provision called "no local presence requirement" which guarantees that services can be traded through modes 1 and 2 without being tied to a commercial presence abroad (unless otherwise specified in the non-conforming measures). This feature is an important one for developing trading partners, as the large majority of their exporters are small and medium-sized firms, which are then able to export through the low-cost information technology channels of the internet on the same footing as larger firms with more capital and international branches. The chapter on Cross-Border Trade in Services contains the basic disciplines of most-favored-nation (MFN) treatment, national treatment, market access, no local presence, and denial of benefits. More recent agreements also include provisions on market access, transparency, and domestic regulation (these obligations apply to both cross-border trade in services and investment in services). The chapter often contains an Annex on Professional Services whose purpose is to facilitate the movement of professionals through provisions to encourage trading partners to recognize the equivalence of their qualifications.

Investment NAFTA-type FTAs have highlighted and captured the interrelated nature of investment in services and goods through a separate investment chapter which covers both within its disciplines. Investment in the NAFTA-type agreements is much broader than "commercial presence" under the WTO GATS, where mode 3 is limited to foreign direct investment (FDI) only. Under the NAFTA approach the definition of investment is broad and asset-based. It is more encompassing than the traditional definition of FDI because it also includes portfolio investment as well as tangible and intangible assets such as intellectually property, among other assets.[11] The chapter on Investment contains disciplines based on three pillars: protection by means of legal security through clear and transparent rules on issues such as expropriation and transfers; guarantee of market access through maintenance of the "status quo" or liberalization of barriers to investment; and dispute settlement provisions specific to investment ("investor-state" provisions).

Temporary entry Contrary to the situation with investment, this chapter under the NAFTA is much narrower than the definition of mode 4 under the WTO GATS. While the latter covers the temporary movement of all natural persons, under the NAFTA-type agreements this has traditionally been limited to business persons. However, these provisions do not include obligations for visas or allow for employment considerations. Generally, there is no market access component in this chapter, although specific quotas may and have been specified separately or in side agreements.[12]

In-depth treatment of specific sectors Two sectors in particular have been signaled out under the NAFTA approach for more in-depth treatment due to their importance for economic development and services trade. These are financial services and telecommunications. The Financial Services chapter covers cross-border trade and a broad definition of investment in financial services. It is self-contained and has its own specific disciplines for the liberalization of trade in financial services as well as its own trade-related regulatory disciplines for financial services (but does not include specific types of regulations). Prudential requirements are outside the scope of this chapter. The Telecommunication chapter contains specific disciplines for the telecommunications sector which are of a "pro-regulatory" nature and a part of competition policy. This chapter in the NAFTA-type agreements

---

11 The definition of investment in NAFTA is broad and asset-based. It includes an exhaustive list of investment assets linked to the activities of an enterprise such as FDI, portfolio investment and various forms of tangible and intangible property, whereas the new US FTAs include an open-ended, asset-based definition of the term investment, which includes FDI, portfolio investment and various forms of tangible and intangible property.

12 It must be noted that, although the definition of mode 4 under the WTO GATS does in principle cover all categories of labor, in fact it has been used by countries to schedule commitments for temporary movement of skilled labor categories only. To date there have been no cases of WTO members that have scheduled commitments for the temporary movement of semi-skilled or lower-skilled workers. And the attempt to negotiate a fuller treatment of mode 4 following the Uruguay Round (1994) proved unsuccessful.

further elaborates on the WTO Reference Paper for Telecom with deeper rules and disciplines. It does not, however, provide for an explicit market access component which is covered for telecommunications in the cross-border and investment chapters.[13]

4.2.2 Innovations in Market Access

Together with their differences in structure, NAFTA-type agreements are also notable for innovations in their approach to market access. This pertains to their comprehensive inclusion of all service sectors within the scope of the agreement, the unconditional application of all the key disciplines of the agreement, a dynamic, in-built provision for ongoing liberalization they contain and the high degree of transparency they bring to the treatment of all exceptions (or non-conforming measures) to the liberalization requirements. These are all discussed in more detail below.

Comprehensive inclusion of all service sectors In contrast to the WTO GATS and "positive list" agreements where inclusion of service sectors and sub-sectors within lists of commitments is completely voluntary as is the type of national treatment and market access commitments that will be accorded to the four modes of supply for each of these sectors, the NAFTA-type approach requires that all service sectors be included within the disciplines of the agreement (other than air transport and services provided by government authorities on a non-competitive basis). As a result of this large degree of freedom under the GATS, where both national treatment and market access are conditional rather than unconditional obligations, there is a large degree of variation in the service agreements following a "positive list" approach with respect to the number and type of commitments included in schedules for traded services. This is not the case under NAFTA, where the requirement for comprehensive sectoral coverage largely shifts the negotiations under this approach from a focus on which sectors to include in liberalization commitments to a focus instead on the residual restrictions those members to the agreement wish to maintain on their service sectors.

---

[13] NAFTA Chapter Thirteen on Telecommunications, which builds on CUSFTA Annex 1404.C, was negotiated before the WTO Reference Paper, and, as such, does not cover all the issues addressed in the Reference Paper.

Unconditional application of disciplines Under the NAFTA approach the main disciplines of the agreement must be applied to all service sectors on an unconditional basis, unless otherwise indicated. All measures affecting trade in services are to be liberalized in order to conform to these disciplines unless otherwise specified in annexes containing reservations, or non-conforming measures. Core disciplines of the agreement for cross-border services trade are MFN treatment, national treatment, market access and no local presence requirement. In the case of investment in goods and services, the core disciplines are MFN treatment, national treatment, no nationality requirements to be applied to senior management and boards of directors and certain prohibited performance requirements. However, this does not mean that NAFTA agreements automatically liberalize all services trade and all investment flows, as is sometimes believed. If countries wish to maintain restrictions on services trade, they are able to do so, subject to the outcome of the negotiations. Those measures that do not comply with core disciplines must then be set out in annexes of non-conforming measures, as mentioned above. This is the so-called "list-or-lose" technique. Non-conforming measures in the annexes can then be (but are not necessarily) liberalized through a commitment to future consultations or periodic negotiations. Additionally, a very few sectors may sometimes be permanently exempted from all disciplines under the NAFTA approach.[14]

Ratchet One very innovative provision in the NAFTA labeled the "rachet clause" effectively provides for ongoing liberalization through the requirement that all measures brought into effect following the conclusion of the agreement in question that provide for greater market access will automatically be considered bound such that the more liberal access must be applied by members to their trading partners on a permanent basis in the future. This requirement makes NAFTA-type agreements dynamic instruments rather than fixed in time like the WTO GATS or other "positive list" agreements, under which all aspects of market opening must be negotiated in future rounds of negotiations and included in future

[14] These two types of measures that violate the core disciplines of the NAFTA-type agreements are set out in two separate annexes: a first annex contains those measures that violate the core disciplines explained above and which are subject to the ratchet mechanism; and a second annex contains those (few) measures or sectors that are permanently exempt from all disciplines. Most of the NAFTA-type agreements have both types of annexes. For more information, see Findlay et al. (2005) and Stephenson (2002).

Positive list or "bottom up"	Negative List or "top down"
Characteristics	Characteristics
– Specific commitments by sectors and modes of supply with national treatment and market access limitations	– Comprehensive sectoral coverage
– MFN treatment (with temporary exemptions)	– Unconditional MFN treatment and national treatment (reservations allowed)
	– No local presence requirement
	– Listing of non-discriminatory quantitative restrictions

Figure 4.2 Modality: contrasting approaches to liberalization in RTAs

schedules of commitments before they are contractually applied to trading partners.

Transparency The NAFTA approach requires that members provide detailed information in a transparent form on the barriers to trade in services that remain in place under the agreement (i.e. the non-conforming measures set out in the annexes). Information must be provided on each measure, including the title and reference to the law in question, the sector it affects, an indication of the core discipline(s) that it violates, as well as a brief description of its contents, thus giving national service providers precise knowledge of foreign markets. This is in considerable contrast to the GATS or "positive list" agreements which only require a brief indication of the type of restriction affecting a given sector. Moreover, in the latter context, the type of conditions and limitations on market access and national treatment included in national schedules can be listed as ceilings on or minimum levels of treatment and thus do not necessarily reflect actual regulatory practice. This possibility results in less transparency for service providers and less legal and economic certainty regarding market access. Under the NAFTA this is not possible, and all remaining restrictions must not only be justified but they must be precisely identified and applied at the level of existing law.

The "negative list" NAFTA approach described above thus innovated in many ways with respect to the "positive list," or "bottom-up," approach of the GATS. Although in reality neither of the two negotiating modalities guarantees full liberalization of services trade and is not presumed to do so unless this objective is explicitly set out by members to a given integration agreement, the NAFTA approach developed a number of innovations in its treatment of services as discussed above that improve upon the "positive list" approach. Two of the major benefits of the NAFTA approach are key ones for the success of any trade agreement. The first lies in its greater ease of use for service providers who are the ones actually trading under the agreement. The second lies in its greater ease of implementation for government officials who must ensure compliance with the disciplines of the agreement.

As mentioned above, members of all but one of the sub-regional agreements negotiated by countries in the Americas have adopted the NAFTA modality of the "negative list" approach for liberalizing services trade as outlined above (see Table 4.1).[15] This stands in contrast to countries in

Table 4.1 Liberalization modality in RTAs in the Americas[16]

Choice of Liberalization Modality	
Negative List Approach	Entry into Force
NAFTA	1994
Costa Rica-Mexico	1995
Canada-Chile	1997
Mexico-Nicaragua	1998
Chile-Mexico	1999
Mexico-Northern Triangle	2001
CACM-Dominican Republic	2001[17]
Chile-CACM	2002[18]
CACM-Panama	2003[19]
Chile-United States	2004
Mexico-Uruguay	2004
CARICOM	2006[20]
Andean Community	2006[21]

15 For more information on the experience of Latin American countries in implementing the trade agreements they have signed with the United States, see Robert (2011).

16 The information in Table 4.1 is up-to-date as February 1, 2012.

17 The agreement entered into force in: Costa Rica on March 7, 2002; El Salvador on October 4, 2001; Guatemala on October 3, 2001; Honduras on December 19, 2001; and Nicaragua on September 3, 2002.

18 The agreement entered into force in 2002 in Costa Rica and El Salvador; in 2008 in Honduras; and in 2010 in Guatemala. The bilateral protocol between Chile and Nicaragua was signed on February 23, 2011.

19 The agreement entered into force in: Costa Rica on November 23, 2008; El Salvador on April 11, 2003; Guatemala on June 22, 2009; Honduras on January 9, 2009; and Nicaragua on November 21, 2009.

20 The CARICOM Single Market entered into force on January 1, 2006.

21 For more information, see: http://www.comunidadandina.org/comercio/comercio_servicios.htm.

Table 4.1 (continued)

Choice of Liberalization Modality	
Negative List Approach	Entry into Force
CAFTA-DR-US	2006[22]
CACM (Agreement on Investment and Trade in Services)	2007[23]
Chile-Panama	2008
Peru-United States (PTPA)	2009
Chile-Peru	2009
Chile-Colombia	2009
Canada-Peru	2009
Colombia-Northern Triangle	2009[24]
Canada-Colombia	2011[25]
Mexico-Peru	2012[26]
	Signed
Colombia–United States (signed)	2006
Panama-United States (signed)	2007
Canada-Panama (signed)	2010
Panama-Peru (signed)	2011[27]
Costa Rica-Peru (signed)	2011[28]
Central America-Mexico (signed)	2011[29]
Positive List Approach	Entry into Force
MERCOSUR	2005

22 The agreement entered into force in: Costa Rica on January 1, 2009; Dominican Republic on March 1, 2007; El Salvador on March 1, 2006; Guatemala on July 1, 2006; and Honduras and Nicaragua on April 1, 2006. For more information on how Costa Rica and the Dominican Republic have been willing to overcome political economy obstacles to take on significant disciplines in the area of services trade in the CAFTA-DR, see Robert and Stephenson (2008).

23 The Agreement on Investment and Trade in Services among the five Central American countries was signed on March 24, 2002. It was updated after the negotiation of the CAFTA-DR, and approved by the Ministers responsible for economic integration on February 13, 2007 in Guatemala City.

24 The agreement entered into force in El Salvador on February 1, 2010; Guatemala on November 13, 2009; and in Honduras on March 27, 2010.

25 The Canada-Colombia FTA entered into force on August 15, 2011.

26 The Mexico-Peru FTA entered into force on February 1, 2012.

27 The Panama-Peru FTA was signed on May 25, 2011.

28 The Costa Rica-Peru FTA was signed on May 26, 2011.

29 On November 22, 2011 the single FTA between Central American countries and Mexico was signed in El Salvador, as part of the convergence efforts to have one single free trade agreement between Central American countries and Mexico. See http://www.sice.oas.org/TPD/CACM_MEX/CACM_MEX_e.asp.

other regions of the world, where the "positive list" approach continues to dominate. However, many of the RTAs that countries of the Americas have exported to trading partners outside the region have also been based on a NAFTA-type, "negative list" approach, which means that the innovations discussed in this section for the treatment of services trade have found their way around the world.

4.2.3 Improving the Early NAFTA Model

Between the years 1994 and 2002, the United States executive was unable to obtain trade negotiating authority from Congress and the U.S. did not initiate any new FTAs[30] after the original NAFTA, partly due to the strong reactions domestically to the feared effects from the passage of the agreement.[31] This gap allowed the negotiators to observe how the NAFTA text was being implemented and to work on improvements to perceived shortcomings. Once new Trade Promotion Authority was granted to the President under the Trade Act of 2002, negotiators incorporated several changes into future NAFTA-type FTAs. Such improvements served to strengthen the original NAFTA template. Specifically, three additional disciplines were added to the chapter on cross-border trade in services that were made applicable as well through cross-referencing to investment in services within the chapter on investment. These include the following:

---

[30] The exception is the U.S.-Jordan FTA which contains one single article on trade in services referring to the GATS. The U.S.-Jordan FTA entered into force on December 17, 2001.

[31] Trade Promotion Authority (previously known as "Fast Track Authority") is granted by Congress to the U.S. President so that the executive branch can negotiate trade agreements that Congress must approve or disapprove but not amend. However, it is not automatically granted; the authority must be requested and voted upon. It was in effect from 1975 to 1994, allowing for the completion of the NAFTA and the Uruguay Round, but lapsed between 1994 and 2002. It was restored in 2002 by the Trade Act of 2002 but expired on July 1, 2007 and has since not been renewed. The five years between 2002 and 2007 allowed the United States executive to negotiate several FTAs, among them the following: Chile-U.S. FTA; U.S.-Singapore FTA; U.S.-Australia FTA; U.S.-Morocco FTA; CAFTA-DR; U.S.-Bahrain FTA; U.S.-Oman FTA and Peru-U.S. Trade Promotion Agreement (PTPA). Three additional FTAs were completed and signed before the Trade Promotion Authority expired, namely the following: Colombia-U.S. Trade Promotion Agreement (CTPA); U.S.-South Korea FTA (KORUS); and Panama-U.S. Trade Promotion Agreement. On October 12, 2011 the United States Congress approved these three FTAs and on October 21, 2011 President Barack Obama signed legislation implementing these agreements. See USTR website at: www.ustr.gov.

- A "market access" discipline with a text similar to that of GATS Article XVI setting out a requirement not to allow restrictions on six types of market access barriers;
- A strengthened provision on "transparency" in the chapter on cross-border trade in services, together with an additional new chapter on transparency covering goods, services and investment;
- A provision on "domestic regulation" with a text similar to that of GATS Article VI, including the "necessity test" clause.
- Inclusion of a separate chapter on electronic commerce covering the object of electronic transmission as "digital products" rather than as "services" for purposes of the agreement.[32]

This new strengthened NAFTA template thus incorporated some of the key features of the WTO GATS that had been missing, including the disciplining of quantitative restrictions and restrictive forms of association on service activities, as well as attempting to ensure that domestic regulations in the forms of qualification and licensing requirements and procedures are based on objective and transparent criteria and are not "more burdensome than necessary to ensure the quality of the service." The strengthened transparency disciplines also were designed to ensure that opaque regulations do not take away from the market opening gains of the services agreements. These new disciplines in the revised NAFTA template were incorporated into all the FTAs concluded by the United States between 2002 and July 2007, when the Trade Promotion Authority expired, namely those in the Americas with Chile, CAFTA-DR and Peru, as well as in FTAs with Colombia and Panama. Canada has also applied the revised NAFTA template in its FTAs with Peru, Colombia and Panama, albeit with its own adjustments. For example, the new provisions on market access and domestic regulation in the cross-border chapter on trade in services do not apply to investment in services. The Canadian

[32] The determination of whether the outcome of an electronic transmission is a "good" or a "service" is still outstanding at the WTO, although there is still a moratorium on the application of duties on electronic transactions. However, the revised NAFTA template defines electronic commerce in the following manner: "For purposes of this Chapter: *digital products* means computer programs, text, video, images, sound recordings, and other products that are digitally encoded and transmitted electronically, regardless of whether a Party treats such products as a good or a service under its domestic law; *electronic* means employing computer processing; and *electronic transmission* or *transmitted electronically* means the transfer of digital products using any electromagnetic or photonic means" (Article 15.6 from the chapter on Electronic Commerce, Chile-U.S. FTA, emphasis in text).

FTAs do include a chapter on transparency but there is no provision on transparency in the cross-border trade in services chapter.

4.3 TAKING THE NAFTA TEMPLATE AROUND THE GLOBE?

Countries of the Americas have negotiated more free trade agreements with partners outside the region than they have with regional partners and at present are turning their attention outward even more. According to the information on the SICE website of the OAS, 32 trade agreements are in force between countries of the Americas, four of these in the form of customs unions and 28 FTAs, while 36 FTAs are in force between countries of the Americas and those outside the region.[33]

The majority of these FTAs with extra-regional partners resemble the negative list NAFTA template because they have been led primarily by five countries – Mexico, Chile, the United States, Canada and Peru – who have all been proponents of this approach in their trade agreements. However, not all of the agreements with extra-regional partners are as similar in structure and content as are the FTAs in the Americas. Countries of the Americas have shown themselves willing to adapt the NAFTA template to the desires and constraints of their trading partners, or, in the case of the European Union, to adopt the template of the EU.

Table 4A.1 in the Appendix sets out a comparison of the main provisions relating to services that are found in a selection of FTAs within the Americas, highlighting how very similar all of these agreements are in form and substance. Table 4A.2 sets out a similar comparison for FTAs negotiated between countries of the Americas and Asian partners, and Table 4A.3 for trade agreements with the European Union.

Many of the FTAs concluded between countries in the Americas and partners in Asia look nearly identical to the NAFTA template or its updated version. This is the case for the U.S.-Singapore FTA in Table 4A.2 (as well as the U.S.-Australia and U.S.-Korea FTAs). Most of the FTAs concluded with Asian partners contain the same basic provisions and disciplines; however there are some variations in the NAFTA template. The FTAs that Chile has signed (with Korea and China) do not have an MFN clause for services, for example, as Chile did not want to extend

[33] See sections on "Trade Agreements" and "Trade Policy Developments" on the OAS Foreign Trade Information System (SICE) website, at www.sice.oas.org.

these same trade benefits to other partners. Chile's FTA with Korea is also missing the provision on domestic regulation. China has insisted upon using the positive list approach to scheduling services commitments in all of its regional agreements, and this is the case for its FTAs with countries in the Americas – Chile, as well as the two other countries with which it has concluded FTAs, Peru and Costa Rica. The ratchet clause of the NAFTA approach is missing from these FTAs with China, as is the Annex on Professional Services. Instead, the agreements with China contain a section to facilitate the "temporary entry of business persons" which includes several categories, including specialists.

It is of note that the Trans-Pacific Strategic Economic Partnership (TPSEP), a NAFTA-type FTA in force since 2006 between Chile, Brunei, New Zealand and Singapore, is being taken as the basis for the TPP or "Trans-Pacific Partnership" negotiations, currently ongoing between nine countries of the Asia-Pacific region. The TPP negotiations were officially launched at the APEC Summit in November 2010 after the U.S. noted an interest in these discussions in 2008.[34] The four TPSEP members were joined by Australia, Malaysia, Peru, the United States and Vietnam, in their objective to create an expanded and "modernized" state-of-the-art or "next generation" free trade agreement, reflecting the realities of the new trade and investment paradigms of the 21st century.

The TPP underwent a substantial widening in 2012, assuming the mantle of a "mega-regional" construct after the formal admission of Canada and Mexico, followed by that of Japan in early 2013. The addition of the United States' two NAFTA partners and the world's third largest economy is far from trivial in economic terms, since such expansion suddenly transformed the TPP into one of the world's largest free trade zones (alongside TTIP, the recently-launched Transatlantic Trade and Investment Initiative). Once completed, the TPP would account for almost a third of global commerce and surpass the European Union in aggregate output terms. At the same time, the TPP is widely regarded as a US-led strategic response to China's increasingly assertive commercial and security interests in the Asia-Pacific region.

The TPP initiative is of considerable importance because it is viewed as one of two possible ways forward for the proposed Free Trade Area of the Asia-Pacific (FTAAP), an initiative that has been endorsed by

---

[34] The TPP negotiations were officially launched at the APEC Summit in November 2010. By the APEC Leaders Meeting of November 2011 a Framework Agreement was concluded. A target date of end 2013 has been set for the completion of these negotiations. For information, see http://www.ustr.gov.

the 21 APEC Leaders.[35] If successful, the TPP would represent a trading agreement among a key nucleus of APEC member economies that could possibly be expanded and garner the support necessary to become an Asia-Pacific wide integration agreement based on an updated and modernized NAFTA model, rather than the alternative ASEAN (and for services, GATS-based) model. Importantly, the TPP will contain an accession clause that will allow a possibility of adhesion for new members in the future.

The United States is highly interested in concluding the TPP not only for its economic benefits in linking with the Asian markets but also for the political and strategic purpose of reinforcing its presence in Asia, a declared priority of the Obama Administration. It is the only active negotiating agenda in which the U.S. is currently engaged and which has been initiated since the lapse of Trade Promotion Authority. The TPP is also considered critical by the Latin American participants in the process – Chile, Peru and very likely Mexico – in their desire to enhance a growing commercial partnership with Asia. The Asian share of total Latin America trade has grown from 5 to 20% over the past 15 years, and the Latin American economies on the Pacific Rim are particularly keen to use the opportunity provided by the TPP negotiations to insert their economies into global value chains of goods and services.[36] Engagement in the TPP is of top importance for Canada and Mexico so that these two NAFTA partners do not find themselves at a disadvantage in the rules of origin, in regional investment and in existing supply chains in North America.

---

[35] The Declaration from the APEC Leaders Meeting in Japan in November 2010 includes the following official endorsement of the FTAAP effort: "We will take concrete steps toward realization of a Free Trade Area of the Asia-Pacific (FTAAP), which is a major instrument to further APEC's regional economic integration agenda. . . ." The Leaders' Statement can be found at: http://www.apec.org/en/Press/News-Releases/2010/1114_leaders.aspx. The most recent APEC Leaders Meeting that took place in Honolulu, Hawaii in November 2011 includes the following reference to the FTAAP: "We further recognize that strengthening regional economic integration also plays a key role in promoting regional peace and stability. We have pursued these objectives in 2011 by addressing next-generation trade and investment issues, including through our trade agreements and a Free Trade Area of the Asia-Pacific, which is a major instrument to further APEC's regional economic integration agenda. " The Leaders' Statement can be found at: http://www.apec.org/Meeting-Papers/Leaders-Declarations/2011/2011_aelm.aspx.

[36] Comments made by the Ambassadors of Chile, Peru and Mexico to the U.S. on the occasion of a seminar on the "Trans-Pacific Partnership: A Western Hemisphere View" organized by the Council of the Americas on January 31, 2012 in Washington, DC.

Additionally, the TPP partners are discussing regulatory coherence as one of the chapters of the future agreement, while Canada has recently launched an ambitious regulatory coherence and cooperation initiative with the United States.[37]

In addition to regulatory coherence, the other "new generation" issues that are being discussed and negotiated in the TPP include: regional connectivity and supply chains; business facilitation; investment, strengthened competition policy, strengthened intellectual property right protection; government procurement, electronic commerce; measures for integration of small and medium-sized enterprises; disciplines on state-owned and state-operated enterprises; technology and innovation; and development and capacity-building.[38] Once finalized, the TPP will be a "state-of-the-art" FTA, based on the NAFTA template but having gone significantly beyond it.

4.4 NEGOTIATING SERVICES WITH THE EUROPEAN UNION?

Negotiating with the EU has been quite a recent phenomenon for countries in the Americas. To date the EU has concluded agreements that cover services with Mexico, Chile, CARIFORUM[39] and more recently with six countries of Central America as well as Colombia, Peru and, in late 2013, Canada.[40] Negotiations with Central America, Colombia and Peru

---

[37] Remarks made by the Minister of Economics Affairs, Embassy of Canada to the U.S. on the occasion of a seminar on the "Trans-Pacific Partnership: A Western Hemisphere View" organized by the Council of the Americas on January 31, 2012 in Washington, DC.

[38] Presentation by Robert Scollay of the University of Auckland, New Zealand, at the Seventh Latin America/Caribbean and Asia-Pacific Economics and Business Association (LAEBA) Annual Meeting, Washington, DC, January 31, 2012.

[39] CARIFORUM States here refers to the 14 member countries of CARICOM (Antigua and Barbuda, the Bahamas, Barbados, Belize, Dominica, Grenada, Guyana, Haiti, Jamaica, Saint Lucia, St. Kitts and Nevis, St. Vincent and the Grenadines, Suriname, and Trinidad and Tobago) and the Dominican Republic.

[40] The EU, Colombia and Peru announced the conclusion of their negotiations for a trade agreement in May 2010 in the framework of the VI EU-Latin America and Caribbean (LAC) Summit. Chief negotiators of the European Commission, Peru and Colombia met in Brussels on March 23–24, 2011 to initial the final texts. The text is available at: http://trade.ec.europa.eu/doclib/press/index.cfm?id=691. Likewise, negotiations with the six countries of Central America (Costa Rica,

were concluded in 2010 and the agreements are in the ratification process. Negotiations are ongoing with MERCOSUR as well as with Canada in the field of investment protection.

The earliest EU agreement with a country in the Americas was that with Mexico (2000). However, the services chapter is more of a framework than a body of obligations, requiring the market access commitments for services to be carried out at a later date, in conjunction with the conclusion of the Doha Round. However, the subsequent EU agreements with countries of the region display a distinct pattern which follows the EU template for services. Though covering essentially the same content as the revised NAFTA template for services, the EU approach is nonetheless quite different in many ways, which are reviewed in this section.

4.4.1 Broader Focus and Heavier Institutional Structure

The EU agreements have a much broader focus than the NAFTA and are conceived as political and development instruments as well as trade promoting agreements. They cover a very broad range of activities and areas. Unlike NAFTA-type FTAs, the EU agreements with countries in the Americas contain sections on political dialogue which extend to cooperation in foreign and security policy, as well as social dialogue. Generally, the agreements are divided into three parts: trade, political issues and economic cooperation.

Similar to the EU itself, the trade agreements negotiated by the EU with other partners are very heavy on institutional structure. They create numerous bodies, including an association committee, a joint consultative committee, special committees for specific disciplines, and an association parliamentary committee. In contrast, the NAFTA-type FTAs usually create only one overall committee to follow the implementation of the agreement, plus a committee on trade capacity-building for those FTAs where this chapter is included.

Like the NAFTA-type FTAs, the EU agreements contain separate chapters for the treatment of each mode of service supply within a broader section called a "title" which covers both trade in services and investment (or establishment as it is often labeled). A chapter on mode 3 or "com-

El Salvador, Guatemala, Honduras, Nicaragua and Panama) and the EU were concluded in May 2010 and announced at the VI EU-LAC Summit. On March 22, 2011, Central America and the European Union initialed the Association Agreement after its legal review. The initialing will be followed by the process of translation, signature and ratification. The text is available at: http://trade.ec.europa.eu/doclib/press/index.cfm?id=689.

mercial presence" contains disciplines for foreign direct investment in goods and services, while a chapter on "cross-border supply of services" is devoted to modes 1 and 2, and a chapter on "temporary presence of natural persons for business purposes" (in some agreements) to facilitate mode 4 is similar to the NAFTA chapter on "temporary entry of business persons."[41] While the U.S. has become less open to dealing with mode 4 in its regional agreements, the EU seems to have moved in the opposite direction.

Unlike the NAFTA-type FTAs, the EU agreements on services/investment concluded with countries in the Americas do not include provisions on investment protection and investor-state dispute settlement, as the EC did not have competence to develop disciplines on foreign direct investment prior to the entry into force of the Lisbon Treaty.[42] The transparency requirements in these agreements are also less stringent and are not set out in a separate chapter, although the agreements do contain a provision on domestic regulation. Similar to the NAFTA template, the EU agreements place high emphasis on financial services and telecommunication services and include separate chapters for these with detailed provisions. However, the EU agreements single out other service sectors as well for special focus, including international maritime transport (in the Chile, CARIFORUM and Central American agreements) and computer services, courier services and tourism services (in the CARIFORUM and Central American agreements). The EU agreements follow a "positive list" approach for the scheduling of service commitments since the EU Commission does not have competence with respect to its member states to negotiate on all services and investment issues.[43] Countries in the

41 The chapter on "temporary presence of natural persons for business purposes" is found in the EU agreements with CARIFORUM and Central America. However, in the case of the EU agreement with Chile, there is only a brief article on "movement of natural persons," with no market access component.

42 Article 207 of the Lisbon Treaty in force since December 1, 2009 brings foreign direct investment under the umbrella of Europe's common commercial policy for the first time, making it the exclusive competence of the European Community.

43 Within the EU, trade in services issues do not fall exclusively under the competence of the Community as they go beyond Articles 113 and 238 of the Treaty that accords supranational treaty-making powers to the Community on behalf of all the member states. Thus when implementing the services provisions and obligations of a trade agreement, these must be approved by each EU member state in accordance with domestic laws. For this reason the EU is required to negotiate on services through a positive list approach, allowing each EU member state to indicate its specific limitations with respect to individual sectors.

Americas have thus been obliged to adapt to this "positive list" scheduling approach when entering into agreements with the EU.

4.4.2 Emphasis on Development Cooperation in EU Agreements

Trade agreements concluded between the European Union and countries in the Americas contain a strong focus on development cooperation. EU agreements underscore the intention to carry out cooperation in nearly every conceivable sphere of economic activity, including energy, transport, customs, statistics, data protection, consumer protection, tourism, mining, science and technology, information technology, audio-visual, investment promotion, small enterprises, illegal immigration, drugs and combating organized crime. Capacity-building is also a big component of EU agreements.

This is particularly the case in the CARIFORUM-EC Economic Partnership Agreement (EPA).[44] The Caribbean countries, for various reasons, were able in their negotiations with the European Union to conclude an agreement that strongly puts into practice the concept of an asymmetrical treatment of levels of development. The EPA highlights several development-related objectives, notably those of contributing to the reduction and eventual eradication of poverty, promoting the gradual integration of CARIFORUM States into the world and improving CARIFORUM States' capacity in trade policy and trade related issues, and the Agreement aims toward the progressive asymmetrical liberalization of trade. Similar to the CAFTA-DR, the EPA builds on and helps to deepen regional integration[45] (Article 4).

Development cooperation (Article 7) is recognized by the Parties as a crucial element of the Partnership. It is specifically stated that this cooperation can take both financial and non-financial forms. Article 8 outlines several broad priority areas for development cooperation between the Parties. With regard to services and investment, the diversification of

---

[44] The CARIFORUM-EC Economic Partnership Agreement was signed on October 15, 2008 by most CARICOM countries, the EU and the Dominican Republic. Guyana signed on October 20, 2008 and Haiti on December 11, 2009. It has applied provisionally since December 29, 2008. The authors are grateful to Alicia Nicholls who provided some of the insights on the innovations of the CARIFORUM-EC EPA for this section. Please also see Sauvé and Ward (2009).

[45] The Regional Preference Clause (Article 238(2)) attempts to help strengthen this intra-CARIFORUM integration by mandating that whatever is given to the EU must be given to all other CARIFORUM states. This is specifically targeted at the relationship between CARICOM and the Dominican Republic.

CARIFORUM's exports through new investment and the development of new service sectors are mentioned. Areas of cooperation are further expounded upon in the development cooperation articles of the individual chapters of the Agreement. Specific tasks that are identified for technical assistance and capacity-building in the tourism section (Article 117) include the upgrading of CARIFORUM's national accounts with the view to facilitating national and regional tourism satellite accounts and the development of internet marketing strategies for small and medium-sized (SME) tourism enterprises. Article 121(2)(f) speaks to establishing mechanisms for promoting investment and joint ventures between service suppliers of the EC and CARIFORUM States, and enhancing the capacities of investment promotion agencies in the latter. The targeted and direct nature of these provisions in the EPA is noteworthy as such provisions in most international investment agreements tend to be indirect and vaguely worded.[46] The more recent agreements between the EU and Central America and the EU and Peru and Colombia also include important provisions for cooperation.

4.5 FINANCIAL SERVICES: A NEW ARCHITECTURAL APPROACH AND IMPROVED COMMITMENTS

The financial services sector has evolved at a rapid pace over the last 25 years, as a result of new technologies, greater competition, and deregulation. On the trade front, the Americas as a region has been at the forefront of a new architectural approach and improved commitments in financial services. NAFTA was the first agreement to address financial services in a comprehensive manner in the region. The CUSFTA provisions were, for the most part, concession-based, which means that each Party granted the other limited concessions. With the exception of insurance, financial services were not covered by national treatment and other key provisions in CUSFTA.

4.5.1 The Americas: A Stand-Alone Chapter on Financial Services

Since NAFTA, several NAFTA-type FTAs signed between countries of the Americas have included a stand-alone chapter on financial services, which is self-contained, and independent of the chapters on investment

46 UNCTAD (2008).

and cross-border trade in services, albeit some provisions included in these two chapters remain relevant.

Scope and coverage

The scope of the chapter on financial services in NAFTA-type agreements reflects the twin objective of liberalizing trade in financial services, while ensuring that the Parties safeguard their capacity to supervise their financial systems. This explains why, although some provisions (such as MFN and transparency) of the chapter are of general application, different rules apply to investment and cross-border trade. The NAFTA-type FTAs cover investment in financial institutions and cross-border trade in financial services. A financial institution is not defined in terms of the activities that an enterprise carries on. Rather, it is defined in terms of how it is regulated in the country in which it is located. If an enterprise carrying on a particular activity is regulated as a financial institution, it is a financial institution covered by the chapter on financial services. In contrast, if an enterprise carrying on the identical activity in another country is not regulated as a financial institution, it is covered by the investment chapter.[47]

The concept of cross-border trade in financial services in the NAFTA-like agreements is identical to the one found in the chapter on cross-border trade in services of these same agreements. It covers cross-border trade as defined by mode 1 under GATS, consumption abroad or mode 2 under GATS, and movement of natural persons or mode 4 under GATS. The definition of financial services is not linked to that of financial institution, which implies that a financial service may or may not be provided by a financial institution.[48]

---

[47] A financial institution is defined as any financial intermediary or other enterprise that is authorized to do business and regulated or supervised as a financial institution under the law of the Party in whose territory it is located, whereas a financial institution of another Party is a financial institution, including a branch, located in the territory of a Party that is controlled by persons of the other Party. It would therefore include a subsidiary in Guatemala of a U.S.-owned bank. The definition would also include a financial institution in El Salvador controlled by the incorporated U.S. subsidiary of an enterprise of a non CAFTA-DR country, such as a European bank. However, it would not include a financial institution controlled by a U.S. branch of a European bank. Therefore, only subsidiaries from third countries can benefit from these FTAs.

[48] In NAFTA, financial services means a service of a financial nature, including insurance, and a service incidental or auxiliary to a service of a financial nature, whereas in the Chile-U.S. FTA, CAFTA-DR, PTPA, Canada-Colombia FTA, Canada-Peru FTA and U.S.-Singapore FTA, financial services is defined as

The NAFTA approach on financial services also innovates in that the chapter on financial services incorporates by reference a number of articles from the chapters on cross-border trade in services (denial of benefits, and transfers and payments[49]) and investment (transfers, expropriation and compensation, special formalities and information requirements, denial of benefits, and investment and environment).[50] Moreover, the investor-state dispute settlement of the investment chapter[51] is incorporated into the chapter on financial services solely for claims that a Party has breached the articles on expropriation and compensation, transfers, or denial of benefits. A joint committee on financial services will review if the prudential carve-out applies to the measure being singled out in the claims.[52]

Rules and disciplines on investment

The provisions which apply to investment include the national treatment obligation, which covers all phases of an investment from establishment to sale.[53] The NAFTA and the Canada-Colombia and Canada-Peru FTAs

---

any service of a financial nature, and financial services include all insurance and insurance-related services, and all banking and other financial services (excluding insurance), as well as services incidental or auxiliary to a service of a financial nature.

49 For the article on transfers and payments in the cross-border trade in services chapter, this applies to CAFTA-DR, PTPA, Canada-Colombia FTA and Canada-Peru FTA.

50 In the Canada-Colombia and Canada-Peru FTAs, the article on investment and environment is entitled health, safety and environmental measures.

51 NAFTA, Chile-U.S. FTA, CAFTA-DR, PTPA, Canada-Colombia FTA, Canada-Peru FTA, and U.S.-Singapore FTA.

52 The provision on scope and coverage in the U.S. NAFTA-based FTAs also states that the chapter does not apply to measures adopted or maintained by a Party relating to activities or services forming part of a public retirement plan or statutory system of social security; or activities or services conducted for the account or with the guarantee or using the financial resources of the Party, including its public entities, except that the chapter on financial services shall apply if a Party allows any of these activities or services to be conducted by its financial institutions in competition with a public entity or a financial institution. Annex 12.1.3(a) of the PTPA further clarifies the language relating to activities or services forming part of a public retirement plan or statutory system of social security. The language in the NAFTA is very similar but does not include the reference to activities conducted in competition between financial institutions or between public and private entities as being covered by the chapter, whereas the Canadian NAFTA-based FTAs further clarify the scope of the chapter on financial services in an Annex (see Annex 11.10.3(a) of the Canada-Colombia and Canada-Peru FTAs).

53 The new FTAs also contain a provision on payment and clearing systems setting out the obligation of each Party to provide national treatment by granting financial institutions of another Party established in its territory access to payment

also contain language on states and provinces (NAFTA Article 1405(4)) or sub-national governments (Article 1102 in the Canada-Colombia and Canada-Peru FTAs) not included in the Chile-U.S. FTA, CAFTA-DR, PTPA and U.S.-Singapore FTA.[54] In addition, NAFTA, the Canada-Colombia FTA and the Canada-Peru FTA include an article on "establishment of financial institutions" (NAFTA Article 1403) or "right of establishment" (Canada-Colombia and Canada-Peru Article 1104) stating that an investor of another Party should be permitted to establish a financial institution in the territory of a Party in the juridical form chosen by such investor without the imposition of numerical restrictions[55] or requirements to take a specific juridical form.[56]

A novel feature included in the most recent FTAs signed by the United States is the article on market access for financial institutions, which is very similar to GATS Article XVI (2) on market access, albeit the

---

and clearing systems operated by public entities, and to official funding and refinancing facilities available in the normal course of ordinary business. The text clearly indicates that this obligation is not intended to confer access to the lender of last resort facilities in the host country.

[54] It is worth noting that the most recent FTAs signed by the United States, including those covered in this chapter, allow the application of the "home-state rule," under which states can discriminate against banks or insurance companies established in other states. Echandi notes that "countries such as El Salvador and Guatemala were interested in allowing their banking groups to penetrate the U.S. market to serve their Salvadoran and Guatemalan communities. Providing best-in-state treatment would have prevented the United States from applying the home-state rule that traditionally has applied to some financial services. . .." See Echandi (2010, p. 287).

[55] Numerical restrictions means limitations imposed, either on the basis of a regional subdivision or on the basis of the entire territory of a Party, on the number of financial institutions whether in the form of numerical quotas, monopolies, exclusive service suppliers or the requirements of an economic needs test.

[56] The Canada-Colombia and Canada-Peru FTAs further clarify that the obligation not to impose requirements to take a specific juridical form does not prevent a Party from imposing conditions or requirements in connection with the establishment of a particular type of entity chosen by an investor of the other Party. Moreover, subject to the article on national treatment, a Party may impose terms and conditions on the establishment of additional financial institutions and determine the institutional and juridical form that shall be used for the supply of specified financial services or the carrying out of specified activities, and may also, in exceptional circumstances, prohibit a particular financial service or activity. Such a prohibition may not apply to all financial services or to a complete financial services sub-sector such as banking. The Canadian FTAs also stipulate that, without prejudice to other forms of prudential regulation, a Party may require that an investor of the other Party be engaged in the business of providing financial services in the territory of that Party.

limitations on foreign capital in financial institutions were not included. However, unlike the GATS, the article does not cover cross-border trade in financial services, only investment.[57]

The article on new financial services in NAFTA and the other FTAs requires a Party to allow financial institutions of another Party to provide any new financial services that it permits its own financial institutions. The Party may determine the institutional and juridical form through which the service will be provided and may require authorization for the supply of the service. Under the Chile-U.S. FTA, as in the GATS-based Chile-EC Association Agreement, "the introduction of a new financial service is permitted, provided that its introduction does not require the party to adopt a new law or modify an existing law. However, the regulatory authorities can refuse the authorization only for prudential reasons."[58]

The FTAs set out reservations, existing non-conforming measures to the obligations on national treatment, MFN, market access for financial institutions (except NAFTA and the Canadian FTAs which do not include such obligation), senior management and boards of directors, and establishment/right of establishment (NAFTA/Canada-Colombia and Canada-Peru). The concept of "ratchet" pioneered by the NAFTA is also included, albeit a note in Chile's non-conforming measures indicates that ratcheting does not apply to market access for financial institutions and the right of establishment of certain financial services. Peru does the same for market access for financial institutions. Chile's chief negotiator for financial services stated that the country "felt some discomfort with ratcheting for requiring a specific juridical form." He noted that "experience in the regulation of financial services shows that requiring a specific juridical form (generally incorporation) is needed to ensure appropriate public disclosure.[59]

---

[57] Under this article, each Party must refrain from imposing any of the quantitative restrictions listed in the provision (see, for example, CAFTA-DR Article 12.4), which "applies horizontally on the basis of a negative list approach, in principle allowing the parties to list all nonconforming measures." In the case of the Chile-U.S. FTA, the approach is slightly different. The article on market access for financial institutions "applies only to commitments in insurance and insurance-related services, following a positive list approach." See R. Sáez (2010, p. 150). Annex 12.9 on specific commitments in the Chile-U.S. FTA borrows from the NAFTA approach and the article on "right of establishment with respect to certain financial services" (NAFTA Article 1403). For banking and other financial services, the approach taken by the Chileans is that of the "negative list" approach of NAFTA.

[58] Ibid., p. 151.

[59] R. Sáez (2010, p. 151).

U.S. NAFTA-type FTAs have led to deeper liberalization on investment related to financial institutions on the part of developing countries in eliminating restrictions on the juridical form of financial services suppliers going beyond the establishment of subsidiaries to allow direct branching, in some cases not immediately, but within a specific time frame. This is particularly true in Latin America, as observed in Chile (life and non-insurance); Colombia and Guatemala (insurance and banking); Costa Rica and El Salvador (insurance); the Dominican Republic (direct insurance and reinsurance); and Peru (all financial services).[60]

Rules and disciplines on cross-border trade

While the disciplines and rules on investment in the chapter on financial services are far-reaching, the two obligations on cross-border trade in financial services are more narrow. First, national treatment is granted only to a limited number of services, that is those explicitly covered and listed in an annex to the agreement. Unlike the NAFTA, the most recent NAFTA-based FTAs do not contain a standstill clause. Therefore, except for listed services, there is no limitation on the Parties adopting more restrictive measures. The second obligation requires Parties to allow consumption abroad but this obligation does not require a Party to permit services providers from another Party to do business or solicit in its territory. Moreover, without prejudice to other means of prudential regulation of cross-border trade in financial services, a Party may require the registration of cross-border financial service suppliers of another Party and of financial instruments.

Commitments on cross-border trade made by countries that have signed an FTA with the United States show that substantial progress has been made. This is particularly true, once again, in the case of Latin American countries. As underlined by Roy, Marchetti, and Lim, these commitments go "beyond the requirements of the WTO Understanding on Commitments in Financial Services in this area by adding commitments on the cross-border supply of insurance intermediation (broking and agency) and of portfolio management services by asset management firms to mutual funds."[61]

Provisions of general application

Finally, as noted above, several provisions in the chapter on financial services in the NAFTA-type FTAs are of general application and apply to

---

60 Marchetti (2008, p. 331).
61 Roy et al. (2009, p. 342).

both cross-border trade in financial services and to financial institutions, investors, and their investments in financial institutions.[62] In the case of MFN, the chapter allows for exceptions. NAFTA and the new NAFTA-based FTAs, as is the case in the GATS Annex on Financial Services, permit a Party to recognize prudential measures of another Party or of a non-Party. Such recognition may be accorded unilaterally; achieved through harmonization or other means; or based upon an agreement or arrangement with another Party or a non-Party.[63] A Party is therefore not bound to accord MFN treatment to another Party.

Transparency is another obligation of general application in the chapter on financial services.[64] As noted by Raúl Sáez, the article on transparency in the new NAFTA-type FTAs builds on NAFTA Article 1411 "but goes further in imposing transparency and dialogue on the regulators," as each Party shall maintain or establish appropriate mechanisms that will respond to inquiries from interested persons regarding measures of general application covered by the chapter. Sáez underlines that there was "some concern (. . .) about how soon Chile's agencies and Central Bank would be able to fully comply; [given that] the obligations required setting up special offices and training personnel, so a two-year grace period after the entry into force of the trade agreement was included" in Annex 12.11 of the Chile-U.S. FTA.[65] In the case of Peru, the grace period is 18 months

---

62 In addition, the NAFTA-type FTAs also include a provision on the establishment of a financial services committee.

63 The text of the chapter on financial services also stipulates that the Party according recognition of prudential measures shall provide adequate opportunity to another Party to demonstrate that circumstances exist in which there are or will be equivalent regulation, oversight, implementation of regulation, and, if appropriate, procedures concerning the sharing of information between the Parties. Where a Party accords recognition of prudential measures, the Party shall provide adequate opportunity to another Party to negotiate accession to the agreement or arrangement, or to negotiate a comparable agreement or arrangement.

64 The provision requires that each Party, to the extent practicable, publish in advance any regulations of general application relating to the subject matter of the chapter that it proposes to adopt; and provide interested persons and another Party a reasonable opportunity to comment on these proposed regulations. Each Party's regulatory authorities must also make available to interested persons their requirements, including any documentation required, for completing applications relating to the supply of financial services. Decisions on completed applications must be made within 120 days and the applicant must be promptly notified. The transparency obligation does not require a Party to furnish or allow access to information on the financial affairs of individual customers or confidential information. In addition, in the CAFTA-DR and the PTPA each Party commits to promote regulatory transparency in financial services.

65 R. Sáez (2010, p. 152).

after the entry into force of the Peru-U.S. Trade Promotion Agreement (PTPA Annex 12.11) and the Canada-Peru FTA (Annex 1111).

The CAFTA-DR is the only FTA to innovate with a provision on domestic regulation specifically related to financial services. It states that, except with respect to non-conforming measures listed in its Schedule to Annex III, each Party shall ensure that all measures of general application to which the chapter applies are administered in a reasonable, objective, and impartial manner.

All the NAFTA-type FTAs also include a provision on self-regulatory organizations[66] and cover state-to-state disputes and investor-state disputes.[67]

4.5.2 RTAs with Asia and the EC: Competing Architectural Approaches

While the NAFTA approach has been embraced by numerous countries of the Americas when negotiating free trade agreements among themselves, no unique model emerges in their trade agreements with Asian and European countries. In fact, several countries, particularly in Latin America, have experimented with competing architectural approaches. For instance, while the U.S.-Singapore FTA adopts the NAFTA structure, the Mexico-Japan contains a chapter on financial services which stipulates that "The

---

[66] It requires a financial institution or a cross-border financial service supplier of another Party to be a member of, participate in, or have access to, a self-regulatory organization to provide a financial service in or into the territory of that Party. The new U.S. FTAs state that the Party shall ensure observance of the national treatment and MFN obligations by such self-regulatory organization, whereas the Canadian FTAs also include the provisions on right of establishment and transparency. The new U.S. FTAs also contain a provision on expedited availability of insurance products stating that the Parties recognize the importance of maintaining and developing regulatory procedures to expedite the offering of insurance services by licensed suppliers. In addition, an article on exceptions in the NAFTA-type FTAs prevents "limits on the application of measures for prudential reasons." Ibid, p. 151.

[67] In the case of Chile, the country's chief negotiator for financial services emphasized that "one major outstanding issue was still unresolved when the financial services chapter was closed: capital controls and the balances-of-payments exceptions." This issue was finally resolved at the highest political level. Annex 10-C (investment chapter) applies to measures adopted by Chile which could be subject to dispute settlement by U.S. investors when applying a restriction on payments and transfers. The claim can be submitted only within one year after the measure is adopted. The objective is to distinguish between volatile and non-volatile capital flows, "reflecting Chile's application of the URR [unremunerated reserve requirements] to address the former in the 1990s." (Ibid., p. 154). The same language can be found in the PTPA.

Parties shall be bound by the terms and conditions that each Party is committed to under the Organisation for Economic Cooperation and Development Code of Liberalisation of Capital Movements, as may be amended, and the GATS, including the Understanding on Commitments in Financial Services, and under other international agreements to which both Parties are parties."[68] To further clarify, a note in the same article states that "Nothing in this Chapter shall be construed to affect the terms and conditions committed to by either Party under the respective agreements referred to in this Article." In contrast, the NAFTA-based Chile-Korea FTA as well as the TPSEP, which contains a chapter on trade in services covering all four modes of supply of a service and negative listing but no chapter on investment, include a work program to negotiate provisions on financial services in the future,[69] whereas the Chile-China FTA excludes financial services from the coverage of the GATS-based Protocol on Cross-Border Trade in Services and does not include any separate provisions on financial services.

The trade agreements between countries of the Americas and the EC have also resulted in different approaches but all based on the GATS. The EC-Mexico agreement is a framework agreement with no substantive provisions on trade in services. It states that "the Joint Council shall decide on the appropriate arrangements for a progressive and reciprocal liberalisation of trade in services, in accordance with the relevant WTO rules, in particular, Article V of the General Agreement on Trade in Services (GATS), and taking due account of the commitments already undertaken by the Parties within the framework of that Agreement."[70] On financial services, "The Parties undertake to establish cooperation in the financial services sector, in conformity with their laws, regulations and policies and in accordance with the rules and disciplines of the GATS, in light of their mutual interest and long and medium-term economic objectives."[71] In contrast, the Chile-EC Association Agreement contains a specific chapter on financial services, which covers all modes of supply and includes key provisions also found in the GATS such as the articles on national treatment and market access, a prudential carve-out, recognition

---

68 See Article 108 of the Mexico-Japan FTA.

69 Unless otherwise agreed by the Parties, these FTAs specify that the negotiations shall begin four years (Chile-Korea FTA, Article 21–5) and two years (TPSEP Agreement, Article 20–2) after the entry into force of the Agreement, respectively. The TPSEP also calls for the negotiations of an investment chapter within two years of the entry into force of the agreement (Article 20.1).

70 See Article 6 of the Agreement.

71 See Article 16 of the Agreement.

as well as other disciplines on new financial services, data processing, and effective and transparent regulation in the financial services sector. The CARIFORUM-EC EPA and the EC-Central America Association Agreement also follow the GATS approach but cover cross-border trade in financial services in the chapter on cross-border trade in services, and investment in financial services in the chapter on commercial presence (CARIFORUM-EC EPA) and establishment (EC-Central America), which covers both goods and services. Both agreements include national treatment and market access obligations in both chapters, and the CARIFORUM-EC EPA also has a separate provision on MFN.[72] In addition, both agreements feature a separate chapter with provisions of general application on the regulatory framework such as transparency and mutual recognition and a separate section in that chapter which contains specific provisions for financial services, for example on new financial services, data processing, and effective and transparent regulation.

Temporary movement of persons: going further with labor mobility

Labor mobility has been an area where the NAFTA did not innovate in the same way as it did in other provisions. Always sensitive, the labor mobility issue became even more so after the implementation of NAFTA to the degree that the FTAs concluded by the United States after 2002 have not treated mode 4 at all. However, Canada has been willing to go much further in its recent FTAs which are very innovative in their treatment of mode 4. Other countries in the Americas have been able to obtain greater opening for labor movement in their negotiations with extra-regional partners in Europe and Asia.

4.5.3 Labor Mobility in FTAs between Countries of the Americas

NAFTA deals with mode 4 through a separate chapter entitled "Temporary Movement of Business Persons" as mentioned in Section 4.2.1, whose

[72] As with goods trade, the MFN clause for cross-border trade in services and commercial presence is asymmetrical. It states that whenever the EU offers better treatment to services providers of another country, this treatment will automatically extend to CARIFORUM services. CARIFORUM countries on the other hand only have to do so where they conclude trade agreements with major trading economies, defined as "any industrialized country, or any country accounting for a share of world merchandise exports above one percent." The MFN clause does not apply to regional agreements in the Caribbean (CARICOM Single Market and Economy (CSME) and the CARICOM-Dominican Republic FTA) although any advantage granted to the EU must also be granted to fellow CARIFORUM countries.

purpose is to facilitate temporary entry for business people between the United States, Canada, and Mexico involved in goods or services trade or in investment activities. The categories defined under NAFTA are limited to: traders and investors; business visitors (BVs); intra-company transferees (ICTs); and professionals. In the case of business visitors, these are allowed short stays of up to 90 days. The novel element of NAFTA with respect to labor mobility is the "Trade NAFTA" or TN visa it introduced.[73] This TN visa was uncapped in 1994 for Canadians and has been uncapped for Mexicans since 2004. Upon demonstrating proof of a job offer, the TN visa permits employment for one year with unlimited renewal.

In addition to the chapter on temporary entry, the NAFTA and subsequent agreements with a similar structure contain an Annex on Professionals, specifically targeted at professional service suppliers. The Annex in these agreements is intended to promote the development of mutually acceptable standards and criteria for licensing and certification of professional service suppliers – based on factors such as educational background, qualifying examinations and experience. Additionally, the Annex encourages NAFTA Parties to provide recommendations for furthering the process of mutual recognition. A qualifying list of professions is set out in an Appendix to the agreement. In the case of NAFTA, 62 different professions are specified, for which the applicant must have the necessary qualification requirements. The United States originally placed a quota on the number of professionals that could be admitted from Mexico at 5,500 per year, but this has since been eliminated.

Under the FTA between the U.S. and Chile, labor mobility was expanded slightly for professional workers and, similar to NAFTA, a new H-1B1 visa was created. The visa provided for an initial stay of 18 months but with unlimited extensions. In addition, an annual quota of 1,800 visas for professionals from Chile was granted in addition to the fixed total of H-1B visas open to skilled workers and professional service providers from all countries. The new visa category created under the FTA is meant for temporary migrants with stays of up to 18 months initially, but with the possibility of unlimited extensions.

The reaction of the public and subsequently the opposition of the U.S. Congress to the labor mobility components of these FTAs that created new visa categories and numerical quotas for skilled professionals were particularly strong. Key congressmen objected that trade agreements had stepped into the realm of immigration matters. As a consequence of this

---

73 Summarized in Stephenson (2008).

outcry, no free trade agreement negotiated by the United States since 2002 has contained a chapter to facilitate the temporary movement of skilled workers.[74] Thus the later FTAs with Central America and the Dominican Republic (CAFTA-DR), as well as with Peru, Colombia, Panama and Korea, contain no chapter on temporary entry. They do however contain an Annex on Professionals with similar objectives as the Annex under NAFTA. However, these Annexes explicitly state that "No provision shall impose any obligation on a party regarding its immigration measures" and the Annexes contain no market access commitments.

In the case of Canada, the other developed country trader in the Americas, the situation has evolved in the opposite manner. Interestingly, and perhaps due to pressures from the private sector and apparent labor shortages in the Canadian market prior to the current crisis, the government has negotiated recent FTAs that go quite far toward providing increased access not only for professionals but also for semi-skilled foreign workers. While the FTA that Canada negotiated with Chile in 1997 looks very much like the NAFTA, with the only categories of workers covered being those of investors, traders and BVs, ICTs and professionals, it was notable in that Canada placed no numerical limits on 72 of these categories of professional labor.

Strikingly, the two recent FTAs negotiated by Canada with Colombia and Peru go much further. They cover all professional categories with

---

[74] The only exception to this is the FTA with Australia where no market access provisions for labor mobility were included in the text itself but a new visa category E-3 was created by an Act of the United States Congress as a result of the United States-Australia Free Trade Agreement (AUSFTA). On May 11, 2005, President Bush signed into law the Emergency Supplemental Appropriations Act for Defense, the Global War on Terror, and Tsunami Relief, 2005 (Pub. L. No. 109–13). Division B of the Emergency Supplemental Appropriations Act is the REAL ID Act of 2005. Section 501 of the REAL ID Act created a new category of E visa, the E-3 visa. The E-3 visa allows for the admission of an alien who is a national of the Commonwealth of Australia and who is entering the U.S. to perform services in a "specialty occupation." The E-3 provisions became effective upon signing of the Act. The E-3 visa is similar in many respects to the H-1B visa. Important differences include the fact that spouses of E-3 visa holders may work in the United States without restrictions (unlike other U.S. non-immigrant visas, even the TN visa issued to Canadian and Mexican citizens), and that the E-3 visa is renewable indefinitely (in two-year increments). Australian citizens applying for an E-3 visa are also no longer subject to the 65,000 annual visa limit for H-1B visas; although there is a separate annual quota of 10,500 E-3 visas, this is believed to be much more generous to Australians than requiring them to compete with all other nations for H-1B visas. Visas issued to spouses and children are not included in the E-3 quota and spouses and children do not need to be Australian citizens.

no numerical limits and no specified length of stay, meaning that visas could in theory be renewed indefinitely. For the first time they also expand coverage of worker categories beyond highly trained professionals to include "technicians." In both the Colombia and Peru FTAs, Canada has listed 50 categories of technicians to be admitted into the Canadian market with no specified length of stay. These technicians must have an educational degree with two years of technical training. Technician categories include, among others, mechanics, construction inspectors, food and beverage supervisors, chefs, plumbers and oil and gas well drillers. This recent innovation in the Americas constitutes a major innovation for the treatment of temporary entry in trade agreements.

4.5.4 Labor Mobility in Agreements Negotiated with Extra-regional Partners

In trade agreements the European Union has negotiated with countries in the Americas, mode 4 is brought within the scope of the agreement in a way similar to that followed under the GATS. Categories of workers included in mode 4 commitments by the EU include the four which are traditional for preferential trade agreements (PTAs) (traders and investors, BVs, ICTs, and independent professionals). In the EU Association Agreement with Chile, besides the coverage of mode 4 in the text of the agreement, there is additionally a specific article on the "movement of natural persons," as well as an Annex on Professionals (Annex VII).[75] In the Annex, the EU specifies 33 categories of professional service providers that it will accept from Chile without numerical limit, for a time period of 3 months, subject to the "necessary academic qualification and experience." Interestingly, Chile did not commit reciprocally to accepting any professionals from the EU.

The CARIFORUM-EC EPA follows a similar structure but expands on the categories of workers to include additional categories important for CARIFORUM members. These include contractual service suppliers, independent professionals and graduate trainees as follows:[76]

---

[75] The specific article on "movement of natural persons" (Article 101) contains only a review requirement: "Two years after the entry into force of this Agreement, the Parties shall review the rules and conditions applicable to movement of natural persons (mode 4) with a view to achieving further liberalization."

[76] It should be mentioned however that several of the EU Member States have attached "economic needs tests" (ENTs) to their commitments on mode 4 entry. Actual access provided, even under the expanded commitments, will depend

- *Contractual service suppliers (CSS)*: Service suppliers who are in possession of a contract for a specific project but who are not being transferred within or employed by a firm. Applicable to a specific list of activities and permits temporary entry for a cumulative period of six months.
- *Independent professionals (IPs)*. A new category, the IPs covers natural persons of the EC Party or of the Signatory CARIFORUM States engaged in the supply of a service and established as self-employed in the territory of that EC Party or Signatory CARIFORUM State who have no commercial presence in the territory of the other Party and who have concluded a bona fide contract (other than through an agency as defined by CPC 872) to supply services with a final consumer in the latter Party requiring their presence on a temporary basis in that Party in order to fulfill the contract to provide services. The provisions for the CSSs category also apply to IPs, i.e. a specific list of activities and temporary stay for up to six months.
- *Graduate trainees*. Graduate trainees, another new category, consist of workers from CARIFORUM States who have a university degree and are temporarily transferred to the parent company or to a commercial establishment for career development or to obtain training in business methods. They may enter for a period of up to one year.

In this agreement the European Union committed to accepting 29 categories of professional services providers without numerical limit from the Caribbean and the Dominican Republic provided they had a university degree and 3 years experience. The CARIFORUM members did not commit reciprocally to accepting any EU professionals. It is interesting to note that the categories of CSS, IPs and Graduate Trainees are not included in the NAFTA or NAFTA-type FTAs.

The agreements negotiated by Mexico and Chile with Japan look very similar in form and content to the NAFTA template. Mode 4 is treated in a chapter on "temporary movement of business persons" and defines the same four categories usually seen in trade agreements (traders and investors, business visitors, intra-corporate transferees, and independent professionals). However, Japan has set a time limit of 3 years for three of these categories, which is a fairly generous length of stay.

Some countries in the Americas started to push the envelope in regional agreements on mode 4 and have begun to innovate even in the most sensi-

---

upon how these ENTs are interpreted and applied in practice. No definitions were supplied with the ENT entries, and some are applied quite restrictively.

tive aspect of services trade. Although the regional agreements still focus almost exclusively on professional service providers, many have gone well beyond the WTO GATS in providing access for a greater number of professional categories. Some also offer the possibility of long-term or even unlimited visa renewals once professionals are settled in the country. Recent FTAs negotiated by Canada open the door even wider to extend access to categories of semi-skilled technicians in the FTAs with Colombia and Peru. The CARIFORUM-EC EPA has opened market access to contractual service suppliers and independent professionals (for 6 months) and to graduate trainees (for 1 year), the latter two new categories not found in the WTO GATS. Australia has innovated in its recent FTA with Chile to cover the spouses and dependents of ICTs and CSSs residing in the country longer than one year. Thus regional trade agreements involving countries in the Americas are moving slowly but surely (other than those with the U.S.) beyond the purely professional categories of labor to include independent professionals, semi-skilled workers, technicians, graduate trainees – and even spouses and dependents – within their scope, and often for considerable periods of time.[77]

4.6 DISPUTE SETTLEMENT: WHY ARE RTAS NOT USED TO SETTLE SERVICES DISPUTES?

One way in which FTAs in the Americas have not innovated is in the area of dispute settlement for services. Almost no disputes involving trade in services have been brought by members under any FTA. While the NAFTA contains dispute settlement provisions that were considered substantive and far-reaching at the time of its adoption, very few disputes of any type have been adjudicated under its purview. In the 18 years since the agreement came into effect in 1994, only three disputes have been brought to arbitration by NAFTA members under NAFTA Chapter Twenty, one of these involving services. Even more striking, a canvassing of the FTAs negotiated post-NAFTA with countries of the Americas indicates that no disputes on services have been brought for adjudication under these agreements.[78] This appears somewhat puzzling, as the large and growing

[77] See Stephenson (2010) for more information on developments and initiatives to provide greater access for professional service suppliers and other categories of workers in recent trade agreements.

[78] In the past 18 years, only three disputes have been brought up under the NAFTA (in force since 1994). See discussion in Macrory (2004) and the NAFTA Secretariat website at www.**nafta**-sec-alena.org and www.**nafta**now.org.

numbers of FTAs should presumably have led to a number of trade frictions. The lack of trade disputes among members of these arrangements being brought to arbitration would seem to indicate either that the agreements are not being used to their full extent, or that the complexity of determining compliance is too great in terms of demands on time and resources compared with the perceived benefits of enforcing negotiated modifications in laws and practices.

Table 4A.4 in the Appendix sets out a summary list of all of the disputes that have been taken to the WTO in the area of services. As of February 2012, these services disputes numbered 22. Of these disputes, the U.S. has been a complainant in nine, the European Communities in four, Canada and Japan in one each, with the other complaints having been brought by developing WTO members. Three disputes involve the sale and distribution of bananas, three disputes involve measures affecting financial information services, three disputes involve distribution services and two disputes involve measures affecting the automotive industry. Interestingly, none of the 22 disputes brought to the WTO involved countries who were parties to regional trading arrangements, other than the dispute on telecommunications between the U.S. and Mexico summarized below.[79] Thus in only one case could the parties to a dispute have chosen between the WTO forum and the regional forum.

Once again, NAFTA has proved to be a testing ground in this regard, as two of its members (United States and Mexico) have been involved in two disputes on services, one of which was taken to the NAFTA for resolution and the other to the WTO for resolution. The services dispute brought by Mexico against the United States for resolution under NAFTA Chapter Twenty centered around a disagreement on cross-border trucking. The second dispute on services which arose between the United States and Mexico centered on practices in the area of telecommunications and was taken by the United States to the WTO for resolution rather than to the NAFTA. It is interesting to compare these two key disputes on services and to try and understand the reasons for the difference in the choice of forum, as is done in the sections below.

---

[79] The only other dispute involving countries who are members of a regional trading arrangement is the complaint brought by Honduras against Nicaragua concerning measures affecting imports from Honduras and Colombia. However, this complaint was brought to the WTO in June 2000, before the Central American Agreement on Investment and Trade in Services (*Tratado Centroamericano sobre Inversiones y Comercio de Servicios*) signed on August 24, 2002 and updated in 2007 to take into account the results of the CAFTA-DR negotiations. For more information, see www.sieca.int.

It is interesting to speculate on the possible reasons for the lack of disputes raised under FTAs in general and on services in particular.[80] Explanations could center on a greater familiarity of governments with the WTO instruments and a greater confidence that the decisions of the WTO dispute settlement body will be understood and respected. Additionally, governments could be swayed by the possibility of retaliation under the WTO if there is no compliance with decisions, which possibility does not exist under most FTAs. There may be a greater degree of comfort and confidence as well in the level of expertise of the panelists to adjudicate disputes at the multilateral level as well as an interest to use the WTO vehicle as a reference point for future jurisprudence on similar issues that might arise in the future in the services area, which would not be the case with decisions arising from the regional FTAs. Lastly, since most of the trade in services takes place between the larger trading nations, the WTO would be the only possible vehicle for the settlement of their disputes, as most of the FTAs to date containing services provisions have been negotiated between larger developed and smaller developing countries but not yet between major trading partners (i.e. Brazil, China, India, Japan, the U.S. and the European Union).

4.6.1 Services Dispute between NAFTA Members on Cross-Border Trucking

Under the NAFTA Annex I, the United States agreed to allow, three years after the signature of the NAFTA, Mexican motor carriers into the four U.S. bordering states – California, Arizona, New Mexico, and Texas – and Mexico would allow U.S. motor carriers into Mexico's six border states. The second part of the commitment was that six years after the entry into force of the NAFTA, Mexican motor carriers would be entitled to travel throughout the United States and U.S. motor carriers would be entitled to travel throughout Mexico. NAFTA also permitted a person of Mexico to establish, three years after the signature of the NAFTA, an enterprise in the United States to provide truck services for the transportation of international cargo between points in the United States; and seven years after the date of entry into force of the NAFTA, bus services between points in the United States. NAFTA also kept in place the moratorium on grants of authority for the provision of truck services by persons of Mexico between

---

[80] The authors are grateful for the insights of Martin Roy of the Services Division in the WTO Secretariat on this question. For relevant sources, see: Porges (2011) and Piérola and Horlick (2007).

points in the United States for the transportation of goods other than international cargo.

On December 17, 1995, President Clinton issued an executive order extending the moratorium on cross-border trucking with Mexico, arguing that Mexican motor carriers were not as safe as U.S. motor carriers, therefore requesting more time to evaluate the situation. As a result, the Mexican government initiated a NAFTA Chapter Twenty state-to-state dispute. An arbitration panel was formed to evaluate Mexico's complaint alleging that the United States had violated NAFTA.

In this dispute brought under the NAFTA, Mexico challenged certain measures maintained by the United States affecting the cross-border supply of trucking services from Mexico to the U.S. Canada exercised its right to participate in the proceedings as a third party. More specifically, Mexico claimed that the United States had violated NAFTA by failing to phase out U.S. restrictions on cross-border trucking services and on Mexican investment in the U.S. trucking industry, as is required by the U.S. commitments in NAFTA Annex I, despite affording Canada national treatment. Therefore, Mexico claimed that the United States was in breach of Articles 1202 (national treatment for cross-border services) and 1203 (MFN treatment for cross-border services). It also stated that the United States had breached Articles 1102 (national treatment) and 1103 (MFN treatment) by refusing to permit investment by Mexican nationals in companies in the U.S. that engage in the transportation of international cargo.

The United States argued that the national treatment language of Article 1202, "in like circumstances," did not apply in the situation because Mexico's regulatory system did not have the same rigorous standards as the regulatory systems of the U.S. and Canada. Therefore, the U.S. claimed that it was justified in treating Mexico's services suppliers differently. The U.S. also claimed that its moratorium could be justified under Chapter Nine (standards) or Article 2101 (general exceptions).

An arbitral panel under Chapter Twenty of the NAFTA issued its final report on February 6, 2001. The Panel found that the U.S. refusal to review and consider for approval applications for authority by Mexican-owned carriers to provide cross-border trucking services was (and remains) a breach of the U.S.'s obligations under Annex I, Article 1202 and Article 1203 of the NAFTA. Secondly, the Panel rejected the U.S.' claim that its actions were justified by the "in like circumstances" language in Articles 1202 and 1203, or by the exceptions set out in Chapter Nine or under Article 2101, concluding that the inadequacies of the Mexican regulatory system were not a sufficient legal justification for the U.S. to maintain a moratorium on the consideration of applications for U.S. operating authority from Mexican-owned and/or domiciled trucking service providers. Thirdly, the panel found that by failing to permit Mexican nationals to invest in U.S. businesses that provide transportation of international cargo within the U.S., the U.S. was (and remains) in breach of its obligations under Annex I, Article 1102 and Article 1103.

After the panel's ruling, the U.S. and Mexico agreed to a Cross-Border Trucking Services Demonstration Program which gave licenses to a select number of Mexican carriers to operate in the U.S under strict regulations. However, the U.S. Congress withdrew funding for the Program on March 11, 2009. In response, Mexico imposed retaliatory tariffs in the amount of $2.4 billion on a number of U.S. agricultural and industrial goods on March 16, 2009. Mexico later expanded the list of U.S. items subject to punitive tariffs. On March 3, 2011, fully a decade after the NAFTA Panel had issued its report, U.S. President Barack Obama and Mexican President Felipe Calderon announced that the two Parties had come to a resolution of this outstanding dispute and that they had reached a preliminary agreement aimed at resolving the bilateral dispute over access of Mexican trucking services to the U.S. market. The final agreement on a new cross-border trucking program was concluded on July 6, 2011. Two days later Mexico lowered by 50% the retaliatory tariffs it had slapped on some U.S. exports. The remaining 50% of the value of the tariffs was lifted on October 21, 2011 after the United States granted on October 14, 2011 long-haul operating authority to the first Mexican carrier under a new pilot program.

4.6.2 Services Dispute between NAFTA Members on Telecommunications

The second dispute that arose on services between these same two NAFTA members involved a complaint by the United States with regard to Mexico on its measures affecting telecommunications services.

In August 2000, the United States sought consultations with Mexico, alleging that Mexico had adopted anti-competitive and discriminatory regulatory measures, had tolerated certain privately established market access barriers and had failed to take needed regulatory action in its basic and value-added telecommunications sectors.[81] In April 2002 a panel was established under the WTO Dispute Settlement Understanding, and two years later in June 2004, the WTO's Dispute Settlement Body adopted the panel's report, which concluded, inter alia, that Mexico had failed to ensure the

---

[81] WTO Document WT/DS204/1 of August 29, 2000.

application of cost-oriented international interconnection rates (in breach of Sections 2.1 and 2.2 of the WTO Reference Paper on Telecommunications, inscribed in Mexico's GATS Schedule of Specific Commitments); had failed to impose regulatory measures to prevent anti-competitive practices on the part of the main telecommunications operator (in breach of Section 1.1 of the Reference Paper, inscribed in Mexico's GATS Schedule of Specific Commitments); and had failed to ensure access to and use of public telecommunications networks on reasonable and non-discriminatory terms (in breach of Section 5 of the GATS Annex on Telecommunications. A similar commitment was made under NAFTA 1302).[82]

It is interesting to speculate on the reasons behind the different choices in the venue for the dispute settlement of these two services complaints summarized above. However, the difference in the outcomes is striking. The United States was able to obtain fairly rapid compliance from Mexico under the WTO dispute settlement mechanism to modify its pricing practices in Telmex, whereas Mexico, despite a clear decision of the NAFTA panel in its favor, was unable to obtain compliance from the United States to modify its practices on trucking for over a decade. While it is difficult to know whether it is the robustness of the dispute settlement process, or the willingness of the parties involved to comply with the panel decision, or a combination of both that made the difference, this contrasting experience may not encourage countries who have the choice of a forum for settling their grievances in the services area to choose an FTA dispute settlement process over the WTO process.

4.7 HAVE FTAS PRODUCED ANY RESULTS? EXAMINING THEIR IMPACT

Assessing the impact of free trade agreements has always been a complex issue.[83] The challenge is even greater for trade in services, where statistics have only been recorded for a short period of time and then only on a limited basis. Statistics on bilateral trade flows in services exist only among a few trading partners. Given the limited datasets available on services trade, it is difficult at the present to run robust regressions.[84] However, to try and obtain some rough indication of whether the FTAs

[82] WTO Document WT/DS204/R of April 2, 2004.

[83] See Baier and Bergstrand (2005) for a comprehensive discussion.

[84] Ideally, the best way to examine the effect of FTAs is with gravity models (for services trade, goods trade and FDI), but the data and computational requirements of such exercises are beyond the scope of this chapter.

entered into by countries in the Americas have had any significant impact on services trade we developed and applied a very simple methodology to calculate "excess growth." This methodology attempts to capture how trade in services has evolved after the entry into force of some key FTAs based on a comparison of the performance of services trade between the same partners and prior to the agreements.[85] It is explained in Box 4.1.

4.7.1 Factors to Take into Account in Applying the "Excess Growth" Methodology

Services trade should hypothetically be stimulated among partners to a free trade agreement in three different ways: either through actual liberalization of services, unleashing greater productivity and competitiveness of services suppliers; through the positive impact of greater security and transparency generated by the binding of market access obligations combined with appropriate regulatory disciplines; or through the greater demand for services trade generated by increased investment flows responding to the signaling effect of the agreement on policy reform and stability and expanded market size for economies of scale. Thus we presume that any subsequent increase in either the demand for, or the supply of services or both, should result in a larger increase in services trade with partner countries rather than with non-partner countries.

However, it must be recognized at the outset that the results obtained from the application of the "excess growth" methodology do not allow for the attribution of a direct casual effect between the entry into force of an FTA and the resulting performance of services exports. The calculation does not necessarily imply any causality. Several factors could enter into play that might impact upon the observed outcomes that would be impossible to isolate within a simple calculation. Such factors include, among others, endogenous changes in demand and the appearance of new services exporters on the world market. Regressions would allow for a better indication of causality but they could not be carried out due to the limitations (time series and partner breakdown) for available statistics on services trade. The "excess growth" methodology does allow us to observe performance of services trade in a pre- and post-FTA situation and does provide some interesting results. These should be taken cautiously and

[85] The authors wish to recognize with gratitude the original contribution of Thibaud Delourme in developing the statistical approach for this methodology and applying it to the regional groupings to obtain the results reported in this section for services trade and goods trade.

BOX 4.1 ON "EXCESS GROWTH METHODOLOGY"

The "excess growth" methodology measures the growth in trade in services between the members of an FTA *as compared with* the growth of trade in services with non-members of the FTA. Calculations of total trade include imports and exports. Data are drawn from international (OECD and IMF balance of payments) and national sources (USTR Dataset and Eurostat) to obtain statistics on trade in services *by trading partner*. Calculations are carried out for: (a) the average growth in total trade in services between a member of a given FTA and the other members, which is labeled intra-zone trade; and (b) the average growth in total trade in services between that same member and the rest of the world, excluding other members, or the extra-zone trade. By subtracting the growth in extra-zone trade from the growth in intra-zone trade, i.e. (a) – (b), it is possible to obtain a measure of "excess growth" which indicates whether trade in services between a member of a FTA and the other members has grown faster (positive excess growth) or slower (negative excess growth) than trade with non-members. This "excess growth" is then calculated for every member. The "total excess growth" is calculated for the regional grouping as a whole by subtracting the growth of total extra-zone trade from the growth of total intra-zone trade. These calculations are carried out for two periods: before and after the agreement enters into force in order to observe the performance of services trade and test whether the existence of an FTA might be a factor in accelerating the growth of intra-zone trade relative to the growth of extra-zone trade or not. The expectation is for the "excess growth" in services trade of the members of an FTA involving services liberalization to be higher after the agreement enters into force than it was prior to the agreement. Results are also shown for the Δ Growth, which is simply the differential in excess growth after and before the FTA: Δ Growth = Excess growth after the agreement minus Excess Growth before the agreement.

only as general indications of trends and are best interpreted in the context of the specific knowledge of each agreement.

The time frames for calculating the "excess growth" figures have been chosen as a function of the longest time period of available and comparable statistics for services trade for the parties to an agreement. The years studied were symmetrical, that is, an attempt was made to cover the same number of years prior to and after the agreement.

We applied the "excess growth" methodology to four different FTAs involving countries of the Americas for which it was possible to gather reliable datasets.[86] As a point of comparison, we also applied the same "excess growth" methodology to examine the change in trade in goods for these same four FTAs. Interestingly, for these agreements, "excess growth" in services (between partner countries) is shown to increase after the FTA entered into force, in some cases significantly. And for members of three out of four FTAs, the differential in "excess growth" is shown to increase more for services than for goods, indicating that the impact of the FTA on stimulating growth in services trade has been greater after its entry into force than its impact on stimulating growth in goods trade. The results of these calculations are set out in Tables 4A.5 through 4A.8 in the Appendix and are summarized below.

4.7.2 Positive "Excess Growth" of Services Trade for Four FTAs

For the case of the U.S. and Chile, applying the methodology indicates that over the five years prior to their FTA agreement (2000–04), total trade in services declined at an average rate of 8.11% a year. At the same time, services trade between the U.S. and the rest of the world increased by 3.67% year and services trade between Chile and the rest of the world by 6.36% a year, resulting in an "excess growth" of -11.78% for the U.S. and -14.47% for Chile. In other words, over the period 2000–04, trade in services between the U.S. and Chile grew at a rate 11.78 percentage points lower than trade between the U.S. and the rest of the world, and 14.47 percentage points lower than trade between Chile and the rest of the world. The "excess growth" for the U.S. and Chile combined was -12.00% over that same period. After the agreement, the negative growth trend is completely reversed. As shown in Table 4A.5, during the five years following the entry into force of the FTA, trade in services between the two trading

[86] Although we examined the "excess growth" trends for NAFTA as well as for the EC-Chile Association Agreement, the results in both cases were not felt to be accurate enough to warrant inclusion in the discussion as it was not possible to carry out the calculations in the same manner as for the other agreements given the limitations in the datasets. As NAFTA was concluded some time ago, there are no time series on services trade available for Mexico and Canada for the years prior to the agreement. And for the EC-Chile agreement, the dataset only allowed for one year's observation prior to its entry into force (2003), which we did not consider a sufficient benchmark for the purpose of the comparison.

partners is calculated to grow by 8.61% a year on average (2004–09). The growth in trade with the rest of the world accelerates too, but not as much, resulting in an "excess growth" of 3.11% for the U.S. and Chile combined, indicating that, for both countries, trade in services has grown at a faster rate than that with other countries, in contrast to the earlier period. The differential in excess growth after and before the FTA is larger for services trade than for goods trade (15.11% compared with 11.08%), indicating that the agreement has stimulated growth of services trade relatively more than goods trade. Once again, these results are purely descriptive and do not necessarily imply any causality. Chile's faster rate of growth in general following the FTA could also have had an impact on this positive outcome.

Similar results appear in the case of the U.S. and Singapore, shown in Table 4A.6. "Excess growth" in services rises from -1.60% during the five years prior to the FTA (2000–04) to −0.09% for the U.S. during the five years following the FTA (2004–09) and for Singapore, from -10.20% to −6.22% over these two same periods. For the U.S. and Singapore combined, the change in "excess growth" during these same time periods moves from -2.48% to 0.94%. We note that, even after the FTA, growth in services trade is at a slower pace than that with the rest of the world, which may partially be explained by the large amount of services already traded between the two countries prior to the trade agreement and the dominant role that services already played in both, with the U.S. and Singapore being the pre-eminent service economies of the world. This also seems to be confirmed by the differential in excess growth after and before the FTA, which is larger for goods trade than for services trade (3.89% compared with 1.54%) for the U.S.-Singapore FTA, as shown in Table 4A.6. However, the growth differential between intra- and extra-FTA trade in services for both the U.S. and Singapore has considerably narrowed after their agreement entered into force.

The agreement between Mexico and Japan (2005) is associated with a significant increase in "excess growth" of trade in services, as seen in Table 4A.7. While the excess growth in services trade for Japan and Mexico combined shows −13.79% during the five years before the FTA (2000–05), it rises to 8.54% during the four years following the agreement (2005–08). The excess growth in goods trade experiences the opposite evolution, slowing dramatically from 24.17% on average during 2000–05 to 0.58% during the four years after the FTA. The differential in excess growth after and before the FTA is strongly positive for services (22.33%) but negative for goods (-23.59%). Thus the FTA appears to have significantly increased the importance of services trade between these two partners.

In the case of the more recent CARIFORUM-EC EPA, results are summarized in Table 4A.8. The "excess growth" for services for the EU and CARIFORUM countries combined rises from -4.96% over the period 2000–08 to 7.64% after the agreement (period 2007–09). This increase is especially important in the case of the CARIFORUM, where their trade with the EU grows at 5.69% a year, as compared with a drop of −7.08% for their trade with the rest of the world. The differential in excess growth after and before the FTA is again in this case strongly positive for services (12.60%), more than double that for trade in goods (5.45%). Thus the agreement appears to have significantly increased the importance of services trade between these two partners. However, this strongly positive outcome is based on a short period of time and cannot necessarily be interpreted as a long-term trend.

In sum, the above four FTAs which we were able to examine on the basis of minimally adequate datasets all show patterns in their services trade growth consistent with the expectation that intra-regional growth in services should increase after a free trade agreement enters into force and that growth of intra-FTA trade relative to trade with outside partners should be higher after the agreement than before. These expectations are confirmed by application of the "excess growth" methodology, which is one method, among many, to try and examine the impact that the formation of an FTA might have on services trade, though admittedly imperfect. Results can also be strongly influenced by changes in the world economy as well as those in the context of the country observed.

4.8 POSSIBILITY FOR CONVERGENCE OF FTAS IN THE AMERICAS?

Several experiments are under way in the Americas of which there is little awareness as of yet to consolidate similar regional trade agreements. Given the large number and overlapping levels of regulatory complexity created by FTAs with various configurations of membership, a bottom-up movement toward convergence has begun recently in the Western Hemisphere. The move toward convergence represents an attempt to rationalize the complications created by numerous sets of disciplines and market access requirements among several like-minded parties to FTAs based on a similar NAFTA-type template.

The effort at convergence in the Americas was first spearheaded under the guise of the *Arco del Pacífico* initiative and involved 11 Latin American countries that border the Pacific and who are parties to several NAFTA-type FTAs. Participating countries were Chile, Colombia, Costa Rica, Ecuador, El Salvador, Guatemala, Honduras, Mexico, Nicaragua, Panama, and Peru. The United States and Canada, although also parties to NAFTA and NAFTA-type FTAs, were not participating in this convergence effort.[87]

The objectives of the *Arco del Pacífico* initiative were three: to deepen existing trade agreements and eventually move toward common rules; to broaden economic cooperation and trade facilitation among participating countries; and to engage more deeply in coordinated economic relations with the Asia-Pacific region.[88] As of February 1, 2012, six ministerial meetings had been held and four working groups had been set up to focus the discussions, including a key one on "trade convergence and economic integration."[89] This working group was given the task of identifying ways of moving toward common rules on accumulation of origin, a complex issue. The group has also been asked to analyze existing trade and integration agreements in the areas of technical barriers to trade, sanitary and phytosanitary measures, customs procedures, trade facilitation, countervailing measures, services, investment, government procurement, competition policy and dispute settlement, in order to see how existing disciplines may be made to converge.

It is worth noting that four ARCO members, Chile, Colombia, Mexico, and Peru, are involved in a more promising initiative. They signed the Declaration of Lima on April 28, 2011, launching the "Pacific Alliance," which creates a framework for "deep integration" that will eventually allow for the freer movement of goods, services, people, and capital among these four members.[90]

A convergence effort among six members of the ARCO, that is, between

---

[87] The U.S. is a party to six FTAs with countries in the Americas (NAFTA with Canada and Mexico, and FTAs with Chile, Peru and the five Central American countries plus the Dominican Republic) and two more approved by the U.S. Congress but not in force as of February 1, 2012 (with Colombia and Panama). There has, however, been an explosion of trade agreements in the region to which the U.S. is not a party, including the discussions of the *Arco del Pacífico*, South American unification efforts and multiple bilateral agreements. The only ongoing negotiation in which the U.S. is currently participating is that of the TPP or the Trans-Pacific Partnership Agreement. Though a relative latecomer to the negotiations of regional agreements, despite the NAFTA, Canada has been actively pursuing FTAs over the recent period and has negotiated six such agreements with countries in the Americas (namely with Chile, Colombia, Costa Rica, Panama and Peru, besides the NAFTA). Canada is involved in ongoing negotiations with CARICOM, Central America (CA-4), and the Dominican Republic.

[88] See chapter IV on "Integration and Trade Initiatives" of ECLAC (2009), pp.103–04.

[89] The other three working groups set up under the *Arco del Pacífico* initiative are: trade facilitation and infrastructure; investment promotion and protection; and competitiveness.

[90] See nota de prensa 5690 of April 28, 2011 on the website of the Government

Mexico and Central America, has already proved successful. In June 2008, on the occasion of the 10th Tuxtla Mechanism Summit, the countries of the region agreed to initiate negotiations aimed at achieving convergence of their free trade agreements into a single instrument. On March 26, 2009, the Vice Ministers of Foreign Trade of Costa Rica, El Salvador, Guatemala, Honduras, Nicaragua, and Mexico agreed on an action plan for the convergence of their free trade agreements. The first round of negotiations was held in May 2010 and the single FTA was signed on November 22, 2011.[91]

4.9 CONCLUSION

There is no doubt that the Americas have been the proving ground for innovations in services agreements. The region has produced a major alternative to the liberalization of services trade in the form of the NAFTA template. A new generation of NAFTA-type agreements has also improved and strengthened the original template, incorporating key features of the WTO GATS for both cross-border trade in services and investment in services.

The NAFTA innovates in several areas with respect to the positive list of GATS, in terms of the structure of the agreement, depth of provisions, liberalizing modality, transparency, in-built liberalizing mechanism, treatment of investment and of mode 4, to name a few elements. The NAFTA template has also been carried around the world in numerous free trade agreements negotiated between countries of the Americas and extra-regional partners, particularly in Asia and the Middle East. One such major initiative is the agreement being negotiated in the TPP, which is viewed as a possible way forward for an eventual FTAAP. With a very high level of ambition by participants for the inclusion of disciplines relevant to the changed paradigm of 21st century for trade and investment flows, the TPP if successfully concluded will be a "state-of-the-art" FTA, based on the NAFTA template but having gone significantly beyond it.

Assessing the impact of free trade agreements remains a complex issue, and particularly for trade in services. This chapter has emphasized that, albeit causality is difficult to prove, the authors' calculations show that for those FTAs with an adequate dataset to merit an examination of trends

---

of Peru: http://www.presidencia.gob.pe/index.asp and also http://alianzapacifico.net/en/.

[91] For more information, see http://www.sice.oas.org/TPD/CACM_MEX/CACM_MEX_e.asp. On January 9, 2012 the government of Mexico issued a decree approving the Single FTA.

prior to and subsequent to the entry into force of an agreement, services trade has increased more between FTA partners than it has with the rest of the world. And examining the differential in growth resulting from the trade agreements shows that services trade increases relatively more than goods trade for most FTA members, indicating that the impact of the FTAs on stimulating growth in services trade has been greater than their impact on stimulating growth in goods trade.

Finally the increasing number of NAFTA-type agreements in the Americas has also given rise to a movement toward convergence and a rationalization of overlapping disciplines and market access opportunities, being led by Mexico and the Central American countries. A more recent trend is characterized by the efforts under way between five Pacific Alliance members – Chile, Colombia, Mexico, Peru and (most recently) Costa Rica, (the so-called Pacific Alliance grouping) – to go beyond convergence and negotiate a deeper relationship based on the establishment of a common market.

Though the Americas region is no longer the main area of the world pursuing regionalism, it nonetheless continues to be at the forefront of experimentation in services rules, disciplines and liberalization. The torch of innovation is no longer being carried by one single country, the United States, but now other countries – Canada, Chile, Mexico, Peru, Central America and the Caribbean – are pushing forward with new developments in the treatment of services in regional trade agreements.

REFERENCES

Baier, Scott L., and Jeffrey H. Bergstrand. 2005. "Do Free Trade Agreements Actually Increase Members' International Trade?" Working Paper 2005–03, Federal Reserve Bank of Atlanta.

Echandi, Roberto. 2010. "The CAFTA-DR-U.S. Negotiations on Financial Services: The Experience of Costa Rica," in Mona Haddad and Constantinos Stephanou, eds., *Financial Services and Preferential Trade Agreements: Lessons from Latin America*, Washington, DC: The World Bank, pp. 243–305.

ECLAC. 2009. *Latin America and the Caribbean in the World Economy, 2008 Trends*. Santiago, Chile: ECLAC.

ECLAC. 2010. *Latin America and the Caribbean in the World Economy, 2009–2010*, Santiago, Chile: ECLAC.

Findlay, Christopher, Sherry Stephenson, and Francisco Javier Prieto. 2005. "Services in Trading Arrangements," in Patrick F.J. Macrory, Arthur E. Appleton, and Michael G. Plummer, eds, *The World Trade Organization: Legal, Economic and Political Analysis, Vol. II*, New York: Springer.

Macrory, Patrick. 2004. "Chapters 19 and 20 of NAFTA: An Overview and Analysis of NAFTA Dispute Settlement," in Kevin C. Kennedy, *The First*

Decade of NAFTA: The Future of Free Trade in North America, Ardsley, NY: Transnational Publishers.

Marchetti, Juan A. 2008. "Financial Services Liberalization in the WTO and PTAs," in Juan A. Marchetti and Martin Roy, eds, *Opening Markets for Trade in Services: Countries and Sectors in Bilateral and WTO Negotiations*, Cambridge: Cambridge University Press, pp. 300–39.

OAS Foreign Trade Information System. www.sice.oas.org.

Piérola, Fernando, and Gary Horlick. 2007. "WTO Dispute Settlement and Dispute Settlement in the 'North-South' Agreements of the Americas: Considerations for Choice of Forum," *Journal of World Trade*, 41(5): 885–908.

Porges, Amy. 2011. "Dispute Settlement", in J.-P. Chauffour and J.-C. Maur, eds., *Preferential Trade Agreements Policies for Development: A Handbook*, Washington, DC: The World Bank, pp. 453–87.

Robert, Maryse. 2011. "The Implementation of Trade in Services and Investment Obligations in Free Trade Agreements: Lessons from Latin America," mimeo. Washington, DC: The Inter-American Development Bank.

Robert, Maryse, and Sherry Stephenson. 2008. "Opening Services Markets at the Regional Level under the CAFTA-DR: The Cases of Costa Rica and the Dominican Republic," in Juan A. Marchetti and Martin Roy, eds., *Opening Markets for Trade in Services: Countries and Sectors in Bilateral and WTO Negotiations*, Cambridge: Cambridge University Press, pp. 537–72.

Roy, Martin, Juan Marchetti, and Hoe Lim. 2009. "Services Liberalization in the New Generation of Preferential Trade Agreements: How Much Further than the GATS," in Antoni Estevadeordal, Kati Suominen, and Robert Teh, eds., *Regional Rules in the Global Trading System*, Cambridge: Cambridge University Press, pp. 316–64.

Sáez, Raúl. 2010. "Trade in Financial Services: The Case of Chile," in Mona Haddad and Constantinos Stephanou, eds., *Financial Services and Preferential Trade Agreements: Lessons from Latin America*, Washington, DC: The World Bank, 123–84.

Sáez, Sebastián. 2005. *Implementing Trade Policy in Latin America: The Case of Chile and Mexico*. Santiago, Chile: ECLAC.

Sáez, Sebastián, ed. 2010. *Trade in Services Negotiations: A Guide for Developing Countries*. Washington, DC: The World Bank.

Sauvé, Pierre, and Natasha Ward. 2009. "The EC-CARIFORUM Economic Partnership Agreement: Assessing the Outcome on Services and Investment," Paper published by the European Centre for International Political Economy, available at http://www.ecipe.org/publications/ecipe-working-papers.

Stephenson, Sherry. 2002. "Can Regional Liberalization of Services go Further than Multilateral Liberalization under the GATS?," *World Trade Review*, 1(2), July.

Stephenson, Sherry. 2008. "Demographic Change and International Labour Mobility in the Pacific Americas", in Graeme Hugo and Soogil Young, eds., *Labour Mobility in the Asia-Pacific Region – Dynamics, Issues and a New APEC Agenda*, Singapore: ISEAS Publishers.

Stephenson, Sherry. 2010. "Increasing Labour Mobility: Options for Developing Countries" in Olivier Cattaneo, Michael Engman, Sebastián Sáez, and Robert M. Stern, eds., *International Trade in Services: New Trends and Opportunities for Developing Countries*, Washington, DC: The World Bank.

UNCTAD. 2008. "Investment Promotion in International Investment Provisions." Geneva: UNCTAD. http://www.unctad.org/en/docs/iteiit20077_en.pdf.

APPENDIX

Table 4A.1 Comparison of treatment of services in RTAs within the Americas

Agreement	Modality*		National Treatment	Most Favored Nation	Market Access	Domestic Regulation	Transparency[94]	Carve-out for subsidies & grants	Ratchet Clause	Mutual Recognition Provisions	Denial of Benefits Clause	Dispute Settlement Provisions	Annex on Professional Services
	Positive List	Negative List											
NAFTA (1994)*	–	✓	✓	✓	–	–	–	✓	✓	✓	✓	✓	✓
Chile-Mexico (1999)	–	✓	✓	✓	–	–	✓	✓	✓	✓	✓	✓	✓
CAFTA-DR (2006–09)*	–	✓	✓	✓	✓	✓	✓	✓	✓	✓	✓	✓	✓
Chile-US (2004)	–	✓	✓	✓	✓	✓	✓	✓	✓	✓	✓	✓	✓
Canada-Peru (2009)	–	✓	✓	✓	✓	✓	✓	✓	✓	✓	✓	✓	✓
Canada-Colombia (2011)	–	✓	✓	✓	✓	✓	✓	✓	✓	✓	✓	✓	✓
Peru-US (PTPA) (2009)	–	✓	✓	✓	✓	✓	✓	✓	✓	✓	✓	✓	✓

Note: * Agreements with more than two parties.

92 The NAFTA Agreement does not have a chapter entitled "transparency", but Chapter Eighteen entitled "Publication, Notification and Administration of Laws" contains transparency provisions, whereas the Canadian FTAs do not contain a provision on transparency in the chapter on cross-border trade in services but do include a chapter on transparency.

Table 4A.2 Comparison of Treatment of Services in RTAs between Countries of the Americas and Asian Partners

Agreement	Modality												
	Positive List	Negative List	National Treatment	Most Favored Nation	Market Access	Domestic Regulation	Transparency	Carve-outs for subsidies & grants	Ratchet Clause	Mutual Recognition Provisions	Denial of Benefits Clause	Dispute Settlement Provisions	Annex on Professional Services
Chile-Korea (2004)	–	✓	✓	–	–	–	✓	✓	✓	✓	✓	✓	✓
US-Singapore (2004)	–	✓	✓	✓	✓	✓	✓	✓	✓	✓	✓	✓	✓
Mexico-Japan (2005)	–	✓	✓	✓	–	✓	✓	✓	✓	–	✓	✓	–
Chile-China (2010)[95]	✓	–	✓	–	✓	✓	✓	✓	–	✓	✓	✓	–
Trans-Pacific Strategic Economic Partnership TPSEP (2006)*	–	✓	✓	✓	✓	✓	✓	✓	✓	✓	✓	✓	✓

Note: * Agreements with more than two parties.

93 The Protocol on Trade in Services between Chile and the People's Republic of China is in force since August 1, 2010. The main agreement between the two countries has been in force since October 1, 2006.

Table 4A.3 Comparison of Treatment of Services in RTAs between Countries of the Americas and the EU

Agreement [96]	Modality												
	Positive List	Negative List	National Treatment	Most Favored Nation	Market Access	Domestic Regulation	Transparency	Carve-outs for subsidies & grants	Ratchet Clause	Mutual Recognition Provisions	Denial of Benefits Clause	Dispute Settlement Provisions	Annex on Professional Services
EC-Chile (2003)	✓	–	✓	–	✓	✓	✓	✓	–	✓	–	✓	–
CARIFORUM-EC EPA (2008)*[97]	✓	–	✓	✓	✓	✓	✓	✓	–	✓	–	✓	–
EC-Central America (AACUE)*	✓	–	✓	–	✓	✓	✓	✓	–	✓	–	✓	–

Note: * Agreements with more than two parties.

94 EC-Mexico is a Framework Agreement. Article 6 on Trade in Services does not contain any substantive disciplines.

95 For services and commercial presence (mode 3), the CARIFORUM countries use a "positive list" approach. However, for non-services investment, CARIFORUM uses a "negative listing" approach.

Table 4A.4 Summary Table of WTO Dispute Settlement Cases with a Services Component

Dispute	Complainant	Relevant GATS Articles	Current Status (as of November 2010)
1. DS413 China – Certain Measures Affecting Electronic Payment Services	United States	Art. XVI and XVII	In consultations on September 14, 2010
2. DS378 China – Measures Affecting Financial Information Services and Foreign Financial Information Suppliers	Canada	Art. XVI, XVII and XVIII	Settled or terminated (withdrawn, mutually agreed solution) on June 20, 2008
3. DS373 China – Measures Affecting Financial Information Services and Foreign Financial Information Suppliers	United States	Art. XVI, XVII, XVIII	Settled or terminated (withdrawn, mutually agreed solution) on December 4, 2008
4. DS372 China – Measures Affecting Financial Information Services and Foreign Financial Information Suppliers	European Communities	Art. XVI:2(a), XVI:2(e), XVII, XVIII	Settled or terminated (withdrawn, mutually agreed solution) on December 4, 2008
5. DS363 China – Measures Affecting Trading Rights and Distribution Services for Certain Publications and Audiovisual Entertainment Products	United States	Art. XVI, XVII	Report(s) adopted, with recommendation that China bring the measure into conformity on January 19, 2010
6. DS309 China – Value-Added Tax on Integrated Circuits	United States	Art. XVII	Settled or terminated (withdrawn, mutually agreed solution) on October 5, 2005
7. DS285 United States of America – Measures Affecting the Cross-Border Supply of Gambling and Betting Services	Antigua & Barbuda	Art. II, VI, VIII, XI, XVI, XVII	Antigua & Barbuda awarded limited cross-retaliation rights against US intellectual property to the tune of $21 million annually on December 21, 2007

Table 4A.4 (continued)

Dispute	Complainant	Relevant GATS Articles	Current Status (as of November 2010)
8. DS237 Turkey – Certain Import Procedures for Fresh Fruit	Ecuador	Art. VI, XVII	Settled or terminated (withdrawn, mutually agreed solution) on November 22, 2002
9. DS204 Mexico – Measures Affecting Telecommunications Services	United States	Art. VI:5, VI, VI:1, XVI, XVI:1, XVI:2, XVII, XVII:1, XVII:2, XVII:3, XVIII	Implementation notified by Mexico on August 31, 2005
10. DS201 Nicaragua – Measures Affecting Imports from Honduras and Colombia	Honduras	Art. II, XVI	Request for consultations on June 6, 2000
11. DS188 Nicaragua – Measures Affecting Imports from Honduras and Colombia	Colombia	Art. II, XVI	Panel established, but not yet composed on May 18, 2000
12. DS182 Ecuador – Provisional Anti-Dumping Measure on Cement from Mexico	Mexico	Art. VI	Request for consultations on October 5, 1999
13. DS168 South Africa – Anti-Dumping Duties on Certain Pharmaceutical Products from India	India	Art. I, VI	Request for consultations on April 1, 1999
14. DS142 Canada – Certain Measures Affecting the Automotive Industry	European Communities	Art. II, VI, XVII	Implementation notified by respondent on March 12, 2001
15. DS139 Canada – Certain Measures Affecting the Automotive Industry	Japan	Art. II, VI, XVII	Implementation notified by respondent on March 12, 2001

16. DS117 Canada – Measures Affecting Film Distribution Services	European Communities	Art. II, III	Request for consultations on January 20, 1998
17. DS105 European Communities – Regime for the Importation, Sale and Distribution of Bananas	Panama	Art. II, XVII	Request for consultations on October 24, 1997
18. DS80 Belgium – Measures Affecting Commercial Telephone Directory Services	United States	Art. II, VI, VIII, XVII	Request for consultations on May 2, 1997
19. DS45 Japan – Measures Affecting Distribution Services	United States	Art. III, VI, XVI, XVII, XXIII:3	Request for consultations on June 13, 1996
20. DS38 United States of America – The Cuban Liberty and Democratic Solidarity Act	European Communities	Art. I, II, III, VI, XI, XVI, XVII	Settled or terminated (withdrawn, mutually agreed solution) on April, 22 1998
21. DS27 European Communities – Regime for the Importation, Sale and Distribution of Bananas	Ecuador, Guatemala, Honduras, Mexico United States	Art. II, IV, XVI, XVII	Compliance proceedings completed with finding(s) of non-compliance by the EC on December 11, 2008
22. DS16 European Communities – Regime for the Importation, Sale and Distribution of Bananas	Guatemala, Honduras, Mexico, United States	Art. II, XVI, XVII	Request for consultations on September 28, 1995

Source: WTO website: http://www.wto.org/english/tratop_e/dispu_e/dispu_agreements_index_e.htm?id=A8#selected_agreement.

Results from "Excess Growth Calculations" for Four FTAs

Table 4A.5 U.S.-CHILE (2004)

			2000–2004	2004–2009	Δ Growth
Average growth of Total Trade					
	US with Chile	*Services*	−8.11%	12.27%	20.38%
		Goods	2.55%	14.64%	12.09%
	Extra-zone Trade	*Services*	3.89%	9.16%	5.27%
		Goods	3.79%	4.78%	0.99%
Excess Growth					
	Services		**−12.00%**	**3.11%**	**15.11%**
	Goods		**−1.23%**	**9.85%**	**11.08%**

Sources: USTR, IMF, OECD.

Table 4A.6 U.S.-SINGAPORE (2004)

			2000–2004	2004–2009	Δ Growth
Average growth of Total Trade					
	US with Singapore	*Services*	2.05%	8.53%	6.48%
		Goods	−2.02%	−2.46%	−0.44%
	Extra-zone Trade	*Services*	4.53%	9.47%	4.94%
		Goods	4.33%	5.39%	1.06%
Excess Growth					
	Services		**−2.48%**	**−0.94%**	**1.54%**
	Goods		**−6.35%**	**−2.46%**	**3.89%**

Sources: USTR, IMF.

Table 4A.7 MEXICO-JAPAN (2005)

			2000–2005	2005–2008	Δ Growth
Average growth of Total Trade					
	Mexico with	*Services*	−8.54%	16.76%	25.30%
	Japan	*Goods*	28.06%	11.70%	−16.36%
	Extra-zone	*Services*	5.26%	8.25%	2.99%
	Trade	Goods	3.89%	11.12%	7.23%
Excess Growth					
	Services		**−13.79%**	**8.54%**	**22.33%**
	Goods		**24.17%**	**0.58%**	**−23.59%**

Sources: USTR, IMF, OECD.

Table 4A.8 CARIFORUM-EC EPA (2008)

			2000–2008	2008–2009	Δ Growth
Average growth of Total Trade					
	EU with	*Services*	5.39%	5.69%	0.30%
	Cariforum	*Goods*	5.32%	−7.08%	−12.40%
	Extra-zone	*Services*	10.35%	−1.95%	−12.30%
	Trade	Goods	10.61%	−7.24%	−17.85%
Excess Growth					
	Services		**−4.96%**	**7.64%**	**12.60%**
	Goods		**−5.29%**	**0.16%**	**5.45%**

Sources: EUROSTAT, IMF, WTO.

5. Services trade in the European Union: internal and external approaches to market opening

Imola Streho*

5.1 INTRA- AND EXTRA-EU TRADE IN SERVICES: CONTEXTUAL CONSIDERATIONS

The European Union is the most important global player in international services trade today.[1] The period since the 1990s has seen a constant rise in the service sector of the EU economy. Services play a major role in EU growth, jobs and exports, accounting for over 70% of Europe's GDP and a similar proportion of aggregate employment. Cross-border services trade represent 25% of the EU's global trade, a level some 20% above the world average.[2] The expansion of EU services trade has in recent decades exceeded service output growth by a sizeable margin.[3]

An important defining characteristic of services trade is the immediacy and proximity of the relationship it entails between the provider and the recipient (consumer) in many transactions. A derivative feature of services is that they are provided via various modes of supply which can trigger and indeed often require the mobility of production factors (capital and labour). In EU law, a specific approach was taken such that in the very

* Associate Professor, Law School and Associate Researcher, Centre d'études européennes, Sciences Po, Paris. I am indebted to Pierre Sauvé for his comments on the first draft and his precious inputs in part III of this chapter. The usual disclaimer applies.

[1] Three main sectors accounts for two-thirds of the total trade in services: transport, travel and other business services (financial services, computer and information services). Statistics Eurostat: http://epp.eurostat.ec.europa.eu/statistics_explained/index.php/International_trade_in_services.

[2] Ibid.

[3] Eurostat, "European Union International Trade in Services. Analytical Aspects. 1997–2005", 2007 edition, http://epp.eurostat.ec.europa.eu/cache/ITY_OFFPUB/KS-EB-07-001/EN/KS-EB-07-001-EN.PDF.

same sector, services can be subject either to the rules of the Treaty of Rome on freedom to provide services or to the freedom of establishment, triggering a different legal regime.

Over the past decade, efforts have intensified within the EU to take full advantage of both intra- and extra-EU trade in services. Several strategies were adopted by the European Commission, culminating in the adoption of the Services Directive at the end of 2006, followed by the Single Market Act in 2011. At the international level, the EU has concluded several bilateral trade agreements of a preferential nature (PTAs) and is currently engaged in negotiating new ones in which services are almost invariably a central component.

5.2 BUILDING THE EUROPEAN INTERNAL MARKET IN SERVICES

> While the European Union has always looked upon services as an essential part of the integration process, it has taken some time for the EU to devote much attention to them.[4]

Since its very origins, primary EU law refers to services. The Treaty of Rome[5] does not offer a definition of what a service is but nonetheless aims at liberalizing trade in services. To achieve this objective, EU law relies on the economic notion of services, which can be defined, as Peter Hill aptly writes: "as a change in the condition of a person, or a good belonging to some economic unit, which is brought about as the result of the activity of some other economic unit, with the prior agreement of the former person or economic unit".[6]

At the core of the European project is the objective of establishing an Internal Market through the economic integration of the founding Member States' market. The project is framed as an international agreement,[7] its peculiar institutional and legal environments allowing such

---

[4] Molle, W., *The Economics of European Integration*, Farnham, Ashgate, 2006, p. 323.

[5] The Treaty of Rome established in 1957 the European Economic Community. The Treaty is also referred to as EECT and since the 1st of December 2009 as Treaty on the Functioning of the European Union, TFEU.

[6] Hill, T. P., "On Goods and Services", *Review of Wealth and Income*, New Haven, Dec. 1997.

[7] Rome Treaty establishing the European Economic Community. Spiermann, O., "The Other Side of the Story: An Unpopular Essay on the Making of the European Community Legal Order", *EJIL*, 1999, 10(4), pp. 763–89. In this piece,

an objective to proceed in a dynamic manner.[8] The unprecedented ambition of the European project was recognized early on, as the region did not aim for free trade[9] but rather for a more advanced stage of economic integration via a customs union and, subsequently, a single Internal Market. In 1993, the objective was revisited and an extra level of integration was added with the aim of establishing a European Economic and Monetary Union.

The first version of the founding Treaty mentions services, but for decades services were considered only as incidental to trade in goods. From the early 1990s, the economic weight of services grew significantly, entailing a notable policy shift towards greater regulatory activity and judicial activism on the basis of the primary law referring to services.

5.2.1 Objectives and Instruments of the European Internal Market in Services

The establishment of a European-wide Internal Market for services required Member States to tackle obstacles to intra-EU trade and the fragmentation of the European services market. Several instruments were included in the Treaty of Rome towards this end, namely a standstill clause and negative and positive integration clause.

The standstill and negative integration clause included in the Treaty allowed the tackling of national obstacles to trade.[10] Both clauses introduced clear prohibitions for Member States and were recognized as having

---

the author establishes a clear link between the early case law of the ECJ and the specificities of the EU treaties. The potential of the preliminary reference allowed the Court to decide cases such as Van Gend en Loos and Costa/Enel. The principles of direct effect and ECJ supremacy established in these cases created a new dynamic which the ECJ explored further. Scholars have also shown that ECJ judges were deciding more as national rather than international court members. Weiler, J.H.H., "The Transformation of Europe", *The Yale Law Journal*, 1991, (8), pp. 2403–83.

[8] All relevant ideas are already clearly embedded in the Schuman Declaration of 9 May 1950, http://europa.eu/about-eu/basic-information/symbols/europe-day/schuman-declaration/index_en.htm as well as in Monnet, J., *Mémoires*, Paris, Fayard, 1976; Delors, J., *1992 Le défi*, Paris, Flammarion, 1990; speeches by Émile Noël in *Hommage à Emile Noël*, Office des publications de la Communauté, 1988.

[9] As opposed to the other European regional trade project; the European Free Trade Association created in 1960 or the original "Outer Seven" (as opposed to the "Inner Six").

[10] The ECJ has early on given a wide interpretation of the negative integration clauses, allowing traders to challenge an important number of obstacles to services trade. In the early 1990s, when case law began to rise in the services field,

direct effect by the European Court of Justice (ECJ), which also gave a wide interpretation of their material scope.

Positive integration clauses inserted in the Treaty allow for harmonization of national regulations at the level of the EU. This instrument proved particularly efficient in advancing the agenda of the Internal Market and facilitated the de-fragmentation of the EU-wide services market.

However, it is the combination of the two instruments that ultimately allowed the establishment of the Internal Market.[11] The active litigation of economic agents on the basis of the negative integration clauses, supported by an equally activist ECJ, paved the way for the removal of national measures inhibiting cross-border services trade. The adoption of secondary law came afterwards, starting with sector-by-sector harmonization of national regulations on services and widespread recourse to the principle of mutual recognition (especially in regard to the recognition of diplomas). Only recently, in 2006, did the EU adopt a Directive which was not sector specific and covered services in the Internal Market.[12]

5.2.2 Building a Single Market for Services

5.2.2.1 The origins

In June 1955, in the negotiating framework that would later lead to the signature of the Treaty of Rome, the governments of the soon to be six founding Member States of the European Economic Community (EEC) decided at the Messine Conference to convene an intergovernmental committee presided over by Paul-Henri Spaak.[13] The committee presented a report on 21 April 1956 which delineated all the foundations of what would subsequently become the Internal Market project in the Treaty of Rome signed in March 1957 and whose main idea was to merge the six national markets.

---

the ECJ gave a wide interpretation of the negative integration clause of the Treaty on services.

[11] Mortelmans, K., "The Common Market, the Internal Market and the Single Market: What's in a Market?", *CMLR*, 1998, 35, pp. 101–36, on this point p. 120, and Weiler, J.H.H., "Epilogue: Towards a Common Law of International Trade", *The EU, the WTO and the NAFTA. Towards a Common Law of International Trade*, Oxford, Oxford University Press, 2000, pp. 201–32, on this point p. 223.

[12] Directive 2006/123 of the European Parliament and the Council, 12 December 2006, on Services in the Internal Market, OJ L 376, p. 36.

[13] Spaak, P.-H., Report of the Heads of Delegation to the Ministers of Foreign Affairs. Intergovernmental Committee on European Integration, commonly called the "Spaak Report", 1956; Spaak was Foreign Affairs Minister of Belgium at that time.

The Spaak Report foresaw the establishment of a sound environment in terms of market competition and the elimination of all forms of protectionism. The report also suggested the need to tackle monopolies and subsidies as well as to liberalize all factors of production, (capital and labour) by allowing their free movement within the European internal market.[14] The report referred to the free movement of both goods and services. Chapter 3 of the report focuses exclusively on services with the following introductory remark: "the importance and growth of services is notable in the economies of the Member States". A short enumeration lists examples of key services, including transport, insurance, banking and other financial services.

While preparing the Spaak Report, committee members referred to the work of the OECE,[15] one of whose aims was to liberalize services then commonly referred to as "invisibles". The Spaak Report advanced several proposals on services. The first and most important challenge was to tackle the liberalization of services that were important components of the production and trade in goods,[16] revealing the predominant perception at the time of the somewhat adjunct nature of services as primarily inputs into other economic activities rather than genuine activities in their own right.[17] Services were thus initially seen as incidental to advancing the main economic priority of the European project which concerned the liberalization of trade in goods.

The second key focus of the Spaak Report was the monitoring of Member States' regulation on services to avoid discrimination on the basis of nationality or residence.[18] The Spaak Report further considered the necessity of putting into place a system of recognition of diplomas and academic titles with a view to facilitating the cross-border movement of skilled labour. This point would assume significant prominence in the EU's positive integration (harmonization) agenda from the 1980s onwards, affirming the central market opening role assumed by the principle of mutual recognition.[19]

---

14 Spaak Report, op. cit., p. 15.

15 It is worth recalling one of the objectives behind the creation of the OECE in 1948, which was the improvement of trade relations between the members. To achieve it several codes were adopted on liberalization of exchanges, invisible transactions and capital movements.

16 Spaak Report, op. cit., p. 41.

17 Goods are described as "top priority" by the Spaak Report.

18 This concern would be placed at the heart of the services-related articles of the future Treaty of Rome.

19 Mutual recognition was also used in earlier case law and secondary law in regard to the free movement of goods. For an extensive study of the principle in the field of services, see Hatzopoulos, V., *Regulating Services in the EU*, Oxford, Oxford University Press, 2012, p. 283 and onwards.

Following the Spaak Report, the group of experts drafting the Treaty of Rome (called the Common Market Group) finalized the articles on services. Despite attempts to include an article with a positive definition of services, the signed version of the Treaty did not feature such a definition. Chapter 3 of the Treaty of Rome contained seven articles dealing with services. This chapter has since remained largely unchanged.

The *standstill clause* of former Article 62 European Economic Community Treaty (EECT) was removed as well as references to the transitional period but otherwise the primary law articulation and reference to *negative and positive integration* remained unchanged in the field of services liberalization. However, one important modification introduced since the Treaty signature has been the use of the ordinary legislative process to adopt EU Directives in the services field. The following lists the relevant articles of the Treaty of Rome governing services in the EU today.

CHAPTER 3 – SERVICES

Article 56 FTFEU

Within the framework of the provisions set out below, restrictions on the freedom to provide services within the Community shall be prohibited[20] in respect of nationals of Member States who are established in a State of the Community other than that of the person for whom the services are intended. The Council may, acting by a qualified majority on a proposal from the Commission, extend the provisions of the chapter to nationals of a third country who provide services and who are established within the Community.

Article 57 TFEU

Services shall be considered to be "services" within the meaning of this Treaty where they are normally provided for remuneration, in so far as they are not governed by the provisions relating to freedom of movement for goods, capital and persons. "Services" shall in particular include: (a) activities of an industrial character; (b) activities of a commercial character; (c) activities of craftsmen; and (d) activities of the professions.[21] Without prejudice to the provisions of the chapter relating to the right of establishment, the person providing a service may, in order to do so, temporarily pursue his activity in the State where the

[20] The trigger of the negative integration clause is the prohibition of restrictions on free provision of services in the EU.

[21] There is no positive and comprehensive definition of services in the Treaty of Rome and it cannot be linked to any other positive legal source. It is a *sui generis* definition of the activity of services with reference to the necessity of remuneration and a cross-border element.

service is provided, under the same conditions as are imposed by that State on its own nationals.[22]

Article 58 TFEU

Freedom to provide services in the field of transport shall be governed by the provisions of the Title relating to transport.[23] The liberalisation of banking and insurance services connected with movements of capital shall be effected in step with the liberalisation of movement of capital.

Article 59 TFEU

In order to achieve the liberalisation of a specific service, the European Parliament and the Council, acting in accordance with the ordinary legislative procedure and after consulting the Economic and Social Committee, shall issue directives. As regards the Directives referred to above, priority shall as a general rule be given to those services which directly affect production costs or the liberalisation of which helps to promote trade in goods.

Article 60 TFEU

The Member States shall endeavour to undertake the liberalisation of services beyond the extent required by the directives issued pursuant to Article 59(1) if their general economic situation and the situation of the economic sector concerned so permit. To this end, the Commission shall make recommendations to the Member States concerned.

Article 61 TFEU

As long as restrictions on freedom to provide services have not been abolished, each Member State shall apply such restrictions without distinction on grounds of nationality or residence[24] to all persons providing services within the meaning of the first paragraph of Article 56 TFEU.

Article 62 TFEU

The provisions of Articles 51 to 54 shall apply to the matters covered by this chapter.[25]

---

[22] We see here reference to the mutually exclusive articles on establishment and provision of services and the reference to the temporary nature of the freedom to provide services.

[23] A specific chapter is inserted in the Treaty of Rome on transport, in Articles 90 to 100 TFEU.

[24] Discriminatory national regulations are prohibited by the Treaty in the field of services also.

[25] Articles 51 to 54 are part of chapter 2 on the freedom of establishment in the EU.

CHAPTER 4 – ESTABLISHMENT

Article 52 TFEU

> The provisions of this chapter and measures taken in pursuance thereof shall not prejudice the applicability of provisions laid down by law, regulation or administrative action providing for special treatment for foreign nationals on grounds of public policy, public security or public health.[26]

The Treaty of Rome included two chapters on services, one entitled "Freedom to provide services" and the other called "Establishment". The approach pursued under the Treaty was to put in place two distinct legal regimes for the same economic activity.[27] As we shall see, the EU construct did not pursue commitments by modes of supply, as is now found in the GATS or PTAs. Such terminology and categorical distinctions for negotiating purposes would come from the GATS negotiating process, itself borrowing from early attempts at developing rules for services in various preferential trade agreements.

The ECJ clarified in a landmark case the differences that could be seen to distinguish the delivery of legal services in the EU under the agreed freedom to provide services versus the freedom of establishment.[28] Such differences lie principally in the duration of the economic activity in question, with the two legal regimes excluding each other mutually. An economic activity which is temporary in nature would be covered by the rules of the Treaty dealing with the free provision of services. This characteristic is explained by the Court in the following terms in the Gebhard case: "the temporary nature of the activities in question has to be determined in the light not only of the duration of the provision of the service but also of its regularity, periodicity or continuity. The fact that the provision of services is temporary does not mean that the service provider within the meaning of the Treaty may not equip himself (or herself) with some form of infrastructure in the host Member State (including an office, chambers or consulting rooms) in so far as such infrastructure is necessary for the purposes of performing the services in question".[29]

---

26 This article establishes a closed list of justifications of restrictive national measures affecting the free provision of services.

27 Both primary law and secondary law refer to services taking into account the two legal regimes. Many directives and regulations on services include sections on freedom of establishment and free provision of services.

28 ECJ 30 November 1995, Gebhard, C-55/94, ECR. p.I-4165, point 27.

29 Wägenbaur, R., "La libéralisation des prestations de service dans la perspective du marché intérieur", *Nuove tendenze del commercio internazionale*,

The main difference between the two legal regimes is that, when covered by the freedom to provide services, the economic activity is subject to the regulation of the home country and if covered by the freedom of establishment it is the regulation of the host country that applies.

5.2.2.2 The early years and the residual approach towards services

Between the 1960s and early 1990s, several initiatives were taken to advance the integration of the European Internal Market. As early as 1961, the Council adopted two General Programs aimed at removing all restrictions on the free provision of services and the freedom of establishment.[30] The Programs pursue the same broad aims as the Spaak Report and the Treaty of Rome, namely the liberalization of services "as instruments for" free trade in goods.

A second Spaak Committee was convened by France and Germany in the early 1980s to advance the European project.[31] The second Spaak Report (Spaak 2) underlines the importance of the Internal Market and the necessity to set up deadlines to remove restrictions thereto. According to the Report, a fragmented Internal Market hampers Europe's competitiveness on the global stage. The Report was the first political document advocating in a concerted manner the necessity of establishing an Internal Market for services.[32]

The second Spaak Report was followed by the ambitious White Paper of 1985. In this document (which had no legal force), the European Commission suggested that the Council set end-1992 as the target date for the completion of the European Internal Market.[33] It also suggested two orientations; first, relying more systematically on the principle of mutual

---

Istituto Universitario di Studi di Torino, Giuffre editore, Milan, 1989, p. 163; Fallon, M., "Vers un principe général de liberté de circulation ? Pour une approche unitaire du droit du marché intérieur", *Annales d'études européennes de l'Université catholique de Louvain*, Brussels, Bruylant, 1996, p. 81; Steindorff, E., "Freedom of Services in the EEC", *Fordham International Law Journal*, 1988, 11, p. 372.

[30] These programs were adopted unanimously by the Council and, despite their lack of legal force, they have an important political influence. OJ no. 2, 15 January 1962, pp. 32 and 36.

[31] Dabin, P., *Le Comité Spaak 2 (dit Comité Dooge): Actes du Comité ad hoc pour les questions institutionnelles créé par le Conseil européen de Fontainebleau (25–26 juin 1984)*, Brussels, 1985.

[32] The wording of the second Spaak Report is quite familiar today as the Lisbon Strategy in 2000, in Europe 2020 and in the 2011 Single Market Act, reference is made to the necessity of an effective and obstacle-free Internal Market for services.

[33] COM (85) 310 final, Completing the Internal Market – White Paper from the Commission to the European Council (Milan, 28–9 June 1985).

recognition and secondly adopting a new approach towards harmonization.[34] Some scholars have called this document "utopic"[35] because of the numerous objectives it sets as well as the exhaustive range of obstacles it targeted for removal. Still, the document would prove decisive in the establishment of the EU Internal Market precisely because of its clear objectives but also because of the reasonable deadline it set for their realization.[36] The White Paper recognizes the importance of services in the economies especially at a time when the European manufacturing sector began its relative decline.

Following the White Paper, for the first time, Member States introduced amendments to the Treaty of Rome leading to the Single European Act. Among others, the voting rule in the Council became qualified majority for the adoption of secondary law in regard to the Internal Market (Article 114 TFEU).[37] This change facilitated the adoption of secondary law and promoted the harmonization of Internal Market rules.[38]

Three years after the White Paper, in 1988, an impact assessment was commissioned regarding the completion of the European Internal Market. The resulting document, called the Cecchini Report, was critical in the emphasis it laid on the potential of the service sector in advancing the European economy in terms of both growth and employment. The Report pointed to a host of national regulations and practices that artificially inhibited the free provision of services and held back competition in the sector.[39] The Report concluded that "much more significant growth is

---

[34] The New Approach departed from the idea that all aspects of trade should be harmonized at European level by identifying priority fields in which harmonization would be relevant.

[35] Schmitt von Sydow, H., "The Basic Strategies of the Commission's White Paper", in Bieber, R., Dehousse, R., Pinder, J., and Weiler, J.H.H., eds., *1992: One European Market ?*, Baden-Baden, Nomos Verlagsgesellschaft, 1998, pp. 79–106.

[36] It is worth noting that the use of deadline proved effective both for the Internal Market for goods and for the establishment of the Custom union of the EU. As in AFAS, the setting of realistic but firm deadlines and of clear intermediary objectives was a successful mix to advance the European integration project.

[37] Jacqué, J.-P., "L'Acte unique européen", *RTDE*, 1986, no. 4, p. 575; Bosco, G., "Commentaire de l'Acte unique européen", *CDE*, 1987, no. 45, p. 355, and Deniniolle, S., "L'acte unique et le marché commun", *Moniteur du commerce international*, février 1988, no. 805/29, p. 17.

[38] Even today, the importance of the change in the voting rule in the Council is acknowledged as one of the key factors in the completion of the Internal Market by 1993. Delors, J., "The Single Market, Cornerstone of the EU, Tribune", *Notre Europe*, 22 November 2012.

[39] "The European Challenge, 1992: The Benefit of a Single Market", Paolo Cecchini, Wildwood House, pour la Commission, 1988, Sommaire du rapport

being artificially held back by regulations and practices which significantly inhibit the free flow of services and thus the free play of competition between companies supplying them".

The continuity and coherence of the European project for completing the Internal Market proceeded very clearly from the adoption of the Treaty of Rome to the Cecchini Report. All the political, institutional as well as legal efforts concurred during three decades to secure the defragmentation of national markets and the establishment of a European-wide services market.

5.2.2.3 The 1990s and the rise of intra EU trade in services

Until the early 1990s, litigation and European Court of Justice (ECJ) decisions on services were limited. This changed progressively as the importance of services grew in the economy of Member States. The relevant articles of the Treaty of Rome were invoked more frequently by traders, economic agents and consumers within the Member States in the framework of domestic litigation. National judges started to refer preliminary references to the ECJ, asking for the interpretation of Articles 56 and 57 TFEU. For much of the recent past, a majority of questions referred to the ECJ on the issue of free movement concerned services-related issues.[40]

5.2.2.3.1ECJ case law on services – the law of prohibition A few important cases were however decided earlier by the ECJ in the services field. The ECJ notably recognized the direct effect of certain Treaty articles on services as early as 1974. As noted earlier, interaction between the provider and the recipient is essential to trade in services. Accordingly, recognition of direct effect has allowed stakeholders to rely on the Treaty articles and challenge national measures that were contrary to EU law. The landmark case on this issue dates from 1974, when the ECJ recognized direct effect to Article 56, paragraph 1 and Article 57, paragraph 3 of the Treaty of Rome in the van Bisbergen case.[41]

Cecchini, SEC (88) 524 final du 13 avril 1988. http://aei.pitt.edu/3813/01/000209_1.pdf.

[40] The ECJ Annual Report shows a steady decrease over the past decade in the number of cases brought to the ECJ on the free movement of goods and an increase in cases relating to the free movement of services.

[41] ECJ 3 December 1974, Van Bisbergen, 33/74, ECR. p. 1299, a Dutch legal representative changed residence from the Netherlands to Belgium. The question arose of whether this person could continue to represent his client in a pending litigation and if Article 56 TFEU could have direct effect.

Recognition of direct effect allowed for the more effective and speedy removal of national regulations restricting the free provision of services. Indeed economic agents (both natural and juridical persons) could invoke Article 56 or 57 of the TFEU before national judges to challenge domestic regulations.[42] Without direct effect, the Treaty would have left them with the possibility of sending complaints to the European Commission requesting an investigation of a specific national regulation and its possible violation of EU law.

The aim of Article 56 TFEU seems clear upon reading. We can rephrase it by saying that national measures restricting the provision of services are prohibited. However, the ECJ's interpretation of this article and especially the concomitant scope of the prohibition evolved over time. Such evolution highlights the central role assumed by the ECJ as a major actor in the European institutional landscape through the teleological interpretation it has given to the relevant Treaty articles on services.

For example, the ECJ gave a flexible interpretation of the private, public or mixed origins of national measures. According to the ECJ, "[t]he abolition, as between Member States, of obstacles to freedom of movement for persons would be compromised if the abolition of State barriers could be neutralized by obstacles resulting from the exercise of their legal autonomy by associations or organizations not governed by public law".[43]

As early as 1974, the ECJ interpreted Article 56 TFEU as prohibiting all discrimination based on the nationality of the service provider.[44] According to the ECJ, both *de jure* (overt) and *de facto* (covert) discrimination are caught by the Treaty prohibition, a distinction that the

---

[42] See Opinion of 13 December 1979 Advocate General Warner in cases Debauve & Coditel, 52/79 & 62/79, ECR. p. 874.

[43] ECJ 19 February 2002, Wouters, C-309/99, ECR. p. I-1577, point 120, quoting cases ECJ 12 December 1974, Walrave & Koch, 36/74, ECR. p. 1405, points 17, 18, 23 & 24; ECJ 14 July 1976, Donà, 13/76, Rec. p. 1333, points 17 et 18; ECJ 15 December 1995, Bosman, C-415/93, ECR. p. I–4921, points 83 & 84, and ECJ 6 June 2000, Angonese, C-281/98, ECR. p. I-4139, point 32. Recently quoted in ECJ 11 December 2007, The International Transport Workers' Federation & The Finnish Seamen's Union, C–438/05, ECR. p. 10779 and ECJ 18 December 2007, Laval un Partneri, C–341/05, ECR p. 11767.

[44] ECJ 3 December 1974, Van Bisbergen, 33/74, ECR. p. 1299; ECJ 3 February 1982, Seco, 62/81 & 63/81, Rec. p. 223 (discrimination on the basis of nationality) and ECJ 18 March 1980, Debauve 52/79, ECR. p. 833. It is settled law that discrimination can arise only through the application of different rules to comparable situations or the application of the same rule to different situations. ECJ 7 May 1998, Lease Plan, C-390/96, ECR. p. I-2553, point 34 and ECJ 3 October 2002, Danner, C-136/00, ECR. p. I–8147.

drafters of the World Trade Organization's (WTO) General Agreement on Trade in Services (GATS) would subsequently adopt. This important distinction was further explained by a member of the ECJ: "By overt discrimination, I mean discrimination which is expressed in the legislation itself, i.e. legislation which expressly applies different requirements to nationals of, or those residents in, another Member State. By covert discrimination, I mean discrimination which results from legislation apparently applying the same requirements, but where the effect of the requirements is to disadvantage nationals of, or those residents in, another Member State".[45]

In the early 1990s, the ECJ revisited the scope of the prohibition of Article 56 TFEU and widened it to all national measures restricting the free provision of services. This evolution of the Court's interpretation of Treaty provisions came about as the number of cases brought before it increased significantly in the services field. The Court underlined in its judgment that most violations to free provision of services were made not by discriminatory but through unduly restrictive national regulations. The new interpretation of the Court is the following: "[. . .] Article [56] of the Treaty requires not only the elimination of all discrimination against a person providing services on the ground of its nationality but also the abolition of any restriction, even if it applies without distinction to national providers of services and to those of other Member States, when it is liable to prohibit or otherwise impede the activities of a provider of services established in another Member State where it lawfully provides similar services".[46]

Recent judgments rendered in the services field show that the ECJ typically proceeds in steps, applying different tests based either on discrimination, market access, additional cost or comparing the effect in law or in fact of national measures before it.[47]

The evolution of case law allowed several national regulations that were restrictive to free trade in services to be challenged, while also advancing various aspects relating to the freedom of establishment of service providers. However, to this day, the question of Treaty interpretation remains

---

45 Point 19 Opinion of the Advocate General 21 February 1991, Säger, 76/90, ECR. p. 4221.

46 Point 12 of the Säger case became a systematic opening in each case of the Court on services. Also used by the EFTA Court 12 December 2003, EFTA Surveillance Authority/Island, E-1/03, EFTA Court Report 2003, p. 143, point 28.

47 ECJ 8 September 2005, Mobistar, C-544/03 & 545/03, ECR. p. I-7723. Meulman, J. and de Waele, H., "A Retreat from Säger? Servicing or Fine-Tuning the Application of Article 49 EC", *LIEI*, 2006, p. 226.

salient: are they intended to liberalize intra-Community trade or rather intended more generally to encourage the unhindered pursuit of commerce in individual Member States?[48]

5.2.2.3.2 ECJ case law on services – the law of justification The Treaty of Rome allows Member States to justify restrictions (non-tariff barriers) to free movement in certain specified circumstances. These justifications are specific to each freedom, for "the freedom to provide services is one of the fundamental principles of the Treaty and may be restricted only by provisions which are justified by the general good and which are imposed on all persons *or* undertakings operating in the said State in so far as that interest is not safeguarded by the provisions to which the provider of the service is subject in the Member State of his establishment".[49] In addition, "such requirements must be objectively justified by the need to ensure that professional rules of conduct are complied with and that the interests which such rules are designed to safeguard are protected".[50]

The key balancing notion of proportionality has also been clarified by the ECJ through its rulings.[51] For example, the ECJ allowed for the maintenance of an important margin of appreciation for Member States when considering the proportionality of national measures targeted at public morality[52] or public health objectives.[53]

As noted earlier, the legal basis for doing so is Article 52 TFEU for the express and closed list of justifications for national measures caught by Article 56 TFEU. The three grounds are public policy, public security or public health, all of which can be maintained despite being subject to the scope of the prohibition arising from Article 56 TFEU. In addition to Treaty-based justification, an open list of justifications has been

---

[48] As noted in its introduction, AG Tesauro in his Opinion of 27 October 1993 in the case Hünermund, C-292/92, ECR. p. 6787.

[49] ECJ 17 December 1981, Webb, 279/80, ECR. p. 3305, point 17.

[50] ECJ 4 December 1986, Commission/France, 220/83, ECR. p. 3663, point 17. ECJ 8 September 2005, Mobistar, C-544/03 & 545/03, ECR. p. I-7723.

[51] Moitinho de Almeida, J.C., "La libre prestation de services dans la jurisprudence de la Cour de Justice des Communautés européennes", *Scritti in onore di Giuseppe Federico Mancini. Vol. II. Diritto dell'Unione europea*, Milan, Dott. A. Giuffrè Editore, 1998, p. 658. Opinion of Advocate General Poiares Maduro 13 July 2006, Ahokeinen & Leppik, C-434/04, points 23 to 26.

[52] ECJ 4 October 1991, Grogan, C-159/90, ECR. p. 4685, point 20, and ECJ 4 March 1994, Schindler C–275/92, ECR. p. 1039, point 61.

[53] Opinion of AG Bot 22 November 2007, Doulamis, C-446/05, points 108 and following.

developed by the ECJ as it builds up its case law on services.[54] Such justifications, labelled as "overriding reasons of public interest", include for example public morality, the protection of consumers and workers, intellectual property, the protection of national treasures with an artistic, historic or archeological value,[55] as well as the protection of fundamental human rights.

The Court explained that "national rules which are not applicable to services without discrimination as regards their origin are compatible with [EU] law only if they can be brought within the scope of an express exemption, such as that contained in Article [52] of the Treaty".[56] The ECJ further stated that "as a fundamental principle of the Treaty, the freedom to provide services may be limited only by rules which are justified by imperative reasons relating to the public interest and which apply to all persons or undertakings pursuing an activity in the State of destination, in so far as that interest is not protected by the rules to which the person providing the services is subject in the Member State in which he is established. In particular, those requirements must be objectively necessary in order to ensure compliance with professional rules and to guarantee the protection of the recipient of services and they must not exceed what is necessary to attain those objectives".[57]

The two lists of justifications (Treaty- and case law-based) do not apply to the same measures, as can be seen from ECJ case law. However, the open-ended nature of the list allows the Court to take into account new overriding reasons which Member States may deem necessary to introduce or maintain otherwise Treaty-incompatible measures in the services field.

5.2.3 Completing the Single Market for Services: Strategy for an Internal Market in Services and the Services Directive

By the end of the 20th century, numerous measures were already in place in the EU with a view to suppressing most of the major obstacles to the Internal Market in services. All economic integration instruments included in the Treaty of Rome were used to this effect; litigation on the basis of

[54] O'Leary, S. and Fernandez-Martin, J., "Judicially-created Exceptions to the Free Provision of Services", *European Business Law Review*, 2000, pp. 347–62.

[55] ECJ 3 February 1982, Seco, 62/81 & 63/81, ECR. p. 223; ECJ 27 March 1990, Rush Portuguesa, C–113/89, ECR. p. I-1417 and ECJ 18 March 1980, Coditel, 62/79, ECR. p. 881.

[56] ECJ 25 July 1991, Mediawet, 288/89, ECR. p. 4007, point 11 and ECJ 26 April 1988 Bond van Adverteerders 352/85 ECR 2085, at paragraphs 32 and 33.

[57] ECJ 21 February 1991, Säger, C-76/90, ECR. p. 4221, point 15.

negative integration clauses arbitrated before national courts and the ECJ[58] and an activist, pro-market opening, advocacy role of the European Commission both as guardian of the treaties and as the initiator of positive integration steps in the services field. The use of all the above instruments enabled the European project to reach a level of economic integration that is unprecedented in its breadth, greater than that achieved under any other regional grouping. However, all is not (or ever) finalized in the quest for EU market integration, as major obstacles continue to hamper the stated aim of taking full advantage of the European Internal Market for services.

5.2.3.1 From action plan to the Internal Market Strategy for Services

In 1996, following the forward dynamic spawned by the Spaak 2 and Cecchini Reports, the Commission produced a document on the untapped potential of services for the economies of the Member States and as a source of employment in Europe.[59] A year later, the Commission produced an action plan on the single market for the attention of the European Council.[60] This was followed in 1999 by the Strategy for the Internal Market, prepared for the European Parliament and the Council.[61] These documents, while less ambitious than the White Paper of 1985, paved the way for the adoption in 2000 by the European Council of the Lisbon Strategy with the fundamental aim to make "the European Union the most dynamic and competitive knowledge-based economy in the world".[62]

As part of the Lisbon Strategy, the Commission continued to explore the possibilities of using the full potential of the Internal Market in services by producing a specific Strategy for the Internal Market for

---

58 "It is clear from the jurisprudence of the Court that any measure liable to prohibit, impede or render less advantageous the supply or use of cross-border services or cross-border establishment within the EU could constitute a barrier. This report therefore includes examples of barriers which are not simply prohibitions, discriminations or conditions which are impossible to meet, but various types of requirements which, if applied to companies from other Member States, would undermine the freedoms to establish or provide services. Some barriers are due to complex, burdensome or non-transparent regulation or practices; most are just due to the wide divergence of national rules." COM (2002) 441 final 30 July 2002, *The State of the Internal Market for Services*, p. 13.

59 *Services: mode d'emploi* CSE (96) 6 final 27 November 1996.

60 Commission Communication, 4 June 1997 to the European Council – (Amsterdam).

61 COM (1999) 624, 24 November 1999.

62 European Council (Lisbon) – June 2000 and set as target date 2010 for its objective. For an evaluation of the Strategy, SEC (2010) 114 final, 2 February 2010.

Services.[63] The Strategy put the Internal Market back at the heart of the European project, emphasizing services trade most particularly, just prior to the major enlargement of the EU in 2004 and the tenth anniversary of the completion of the Internal Market in goods. The Lisbon Strategy features various steps aimed at boosting EU-wide competitiveness, among them the identification of obstacles to intra-EU trade to which Member States and civil society stakeholders could react.

The Commission's report of 2002 noted that "[t]he overall aim (of the report) is to describe the realities of the Internal Market as seen by providers and users of services. It does not at this stage seek to assess whether any individual barrier is justifiable or not. A wide range of difficulties was identified that both services providers and consumers were facing".

The services Strategy put aside, for the first time, the sector-specific approach and considered services globally and in an interconnected environment. It suggested the establishment of a common regulatory framework but with enough flexibility to consider new and innovative types of services as well.

This proposed regulatory framework was presented by the Commission to the European Parliament and the Council under the form of a draft Directive on services in the Internal Market.[64] For the first time, an annex was attached on an "Extended Impact Assessment",[65] which emphasized the benefits to be derived from greater intra-EU trade in services under the draft Directive. It would take two years to finalize the Directive which, in its final version, was more modest than foreseen under the original draft. However, the Directive is widely considered as landmark EU legislation.

5.2.3.2 The Services Directive

The aim of the draft Services Directive was to establish a regulatory framework that could tackle the obstacles to the free movement of services between Member States and offer a reliable environment for both service providers and the recipients of services (consumers). To this end, a draft

---

[63] COM (2000) 888 final 29 December 2000, *An Internal Market Strategy for Services*, COM (2002) 441 final 30 July 2002, *The State of the Internal Market for Services*, p. 13, which is the first stage of the Strategy.

[64] Commission – draft Directive to the EP and the Council on services in the Internal Market to be adopted following a co-decision COM (2004) 2 final 13 January 2004 – [SEC (2004) 21] influenced by general follow-up documents on the Strategy for the Internal Market COM (2003) 238 final 7 May 2003 and COM (2004) 22 final January 2004.

[65] *Extended Impact Assessment*, presented on the same day as the draft Directive, 13 January 2004, SEC (2004) 21.

framework Directive was prepared that initially covered all service sectors. In drafting the Directive, the European Commission took a pragmatic (if ambitious) approach, attempting in one single instrument to cover all services instead of adopting a set of instruments to cover each sector specifically.[66] The framework Directive aimed to create a dynamic environment to tackle the remaining obstacles to the free movement of services within the EU with a minimum of regulatory instruments (exercising so-called "regulatory or judicial economy").

The draft framework Directive for the most part codified ECJ case law on the free movement of services and included an important principle as a central rule, that of the country of origin.[67] This principle is supposed to create a dynamic for tackling the remaining obstacles in the service sector[68] but without the need to adopt European-wide harmonized rules, such that each country can keep its own domestic regulatory frameworks so long as they broadly approximate EU-wide aims. The Directive calls however for further collaboration in the field of consumer protection. In practice, the principle applies as follows: service providers comply with the regulatory requirements of their home state[69] applicable to the services they supply. The country of origin principle allows the provider to offer its services in other Member States without additional regulatory requirements.[70] The draft Directive nevertheless included some exceptions and temporary arrangements in this regard.[71]

The ECJ recognized quite early in its case law the principle of mutual recognition in the free provision of services.[72] According to this principle,

---

[66] The advantage of the framework Directive is underlined by the Commission, as it is in line with ECJ case law which is not sector-specific and also avoids over-regulation in the services field. Recital 7 of the Directive.

[67] Also called "automatic mutual recognition principle". De Witte, B., "Setting the Scene. How did Services get to *Bolkenstein* and Why?", *EUI Working Papers, Law* 2007/20, p. 8; Hatzopoulos, V., "Que reste-t-il de la directive sur les services?", *CDE*, 2007, no. 3/4, p. 303 and Micossi, S., "Fixing the Services Directive", *CEPS Policy Brief*, 2006, no. 100, p. 7.

[68] Those identified by the 2002 Report of the Commission and the case law of the ECJ.

[69] According the case law of the ECJ, it is the Member State where the services provider is established.

[70] The principle applies somewhat differently when the service activity is done under the freedom of establishment; indeed the draft Directive relies on the existence of a single contact point to facilitate establishment in other Member States.

[71] COM (2004) 2 final, p. 4, Articles 17, 18 and 19.

[72] Mutual recognition was also considered in the positive integration instruments on services, for example the Directives on insurance and banking both refer

the host country of the service provider should take into account the regulatory framework with which the services provider has already complied in its home country.[73] The approach taken by the ECJ has been to avoid instances where service providers would be subject to dual regulatory burdens in home and host country markets.[74] However, host countries can always request additional regulatory requirements if they are justified and applied in a proportional manner.

In 2006, following protracted discussions in the European Parliament and the Council, the European Commission drafted a second version of the Directive,[75] signed in December of the same year. The final version of the framework Directive was less ambitious and innovative compared with the original version.[76] The material scope of the Directive is for example much reduced and several sectors are now excluded, among them financial services, electronic communications, energy, social services, and gambling activities. The Directive does not replace Directives that apply to regulated services or certain specific services which are covered by separate (sector-specific) Directives.[77] The most important change was the removal of the country of origin principle, which made the draft framework Directive potentially dynamic according to the impact assessment. The final version of the framework Directive "establishes general provisions facilitating the exercise of the freedom of establishment for service providers and the free movement of services".[78] Therefore, the Directive does not harmonize national law but is an additional vehicle of negative integration. The purpose of the Directive is to further eliminate barriers to the freedom of establishment for service providers and the free movement of services between Member States. The Directive "directs" the Member States to "screen" their national legislation and remove obstacles to the freedom

---

to the system of "unique licence" delivered by the home country where the services provider has its residence. Peglow, K., "La libre prestation de services dans la directive 2006/123. Réflexion sur l'insertion de la directive dans le droit communautaire existant", *RTDE*, 2008, pp. 67–118.

[73] ECJ 18 January 1979, Van Wesemael, 110–111/78, ECR. p. 35.

[74] ECJ 11 December 2003, Schnitzer, C-215/01, ECR, 14847.

[75] COM (2006) 160 final, 4 April 2006.

[76] The legal basis of the framework Directive are Articles 52 and 64 TEUF.

[77] We can consider this as a *lex specialis* of the Services Directive, Directive 2005/36/EC on regulated services.

[78] Article 1, paragraph 1 of the Directive. With such a limited impact, certain authors even questioned the need to keep the framework Directive. Gareth, D., "The Services Directive: Extending the Country of Origin Principle, and Reforming Public Administration", *ELR*, 2007, p. 239.

of services.[79] Ultimately, the Services Directive calls for rationalization of regulation in the services field.

However, according to the Directive, the free movement of services can be subject to host country requirements when justified by public order, public health, public security or environmental protection considerations.[80] This closed list of justifications is for many observers the main innovation of the framework Directive as it reduces the possible scope of restrictive national measures on the free movement of services to four grounds and arguably suppresses the open list of justifications created by the ECJ through its case law through the overriding concept of "general interest".[81] This has led some observers to argue that the Directive has produced a deregulatory shift compared with the existing legal environment on services in the EU.[82]

The other aspects of the draft Services Directive, especially those calling for better administrative collaboration, were left untouched (Article 5), along with the single contact point (Article 6) or the right to information (Article 7).

Overall, the Services Directive signed in December 2006, without the overarching principle of the country of origin,' is significantly less ambitious than the dynamic instrument initially foreseen by the Commission to advance the Lisbon Strategy and achieve the removal of the remaining major obstacles to the free movement of services. However, if the ECJ revisits its case law on the justifications to restrictive national measures to services and does not accept any other justification beyond those listed in the Services Directive, we might see important changes in the European regulatory environment for services providers.

Despite the difficulties encountered in adopting the Services Directive, the European Commission put forward a new action plan to maintain forward advances in the functioning of the European Internal Market.[83] The action plan follows up on a study carried out in 2010 at the behest

---

79 Merteen, H., "A Comparison of the Services Directive with the Case Law of the Court of Justice: A Case Study", *Griffin's View*, 2006, 7, p. 141. http://papers.ssrn.com/sol3/papers.cfm?abstract_id=1537681.

80 Article 16, paragraph 3 of the Directive.

81 ECJ 3 October 2000, Corsten, C-58/98, ECR. p. 7919.

82 De Witte, B., "Setting the Scene. How did Services Get to Bolkenstein and Why?", *EUI WP*, Law 2007/20.

83 COM (2011) 206 final, 13 April 2011, Single Market Act, Twelve levers to boost growth and strengthen confidence, "Working together to create new growth", SEC (2011) 467 final and COM (2012) 573 final, 3 October 2012, Single Market Act II, Together for new growth.

of the President of the European Commission.[84] The study found that many obstacles continued to hamper the full realization of the benefits of the European Internal Market and cautioned that past achievements and the existing level of completion of the Internal Market should not be taken for granted. The study argued for the need to reboot the Internal Market.

The Commission put 50 proposals forward for debate. These were set out in a communication entitled "Towards a Single Market Act" in 2010. The public debate took place at European, national and local levels. There were more than 800 responses to the call for public consultations on the Single Market Act, reflecting the points of view of Member States, non-governmental organizations, social partners at national and European level, local and regional authorities, industrial and professional organizations, trade unions, businesses, consumer organizations, think tanks, academics and a number of individuals.

The consultations revealed high expectations from civil society, in terms of both the development of the Single Market's potential to foster growth and employment as well as its social dimension and the concomitant need to protect and preserve the adequate supply of public services. The Commission formalized the results of the consultation process through the Single European Act of 2011, which was followed by a second Act in 2012, both of which featured a number of actions directed towards the service sector.[85]

In conclusion, the EU still needs to make active use of both negative and positive integration instruments to reap the full benefits of the European Internal Market in services. Of central importance in this regard is the continued central influence that the European Commission continues to exercise in promoting new policy initiatives as well as the equally critical role played by the ECJ in interpreting primary and secondary EU law in the field of services.

---

84 The Monti Report: A New Strategy for the Internal Market, May 2010.

85 The key action foreseen by the first document is the revision of the legislation on the European standardisation system to extend it to services and make standardisation procedures more effective, efficient and inclusive. The document underlines also the necessity for a full and complete implementation of the Services Directive in all Member States including the establishment of Points of Single Contact as foreseen by the directive. The second document add another key action to support online services by making payment services in the EU more effective.

5.2.4 Services in the EU: From an Accessory Role to a Central Freedom

As noted above and throughout this section, the ECJ has proven central to the advancement of the European Internal Market in services through negative integration. However, judicial activism may not be enough to create a de-fragmented Internal Market in services. A general overview of the establishment of the Internal Market in services actually shows similar momentum to the construction of the Internal Market in goods, but two decades later in time. If one were to try to establish the steps for constructing the Internal Market in services following the characterization of "the Constitution of the Common Market Place" (for goods) put forward by Weiler (1999),[86] four distinct periods could be identified.

The first, "foundational", period for services is quite long, taking nearly two decades (from 1974 to 1990) and its central point was the interpretation of the Treaty of Rome as prohibiting discrimination in intra-EU trade in services and some sector-specific harmonization in the field via mutual recognition.

A second, shorter, period stretching from 1991 to 1999 saw significant judicial activism, starting with the Säger judgment. Worth noting is the similarity between this judgment and the foundational period identified for goods two decades before. While not bringing significant changes to the ECJ's interpretation of the negative integration clause, a third period saw a distinct rise in the action and visibility of the European legislator in the services field. This period culminated in the adoption of the Services Directive in 2006.

Since the Directive's adoption and the deadline for its transposition into domestic laws in 2009, a fourth and final period has seen a continued push for a deepening of the Internal Market in services as a core policy concern of the EU's integration agenda. The current period combines continued reliance on consolidated case law on services and a more widely regulated European environment which still faces many challenges due to the limits of the horizontal Directive and the difficulties encountered in its transposition.[87]

---

86 The evolution of the establishment of the Internal Market in services is done following the model drafted for goods by Weiler, J.H.H., "The Constitution of the Common Market Place: The Free Movement of Goods: Text and Context in the Evolution of the Free Movement of Goods", in Craig, P., and De Burca, G., éds., *The Evolution of EU Law*, Oxford, Oxford University Press, 1999, pp. 349–76.

87 The European Commission put in place an unprecedented monitoring to ensure the correct transposition of the Services Directive in all Member States by

The building of the European Internal Market for services is a work in progress that has been ongoing for six decades. This long march has required the constant involvement of the European institutions, Member States and economic agents as well as consumer organizations. The agenda for the completion of the Internal Market in services continues to progress thanks to the important set of legal sources now available at the EU level with the Treaty of Rome, the Services Directive, a number of sector-specific Directives and ECJ jurisprudence. Without this set of legal instruments and the constant interaction of relevant European institutions, it is doubtful that the EU's Internal Market for services could have deepened as much as it has.

5.3 THE EU'S EXTERNAL AGENDA IN SERVICES TRADE[88]

As the world's leading exporter of services, the EU assigns to services trade and investment liberalization a central place in its trade diplomacy. The aims the EU pursues with third parties in the services realm are of essence different and more recent than those enshrined in the EU's six-decade-old foundational Treaty. Indeed, while the Treaty of Rome laid down clear and ambitious aims for the Internal Market and intra-EU trade in services, the legal sources from which the EU derives its international negotiating agenda are more modest. The EU agenda on international trade in services also came later in time, and only gained significant traction once the broad contours of the EC-1992 Single Market objectives came into being, a process that coincided with the launch of the Uruguay Round negotiations on trade in services.[89]

The EU's approach in services trade has been, and remains, anchored in the pursuit of negotiating advances under the multilateral framework contained in the World Trade Organization's (WTO) General Agreement on

the end of 2009. However, despite the coordinated efforts, the task has proven very difficult as the Services Directive requested certain Member States to change not only their regulations on services but also to adapt their administrative procedures or organisation. Peglow, K., "La libre prestation de services dans la directive n°2006/123/CE. Réflexion sur l'insertion de la directive dans le droit communautaire existant", *RTDE*, 2008, pp. 67–118.

[88] By opposition to intra-EU trade, international trade in services covers all major trading relation of the EU with third countries (countries outside the EU).

[89] Eeckhout, P., "Constitutional Concepts for Free Trade in Services", in De Burca, G., and Scott, J., eds., *The EU and the WTO: Legal and Constitutional Issues*, Oxford, Hart Publishing, 2001, p. 212.

Trade in Services, a body of rules whose development the EU helped shape. While the EU continued to profess its faith in the WTO process, and in fact maintained a moratorium on participation in preferential trade liberalization initiatives in the early years of the Doha Development Agenda, the protracted stalemate in WTO talks since the mid-2000s has prompted the EU to respond to private sector pressure and engage in a large and growing network of bilateral, regional and, most recently, plurilateral initiatives aimed at WTO+ rule-making and market opening advances in the services field.[90]

5.3.1 The EU and the GATS

The EU's growing interest in services as an engine of growth and pro-competitive regulation and its decision to lend support to what remained primarily a US push to place services on the global trade agenda paralleled the rising tide of intra- and extra-EU services trade observed from the middle of the 1970s onwards. The American position found increasing (albeit uneven) resonance within the EU.[91] The then US Trade Representative (USTR), William Brock, advanced a two-pronged agenda, focusing in turn on the development of a body of multilateral provisions and an institutional framework to govern international services transactions, followed by a process aimed at securing the reduction or elimination of obstacles, both discriminatory and non-discriminatory, to international trade in services.[92] The American efforts proved successful

---

90 As we shall see throughout this part, the reasons, circumstances, timing and content of the EU's trade agreements vary a great deal and seem to concur with the findings of VanGrasstek, Craig, "The Political Economy of Services in Regional Trade Agreements", OECD Trade Policy Working Papers, 2011, 112, who speaks about the EU's trade agreements as "multifaceted undertakings".

91 In the USA, influential businessmen advocated the inclusion of services in the Trade Act of 1974. Feketekuty, G., *International Trade in Services: An Overview and Blueprint for Negotiations*, Cambridge, MA, An American Entreprise Institut/Ballinger Publication, 1988, appendix, pp. 300–01.

92 Brock, W.E., "A Simple Plan for Negotiating on Trade in Services", *The World Economy*, 1982, 237–8, in Malmgren, H.B., "Negotiating International Rules for Trade in Services", *The World Economy*, 1985, 8, 19 and Gibbs, M., and Mashayekhi, M., "Services: Cooperation for Development", *Journal of World Trade Law*, 1988, 22, 86. Some authors contested this approach as unnecessary; according to them, services do not need a separate agreement since they were either embodied in goods or persons; Grubel, H.G., "All Traded Services are Embodied in Materials or People", *World Economy*, 1987, 3, 319 and Berr, C.J., and Reboud, L., "Les services", Flory, T., ed., *La Communauté européenne et le GATT. Évaluations des accords du cycle d'Uruguay*, Apogée, publication du centre de recherches européenne de l'Université Rennes I, 1995, p. 120.

as services were placed on the agenda of the GATT Ministerial meeting in 1984.[93]

The EU would ultimately join the US in advocating the inclusion of services in the multilateral negotiating agenda but with a number of specificities reflecting, *inter alia*, the mixed competence prevailing in services regulation between the Commission and the Member States, the still dominant presence of state-owned service providers in key service sectors (e.g. energy, telecommunications, postal services, air transport), the more defensive attitudes of Southern European Member States towards an ambitious liberalizing agenda, the lack of a clear intra-EU roadmap for full market integration in services (which would soon be articulated in the EC-1992 Single Market drive), as well as the calls for key sectors, particularly audiovisual and cultural industries, to be left outside the negotiations in light of their sensitive nature.[94]

Despite the strong reluctance of numerous developing countries, services were placed on the Uruguay Round's negotiating agenda, agreed by ministers in Punta del Este in September 1986,[95] and which called for the "progressive liberalization" and if possible abolition of non-tariff barriers inhibiting international trade in services.[96]

---

[93] Krommenacker, R.J., "Multilateral Services Negotiations: From Interest-Lateralism to Reasoned Multilateralism in the Context of Servicization", Petersmann, E.-U., and Hilf, M., eds., *The New GATT Round of Multilateral Trade Negotiations – Legal and Economic Problems*, Deventer, Kluwer, 1988, p. 457.

[94] This specificity of the EU position is still topical today and high on the agenda of any EU negotiations in the field of international trade in services.

[95] The Uruguay Round Ministerial Declaration [MIN(86)/6] at Punta del Este was a very carefully drafted declaration: "Negotiations in this area shall aim to establish a multilateral framework of principles and rules for trade in services, including elaboration of possible disciplines for individual sectors, with a view to expansion of such trade under conditions of transparency and progressive liberalization and as means of promoting economic growth of all trading partners and the development of developing countries. Such a framework shall respect the policy objectives of national laws and regulations applying to services and shall take into account the work of relevant international organizations. GATT procedures and practices shall apply to these negotiations. A Group of Negotiations on Services is established to deal with these matters. Participation in the negotiations under this Part of the Declaration will be open to the same countries as under Part I. GATT secretariat support will be provided, with technical support from other organizations as decided by the Group of Negotiations on Services."

[96] Petersmann, E.U., "The Transformation of the World Trading System through the 1994 Agreement Establishing the WTO", *European Journal of International Law*, 1995, 2, p. 200. The author lists the types of restrictions on trade in services that should be tackled, especially with regard to market access.

At the time of the Uruguay Round's launch, a number of scholars had suggested that the EU legal framework be used as a model for the progressive liberalization of trade in services.[97] However, it quickly became obvious that the objectives of the multilateral journey initiated in Punta del Este, which aimed at securing progressively freer trade and investment in services through periodic negotiating rounds, were significantly less ambitious than the EU's internal quest to integrate the markets of its Member States via a *sui generis* institutional and legal environment.[98]

The Uruguay Round negotiations in services proved challenging for the EU from the outset as it needed to clarify its own mandate. Indeed the Treaty of Rome included since its inception a legal basis for the negotiation of international trade agreements within the ambit of the EU's common commercial policy (CCP). However, the relevant chapter of the Treaty referred to trade in goods and not to services.[99] An opinion was requested from the European Court of Justice to establish the nature of the EU's competence in the services field and decide if the EU only (i.e. exclusive Community competence) or the EU and Member States (i.e. shared competence) should characterize the conduct of the negotiations.

In Opinion 1/94, the ECJ considered the definition of services being contemplated under the multilateral negotiations, which referred to four modes of supplying services. The ECJ established that "[a]s regards

Ehlermann, C.D., and Campogrande, G., "Rules on Services in the EEC: A Model for Negotiating World-Wide Rules", in Petersmann, E.-U., and Hilf, M., eds., *The New GATT Round of Multilateral Trade Negotiations – Legal and Economic Problems*, Deventer, Kluwer, 1988, pp. 481–98.

[97] Ehlermann and Campogrande (1988), op. cit, p. 484.

[98] We refer here to the unprecedented decision-making process of the EU (the use of qualified majority in the Council), as well as the judicial system presented in the Rome Treaty. We also have in mind the founding principles of EU law, i.e. direct effect (ECJ 5 February 1963, Van Gend en Loos, 26/62, ECR. p. 1) and supremacy (ECJ 15 July 1964, Costa v ENEL, 6/64, ECR. p. 585), which create a unique regional legal environment in the EU that knows no parallel at the multilateral level.

[99] Jacobs, F., "The Completion of the Internal Market v the Incomplete Common Commercial Policy", in Kostadinidis, S., ed., *The Legal Regulation of the EC's External Relations after the Completion of the Internal Market*, Aldershot, Dartmouth, 1996, pp. 3–18. Some authors have suggested the need for a flexible interpretation of this chapter of the Treaty of Rome since international trade is constantly evolving: Eeckhout, P., *The European Internal Market and International Trade: A Legal Analysis*, Oxford, European Community Law Series, 1994, p. 399 and Timmermans, C.W.A., "Common Commercial Policy (article 113 EEC) and the International Trade in Services", *Du droit international au droit de l'intégration. Liber Amicorum Pierre Pescatore*, Baden-Baden, Nomos Verlagsgesellschaft, 1987, p. 684.

cross-frontier supplies, the service is rendered by a supplier established in one country to a consumer residing in another. The supplier does not move to the consumer's country; nor, conversely, does the consumer move to the supplier's country. That situation is, therefore, not unlike trade in goods, which is unquestionably covered by the common commercial policy within the meaning of the Treaty". However, the ECJ noted that "[t]he same cannot be said of the other three modes of supplying services covered by the GATS, namely, consumption abroad, commercial presence and the presence of natural persons. . . [which] are not covered by the common commercial policy".[100] The Treaty of Rome Treaty was amended in the light of the ECJ's opinion and, since 1997, the CCP refers to trade in both goods and services.[101]

The Uruguay Round produced a services agreement – the GATS 1994 – that lies outside the scope of the GATT 1994. Presented in a separate, parallel, document, the GATS follows closely the structure of the original GATT but with several important distinctions uniquely tailored to meet the specificities of services trade. Negotiated in the heyday of the Washington consensus and of Francis Fukuyama's proclaimed "end of history", the GATS has a wide scope, with all services (including audiovisual services) covered by the final agreement.[102] Article 1 of the GATS states that "trade in services is defined by the supply of a service" through four modes of supply: cross-border supply; consumption abroad; commercial presence and movement of persons. However, the Agreement affirms the pragmatic principle of "progressive liberalization", affording scope for Parties to schedule specific commitments on national treatment and market access (subject to any scheduled limitations thereto) while also retaining considerable regulatory immunity in non-scheduled sectors, subsectors and/or modes of supply. The GATS further features a number of annexes dealing with sectoral (e.g. finance, telecommunications, maritime and air transport) or horizontal (labour mobility and MFN exemptions)

---

[100] ECJ 15 November 1994, Opinion 1/94, ECR. p. I-5267, points 44 and 46.

[101] The relevant article is 207 TFEU, the former Article 133 of the ECT, and whose paragraph 4 sets apart audiovisual and cultural services as well as social, education and health services.

[102] Article I, paragraph 3 (b), "except services supplied in the exercise of governmental authority". Feketekuty, G., "Assessing and Improving the Architecture of GATS", in Sauvé, P., and Stern, R., eds., *GATS 2000. New Directions in Service Trade Liberalization*, Washington, DC, Brookings Institution Press, 2000, p. 104.

specificities, all of which are subject to renegotiation through periodic multilateral negotiating rounds.[103]

GATS Article VII codifies the principle of mutual recognition. As noted earlier, such a principle was a centrally important means of promoting regulatory approximation in intra-EU trade in services. Entitled "Recognition", GATS Article VII encourages Parties to take into account the "education, experience, licenses, certification obtained from a particular country". Article XVI of the GATS establishes the cornerstone concept of "market access", once more a notion familiar within the intra-EU trade environment.[104] The GATS, alongside agricultural talks, foresaw a built-in negotiating mandate, such that services negotiations resumed prior to (and were subsequently incorporated into) the late 2001 launch of the Doha Development Agenda.

5.3.2 The EU and its Main Bilateral and Regional Partners in Services Trade

An important derivative consequence of the stalled Doha Round has been the surge in preferential agreements of a bilateral and regional (and often trans-regional, such as the Trans-Pacific Partnership currently under negotiation) nature, most of which now routinely extend to services. At the end of 2012, some 103 services-related PTAs had been notified to the WTO. The above trend is one in which the EU has been particularly active around the globe in recent years. In pursuing services liberalization along preferential lines, the EU has had several key policy motivations.

One important subset of agreements can be categorized as either precursors to EU accession or as responses to neighbourhood policy impulses. To varying degrees, such agreements help EU trading partners to converge towards the "*acquis communautaire*", prompting them to embed EU-

---

103 The architecture was considered by some scholars as "à la carte" and potentially less effective. Sauvé, P., "Regional *versus* Multilateral Approaches to Services and Investment Liberalization: Anything to Worry about?" *Regionalism and Multilateralism after the Uruguay Round*, 1997, 429.

104 Some scholars have underlined that for the first time a multilateral trade agreement targets more than discriminatory obstacles to trade but have also regretted the lack of definition of the concept of market access. Hoekman, B., "Services and Intellectual Property Rights", Collins, S., and Bosworth, B., eds., *The New GATT. Implications for the US*, Washington DC, The Brookings Institution, 1994, pp. 85 and 89. The concept of market access was considered in the litigation on gambling WT/DS285; cf. comments of the litigation "Gambling – with Regulation and Market Access in the GATS", *Legal Issues of Economic Integration*, 2005, pp. 231–4.

compatible or proximate features in domestic laws and regulations. In the context, talks regarding the creation of so-called Association Agreements of which Deep and Comprehensive Free Trade Areas (DCFTA) are invariably important constituent parts and which typically extend to services trade have been initiated with a diverse set of actors in the EU's immediate periphery. This includes Ukraine, with whom the EU concluded an agreement in 2012 which has yet to enter into force, as well as ongoing talks with Morocco, Moldova, as well as with three countries in the South Caucasus region – Armenia, Georgia and Azerbaijan (the latter as a non-WTO Member).

A second impulse guiding the selection of partners with whom the EU has entered into PTAs extending to services relates to the policy aim of neutralizing the preferences granted to the EU's major trading partners and competitors, particularly the United States. Agreements fitting this pattern, almost invariably negotiated or concluded *after* the completion of a PTA between the United States and key EU trading partners, respond to EU business interests in enjoying the same degree of preferential access afforded to US firms in third country markets. Agreements of this type include those signed with Mexico (concluded in 1997 in the wake of the North American Free Trade Agreement (NAFTA) of 1994 but whose generally modest provisions and commitments in the services field were added in 2001 and are arguably still in need of a major qualitative upgrade); Chile,[105] a considerably more ambitious and innovative agreement in the services field which entered into force in 2003, fresh on the heels of the US-Chile FTA concluded in 2002; as well as with South Korea, the first of a newer generation of comprehensive EU PTAs with extensive disciplines and provisions on services trade and investment which was negotiated in parallel to the US-Korea FTA but which actually entered into force before the latter agreement in July 2011.

Of the three bilateral PTAs with putatively preference-neutralizing aims, the agreement with South Korea is arguably the most important, targeting a range of sophisticated services in a country that is the EU's sixth most important trading partner and for whom the EU represents the fourth most important export market.[106]

In 2012, the EU also completed negotiations on an FTA with the Andean countries of Peru and Colombia, both of whom had previously

---

[105] The text of the agreement can be found at: http://eurlex.europa.eu/LexUriServ/LexUriServ.do?uri=OJ:L:2002:352:0003:1439:EN:PDF.

[106] The text of the FTA can be found at: http://eur-lex.europa.eu/JOHtml.do?uri=OJ:L:2011:127:SOM:EN:HTML.

signed FTAs with the United States which came into force in 2009 and 2011 respectively. Finally, in the wake of a failed attempt at negotiating a bloc-to-bloc agreement with the ten-country Association of South East Asian Nations (ASEAN) grouping, the negotiation of which was halted in March 2009, the EU embarked on a series of bilateral negotiations with three ASEAN Member States – Malaysia, Singapore and Vietnam. In December 2012, the EU completed negotiations with Singapore on an FTA featuring an ambitious services chapter (which can once again be seen as neutralizing the preferences granted by Singapore to the United States in an FTA that entered into force in 2004). The EU-Singapore FTA has yet to enter into force. Meanwhile, FTA negotiations are proceeding with both Malaysia and Vietnam.

On the bilateral front, the EU has also been negotiating – but has yet to conclude talks – with a number of major trading partners. These include Canada, with whom the EU is close to concluding a Comprehensive Economic and Trade Agreement (CETA) whose negotiation was launched in May 2009[107] and which promises several novel advances in the EU's treatment of services and investment in PTAs, notably the first ever adoption of a negative list approach to market opening in services markets (in respect of both cross-border trade and investment in services). The EU is Canada's second largest trading partner while Canada is the EU's eleventh biggest trading partner.

A second pending PTA of importance in the services field is that which the EU has been negotiating, so far inconclusively, with India since 2007. Finally, the EU has recently launched negotiations with the United States on what would represent, if successfully concluded, its most ambitious ever bilateral PTA. Services trade and the quest for trade- and investment-facilitating regulatory convergence and cooperation are at the core of the proposed Transatlantic Trade and Investment Partnership (TTIP) talks that got under way in July 2013 among the world's two dominant forces in services trade.[108]

The quest to deepen bilateral trade relations with the United States

---

[107] Joint Report on the EU and Canada Scoping Exercise, 2009, http://trade.ec.europa.eu/doclib/docs/2009/march/tradoc_142470.pdf. Biuković, L., and Mathis, J., "Enhanced Regulatory Cooperation in the Canada: EU Comprehensive Trade Agreement", *Legal Issues of Economic Integration*, 2012, 1, pp. 1–2 and more preciously on services in the CETA, J. Anthony VanDuzer, "A Critical Look at the Prospects for Robust Rules for Services in Preferential Trading Agreements", *Legal Issues of Economic Integration*, 2012, 1, pp. 29–49.

[108] For more data: http://ec.europa.eu/trade/policy/countries-and-regions/countries/united-states/.

dates back to the 1990s when, parallel to the conclusion of the Uruguay Round and the entering into force of the GATS and the NAFTA, the EU and the US decided in 1995 to launch the New Transatlantic Agenda (NTA). The NTA's main objective was the creation of a New Transatlantic Marketplace (NTMA) whose core focus would be to tackle trade-inhibiting non-tariff barriers and to promote the liberalization of services trade on the basis of the home country principle. Such a non-legally binding agenda progressed slowly and the ambitious NTMA objective was eventually shelved, giving way to the Transatlantic Dialogue focused on regulatory dialogue and the quest for mutual recognition agreements in the goods trade area.

The Doha Round stalemate has arguably revived interest in renewed transatlantic trade talks. At the end of 2011, a High Level Working Group on Jobs and Growth was jointly established by the EU's Trade Commissioner and the Office of the USTR, whose final report was issued in early 2013,[109] calling for a re-launch of transatlantic trade discussions and the negotiation of a comprehensive, legally binding, agreement on trade and investment issues[110] for which the European Commission secured a negotiating mandate from the European Council in June 2013.[111]

A third set of PTAs covering services that the EU has been involved with has sought to achieve economies of scale in rule-making and market opening through negotiations conducted on a trans-regional, bloc-to-bloc, basis. Such a Strategy, pursued to date with ASEAN, the member countries of the Common Market of the South (MERCOSUR) and Central America (via the EU-Central America FTA) has generated mixed results. As noted earlier, faced with a regional grouping characterized by a marked diversity of income levels and implementation capacities,[112] the EU dropped the idea of a bloc-to-bloc compact with ASEAN in 2009 in favour of a series of bilateral PTAs with selected ASEAN Member States, of which only one (Singapore) has been concluded to date.

Negotiations with the Member States of MERCOSUR, which were

---

109 The interim report can be found at: http://trade.ec.europa.eu/doclib/docs/2012/june/tradoc_149557.pdf. The final report can be found at: http://trade.ec.europa.eu/doclib/docs/2013/february/tradoc_150519.pdf.

110 An independent economic impact assessment of the TTIP was also carried out and presented in 2013: http://trade.ec.europa.eu/doclib/docs/2013/march/tradoc_150737.pdf.

111 For information on the negotiation guidelines: http://europa.eu/rapid/press-release_IP-13-548_en.htm.

112 ASEAN is characterized by extreme gaps in per capita income levels, a 45 to 1 ratio (in PPP terms) between Singapore, the regional grouping's richest member state, than in Myanmar, its poorest.

launched as far back as 1999 and which resumed in 2010 after a three-year hiatus, have encountered recurring challenges since their inception, owing largely to unbridgeable divides on issues linked to agricultural trade. To date, the FTA agreed in June 2012 (but not yet implemented) between the EU and the member countries of the Central American Common Market has been the only successful bloc-to-bloc agreement the EU has completed. Interestingly, the latter agreement came in the aftermath of the FTA concluded in 2004 between the five members of the Central American Common Market, the Dominican Republic and the United States (CAFTA-DR), such that beyond the objective of negotiating on a bloc-to-bloc basis, preference neutralization imperatives could also be argued to lie behind the EU's negotiating strategy in Central America.

A fourth and final set of PTAs addressing services that have been entered into or pursued by the EU relates to a series of negotiations the EU has had to initiate in the wake of an adverse ruling regarding the WTO (in)compatibility of its non-reciprocal trade relationship with countries from the African-Caribbean-Pacific (ACP) grouping. Such a ruling by the WTO's Dispute Settlement Body prompted the EU to pursue a series of reciprocal Economic Partnership Agreements with seven regional groupings of ACP countries – five in Africa, one in the Pacific and one in the Caribbean.

The 2008 CARIFORUM[113]-EU EPA[114] is the only comprehensive agreement featuring services and investment disciplines to have been concluded with ACP countries to date.[115] The CARIFORUM-EU EPA

---

113 Antigua and Barbuda, Bahamas, Barbados, Belize, Dominica, Dominican Republic, Grenada, Guyana, Haiti, Jamaica, St Lucia, St Vincent and the Grenadines, St Kitts and Nevis, Suriname, Trinidad and Tobago.

114 The text of the EPA can be found at: http://eur-lex.europa.eu/LexUriServ/LexUriServ.do?uri=OJ:L:2008:289:0003:1955:EN:PDF.

115 A number of factors may be seen as explaining why, among all ACP regional groupings, the CARIFORUM countries were both willing and able to conclude a comprehensive EPA with the EU. Chief among these were the strong commitment manifested in negotiating an EPA by the region's political leadership and the high level of technical preparation on offer in the region, honed largely in the context of the failed Free Trade Area of the Americas (FTAA) negotiations. A complex set of dynamics served to reinforce such a commitment. There was, first, the region's desire to bind existing levels of access to the EU market and to preclude the possibility that such preferential access become the target of WTO dispute settlement procedures. Second, the region deliberately sought to expand its access to the EC's lucrative services market. Third, the region needed to diversify its export base and derive higher value from its exports in the face of the combined effects of preference erosion and the decline in EC agricultural support policies for Caribbean producers of bananas and sugar. Fourth, given

marked a new sort of PTA as both sides agreed to open their markets but in an asymmetric manner, taking into account marked differences in economic development levels between the Parties.[116] The agreement features a number of novel advances in the services field, notably in its treatment of labour mobility, its detailed provisions on tourism services (including competition-related provisions to be applied in the sector), as well as significant doses of aid for trade linked to implementation priorities of the CARIFORUM Parties.[117]

---

that the process of intra-Caribbean regional integration was considered by many as suboptimal and suffering from an implementation deficit, the EPA's emphasis on regional groupings was seen as offering a desirable boost to the CARIFORUM integration process. Fifth, by supporting the creation and/or strengthening of regional regimes in a number of disciplines such as, *inter alia*, competition policy, government procurement, services and investment, the EPA came to be seen as offering a tool with which to advance CARIFORUM competitiveness, promote productive capacity and innovation in new products and production systems. Sixth, the region as a whole bought into the EPA's "signalling" properties, viewing it as a powerful means to reassure foreign investors and development partners over the region's commitment to continued economic reforms. Another factor that facilitated the conclusion of a comprehensive EPA was that the negotiations pitted two partners that had both reached an advanced stage in their own internal process of regional integration, including in terms of the requisite machinery of regional inter-governmental cooperation. In addition, CARIFORUM was not as troubled as other ACP regions by the problem of overlapping regionalism, in which member countries are part of different integration groupings. CARIFORUM's capacity to negotiate a comprehensive EPA was furthermore facilitated by the fact that the region had already acquired significant experience in negotiating trade issues in several negotiating fora. Within the CARICOM grouping, the negotiation of the Single Market helped to identify barriers to internal trade as well as highlight the sectors with the greatest export potential. Hence, CARICOM Members had a head start in identifying their key negotiating priorities, both offensive and defensive. Likewise, the negotiation of the CARICOM-Dominican Republic FTA provided further insights on the level of existing barriers to trade within the CARIFORUM region and clear indications of what the future liberalization agenda should look like within the sub-region. All of these above processes, together with experience gained in multilateral negotiations at the WTO, contributed to improving the quality of the region's negotiating skills and boosted the region's comfort level in dealing with many of the policy areas, old and new, that would become subject to EPA negotiations.

116 Zampetti, A.B., and Lodge, J., eds., *The CARIFORUM-EU Economic Partnership. A Practitioner's Analysis*, New York, Kluwer, 2011.

117 Sauvé, P., and Ward, N., "The EC-CARIFORUM EPA: Assessing the Outcome on Services and Investment", European Center for International Political Economy (ECIPE), 2009.

5.3.3 The EU and the Plurilateral Negotiations on Services

The lack of forward movement in the Doha Round and increasing frustration over the quest for an explicit multilateral consensus in the WTO have recently prompted a number of countries, as well as the EU, to advocate an agenda of "progressive liberalization" of services trade outside the GATS framework.

In early 2012, a group of WTO Members dubbed the "Really Good Friends of Services"[118] agreed to launch a plurilateral negotiation on services.[119] The main idea behind the latter initiative is to (re)create a dynamic in the centrally important and vibrant field of services and achieve a critical mass of participants and trade coverage sufficient for the resulting negotiations to be ultimately embedded within the WTO and its benefits extended to all WTO Members on an MFN basis.

As the world's two leading services exporters, the US and the EU can expect to reap the largest gains from a possible plurilateral agreement[120] which, because of its perceived exclusionary, club-like, nature, has been roundly criticized within emerging country circles.[121]

The EU has tried to strike a more open stance on plurilateral negotiations, encouraging broad participation in the talks and the pursuit of a GATS-compatible set of rules so as to facilitate the agreement's future WTO-anchoring. In so doing, the EU showed caution in not being seen as contributing to the further undermining of the Doha Round by participating in the plurilateral initiative.[122] Rebranded TISA (or the Trade in

---

[118] Australia, Canada, Chile, Colombia, Costa Rica (joined end of 2012), European Union, Hong Kong, Iceland, Israel (joined end of 2012), Japan, Mexico, New Zealand, Norway, Panama (joined end of 2012), Pakistan, Peru (joined end of 2012), Singapore (left the group in July 2012), South Korea, Switzerland, Taiwan, Turkey (joined end of 2012) and the United States.

[119] Also known as "new type of services agreement"; Vastine, J.R., "A New Form of Services Trade Agreement Moving Ahead in Geneva: The International Services Agreement", *Economic Policy Vignette, 2012–11–04*, Center for Business and Public Policy, McDonough School of Business, Georgetown University, 9 September 2012, http://www.gcbpp.org/files/EPV/Vastine_ISA_11042012.pdf.

[120] Hufbauer, G.C., Jensen, J.B., and Stephenson, S., "Framework for the International Services Agreement", Final Draft, Washington, DC, Peterson Institute for International Economics, 24 February, 2012, 22.

[121] Devarakonda, R.K., "Tale of Two Approaches: The WTO Torn Asunder", *Ibsanews*, 2012, http://www.ibsanews.com/tale-of-two-approaches-the-wto-torn-asunder/.

[122] Therefore the "multilateralization" of the ISA is ultimately the way forward according to the EU.

Services Agreement), the plurilateral agreement's negotiating process was formally launched in the spring of 2013.

The European Commission turned to the European Council for a negotiating mandate. The latter was granted in March 2013. The EU continues to underline the importance of persuading major non-participant countries such as Brazil, China, India but also ASEAN countries to eventually join the plurilateral negotiations (through the inclusion of a TISA accession clause). The EU's position also advocates new and improved market access. Another major concern of the EU is to multilateralize TISA; therefore the core concepts, definitions as well as the overall negotiating architecture of the GATS should be preserved in TISA, while deepening (GATS+) commitments and advancing new rules for services trade in the digital age.[123] The EU also decided to carry out a Trade Sustainability Impact Assessment of TISA and in June 2013 the European Commission launched a public dialogue on TISA to solicit private, academic and other non-governmental views on the proposed agreement.[124]

For the EU, the success of the plurilateral negotiations means preserving the WTO *acquis*[125] while progressing both the liberalization commitments of Parties, including in sectors not yet subject to GATS commitments.[126]

5.4 CONCLUDING REMARKS

While the EU is the world's leading actor in the field of international trade in services, advances in the governance of services trade have been significantly greater on the internal EU front than in the Union's trade relations with third countries. This is to be expected given the nature of the European integration process and its stated aim of achieving a single market for services characterized by the deepest level of regulatory con-

---

[123] "Negotiations for a Plurilateral Agreement on Trade in Services", European Commission, MEMO/12/107, 15 February 2013, http://trade.ec.europa.eu/doclib/docs/2013/february/tradoc_150552.pdf.

[124] The European Commission calls the ISA the Trade in Services Agreement (TiSA), http://trade.ec.europa.eu/doclib/docs/2013/june/tradoc_151374.pdf.

[125] Chambovey, D., "Swiss Negotiator: Regional Trade Deals are Good for Multilateralism", *Euractiv*, 2012, October, http://www.euractiv.com/special report-free-trade-growth/swiss-negotiator-regional-trade-interview-515255.

[126] For a fuller discussion of TISA and its prospects, see Sauvé, P. (2013), "A Plurilateral Agenda for Services? Assessing the Case for a Trade in Services Agreement (TISA)", NCCR-Trade Working Paper No. 2013/29, (May), Bern: World Trade Institute. Available at http://www.nccr-trade.org/fileadmin/user_upload/nccr-trade.ch/wp2/publications/TISA_P_Sauve.pdf.

vergence and approximation on offer in any of the world's major regional groupings. This chapter has thus naturally drawn attention to differences in the legal sources, instruments, institutional settings and the strategic approaches to intra- and extra-EU trade in services.

Ever since the entry into force of the 1957 Treaty of Rome, the EU has developed an increasingly complete arsenal of legal rules, tools and institutional means to advance the agenda of services liberalization and market integration within the EU, guided by the ultimate aim of creating an Internal Market for services. All of the legal instruments available under the Treaty of Rome, from the standstill clause to negative and positive integration clauses, were and remain necessary to liberalize intra-EU trade in services and establish an internal services market. Equally important has been and remains the active role of key institutions such as the European Commission, which has advanced a set of Directives to prise open service markets in services, and the ECJ, whose critically central task has been to interpret negative integration clauses and ensure compliance with relevant EU law.

On the world stage, originally, the EU relied on the multilateral framework of the GATT/WTO, to liberalize international trade in services, but recently the EU decided to explore other means to advance its agenda despite the stalled multilateral discussions. Hence, the EU is using several tools in bilateral, interregional relations to create the most adequate agreement with its partner. Depending on the historical links between the EU and its trading partner, the partner economic capacities, the trade agenda in discussion, the EU deploys an impressive set of agreements and chose with care the framework that it agrees with each of its partner.

The latest developments on the agenda of the EU in the field of international trade in services are quite unprecedented. Mid 2013, the EU launched negotiations for a very ambitious and unparalleled FTA with its most important trading partner the USA. At the same time, alongside the USA, the EU is actively participating to the informal plurilateral discussions to create a new and more ambitious trade agreement on services outside of the WTO and hence advance the agenda of progressive trade liberalization in services on the global stage.

These recent developments shade light on the EU as an ambitious and quite unique trade partner in the field of services. The EU agenda for liberalization is clear but not at any price, several parallel objectives are also pushed but the EU during these new negotiations, like safeguarding its norms, standards and EU wide regulations as well as keeping its central priority getting back ultimately in the dynamic of multitaleral trade negotiations within the WTO.

6. Services preferences in Africa: perspectives and challenges

Pierre Sauvé and Natasha Ward

6.1 INTRODUCTION

The world has witnessed a fevered push towards the preferential liberalization of trade and investment over the past two decades. Since the advent in 1994 of the WTO's General Agreement on Trade in Services (and in a few instances before it), the above push typically extends to trade in services.[1] The focus on services has come in light of increasing recognition both of their rising salience in world trade and investment and, most importantly, of the central influence that an efficient service infrastructure can exert on economy-wide performance.

If there was one region of the developing world where a focus on services as a means to lower punitively high trade costs, enhance the efficiency of resource use in upstream and downstream sectors, from extractive industries to agriculture, fisheries, manufacturing and other service sectors, and exploit new sources of comparative advantage, especially in labor-intensive services, it should be Africa. Yet the continent, North and South of the Sahara, has to date (and with few exceptions) largely eschewed *negotiated* market opening and rule-making in services trade and investment.

The African continent is indeed a reluctant latecomer to negotiations aimed at the progressive liberalization of trade and investment in services, a trend that sets it apart from most other regions of the developing world that have long chosen to anchor domestic reform efforts in legally binding commitments under international trade agreements. They have typically done so with a view to affording greater predictability to ongoing reforms and buttressing investment climates.

This chapter takes stock of the state of play of preferential services

[1] See Chapter 1 by Roy and Chapter 10 by Sauvé and Shingal for a discussion of recent trends in service sector PTAs.

trade and investment negotiations in Africa. The chapter is structured as follows. Section 6.2 explores the factors that lie behind the reluctance of African governments to bind service sector policy under international treaties. Section 6.3 chronicles several ongoing initiatives aimed at deepening intra-regional trade and investment among the eight regional economic cooperation areas (RECs) found on the continent. The analysis on offer reveals a starkly uneven pace of negotiating advances and policy implementation. Much, indeed, remains to be done to ensure that the ambitious blueprints for deepened integration across goods, services, investment and labor markets mutate from lofty political intent to concrete implementation. Section 6.4 shifts the focus to external liberalization efforts engaging Africa with the rest of the world in services trade. By far the most important ongoing initiative is the series of negotiations under way with the European Community (EC) with a view to concluding WTO-compatible Economic Partnership Agreements (EPAs) featuring comprehensive (and potentially WTO+) disciplines on services trade and investment. Section 6.5 devotes particular attention to the EC-CARIFORUM EPA, the only negotiation between EC and ACP member states to have produced disciplines on services trade and investment to date. The chapter draws attention to several novel features of the latter agreement and discusses the possible implications of such a precedent for Africa's ongoing processes of integration in services markets at both the intra- and extra-regional levels. Section 6.6 offers a broader discussion of a range of policy challenges confronting African governments in designing development-enhancing strategies of engagement in services trade negotiations. In particular, the section suggests a number of options worthy of consideration in pursuing more comprehensive negotiating agendas, notably in light of the EC-CARIFORUM precedent and the likely need for adaptation flowing from a number of contextual, on the ground, considerations specific to the African continent. The section also draws attention to the need for African governments to pay special attention to the timing and sequencing of their market opening strategies in services and to be clear on how best to articulate and leverage the interplay between internal and external liberalization processes in services markets. Section 6.7 offers a few concluding remarks.

6.2 A MARKED RELUCTANCE TO COMMIT TO NEGOTIATED MARKET OPENING

Until very recently, African countries have shown a marked reluctance to incorporate provisions that liberalize or create disciplines for trade and investment in services in their regional integration arrangements. The vast majority of preferential compacts to which countries in the region are Parties do not contain provisions on trade in services. However, recent developments suggest that there has been some evolution of thought on the value of negotiating services pacts, at least within the intra-regional context.

While there has been progress in liberalizing some elements of services trade in the intra-regional context, for the most part, such market-opening continues to be driven primarily by autonomous decisions at the national level. Resistance to incorporating comprehensive services commitments and rules into PTAs has been most evident in agreements negotiated with developed countries. This is most vividly the case for ongoing negotiations between the EC and its African ACP partner countries, none of whom have to date reached agreement on a comprehensive economic partnership agreement extending to services trade and investment.

The reluctance depicted above reflects a number of defensive concerns common to countries beyond the African theatre but which have gained important policy traction throughout the continent. These include a fear that services trade liberalization may deprive African governments of needed policy space to incubate nascent service industries and the required freedom to regulate services markets in the public interest; recurring (and legitimate) concerns over the inadequacy of existing regulatory frameworks in implementing entry- and competition-promoting liberalization commitments; as well as a more general sense that the preconditions for facilitating increased trade in services have in many African economies yet to be put in place (Hoekman and Mattoo 2011).

Moreover, where services provisions do exist in preferential trade agreements (PTAs), the dominant pattern is for Parties to go no further than to reaffirm the level of commitments made under the GATS, with little or no additional disciplines or rules elaborated at the PTA level (see Table 6.1). With the notable exception of the Morocco-United States Free Trade Agreement of 2004 (which entered into force on 1 January 2006) featuring comprehensive, NAFTA-type, chapters on cross-border trade and investment in services,[2] the above pattern has obtained regardless of whether or not the PTAs in question involve Sub-Saharan or Northern African countries.

Among other reasons fuelling Africa's high level of policy precaution towards services trade – once again not unique to the continent but especially salient given the limited range of offensive export interests that

---

[2] See http://www.ustr.gov/trade-agreements/free-trade-agreements/morocco-fta.

Table 6.1 Main features of services liberalization and disciplines in African PTAs

Reaffirmation of GATS Commitments	Commitment to Future Liberalization	Provisions on Right of Residence and Right of Establishment	Liberalization Commitments and New Disciplines
SADC*	EC–Central African Interim EPA	ECOWAS	US–Morocco
SACU–EFTA	EC–EAC Interim EPA	EAC	EAC
Morocco–Turkey	EC–ESA Interim EPA		
Morocco–EC	EC–SADC Interim EPA		
Egypt–EFTA	SADC–EAC–COMESA Tripartite FTA		
Egypt–Turkey			
South Africa–EC*			
COMESA *			
Tunisia–EFTA			

Note: * Also commits to future liberalization.

characterize many countries in the region – is the fact that the key motivation of reciprocal access that pervades trade in goods negotiations appears less compelling for trade in services. Though there is a wealth of literature suggesting why governments may actively seek trade negotiations to improve their terms of trade, implement reforms that are opposed by strong domestic interests, and use international commitments to lock-in recent or foreseen policy reforms, in practice such rationales all seem to be less persuasive for services.[3]

The very structure of many African economies, largely attuned to agricultural and industrial activities and with generally weaker, more informal, tertiary activities, may prompt governments to believe that there is little to gain from making concessions in services. This may be particularly the case where domestic service suppliers are small and/or weakly competitive. In a number of sub-regions of the continent, there may be the added political dimension that only a narrow subset of larger regional PTA partners might be in a position to take advantage of a services pact. For example, within the Southern Africa Development Community (SADC), South Africa is widely seen as the country with the most to gain

[3] For a fuller discussion of the limits of reciprocal bargaining in services trade, see Hoekman and Messerlin (2000).

from regional services liberalization. The same logic extends to Nigeria within the Economic Community of Western African States (ECOWAS) or to Kenya within the East African Community (EAC). Concerns over the ability of the domestic service-providing firms to compete regionally, let alone globally, typically underlie such fears.

The relatively smaller share of the tertiary sector in many African economies tends as well to result in services being assigned a lower priority than goods in trade policy formulation. Continued high dependence on agriculture and various extractive industries means that services do not feature prominently in many African countries' export, trade or industrial policies. Such a policy bias tends to be largely replicated at the regional level.

The above should not be read as intimating that African policy-makers are oblivious to the benefits of service sector reforms. The fact that unilateralism has been (and remains) the policy option of choice in many African countries services markets supports the above claim. Moreover, Sub-Saharan Africa (AFR) is not on the whole the region of the world that maintains the highest overall level of restrictions on services trade. Key service sectors are less contestable in much of the Middle East and North Africa (PAFTA), South Asia (SAR), and East Asia and the Pacific (EAP).

Still, one is left with a sense, epitomized in the current EPA imbroglio with the EC over the fate of Economic Partnership Agreements (EPAs), that engagement in services negotiations is not widely considered as a priority means of anchoring domestic reforms in services markets. Autonomous reforms are preferred as they are seen as reducing the need for reciprocity-driven negotiations. Engaging in deeper regulatory cooperation is another avenue that is being explored by African policy-makers. Promoting regulatory convergence and, where feasible, policy harmonization, has notably been explored through the establishment of various land transport corridors given the sector's central impact on trade facilitation and its strong links to agriculture, mining and manufacturing. However, neither of the above approaches – unilateralism and non-binding regulatory convergence – is devoid of pitfalls. Autonomous reforms may help address issues facing established service providers (both domestic and foreign), but will do little in expanding markets or tackling impediments abroad. For their part, gains from closer regulatory cooperation will typically depend heavily on the willingness (and capacity) of partners to implement promised reforms. The gains from services liberalization typically need to rest on concurrent investments in strengthening regulatory regimes and institutions so as to ensure that the market generates outcomes which support competition, tackle market failures in an economically efficient manner while also addressing non-trade objectives such as social equity. Concerns over the adequacy of many African countries' regulatory regimes and the ability to regulate contestable services markets clearly constrain effective participation in services negotiations (Brenton et al. 2010). Indeed, the appetite for services liberalization faces acute human resource, technical, institutional and financial constraints in many parts of the continent, particularly so in least-developed countries.

The fact that Africa currently collectively accounts for less than 3% of world commercial service exports and, more significant still, that 33 of the world's 49 least developed countries (LDCs) are found on the continent, clearly goes some way to explaining the generally low level of appetite for – and defensive posture towards – services negotiations. To some degree, such policy precaution reflects the limited pressure that many African governments have faced at the negotiating table. This is particularly the case at the multilateral level, where notions of a "round for free" or the working assumption that LDCs need not make new or improved commitments in services under the WTO's Doha Development Agenda (DDA), explains – indeed almost justifies – why Africa stands out as the region with the greatest revealed preference for maintaining a large wedge between domestically decreed (i.e. applied regulations) and internationally bound polices in services trade and for refusing to improve on its Uruguay Round commitments in the DDA.

The above (arguably perverse) negotiating incentives, and the putative development assumptions on which they rest, require greater critical scrutiny; all the more so when one considers that the development prospects of low-income countries, a majority of which are found on the African continent, can hardly be best served by maintaining the highest aggregate and sector-specific levels of trade and investment restrictiveness in key service sectors.

A final factor at play may be the low(er) level of engagement of the African business community. To some extent, this mirrors the unbalanced economic structure of many African economies depicted above. If services negotiations and their regulatory intricacies remain relatively novel for African policy-makers, this is even more so for the continent's business community. While there is generally adequate awareness within business support organizations, most service-supplying firms lack knowledge on how trade negotiations can serve as a tool to secure enhanced access to foreign markets, address discriminatory practices therein and promote tangible improvements in (pro-competitive) regulatory frameworks in the domestic market. Durable improvements in African countries' trade policy formulation processes require that greater efforts be directed towards reaching out to private sector stakeholders in the service sector and in making stakeholder dialogues more inclusive.

Moreover, by their very nature services form a highly heterogeneous sector. As such, some service industries have developed powerful lobbies, notably in banking and the regulated professions, while others have considerably less voice in shaping trade policy, particularly those sectors whose regulatory burden may be lighter. While a few national coalitions of services industries (CSIs) have been established to attempt to remedy the above deficit, in most countries of the continent no single voice addresses services issues in a coherent manner at the national or regional level. As is the case in most parts of the world, this results in a silo approach to the design of service sector policy, with industries liaising directly with their respective sectoral (regulating) ministries or agencies. Such a configuration heightens the scope for vertical protectionist or regulatory capture. It can also inhibit the emergence of whole-of-government approaches focused on lifting sector-specific constraints negatively affecting economy-wide performance.

6.3 TRENDS IN INTRA-REGIONAL INTEGRATION IN SERVICES

A significant share of the trade and market integration that has taken place in Africa has been driven by the 1991 Treaty of Abuja, through which the 54 members of the African Union established the African Economic Community. The Treaty envisages a six-stage integration process culminating in the creation of an African Common Market which is to be strengthened and consolidated through provisions governing the free movement of people, goods, capital and services as well as the rights of residency and establishment (see Table 6.2). The African Union recognizes eight regional economic communities (RECs)[4] as the building blocks of the African Economic Community.[5] To get a better sense of the progress

[4] According to the United Nations Economic Commission for Africa, RECs have much broader agendas and objectives than conventional PTAs. As such, the strategic and political rationales which underpin the existence of the RECs may at times take precedence over economic integration aims. See United Nations Economic Commission for Africa (2010), p. 404.

[5] These eight RECs are: the Economic Community of West African States (ECOWAS); the Economic Community of Central African States (ECCAS); the Common Market for Eastern and Southern Africa (COMESA); the South African Development Community (SADC); and the East African Community (EAC); the Community of Sahel-Saharan States (CEN-SAD); the Arab Maghreb Union (UMA) and Intergovernmental Authority on Development (IGAD).

Table 6.2 Main stages of trade and market integration under the Abuja Treaty

Stage	Activity
1	Strengthening of RECs
2	Intra-REC integration Inter-REC harmonization
3	Establishment of PTAs in each REC Establishment of Customs Unions in each REC
4	Harmonization and Co-ordination of Customs Unions to establish a continent-wide Customs Union
5	Establishment of a Common Market
6	Strengthening and Consolidation of the Common Market Establishment of an African Monetary Union Adoption of a Common Currency

registered in liberalizing services trade in the intra-regional context, developments within the RECs need to be scrutinized more closely.

6.3.1 ECOWAS

The Economic Community of West African States (ECOWAS) ranks among the most advanced African regional grouping in services liberalization. The ECOWAS Treaty requires the Community to ensure the removal of obstacles to the free movement of persons, goods, services and capital, and to guarantee the right of residence and establishment. To date, ECOWAS has signed three supplementary Protocols on the free movement of persons, residence and establishment. The first Protocol provides for the free entry of Community citizens for a period of 90 days without a visa.[6] The second Protocol allows Community residents to reside in, seek and carry out income-earning employment in any member state.[7] The Protocol specifically refers to migrant workers, who are defined as nationals of Community member states who seek or propose to hold, are holding or have held employment. Special provisions are made for three categories of migrant workers – itinerant workers, seasonal workers and border workers. The third Protocol provides for the right of establishment

[6] Protocol A/P.1/5/79 relating to free movement of persons, residence and establishment, 1979.

[7] Supplementary Protocol A/SP.1/7/86 on the second phase (right of residence) of the protocol on free movement of persons, the right of residence and establishment, 1986.

and access for enterprises.[8] As is allowed under GATS Article V.6, the Protocol adopts a fairly restrictive rule of origin (denial of benefits clause) for investment limiting ECOWAS privileges to Community enterprises that are: (i) incorporated in accordance with the laws and regulations of the member states; (ii) have their headquarters, central seat of establishment or principal establishment within the Community; and (iii) conduct substantial business operations within any member state. The third Protocol also commits member states to offer non-discriminatory treatment to nationals and companies of other member states in matters related to establishment and provision of services. Provision is further made for the protection and promotion of capital for investment or for capital already invested in the establishment of an enterprise. Finally, the Protocol incorporates rules governing the movement of capital.

6.3.2 West African Economic and Monetary Union (WAEMU)[9]

The Treaty establishing WAEMU, which is a smaller subset of the ECOWAS member states, confers the right of free movement of people, the right to provide services, the right of establishment and the right of residence to natural and juridical persons of its eight member states.[10] It further provides for non-discrimination in respect of the right to seek and engage in employment.

6.3.3 East African Community (EAC)[11]

The five EAC member states have taken a progressive approach to liberalization, committing to the four freedoms – of goods, services, people and capital – plus the right of residence and establishment.[12] The EAC Protocol additionally sets forth the rules governing trade in services and member states have made GATS-style commitments with phase-in periods commencing from 2010 to 2015. The initial round of intra-EAC services liberalization focused on seven core sectors: business, communications,

---

[8] Supplementary Protocol A/SP.2/5/90 on the implementation of the third phase (right of establishment) of the protocol on free movement of persons, right of residence and establishment, 1990.

[9] See http://www.uemoa.int/Pages/Home.aspx.

[10] Treaty Establishing the West African Economic and Monetary Union, 1996, Articles 91–3.

[11] See http://www.eac.int/.

[12] Protocol on the Establishment of the East African Community Market, 2009, Parts C, D, G and E.

distribution, educational, financial, tourism and travel-related, and transport services.[13] Member states have pledged to make additional commitments on the elimination of restrictions beyond these initial seven sectors after the entry into force of the Protocol.

6.3.4 Other regional initiatives

Other intra-Sub-Saharan African PTAs have pledged to embark on the liberalization of services in the future. This is the case, notably, of the Common Market of Eastern and Southern Africa (COMESA) Agreement, which features provisions calling on Parties to negotiate a protocol on services and the right of establishment.[14] The Southern African Development Community's (SADC) Protocol on Trade also affirms the intention of the member states to liberalize their services trade.[15]

6.3.4.1 Common Market for Eastern and Southern Africa (COMESA)

For some years, the 19 member states of COMESA[16] have been working on a GATS-type agreement on services to be coupled with separate disciplines on investment. This work culminated in June 2009 in the adoption by the COMESA Council of Regulations on Trade in Services.[17] Novel

---

13 Government of Uganda (2010), p. 8.

14 COMESA Treaty, 1993, 164(2).

15 Protocol on Trade in the Southern African Development Community, 1996, Article 23.

16 See http://www.comesa.int/.

17 The COMESA Council decided in June 2009 to: "(i) prepare negotiating guidelines that could include possible priority sectors, modalities for negotiations and any existing commitments; (ii) submit the guidelines to member states who should give their inputs within two weeks of receiving the guidelines; (iii) write a letter to member states advising that the region had adopted a positive list approach to services liberalisation and upon adoption of the Framework. Member states shall submit their requests and offers to the Secretariat; (iv) consider the possibility of drawing a matrix of specific commitments on trade in services made by member states including at the WTO and other regional organisations; (v) consider the possibility of convening a meeting for negotiations after receiving the request and offers; and (vi) arrange capacity building activities for preparing schedules of specific commitment for interested member states. The Council further decided that: (i) the liberalization process shall be concluded by the Committee on Trade in Services and according to negotiating modalities to be established by member states taking into account the different levels of development among the member states and Special and Differential Treatment may be granted based on the level of commitments that will be submitted at a later stage of negotiations and (ii) the Liberalisation process under paragraph 1, shall be conducted with the aim of promoting the economic growth and development of the member states, in conformity

aspects of the COMESA Regulations include the decision to liberalize air transport services, a trend found in few PTAs elsewhere on the continent and beyond; the improvement of procedures relating to the establishment of enquiry points to address service suppliers as opposed to governments and a "best endeavors" clause to process licensing and other services-related applications electronically.[18] In addition, the categories of natural persons covered by Mode 4 services trade have been defined clearly.

COMESA's achievements to date include the adoption of guidelines for the negotiation of trade in services which would guide countries in the preparation of schedules of specific commitments and a negotiating roadmap. In addition, negotiations are set to commence on seven priority sectors in which member states will forego the right to maintain any restrictions beyond agreed transition periods. The priority sectors owe to their central infrastructural functions and their role in strengthening the competitiveness of economies. They are: financial, communication, business, transport, tourism, energy and construction and related engineering services. Efforts are currently being directed towards the preparation of negotiating offers.

6.3.4.2 Southern African Development Community (SADC)

The 14 member states of SADC[19] have reaffirmed their GATS commitments and committed to deepening service sector liberalization within the region. SADC member states are slated to commence the negotiation of WTO+ commitments upon the signature of a Protocol on Trade in Services by Heads of State/Government. The Protocol sets out the framework for the liberalization of services trade and serves as a basis for negotiations. Negotiations are scheduled to focus on six priority sectors: construction, communication, transport, tourism, financial and energy-related services.

6.3.4.3 Tripartite Agreement

The member states of COMESA, the EAC and SADC have embarked on the ambitious path of establishing a PTA among the three RECs.[20]

---

with the principle of asymmetry. Special flexibility to such member states may *inter alia* take the form of: (a) a transition period for liberalization; and (b) opening fewer sectors or types of transactions." (COMESA 2009, pp. 11–12)

[18] Markus Jelitto, Presentation at the USAID/ GIZ/ Southern Africa Institute of International Affairs Services Roundtable, Johannesburg, July 13, 2011.

[19] See http://www.sadc.int/index/browse/page/52.

[20] COMESA, EAC and SADC Heads of State/Government formally launched negotiations on the Tripartite FTA on June 12, 2011.

This PTA represents one of the three pillars of the so-called Tripartite Agreement, with the other two being joint investments in infrastructure development with a view to enhancing trade connectivity and reducing the cost of doing business as well as industrial development initiatives to address productive (i.e. supply-side) capacity constraints.[21]

The impetus driving the creation of such a continent-wide PTA is the realization that the regional integration processes of the three RECs share a great number of similarities (in some cases identical priority sectors for instance) and that overlapping/multiple membership in the RECs required increased cooperation in policy development and implementation. Clearly the intention is to promote economies of scale and scope in regional integration efforts, achieve a higher level of coordination in the creation of regional rule-making architectures, while also supplying a host of regional public goods in the form of trade-facilitating transport and infrastructural projects such as the improvement of the operations of trade corridors.

There is little doubt that linking three incipient integration processes, none of which is individually much advanced, is likely to prove challenging given the differing levels of liberalization within each REC (see Box 6.1). This may perhaps account for the decision to delay the onset of services discussions until the second phase of Tripartite negotiations. However, it bears noting that services-related issues have not been completely sidelined. Some thematic areas such as the movement of business persons have been prioritized for negotiation in the first phase. Work is also proceeding on the liberalization of air transport services and the Tripartite has established a Joint Competition Authority to oversee the full implementation of the Yamoussoukro Decision on the Liberalization of Air Transport Services.[22] Moreover, through a broad ongoing initiative on trade facilitation, a host of barriers to road transport services are being addressed such as the harmonization of commercial truck driver immigration requirements and regulations. The latter two areas fall squarely within the remit of the infrastructure development pillar but in a manner that can yield clearly positive trade- and investment-facilitating dividends.

As regards other RECs, there has generally been very little progress on services liberalization. Political instability and resource constraints (including trade-related human capital) have held back or postponed the implementation of agreed Protocols designed to facilitate the movement of

---

21 Tripartite FTA Secretariat (2011), p. 4.

22 The Yamoussoukro Decision of 2000 is a multilateral agreement among most of the 54 African states which provides for the gradual liberalization of scheduled and non-scheduled intra-African air transport services. See Schlumberger (2010), pp. 6–11.

BOX 6.1 A BRIDGE TOO FAR? A PROPOSED TRIPARTITE AGREEMENT ON SERVICES

The negotiation of a services agreement within the Tripartite Arrangement seems to be particularly ambitious in terms of its geographic scope. An important lesson emerging from the intra-African PTA experience is that it appears to be easier for a small number of states such as the five EAC member states to negotiate a services agreement. Moreover, this success was further buttressed by strong political will within that REC.

By contrast, opening the services markets of 26 member states is bound to be fraught with significant difficulty. Even the circumstances surrounding the creation of the services component of the Tripartite Arrangement are different as the RECs manifest varying levels of ambition, with the EAC being the most ambitious and SADC appearing to be the least so. This is further compounded by the slow pace of progress in the RECs, with the exception of the EAC. Hence, it is anticipated that the extension of the Tripartite PTA to include services is likely to provide a strong challenge to member states. This is especially so as the outcomes and impact of services negotiations on the member states at the level of the RECs are at the moment unclear in the case of the EAC or simply unknown in the case of both COMESA and SADC (Kruger 2011). For this reason, the Tripartite services negotiations can only realistically commence after the completion (or significant advancement) of the integration process within the three RECs it aims to federate as the wider liberalization initiative needs to build on existing regional efforts and architectures.

There is likely to be an element of duplication involved in following this route. In addition, just as regulatory cooperation and coherence are key to reaping the benefits of services liberalization at the level of the REC, they will be even more so at the Tripartite level where the potential for ill-conceived or trade- and investment-restrictive regulations to detract from the economic benefits of increased competition may be higher with more member states being involved. Moreover, the risk of getting key elements of an integrated framework wrong could impose non-negligible (and difficult to reverse) costs on service providers. Achieving regulatory cooperation and coherence in the Tripartite context is likely to represent an uphill task for regulatory authorities as the human, technical and financial resources required to support such an ambitious undertaking will be considerable. The latter challenge represents a prime area where targeted donor support could provide much needed technical assistance. The experience of Kenya provides insights into difficulties at the national level of complying with a services PTA. While Kenya has reportedly made significant progress in implementing the EAC services provisions, it is struggling to establish the legislative and regulatory framework to support the EAC Protocol due to resource constraints (Ndegwa 2011).

Another important element in this scenario is the approach to the Tripartite services negotiations. It is not clear whether the Tripartite will see the RECs extending the preferences of each REC to other Parties to the Agreement or whether the RECs will be trying to secure a deeper level of commitments from each other (Kruger 2011). It will also be of interest to see how the unique elements of each REC's services agreements are incorporated into the Tripartite framework. Certainly, these critical elements ought to be subject to careful consideration well in advance of the negotiations to ensure that the services provisions in the Tripartite FTA go beyond those in the RECs' FTAs. In the absence of such enhanced commitments, the added value of the Tripartite FTA's services pact (other than having expanded the geographic coverage of the concessions) might be questionable.

Overall, while the creation of a services pact in the Tripartite context is laudable and there are likely to be significant gains as a more competitive services sector supports economic activity throughout the enlarged region, the question remains whether there is sufficient political will to bring a services pact of such magnitude into being and whether member states will be able to mobilize sufficient resources to support the heavy institutional demands created by such an integrated market. The key challenge will be to devise a formula for the Tripartite negotiations which would be sufficiently ambitious so as to add value beyond the services agreements at the level of the RECs while at the same time still providing comfort to more reluctant member states.

goods and services in the Economic Community of Central African States (ECCAS).[23] Similarly the Inter-Governmental Authority on Development (IGAD) has not made much headway: this REC is currently planning a provision on a free movement of persons, services, goods and capital to be implemented through a Protocol. While the Treaty establishing the Community of Sahel-Saharan States (CEN-SAD) has as one of its main objectives the free movement of people and services, the CEN-SAD has yet to move beyond the process of drafting a Protocol on the free movement of people.

6.4 TRENDS IN EXTRA-REGIONAL INTEGRATION IN SERVICES

In PTAs concluded between African countries and other *developing* countries outside the region, the Parties to the agreement tend to merely reaffirm their GATS commitments. Examples include the Egypt–Turkey FTA and the Morocco–Turkey FTA. In line with most of the African bilateral trade agreements which cover services, the Agadir Agreement among Jordan, Tunisia, Egypt and Morocco also reflects the GATS status quo. It is doubtful whether such agreements have generated much in the way of tangible new market access opportunities, nor do they appear to have generated much trade-facilitation traction through various regulatory cooperation initiatives.

Meanwhile, with few exceptions, the vast majority of PTAs concluded with *developed* countries outside of the African region feature little by way of WTO+ advances. In fact, a recurring thread running through the services chapters of the latter category of PTAs is the reaffirmation of the Parties' GATS obligations. As noted earlier, the only PTA representing a clear break with the above pattern is the US–Morocco FTA of 2004. This should perhaps come as no surprise given the predominance of the NAFTA model championed by the United States, Canada and a number of South and Central American countries in their PTAs. The US–Morocco FTA is as encompassing as any of the latest generation of US FTAs, featuring all of the traditional panoply of provisions found in agreements commonly found in the Western Hemisphere: most favored nation (MFN) treatment, national treatment and market access obligations on cross-border trade in services and investment, a negative list approach to reserving non-conforming measures affecting both cross-border services

---

[23] See United Nations Economic Commission for Africa (2010), pp. 14–19.

and investment, disciplines on domestic regulation, separate chapters on telecommunications, financial services and electronic commerce, a denial of benefits clause with a liberal, substantial business operations, requirement as mandated by Article V.6 of GATS), prohibition of local presence requirements and a ratchet clause.[24] One notable exception is the lack of a chapter governing the temporary entry of business people. This reflects the fact that, since 2004, the US Congress no longer directs the United States Trade Representative to address Mode 4 issues in the country's PTAs.

Neither the member states of the EC nor those of the European Free Trade Association (EFTA) have so far been able to achieve a similar outcome in their PTAs with African countries. This can be seen in the Southern African Customs Union (SACU)–EFTA PTA, which merely codifies the GATS *status quo* and contains no new disciplines or expanded sectoral coverage in the services realm. A similar pattern is discernible in the EC–South Africa Trade, Development and Cooperation Agreement (TDA),[25] the EC–Morocco, Egypt–EFTA and Tunisia–EFTA free trade agreements.

An important development for the region was the December 2007 expiry of the WTO waiver granted to the EC for its preferential treatment of ACP partners. While the WTO decision related solely to trade in goods between the EC and its ACP partners, it nonetheless led to the launch of talks towards WTO-compatible comprehensive Economic Partnership Agreements (EPAs) whose stated aim is to extend the scope of EC-ACP ties in services trade and investment. To date, among all ACP partners, only the member states of CARIFORUM have agreed to a services compact as part of an EPA. None of the African member countries and sub-regions has so far agreed to such an anchoring.

Unlike the CARIFORUM group of the ACP, which considered an EPA with the EC as a unique opportunity to gain commercially relevant market access for services exports in line with the economic structure of the bulk of the region's economies, the four African ACP sub-regions have professed strong reluctance to making services commitments in their EPAs with the EC. Rather, SADC, the Eastern and Southern Africa (ESA), the EAC and the Central African sub-regions have all concluded interim EPAs dealing solely with trade in goods and signaled a commitment to *future* negotiations on services. Moreover, of the four African sub-regions, only

---

24 For a description of US private sector views of the Morocco–US FTA, see http://www.uscsi.org/publications/papers/06-15-04.htm.

25 The 1999 EC-South Africa TDA called for future negotiations on services between the two partners. To date, no such negotiations have taken place.

the Central African states have to date reached agreement on a specific timeframe for concluding this element of the EPA negotiations – January 1, 2009. This deadline has since lapsed and negotiations have continued as with all other sub-regions but in the absence of a clear negotiating timetable. It bears noting that in those instances where individual African states have concluded an interim EPA with the EC, due to the overall lack of consensus among the sub-regional grouping to which they belong, the commitment to negotiate on services is often weaker still. For instance, in the interim EPAs concluded by both Ghana and Côte d'Ivoire, there is little more than a commitment to facilitate measures leading to the conclusion of a global EPA including provisions on services trade.

Nevertheless, negotiations on disciplines and commitments on services and investment are currently under way in all regions. However, not all members of all sub-regions are involved in such negotiations. For example, only Botswana, Lesotho, Swaziland and Mozambique are engaged in the EC-SADC services discussions. Moreover, to add to the hemispheric confusion, a number of SADC member states are currently negotiating on services and investment with partners in the other sub-regions. For instance, Malawi is engaged in the EC-ESA negotiations. However, other member states such as Angola, South Africa and Namibia are not actively participating in this area of negotiations, but merely serving as observers.

The section that follows explores what a comprehensive EPA conducted along the lines of the recently concluded EPA between the EC and the member states of CARIFORUM could portend for the African ACP sub-regions.

6.5 THE EC-CARIFORUM ECONOMIC PARTNERSHIP AGREEMENT: POSSIBLE IMPACTS ON AFRICAN INTEGRATION PROCESSES[26]

The expiry of the World Trade Organization (WTO) waiver on December 31, 2007, which provided legal cover for the EC's preferential trade regime for goods originating from the ACP countries, coupled with the improbable likelihood of securing the waiver's renewal, signaled the end of non-reciprocal EC-ACP trade relations. Such a change in ACP countries' trading environment has so far spawned vastly different responses

[26] This section draws on Sauvé and Ward (2009).

within the six ACP negotiating regions. These run the gamut from the CARIFORUM[27] group's decision to enter into a comprehensive EPA with the EC to the Interim EPAs signed by some members of the Pacific Region, SADC, West Africa, ESA and EAC, all of which as noted above apply solely to goods trade, leaving open the possibility of concluding more comprehensive EPAs in future.

The lack of consensus within the latter regions was vividly illustrated by the decision of some non-LDCs to opt out of the interim EPAs, foregoing their preferential access to EC markets. Meanwhile, a number of least developed ACP members (LDCs) saw limited value-added in entering into EPAs, preferring instead to continue to export under the EC's Everything But Arms (EBA) initiative, affording them non-reciprocal duty-free access to the EC market (but in goods trade only).

The signature on December 16, 2007 of the EC-CARIFORUM Economic Partnership Agreement (EPA) drew the curtain on 30 years of preferential access to European markets enjoyed by Caribbean producers. Failure to negotiate a WTO-consistent trade regime was a luxury the CARIFORUM region could ill afford since the application of Europe's Generalized System of Preferences (GSP) would have disrupted trade as the majority of the region's exports to Europe would need to contend with higher levels of GSP import duties. The challenge for the region was thus to negotiate "a development friendly, asymmetrical, reciprocal agreement whose net welfare benefit. . . would be greater than that under the best available GSP' (Gonzales 2008, p. 2).

In several regards, the CARIFORUM EPA exceeded the thresholds laid down under GATT Article 24 and GATS Article V to determine WTO-compatibility. The EPA also features many WTO-plus (i.e. improvements on existing rules and/or commitments) and GATS-X (i.e. new rules, sectors or commitments not covered by the GATS) provisions. The CARIFORUM EPA represents a significant departure from earlier trade arrangements between the EC and the CARIFORUM region by moving beyond goods trade and incorporating areas such as trade in services, investment, government procurement, competition policy and trade-related intellectual property matters.

Indeed, even while allowing for inevitable differences in the design

27 CARIFORUM stands for the Caribbean Group of the African, Caribbean and Pacific Forum. It refers to the 14 member states of CARICOM (Antigua and Barbuda, Bahamas, Barbados, Belize, Dominica, Grenada, Guyana, Haiti, Jamaica, St. Kitts and Nevis, St. Lucia, St. Vincent and the Grenadines, Suriname and Trinidad and Tobago) plus the Dominican Republic and for the purposes of the EPA negotiations excluded Cuba.

and substantive content of EPAs to be concluded with the African and Pacific regions owing to differences in economic structures, development levels and collective preferences, the argument can be made that the EC-CARIFORUM EPA has arguably set the bar for all subsequent EPA negotiations and perhaps indeed for future preferential trade agreements entered into by the EC.

Given the precedent-setting value of the EC-CARIFORUM EPA, some of the questions that are bound to be uppermost in the minds of trade officials of Sub-Saharan African countries are: (i) what lessons can Sub-Saharan African countries draw from the GATS+ and GATS-X provisions found in the EC-CARIFORUM EPA; and (ii) which WTO+ or GATS-X elements found in the EC-CARIFORUM EPA elements hold the potential, if replicated in African EPAs, to stimulate development in these countries?

6.5.1 Precedence and Innovation in Services Rule-design

The EC-CARIFORUM EPA represents an important, precedent-setting, evolution in preferential trade agreements. The Parties essentially worked within the construct of a PTA to bring about a development dimension to their international trading arrangements. The Agreement underscores the fact that PTAs involving highly unequal partners can nonetheless generate outcomes that offer tangible benefits to the weaker side. Such an approach may heighten the interest of lesser developed ACP partners in concluding EPAs and potentially improving the terms on which they become increasingly integrated into regional and/or global production networks.

In several respects, the EPA can be considered a WTO+ agreement as it goes beyond the commitments and rules governing services trade in the WTO and creates a detailed (if far from comprehensive or fully coherent) framework of rules on investment.[28] The EPA also marks important advances, with novel forms of variable geometry, in addressing the issues

---

[28] Reflecting as it did at the time the still incomplete nature of Community competence over investment policy matters (such competence was shared with EC member states), the EC-CARIFORUM EPA does not cover issues relating to investment protection nor does it provide recourse to investor-state dispute settlement procedures. The latter continue to be covered by the dense network of bilateral investment treaties entered into and implemented by EC member states. The entry into force of the Lisbon Treaty in 2010 has extended full Community competence to the EC in the investment field, such that the texture and substantive remit of future EPA (and all other EC PTA) rules on investment may likely diverge significantly from the more limited architecture of investment rules embedded in the CARIFORUM EPA.

of competition policy, government procurement, and in featuring an innovative set of cooperation activities for cultural industries, all areas that have encountered repeated and, in some cases, protracted, difficulties at the multilateral level.

The GATS+ character of liberalization is evident in CARIFORUM member states' commitments on a wider range of service and investment activities, particularly in key infrastructural sectors. EPA progress is significantly more limited however as regards the depth of commitments scheduled in areas where the Parties had already made GATS commitments. The GATS+ nature of EPA advances is also illustrated by improvements in access to the EC market for commercial presence and, especially, in regard to the temporary entry of natural persons and the treatment of cultural industries, even as the latter do not *per se* involve the granting of new market access commitments. The EC-CARIFORUM EPA has also broken important new ground in the tourism sector, an area of critical importance to CARIFORUM members (and most developing countries). The Agreement features a chapter dedicated to the sector in which a novel set of disciplines targeting the potentially anti-competitive conduct of large tourism intermediaries has been adopted. The latter disciplines complement the EPA's market access and national treatment commitments in the sector. Such disciplines have led to calls for the adoption of a GATS sectoral annex for the tourism sector, highlighting how PTAs can incubate best practices liable to migrate to the WTO level.

The EC-CARIFORUM EPA can be described as a successful attempt to give operational meaning to the principles and objectives of GATS Article IV (Increasing Participation of Developing Countries). This is so inasmuch as the EC has made evident efforts to respond to demands to open sectors and modes of supply of relevance to CARIFORUM states. This can also be seen in the EPA's concrete mechanisms to support the strengthening of domestic services capacity in a number of sectors and the improvement of CARIFORUM's access to distribution channels and information networks in the EC.

The biggest challenge facing CARIFORUM states lies in implementing the terms of the EPA. On the financial side, the funds and technical assistance made available through the European Development Fund (EDF) should help to ease the adjustment burden flowing from the agreement and help CARIFORUM service suppliers and investors to take advantage of newly opened market opportunities in EC markets. If the CARIFORUM region applies a similar level of commitment to the implementation process as it did to the EPA's negotiating process, the adjustment challenges arising from the Agreement should prove surmountable. In entering into the EPA, CARIFORUM states at the highest level appeared convinced that there was simply no turning back and that survival in the global economy required a strategic repositioning of the region based in part on some of the tangible advantages that the EPA could confer, notably in the services sector. Such pragmatism on the part of a small player eager to confront its vulnerabilities and diversify its economic tissue, while also affording its ample supply of qualified workers, professionals and artists greater mobility and opportunities in world markets, explains why CARIFORUM states ultimately opted for a comprehensive EPA. Whether a similar political resolve or innate export potential holds throughout the African region and its several RECs remains an open question.

6.6 POSSIBLE LESSONS FOR AFRICAN EPAS IN SERVICES TRADE

For the African members of the ACP grouping, it has long been clear that the EC considers EPAs as the best available option for structuring its trade, regulatory and development cooperation relationship with ACP partners. The African regional groupings thus need to evaluate what trading arrangements are best suited to satisfying their development goals based on a comprehensive strategy for sustainable development and poverty alleviation.

Countries in Sub-Saharan Africa are confronted with a range of options in deciding the basis upon which to pursue their trading relations with the EC. These include agreeing to a comprehensive, (asymmetrically) reciprocal EPA that delves beyond trade in goods into areas such as investment, services, government procurement, competition policy as well as cooperation in cultural matters, together with the attendant development assistance and technical cooperation provisions attached to the above.

Another option involves continued reliance on the EC's GSP scheme or, for the least developed ACP countries, continued benefits under the EC's Everything But Arms (EBA) initiative, the latter two forms of preferential treatment however being confined to goods trade only and not being permanent (i.e. they are not politically reversible) in character.

As regards more specifically the services and investment chapters of prospective EPAs, two main questions facing African ACP members are: (i) whether they can use such instruments and their likely development finance and technical assistance attributes as useful developmental tools in addressing areas of priority export interest or in tackling key growth-impeding infrastructure bottlenecks; and (ii) how best to articulate and make cohere greater engagement with the EC, which for most African countries remains a predominant trade and investment partner, with the multiplicity of ongoing intra-African integration initiatives.

While there is no legal obligation stemming from WTO law compelling African countries to negotiate chapters on services, investment and other behind the border issues in an EPA context, there is little doubt that the EC expects their EPAs with ACP partners to be comprehensive in scope and thus to extend to trade and investment in services.

Given the marked differences in the economic make-up between the African groupings and the CARIFORUM, the services and investment chapters of EPAs concluded with African partners need not (and probably cannot) be as extensive as those found in the EC-CARIFORUM agreement, and the various formulas of variable geometry that the latter agreement has generated could be further adjusted to relax the reciprocal nature of the EPA's rules and market access commitments, while nonetheless satisfying the requirements of GATS Article V.

Embedding such chapters in a flexible manner in African EPAs could prove useful in enhancing domestic and regional investment climates and in promoting greater competition through new entry in service sectors of crucial importance to economy-wide performance, including in agriculture, fisheries, mining and manufacturing and in helping promote needed economic diversification.

An EPA compact on services and investment cannot be viewed merely as a stand-alone element. It must, rather, be seen as part of any determined effort at enhancing the infrastructure for trade and lowering the overall cost of producing goods and other services and bringing them to markets at home and abroad. The aid for trade components embedded in the EC-CARIFORUM EPA, including those specific to services and investment, are likely to be replicated in an African context. This would help ensure that efforts at progressively opening up key services markets are coupled with needed investments in capacity strengthening in service sectors, both in regulatory terms and in terms of private sector supply capacities.

In pondering whether to engage in EPA negotiations with the EC in these areas, African countries must determine the likelihood that the WTO process might yield equally tangible forms of needed capacity-building benefits. They must also weigh such benefits against the possible costs (and benefits) stemming from the deeper liberalization of services trade and investment likely to emerge from EPA negotiations (and needed to satisfy the substantial sectoral coverage and liberalization requirements of GATS Article V) relative to the WTO, where African members, especially LDCs, face considerably weaker pressure to make market opening commitments.

In solving the above equation, a number of important elements ought to be considered. First is the need to ensure that both the wider EPA and its services and investment chapters provide for development cooperation benefits that adequately support the implementation of any commitments made. A balance must indeed be found between the agreed rules and the commitments scheduled in services and investment chapters, while also maintaining conditions of asymmetrical reciprocity.

Second, African EPA partners must get the timing and sequencing of their liberalization right. This is critically important in both the intra-regional and the EPA contexts. More so than the CARIFORUM states, most African economies will need more time to allow for the building up of regulatory and productive (i.e. private sector supply) capacities in services. Perhaps a first step would be to work within the EPA at building up such capacities and to backlog liberalization commitments on the part of African ACP members until such time as such capacity-building efforts have generated visible institutional traction. Such a process could entail the gradual opening of those sectors in which the two elements noted above already exist – i.e. a readiness to open up progressively and the needed funding to ensure that regulatory, implementation and supply capacities are properly buttressed. Such a policy course is certainly in consonance with the advice that market access negotiations ought to be complemented by parallel processes that focus not only on improving services regulations and enforcement, but also on putting into place the regulatory cooperation that may be needed to allow greater trade to occur.[29]

Third, the services and investment provisions in the EC-CARIFORUM EPA represent one of a range of possibilities for structuring relations in trade in services and investment policy. If, as seems likely, more flexibility is required, African EPA partners should pay particular attention to formulating their own proposals on the nature of required flexibilities.

The experience of the CARIFORUM countries offers several useful insights which can assist their African counterparts in the negotiations. For starters, the EC-CARIFORUM experience has shown that an EPA can be development friendly; however, there is nothing automatic in securing such an outcome and it requires vigilance at the negotiating table. African countries must be clear about their development strategy, place themselves in a position to articulate such a strategy and allow it to inform the development thrust contained in an EPA's services and investment chapters. Consequently, African countries need to engage in the necessary technical work to clearly identify their offensive and defensive interests

---

[29] See Hoekman and Mattoo (2011).

and be clear on how they would want to see such interests crystallized in the context of an EPA's services and investment chapters.

Fears that the conclusion of an EPA will necessarily give rise to a more demanding or sovereignty-threatening framework of general trade and investment disciplines may be assuaged by two observations. On the one hand, the likelihood of the inclusion of investment and services rules in an EPA that are more fully developed or more constraining of domestic policy space than those found at the multilateral level appears low. In the EC-CARIFORUM EPA, there has been minimal progress on the bulk of the unfinished rule-making agenda of GATS, be it in the area of subsidy disciplines, emergency safeguards or domestic regulation/necessity.

On the other hand, the conclusion of a services and investment pact within the context of an EPA may be an effective means of redressing perceived imbalances in existing regulatory frameworks that might otherwise disadvantage African ACP member states. For instance, the perception that bilateral investment treaties (BITs) provide more rights than obligations to investors led CARIFORUM countries to use the EPA to embed greater rights for host countries.[30]

The CARIFORUM-EC EPA also illustrates that asymmetrical commitments and variable geometry in rule-making offer useful tools to structure services trade and investment relations between unequal trading partners. Significantly, such tools may be tweaked to encourage deeper and faster integration among developing countries before embarking on a later stage of integration between developing country partners and the EC. Such a process may arguably result in increased predictability and transparency in the intra-regional services and investment environment and confer first-mover advantages on intra-regional suppliers (within the services and investment protocols of ongoing RECs) before external liberalization with the EC (or other developed countries) proceeds. The CARIFORUM experience is a case in point: thanks to earlier progress secured (within the CARICOM Single Market Initiative), deeper levels of (prior) intra-regional integration arguably made the conclusion of an EPA with the EC significantly easier and less politically contentious. Hence an EPA can serve as the impetus for the more expeditious creation of more commercially meaningful intra-regional services and investment ties and strengthened regional regulatory frameworks tailored to the specific needs of Africa's various sub-regional country groupings.

Finally, a key lesson emerging from the EC-CARIFORUM service and investment compact is that EPAs may be a platform for the

30 EC-CARIFORUM EPA, Article 72.

internationalization of the regulation of key service industries on a sector-by-sector basis. Actively strengthening regulatory frameworks can bring two benefits. First, developing country partners can, in an EPA context, push to ensure that their interests are taken on board in the tailoring of agreed regulatory frameworks. Second, they can ensure that fledgling regulatory frameworks governing key service markets are strengthened through targeted technical assistance funding and capacity-building activities.

By insisting on the need to work towards sounder regulatory frameworks in sectors in which they have offensive interests, such as tourism, creative industries or labor mobility, African countries can better ensure that any future EPA disciplines on services and investment are not unduly skewed towards developed country objectives and interests. Given that the negotiation and implementation capacity of African countries is in most instances severely constrained, one priority issue area should be the provision of needed development cooperation assistance to ensure the fulfillment of commitments in this regard. Many African countries have consistently identified weak regulatory capacity as a particular area which has hindered tangible progress and fuller engagement on the services front. A comprehensive EPA may represent a useful opportunity to push ahead in this specific area as the combination of binding commitments on the part of the African countries coupled with the provision of development assistance and financing from the EC holds potential for stimulating economic diversification into services.

While CARIFORUM states and African countries may share a number of common characteristics and negotiating interests, the negotiation contexts for these two groups of countries nonetheless reveal significant differences. One can point to several instances where similarities in legislation and regulatory frameworks between the EC and CARICOM likely facilitated the attainment of GATS+ and GATS-X outcomes in the EPA context. The level of regional integration achieved within CARICOM prior to entering into the EPA ensured that the region had either already put in place its own institutional arrangements on some of the GATS+/GATS-X issues at play in the negotiations (e.g. competition policy, a single market for services, intra-regional labor mobility and mutual recognition of professional qualifications, etc.) or was working on doing so (e.g. government procurement). Taking the next step of concluding a comprehensive EPA with the EC was thus hardly revolutionary.

The above combination of circumstances and the extent of regulatory convergence between regions characterized by sophisticated internal processes of integration and the attendant institutional machinery are less likely to obtain within African negotiating sub-groups. As a consequence, certain elements of the EC-CARIFORUM EPA, such as disciplines on competition policy, transparency in public procurement or regulatory frameworks in certain sectors (such as e-commerce/digital trade), may not always be ripe for inclusion in an EC-African EPA. Accordingly, the range of behind the border issues to be tackled under such agreements may need to be narrowed.

6.7 CONCLUDING REMARKS

With few exceptions, the *negotiated* opening of services markets has not progressed much to date on the African continent, both North and South of the Sahara. This is notably the case at the level of intra-regional trade, where services tend to remain the weakest element of a large number of fledgling integration schemes. It is perhaps even more characteristic of Africa's relations with the outside world, most notably in the context of the stalled EPA negotiations with the EC, which have been marked by significant reluctance to anchor ongoing domestic reforms in legally binding treaty provisions.

African governments continue on the whole to profess considerable policy precaution in the field of services trade and investment, preferring to experiment with reversible autonomous policy change. Such revealed policy preferences are in many ways rational. They are, after all, to be expected of countries (e.g. LDCs) who have been told repeatedly at the WTO that they could sit back and enjoy a "round for free". Policy precaution also correlates with many salient characteristics of the continent's economic DNA, where heavy (excessive) reliance on agriculture and extractive industries, punishing trade costs, particularly in landlocked countries, weakly competitive domestic service industries, a continued lack of negotiating capacity and, more important still, weak or incomplete regulatory regimes and equally deficient regulatory enforcement capacities, all impart a cautious bias to service sector policy.

Still, it is hard to see how governments in the region will meaningfully take up the imperative of economic diversification, support the insertion of African producers into regional and global supply chains in agri-food and manufacturing, take advantage of a new international division of labor in remotely supplied services, meaningfully improve the transparency and efficiency of domestic and regional regulatory regimes and live up to the lofty aims embedded in the numerous integration schemes under negotiation without a serious commitment to the progressive liberalization of services trade and investment throughout the continent.

Continued reliance on autonomous reforms may well go some way towards securing the above objectives. At the same time, to reap the regional and global public goods likely to emanate from collective action on issues of regulatory cooperation and trade facilitation – the core of today's services trade and investment agenda – African economies can ill afford to stay forever on the policy sidelines. While greater engagement in negotiated market opening and rule-making in services carries inevitable downside risks and needs to be sequenced properly so as to promote orderly adjustment, the progressive liberalization of services trade and investment affords African policy-makers with a centrally important *quid pro quo* with which to address trade policy priorities in more traditional sectors of export interest, address the many obstacles that lie in the way of service sector export growth (which autonomous virtue cannot affect), while also committing the region to a path of deepened regulatory cooperation in sectors likely to exert far-reaching effects on allocative efficiency and economy-wide performance.

Greater engagement in services trade negotiations, both intra- and extra-regionally, including at the multilateral level, is also most likely to involve the supply of targeted forms of trade-related technical assistance and capacity strengthening without which durable improvements in service sector performance may not quickly materialize.

REFERENCES

Borchert, I., B. Gootiiz and A. Mattoo (2010), "Restrictions on Services Trade and FDI in Developing Countries", Mimeo, World Bank.

Brenton, Paul, Nora Dihel, Larry Hinkle and Nicholas Strychacz (2010), "Africa's Trade in Services and the Opportunities and Risks of Economic Partnership Agreements", *Africa Trade Policy Notes – No. 6*, Washington, DC: World Bank.

COMESA (2009), *Official Gazette of the Common Market for Eastern and Southern Africa (COMESA)*, 15(4), 9 June.

Gonzales, Anthony Peter (2008), "Choosing a Comprehensive EPA", available at http://www.crnm.org/documents/ACP_EC_EPA/epa_agreement/Choosing_a_Comprehensive_EPA_by%20AGonzales.pdf.

Gootiiz, B. and A. Mattoo (2009), "Services in Doha: What is on the Table?", *Journal of World Trade*, 43(5): 1013–30.

Government of Uganda (2010), "Brief on Trade in Services under the East African Community Common Market", Kampala: Ministry of East African Community Affairs, unpublished.

Hoekman, Bernard and Aaditya Mattoo (2011), "Services Trade Liberalization and Regulatory Reform: Reinvigorating International Co-operation", *World Bank Policy Research Working Paper* 5517, Washington, DC: World Bank.

Hoekman, Bernard and Patrick Messerlin (2000), "Liberalizing Trade in Services: Reciprocal Negotiations and Regulatory Reform", in P. Sauvé and R.M. Stern,

eds., *GATS 2000: New Directions in Services Trade Liberalization*, Washington, DC: Brookings Institution, pp. 487–508.
Kruger, Paul (2011), "Services Negotiations under the Tripartite Agreement: Issues to Consider", Stellenbosch: TRALAC.
Ndegwa, Barrack (2011), Integration Secretary, Ministry of East African Community, Kenya, Opening Remarks at the ILEAP/ICTSD/GIZ Workshop on Positioning Services Reforms and Negotiations for Development, Nairobi, Kenya, November 14–16, 2011.
Sauvé, Pierre and Natasha Ward (2009), "Services and Investment in the EC-CARIFORUM Economic Partnership Agreement: Innovation in Rule-design and Implications for Africa", in G. Faber and J. Orbie, eds., *Beyond Market Access for Economic Development: EU-Africa Relations in Transition*, London: Routledge, pp. 137–72.
Schlumberger, Charles (2010), *Open Skies for Africa: Implementing the Yamoussoukro Decision*, Washington, DC: The World Bank.
Tripartite FTA Secretariat (2011), *Brief on the Tripartite Free Trade Area*, Lusaka: Tripartite FTA Secretariat.
United Nations Economic Commission for Africa (2010), *Assessing Regional Integration in Africa IV: 2010 Enhancing Intra-Regional Trade*, Addis Ababa: UNECA.
World Trade Organization (2011), *International Trade Statistics 2011*, Geneva: World Trade Organization. Available at http://www.wto.org/english/res_e/statis_e/its2011_e/its11_toc_e.htm.

7. Mapping the universe of services disciplines in Asian PTAs[1]

Rupa Chanda[2]

7.1 INTRODUCTION

In the past decade, there has been a surge in preferential trade agreements (PTAs) around the world. A notable development in this regard has been the trend towards more broad-based or comprehensive PTAs, which go beyond goods to include services, investment, and other "new age" issues such as government procurement, digital trade, and competition policy. There were 118 PTAs featuring provisions on trade and investment in services notified to the WTO as of June 2013, representing 45% of all notified PTAs. Most were between developed and developing countries but a growing number are being conducted between developing countries.[3]

Asia has been an important participant in these trends. The region has witnessed an upswing in bilateral, regional, and cross-regional agreements. As of July 2013, 82 FTAs had been concluded in Asia, up from only three in 2000, with another 20 new agreements either under negotiation or proposed, thus clearly putting Asia at the forefront of PTA activity.[4] Many of these PTAs have a services and investment component and involve important developed and developing countries in the region, including

[1] In this chapter, the term PTAs is used to describe all types of agreements, including free trade agreements, economic partnership agreements, and comprehensive economic cooperation agreements.

[2] The author wishes to thank Pralok Gupta, doctoral student at IIM Bangalore, for his research assistance and help in finalizing all the data tables and compiling information on the status of PTAs; Shahana Mukherjee and Josmy Joseph for their enumeration of commitments in the General Agreement on Trade in Services (GATS) and in PTAs; and Kirthiga Balasubramaniam for help with updating and revising the chapter.

[3] Author's calculations based on the WTO RTA database. http://rtais.wto.org/UI/PublicAllRTAList.aspx

[4] Author's calculations based on the WTO RTA database. http://rtais.wto.org/UI/PublicAllRTAList.aspx

China, India, Japan, Korea, Singapore, the Philippines, and Thailand as well as important regional players such as ASEAN.[5]

The spate of Asian PTAs and, in particular, the widening of their ambit to areas such as services and investment can be attributed to several factors. These include the slow pace of negotiations under the Doha Development Round and the failure to achieve substantive progress in the new areas; the pursuit of broad-based PTAs by the EU and the US, in turn leading Asian countries to pursue preferential market access under similar agreements; and the perceived need to deepen integration through liberalization of investment, labour, and regulatory cooperation to support regional and bilateral production networks. The inclusion of services and investment issues reflects increased policy interest in the service sector, growing recognition of the role played by services in economic development, and the importance of dismantling services trade and investment barriers. These trends also reflect the growing use of broader PTAs in Asia as a policy tool for addressing longer-term objectives such as trade and investment facilitation, strategic diversification of trade flows, enhancing negotiating and regulatory capacity, and for providing the impetus for unilateral liberalization.

There has been much analysis of the trade-creating and trade-diverting effects of PTAs in goods and how PTAs compare to most-favoured nation (MFN) based market access commitments and trade rules under the World Trade Organization (WTO). In contrast, comparatively little analysis has been undertaken of PTAs in services, mainly owing to the empirical challenges involved in assessing MFN or preferential trade flows in services. However, given the growing number of PTAs involving services and this being the likely trend for the future, an understanding of the relationship and dynamics between multilateral and regional or preferential trade rules and commitments in services (and related cross-cutting areas) is required. Such an analysis is needed given the significance of regulatory barriers in shaping services trade flows and thus the role of regulatory disciplines in governing services trade. Such analysis is also required given the incipient nature of many GATS disciplines and the rather low levels of binding GATS commitments and offers and thus the possibilities for cross-learning between the multilateral and the preferential trading system with regard to rule making, negotiating modalities and templates, and the scope for deepening and widening commitments in services on a preferential or multilateral basis. Such analysis would enable one to understand whether

---

[5] See Fink and Molinuevo (2007) for Asia and Roy, Marchetti, and Lim (2007) for advances in specific sectors.

and to what extent PTAs complement, undermine, compete with, or aid multilateral negotiations in services.

7.1.1 Scope and Objectives

The present chapter attempts to fill the gap in the existing literature on services trade noted above. It does so through an in-depth analysis of eight Asian PTAs: seven intraregional and one cross-regional; seven bilateral and one regional; seven concluded and one under negotiation; and involving a mix of developed and developing countries under North–North (N–N), North–South (N–S), and South–South (S–S) agreements. The selected agreements include the India–Korea CEPA (N–S), India–Singapore CECA (N–S), Japan–Singapore CECA (N–N), Japan–Philippines EPA (N–S), China–Pakistan FTA (S–S), China–ASEAN FTA (regional, S–S), India–Sri Lanka CEPA (S–S), and the US–Korea FTA (cross-regional, N–N).

The selection of these PTAs reflects several considerations. The most important reason underlying their selection was the need to include agreements which involved different combinations of partners in terms of income levels, i.e. a mix of North–North, North–South, and South–South agreements, as noted above. The second consideration was to include at least one regional PTA along with the usual bilateral PTAs. Hence, China–ASEAN was chosen as a PTA involving a regional bloc with another country within Asia. A third consideration was the need to include at least one extra-regional PTA, as captured by the US–Korea FTA. A final consideration was the need to include agreements at different stages of completion, some concluded and already in force (recent or earlier), and some still under negotiation. The India–Sri Lanka CEPA was chosen to cover a PTA where there are no commitments as yet but where a detailed framework is available for comparison with the GATS, while under the other PTAs, there is scope to discuss the commitments made vis-à-vis those under the GATS.

The analysis of the selected PTAs focuses on three aspects. These relate to:

(1) negotiating architecture and scheduling modalities;
(2) overall framework of disciplines and chapters on cross-cutting issues; and
(3) scope and depth of commitments made under these PTAs compared to those undertaken by these same countries under the GATS.

The wider objective of this analysis is to gain a better understanding of the evolving universe of rules and negotiating architectures in services and the extent to which PTAs have gone beyond the GATS in rule making and commitments and thus might provide scope to adopt best practices for future WTO negotiations. For this purpose, the comparative analysis specifically addresses several questions. How equivalent are PTA provisions to those found in the GATS? Do the PTA rules promote "open regionalism" and to what extent are they discriminatory towards non-member countries? Do the PTAs involve advances in rule making relative to the GATS and, if so, in what manner? What differing approaches and negotiating architectures are used in these PTAs compared to those under the GATS? Where do the PTAs fall short with regard to rule making or market access commitments? Are these similar to those found under the GATS? What differences and similarities emerge relative to the GATS with respect to concerns in specific sectors and on specific issues? And to what extent and in what manner do the PTAs enable countries to evolve more pro-competitive regulations and to build negotiating and regulatory capacity which could be useful for multilateral services negotiations? In examining these issues, an attempt is made to identify commonalities and differences between these selected PTAs and the GATS and also to identify patterns with regard to the scope and depth of commitments and of rule making with respect to the nature of the countries (developed or developing) involved in the PTAs.

7.1.2 Outline

Following this introduction, Section 7.2 of the chapter provides an overview of the status of services PTAs in Asia, including those discussed in this chapter. Section 7.3 provides an analysis of the architecture of the selected agreements, in terms of the negotiating approach, carve-outs, and generally applicable or excluded measures for the selected agreements. Section 7.4 discusses the overall framework of these PTAs vis-à-vis the GATS and examines key disciplines and specific chapters on cross-cutting issues such as movement of natural persons and investment to identify similarities and differences between the multilateral and preferential frameworks and their implications. Section 7.5 discusses the scope and coverage of commitments, by sectors and by modes under the PTAs, both quantitatively and qualitatively, in comparison with the Uruguay Round commitments and latest GATS offers made by these same countries and what this implies about the countries' preferential versus multilateral negotiating stance and preparedness. The final section concludes the chapter by summarizing the main take-home messages from this analysis and by identifying what PTAs have to offer for global rule making and services negotiations.

7.2 STATUS OF PTAS IN SERVICES IN ASIA

The rise of services PTAs in Asia is a recent phenomenon. Until 2000, the only trade agreement in services in Asia was the ASEAN Framework Agreement on Trade in Services or AFAS. However, since then over 30 agreements covering services – of which at least one Asian country is a member – have been signed or are at different stages of negotiation.[6] All the key countries in South, South East and East Asia, including China, India, Japan, the Republic of Korea, and Singapore, have entered into a large number of FTAs. This spurt has mostly occurred in the post-2000 period. Increasingly, many of these agreements are "broad-based" in that they include areas such as services, investment and other emerging issues.

Table 7.1 illustrates the share of PTAs which cover services for selected Asian countries. It is evident that for the most advanced countries in the region, namely, Japan, the Republic of Korea, and Singapore, more than 90% of the PTAs cover services. For almost all the selected countries, over half of the PTAs cover services. This includes all the major developing countries in Asia, such as China, India, and the ASEAN countries. Hence, services are an increasingly important area of negotiating interest not only for the advanced Asian countries but also for the emerging economies in Asia.

The status of the eight PTAs selected for discussion in this chapter is highlighted in Table 7.2. These are all PTAs that have been signed since 2000, particularly in the last five to six years. Most have come into effect very recently.

7.3 COVERAGE OF DISCIPLINES AND CROSS-CUTTING ISSUES IN SELECTED ASIAN PTAS

One of the most important areas to examine is the overall framework of rules and provisions under the PTAs covering services and the extent to which there is convergence or divergence from the coverage of similar rules and disciplines under the GATS. The following discussion takes a step-by-step approach to examining these similarities and differences among the PTAs and between the PTAs and the GATS.

---

6 http://www.aric.adb.org/10.php.

Table 7.1 RTAs featuring services for selected Asian countries, April 2012

Country	Notified RTAs in force	RTAs for which an early announcement has been made	Total no. of RTAs	Total no. of RTAs featuring services provisions	Services provisions RTAs as a percentage of total no. of RTAs
Bangladesh	6	1	7	0	0
Cambodia	6	0	6	3	50
China	11	4	15	11	73
Hong Kong	3	0	3	3	100
India	16	4	20	4	20
Indonesia	8	1	9	4	44
Japan	13	4	17	13	77
Korea	13	3	16	9	56
Malaysia	13	1	14	9	64
Pakistan	8	0	8	2	25
Philippines	9	0	9	4	44
Singapore	21	3	24	18	75
Sri Lanka	7	1	8	0	0
Thailand	11	2	13	7	54

Note: The number of FTAs for each country may not exactly match the figures provided in Table 7.1 owing to slight differences in the treatment of agreements which are under negotiation. However, the overall numbers are broadly similar.

Source: WTO RTA Database, available at http://rtais.wto.org/UI/PublicMaintainRTAHome.aspx, accessed on December 20, 2013.

7.3.1 Key Disciplines: Some General Insights

This section examines key disciplines under the GATS, whether these are covered under the selected PTAs and also the manner in which they are covered. This analysis is used to draw some broad inferences about the approaches and the possible underlying reasons for the approaches adopted. It also tries to identify patterns based on the typology of these PTAs in terms of the countries involved. The aim is to highlight, through comparisons with the GATS, whether PTAs in services have made possible more comprehensive rule making than under the GATS, and to what extent they may have used the GATS as a benchmark for rule making. By providing comparisons among the PTAs on each of these issues, the aim

Table 7.2 Status of selected Asian PTAs

FTA Name	Under negotiation	Signed	In effect	Notified to the WTO	Year		
					Negotiation	Signed	In effect
India–Korea CEPA		✓	✓	✓		2009	2010
India–Singapore CECA		✓	✓	✓		2005	2005
Japan–Singapore CECA		✓	✓	✓		2002	2002
Japan–Philippines EPA		✓	✓	✓		2006	2008
China–Pakistan FTA		✓	✓	✓		2009	2009
China–ASEAN FTA		✓	✓	✓		2004	2005
India–Sri Lanka CEPA	✓				2005		
US–Korea FTA		✓				2007	2012

Source: http://www.aric.adb.org/10.php. (accessed October 3, 2012).

is to highlight how levels of development, differences in bargaining power and asymmetries in size, might among other things influence the approach to services liberalization under PTAs.

An examination of the eight PTAs selected for this study reveals that although they differ in terms of the nature of the countries involved (and as will be seen later also in terms of the scope and depth of scheduled commitments), they are broadly similar to each other and to the GATS with regard to the framework of rules and provisions. Table 7.3 summarizes the coverage of all major disciplines and provisions in the services chapters of the selected PTAs.

As shown in Table 7.3, the disciplines on market access and national treatment (which are the basic pillars of the GATS liberalization architecture), in the services chapter of all eight of the selected PTAs, are closest in wording and intent to that found under the GATS. In addition, general rules and obligations which are common across the selected PTAs and which are again quite similar in scope and intent to that found in the GATs are those on transparency, domestic regulation, payments and transfers, restrictions to safeguard the balance of payments, general exceptions, and rule of origin (denial of benefits). These latter disciplines involve broadly similar terms and conditions across all the PTAs, and the wording

Table 7.3 Coverage of key disciplines in services chapters of selected PTAs

Disciplines	North–South PTAs			South–South PTAs			North–North PTAs	
	India–Singapore CECA	India–Korea CEPA	Japan–Philippines EPA	India–Sri Lanka CEPA	China–ASEAN FTA	China–Pakistan FTA	Japan–Singapore CECA	US–Korea FTA
MFN	X	X	X	X	No	No	No	X
National treatment	X	X	X	X	X	X	X	X
Transparency	X	X	X	X	X	X	No	X
Market access non-discriminatory	X	X	X	X	X	X	X	X
Domestic regulation	X	X	X (Authoriza-tion, licensing, qualifica-tion)	X	X	X	X	X (specific to development and application of domestic regulation)
Safeguard measures	X	X	No (included in investment chapter)	X	X	X	No (included in investment chapter)	No
Recognition	X	X	X	X	X	X	No (separate chapter on MNP where	X

Table 7.3 (continued)

Disciplines	North–South PTAs			South–South PTAs			North–North PTAs	
	India–Singapore CECA	India–Korea CEPA	Japan–Philippines EPA	India–Sri Lanka CEPA	China–ASEAN FTA	China–Pakistan FTA	Japan–Singapore CECA	US–Korea FTA
							mutual recognition is covered)	
Subsidies	X	X	No	X	X	No	No	No
Government procurement	X	No	No (separate chapter)	X	No	No	No (separate chapter)	No (separate chapter)
Monopolies and exclusive suppliers	X	X	X	X	X	X	X	No
Business practices	X	X	No	X	X	X	X	No
Payments and transfers	X	X	X	X	X	X	X	X
General exceptions	X	X	X	X	X	X	X	X
Rule of origin (denial of benefit)	X	X	X	X	X	X	X	X

Restrictions to safeguard the balance of payments	X	X	X	X	X	X	X	X
Dispute settlement	No (separate chapter and included in investment chapter)	No (separate chapter and included in investment chapter)	No (separate chapter)	No (separate chapter and included in investment chapter)	X (reference to separate chapter on dispute settlement)	X	No (separate chapter and included in investment chapter)	No (separate chapter and included in investment chapter with additional annexes on specific issues)
Selected additional provisions not found in GATS	Services–investment linkage	Services–investment linkage	Sub-committee on trade in services	Services–investment linkage, sub-committee on trade in services	Cooperation (for enhancing capacity and efficiency) Different levels of government	Cooperation (for enhancing capacity and efficiency), Committee on Trade in Services	Service suppliers of any non-party	Non-conforming measures, local presence

Source: Based on an analysis of the legal texts of the selected PTAs.

is also very similar – in several cases, exactly the same as that employed under the GATS. Several of the PTAs specifically refer to the pertinent article under the GATS for further definitions and clarifications, clearly indicating that the GATS has been used as a benchmark for establishing the framework of these preferential services agreements. Therefore, the PTAs do not deviate much from the GATS or from one another in terms of the basic liberalization framework they follow, which is defined by the market access and national treatment obligations. They also do not deviate much with regard to coverage of key issues such as domestic regulation which indicates recognition of the latter as the key impediment to services trade and investment and the importance of including obligations such as objectivity and transparency in applying domestic regulations and not nullifying the services commitments made.

A slightly different approach is evident in the case of some other disciplines such as those on monopolies and exclusive suppliers, transparency, business practices, and recognition, which may not always be present in the services chapter. Of the selected PTAs, at least six contain such provisions, but in several cases they are present outside the services chapter. For example, although the provision on business practices is not included in the services chapter of the Japan–Philippines Economic Partnership Agreement (JPEPA), the intent of this provision is captured in provisions under a different chapter entitled Business Environment in the JPEPA text. Likewise, although recognition is not explicitly covered in the services chapter of the Japan–Singapore agreement, there is a provision on recognition under the chapter on movement of natural persons, with wording similar to that found under the GATS or other PTAs for disciplines on mutual recognition. It is worth noting that, even when some of these provisions, such as those on recognition, are included in the services chapter, they may also be present in other chapters, signifying their importance. This approach to the coverage of key disciplines suggests that some provisions have been included where they have a more direct bearing on the mode or sector or cross-cutting issue under discussion, thus potentially allowing for more detail and linkages to be established with relevant issues.

The disciplines within the services chapter which tend to be least common across the selected PTAs are those on subsidies, emergency safeguard measures, government procurement, MFN, and dispute settlement. Here three different approaches are evident.

The first is the tendency to have completely separate chapters on these issues, in addition to which these disciplines are often incorporated in chapters on other issues. This approach is most evident for the provision on dispute settlement. All but one of the selected agreements have a separate chapter on dispute settlement in addition to which dispute settlement provisions are found with a considerable amount of detail in chapters on investment or chapters on financial services, often with additional annexes on specific dispute-related issues. This approach clearly indicates that issues which are significant and cross-cutting are covered in most PTAs by an overarching chapter and by explicitly indicating linkages with other important issues or sectors, thus providing scope for additional detail and customization.

The second approach seen is to cover the discipline outside the services text in a separate chapter, or to leave out the discipline altogether from the scope of the agreement (along with carve-outs for the same). This is applicable to the case of government procurement where, as shown in Table 7.4, either the PTAs contain a separate chapter on government procurement where disciplines are approached in a cross-cutting manner or there is no discipline. Even where provisions are included in the services text, the wording remains general as in the GATS, only noting that services procured for governmental purposes and not for commercial reasons are excluded, with no additional detail or rule making. The overall approach suggests that issues such as government procurement remain sensitive in many PTAs and there is no uniform approach.

The third approach identified is to either cover the provision within the chapter on services (usually rather loosely) or to exclude it altogether from the agreement, with no separate coverage under specific chapters on these issues or in other related chapters where these provisions have a bearing. This approach has been taken in the cases of subsidies and emergency safeguard measures where there are either rather general provisions included within the services chapter or no coverage of these disciplines at all. In one of the selected PTAs, safeguards are discussed in the context of the investment chapter. The latter approach suggests that there are differing views between PTA participants on such disciplines, as has also been the case in the multilateral negotiations. This indicates that basic sensitivities and differences of opinion remain under the PTAs and that there has not been much advancement in rule making in these domains.

It is interesting to note some of the patterns which emerge in terms of the coverage of disciplines, with regard to the nature of countries involved in the PTAs. While there is generally little difference in the coverage of the main provisions between the three North–South, the three South–South, and the two North–North agreements under discussion, a difference emerges in the provisions on government procurement, emergency safeguards, and subsidies, the areas where, as mentioned earlier, the sensitivities and non-uniformity of approaches are most evident. Both the North–North agreements (Japan–Singapore and US–Korea) as well as the one North–South agreement involving Japan (JPEPA) have separate chapters on government procurement, while none of the South–South PTAs has such provisions. Hence, government procurement is clearly an issue that is of negotiating interest for the developed countries (as also borne out by the multilateral discussion and differences seen between developed and developing countries on this subject).

While it is difficult to infer anything conclusive regarding the motivations and objectives of the different countries or the patterns that emerge based on the typology of the PTAs (N–N, N–S, S–S) given the small sample of PTAs, some differences and possible explanations are worth noting. For instance, while both the North–South and North–North PTAs involving Japan have government procurement chapters, the same is not true of Korea, whose North–South PTA with India does not cover government procurement either as a discipline in the services chapter or as a separate chapter, while its N–N PTA with the US includes a separate government procurement chapter. This suggests that, for a particular country, the approach to certain disciplines such as government procurement may vary across PTAs depending on its negotiating partner, which may also reflect differences in objectives, concerns, and bargaining power between different PTAs signed by a country.

Likewise, it is interesting to note that neither of the North–North PTAs contains provisions for safeguard measures within the services text, while this provision is included (though rather loosely as will be discussed later) in all the South–South PTAs and the two North–South PTAs excluding Japan. This pattern might reflect the fact that PTAs involving developing countries may be subject to more concerns over application of safeguard measures and thus the need to include explicit provisions to prevent the introduction of such measures. The absence of safeguard-related provisions in the two North–North agreements could also reflect the greater regulatory capacity on both sides to deal with such measures. Once again, it is noteworthy that both of Japan's PTAs cover safeguards in the context of the investment chapter, specifically with regard to cross-border movement of financial capital for reasons of macroeconomic management and stability.

There are additional provisions in the selected PTAs which are not present in the GATS. In the North–South and South–South PTAs, these additional provisions mainly pertain to institutional issues such as setting up of sub-committees on services trade or cooperation, or recognizing the linkages between services and investment in so far as explicitly noting the applicability of provisions in the investment chapter of the PTA to commercial presence-based delivery of services (i.e. the cross-cutting nature of key investment provisions). It is worth noting that all three PTAs involving India include a services-investment linkage provision, which is not seen in any of the other South–South or North–South PTAs. The two North–North PTAs involve additional provisions which allow for extending privileges to third party firms operating in the partner countries or regarding non-applicability of market access and national treatment conditions to any non-conforming measures at various levels of government. What is evident here is that PTAs involving developing countries tend to focus on developing regulatory capacity while the developed–developed country PTAs may involve more detailed provisions, whose implementation presumes a certain level of regulatory capacity.

Overall, even from the small sample of PTAs selected for discussion, it is clear that: (i) some disciplines such as government procurement or subsidies are not uniformly seen to be integral to services liberalization; (ii) some disciplines such as dispute settlement are seen to be generally applicable, thus warranting a cross-cutting approach within the overall PTA; and (iii) some disciplines such as safeguards or recognition are seen to be pertinent to specific issues, thus requiring explicit inclusion in relevant parts of the agreement. Although the sample size is small, there appear to be some broad differences between agreements involving only developed countries and those involving developing countries, where the former seem to go a bit further in terms of having specific chapters and additional annexes on the so-called "Singapore Issues" of transparency in government procurement and investment. Finally, countries seem to follow a similar approach across PTAs in terms of the disciplines covered and the manner in which this is done, although differences may arise on specific disciplines especially in cases where the partner may have more negotiating leverage (like the US).

7.3.2 Important Cross-cutting Issues: Some General Insights

An examination of the eight selected PTAs reveals that there are some cross-cutting issues which are uniformly addressed across agreements in the form of chapters or additional annexes, but there are also differences when it comes to the more "new age" regulatory issues. Table 7.4 provides an overview of the status of chapters or annexes in each of these PTAs.

As can be seen in Table 7.4, the most prevalent issue, which is covered in a chapter in all these PTAs, is that of dispute settlement, indicating the importance of legal frameworks for operationalizing and enforcing commitments and rules under all agreements. Next most important are the issues of investment and movement of natural persons, which are present in all but two agreements (China–Pakistan and China–ASEAN). All types of PTAs, N–S, N–N, and S–S, have chapters on these two

Table 7.4 Presence of chapters and annexes in selected PTAs

FTA Name	Investment	Movement of Natural Persons	Government Procurement	Competition	Cooperation	Dispute Settlement	Financial Services	Telecommunication Services	Other issues
India–Korea CEPA	✓	✓		✓	✓	✓		✓	"Other" includes audiovisual co-production
India–Singapore CECA	✓	✓				✓			"Other" includes air services, e-commerce, education and media
Japan–Singapore CECA	✓	✓	✓	✓		✓	✓	✓	"Other" includes ICT, broadcasting, tourism etc.
Japan–Philippines EPA	✓	✓	✓	✓	✓	✓			
China–Pakistan FTA						✓			
China–ASEAN FTA						✓			
India–Sri Lanka CEPA	✓	✓			✓	✓			"Other" includes air services
US–Korea FTA	✓	✓	✓	✓		✓	✓	✓	"Other" includes E-commerce, labour and environment

Source: Based on an analysis of the legal texts of the selected PTAs.

issues. Cooperation chapters mostly feature in N–S and S–S agreements, although, as highlighted earlier, there are provisions on cooperation within the services text in several PTAs (e.g. China–Pakistan, China–ASEAN), even if there is no separate chapter on cooperation. But it is worth noting that neither of the N–N PTAs included in this sample have chapters on cooperation (or provisions within the services text on cooperation), indicating that a certain level of regulatory capacity and institutional development has already been achieved by such countries. Competition policy and government procurement are the least common areas to be covered under separate chapters. Government procurement chapters are present in both the N–N PTAs and in the one N–S PTA featuring Japan (as also highlighted earlier), but are not present in any of the S–S PTAs. Competition policy chapters, similarly, are only found in the N–N PTAs or the N–S PTAs involving Japan and Korea, and are not present in any of the S–S PTAs. Thus as highlighted earlier, government procurement and competition are clearly not priority areas for agreements involving only developing countries, and are probably more sensitive issues for the latter.

As regards additional chapters or annexes, it is evident that only agreements involving developed countries contain annexes on financial services, while none of the N–S or S–S PTAs has a financial services chapter or annex. In the case of telecom services, barring the India–Korea PTA, there is no such annex in any of the other PTAs involving developing countries, whereas both the N–N PTAs in the sample have such a chapter. What this reveals is that on issues or in sectors that involve considerable regulatory cooperation and institutional capacity, developed country PTAs are most likely to go further by including specific chapters (with elaborate rules as will be seen later). Annexes or chapters on "other" sectors or issues mainly relate to emerging areas such as audiovisual, e-commerce, information and communication technology, education, and environmental services, areas such as air transport services where bilateral cooperation is important, or sectors such as tourism where there is considerable commercial potential and scope for cooperation. It is interesting to note that all the PTAs involving India, whether with developed or developing countries, contain chapters on quite a variety of "other" issues or sectors, possibly reflecting India's competitiveness in services and its interest in leveraging its PTAs to explore commercial and collaborative opportunities in a range of service sectors. Both the N–N PTAs also include chapters on "other" issues, either relating to technology-intensive or commercial considerations (Japan–Singapore) or to social and environmental considerations (US–Korea). It is also worth noting that only the PTA with the US incorporates social and environmental issues. None of the intraregional Asian PTAs (including the other PTA involving Korea) cover such non-economic issues in additional chapters. Thus, the variation with regard to the inclusion of additional chapters in PTAs possibly also reflects differences in negotiating approaches and bargaining power for the same country under different PTAs depending on its negotiating partner.

A comparison of the above coverage of chapters and annexes in the selected PTAs with that under the GATS indicates that PTAs have generally gone beyond the GATS in inscribing more sector- or issue-specific provisions. Issues such as competition or cooperation are neither included as annexes nor as provisions within the services chapter of the GATS. Sensitive issues such as environment and labour are not covered under the GATS annexes. This expanded framework of rules in the form of additional chapters under PTAs confirms the well-known fact that countries are able to introduce sensitive issues into PTAs which are difficult to incorporate into the multilateral framework (labour and environment) and that the ability to do this is related to the bargaining power of the partner countries (US in US–Korea). The difference in the scope of chapters under these PTAs from that found under the GATS indicates that PTAs have been able to address technological advancements and new opportunities such as e-commerce, ICT, and audiovisual services, and further that PTAs have been able to address specific concerns and interests of the negotiating partners by including specific sectoral chapters. But the area where the deviation from the GATS is most striking is that of investment. The GATS does not contain any separate annex on investment, while almost all the PTAs contain separate chapters on investment with detailed provisions on rights of investors and judicial procedures to be followed in the case of investor disputes (as will be discussed later, in addition to explicit provisions in the services chapter on services–investment linkages as highlighted earlier). Thus, the PTAs do advance rule making by expanding the scope of the negotiating framework by including chapters and provisions on additional issues, particularly with respect to investment and emerging areas in services trade.

7.3.3 Carve-outs and Broader Scope and Coverage Issues in the Selected PTAs

While it is important to examine the extent to which the PTAs are similar in scope across disciplines and additional issues or sectors, it is equally important to examine to what extent they leave out sectors and subsectors. Across all the selected PTAs, air transport services, other than three subsectors, namely aircraft repair and maintenance services, computer reservation system services, and sales and marketing are excluded.[7] This exclusion is the same as that under the GATS. What is interesting to note is that, while air transport services, given their dependence on bilateral air service agreements and the presence of other international regulatory frameworks to govern this sector, are not conducive to multilateral discussions, even under PTAs, they are carved out. However, in some of the PTAs, air services are separately addressed through an additional chapter addressing sector-specific liberalization issues. Another area that is commonly excluded is cabotage in maritime transport services, as is also the case under the GATs. There is also a carve-out for financial services in two of the agreements involving India, although the India–Singapore CECA does not carve out this sector, reflecting the importance of this sector for Singapore. Thus carve-outs in the PTAs reflect concerns and sensitivities similar to those under the GATS. However, as shown earlier, PTAs tend to include customized chapters on many other services and cross-cutting issues. Hence, they have the scope to go further on rule making or intent than the GATS (though, as will be highlighted later when examining the content of these provisions, these additional chapters may remain best-endeavour in nature).

Apart from these carve-outs, the PTAs are also very similar to the GATS in the way they define their scope and coverage. The services chapters across all the PTAs in this sample commence by highlighting the scope and coverage. In all the PTAs, in addition to excluding air transport services (barring the three selected segments noted above) and cabotage services, the texts clearly note that the measures *will not apply to subsidies provided by governments or state enterprises* (including grants, government-supported loans, guarantees and insurance) or to *measures relating to immigration laws and regulations*, and *measures affecting natural persons seeking employment or nationality or residence in the partner country's market*. Some of the PTAs also note that the measures affecting trade in services will not apply to government procurement (although there may be chapters specifically on some of these excluded areas where specific negotiating issues and progressive liberalization are addressed). In addition, all the PTAs conform with the GATS in that they exclude services supplied in the exercise of governmental authority which are not supplied on a commercial basis or in competition with one or more service suppliers, with this exclusion being applicable to all levels of government, central, state, local, and provincial. Thus the GATS text appears to be a reference for the PTA texts with regard to broader scope and coverage issues.

---

7 Based on an analysis of the legal texts of the selected PTAs.

7.4 THE SUBSTANTIVE CONTENT OF DISCIPLINES AND CHAPTERS IN SELECTED PTAS

While it is useful to examine the scope of disciplines and chapters, it is the substantive content of these disciplines and chapters that determines whether the PTAs do indeed go further than the GATS when it comes to rule making and liberalization intent. The discussion that follows in this section has two parts. The first takes a closer look at the content of key disciplines found in the services chapter of the PTAs and compares this with the content of the same disciplines in the GATS text, to see to what extent they are broadly similar and to what extent they diverge, what these differences might imply, and whether there are any identifiable patterns with regard to the nature of countries involved and the content of these disciplines. The discussion also examines some new provisions which are found in the selected PTAs, but are absent from the GATS. The second part of the discussion in this section examines the substantive content of chapters on key issues (such as investment or movement of natural persons) in the selected PTAs to assess the extent to which they are similar to or different from the annexes on similar issues under the GATS. Once again there is an attempt to identify the relationship, if any, between the types of countries involved in the PTAs and the content of these chapters.

7.4.1 Content of Key Disciplines: Some Insights

The following discussion highlights and compares the content for the disciplines on: MFN, market access, national treatment, domestic regulation, transparency, mutual recognition, other areas (subsidies, government procurement, emergency safeguard measures), and additional issues (services–investment linkages, cooperation, institutional issues), as highlighted in Table 7.4 above.

7.4.1.1 Most-favoured nation provision

The MFN provision is one of the fundamental principles of the multilateral trading system and thus also of the GATS. Under the GATS, the MFN provision states that each member will accord immediately and unconditionally similar treatment to third country services and service suppliers with respect to measures covered by the GATS. If one examines the text of the MFN provision or "Review of MFN commitments" as it is termed in some of the selected PTAs, one finds that, while the broader intent of extending similar treatment to third parties is present in the PTA provisions on MFN, there are slight differences in wording and nuancing of the intent. For instance, the India–Korea CEPA and the India–

Singapore CECA state that if one of the parties enters into an agreement on services trade with a third party, it will give *consideration to a request by the other party* for incorporation of no less favourable treatment than that provided in the new agreement, while maintaining the balance of concessions in the overall agreement. This is not as clear a mandate to extend similar treatment as it only says that consideration will be given to such extension requests by the signatories of the India–Korea CEPA or India–Singapore CECA. Likewise, the India–Sri Lanka CEPA has a loose provision on MFN. In contrast, the Japan–Philippines EPA contains the more standard GATS form of MFN provision, wherein parties are to accord no less favourable treatment to third parties with exceptions for those activities, sectors or subsectors listed in the annex on MFN exemptions. Hence, it is a stronger version of MFN than that found in the India–Singapore and India–Korea PTAs. The US–Korea PTA's MFN provision similarly is closer to the wording found under the GATS. There is one difference though between even the stronger versions and the GATS MFN provision in that none of the PTAs uses the terms "unconditionally" and "immediately" as would be expected given their preferential nature. They are always somewhat softer than the GATS. It is important to note, however, that the MFN provision is pertinent only to the extent that the commitments made under the PTAs go beyond the level of unilateral liberalization and are truly preferential in nature, in which case the extent to which MFN is accorded or not becomes important for determining the possibilities for trade creation or diversion.

7.4.1.2 National treatment

The national treatment under the GATS requires members to accord no less favourable treatment to services and service suppliers of other members than what is accorded to their own, subject to conditions and qualifications set out in the sectoral commitment schedules. Formally identical or formally different treatment may be accorded. Less favourable is further defined as relating to treatment which modifies the conditions of competition in favour of the member country's services or service suppliers. Further, countries would not be required to compensate for any inherent competitive disadvantage resulting from the foreign character of the relevant services or suppliers.

The selected PTAs almost all adhere to this content and wording in their provisions on national treatment. The one difference that emerges is that the clause on not being required to compensate for inherent competitive disadvantages is brought explicitly into the national treatment clause in some of the PTAs, while it is present as a footnote to this provision in the GATS. The question is whether this can be interpreted as not only clarificatory in nature but as an integral part of understanding measures affecting services and service suppliers in that measures may have differential effects owing to inherent disadvantages on account of being foreign, though they may not be per se discriminatory. This is an important issue in services trade and the PTAs make this recognition explicit.

In some of the PTAs, additional clauses are present. The India–Singapore, India–Korea, and India–Sri Lanka agreements include two additional clauses. The first of these clauses states that subsequent establishment, acquisition and expansion of investments by a service supplier that is incorporated, constituted, set up or otherwise in one of the parties and owned by a service supplier of the other party is to be treated as an investment of the other party for purposes of determining applicable treatment. Thus, these PTAs are forward-looking in extending similar or better treatment to new investments in services by any one of the parties in the other party's market. It is also worth noting that, while allowing for better treatment of future investments, the footnote to this clause also states that such improvements would not mean automatic additions to India's schedule of specific commitments. Thus, there is a possibility of progressive liberalization but without requiring grandfathering of earlier investments under similar, more liberal, terms and conditions. The second additional clause in these three PTAs pertains to the applicability of the national treatment provisions at the regional and local levels, thus addressing sub-federal issues in the application of measures affecting services trade and investment in countries like India.

The US–Korea agreement is also quite different in wording and scope of national treatment from the other PTAs in this sample. It excludes the use of the term "services" and makes mention only of "service suppliers", thus narrowing the scope potentially to modes where there is explicit presence of service suppliers (modes 3 and 4 in particular). Like the Indian PTAs, it has an additional clause which states that this national treatment provision would apply at the level of the regional government, in like circumstances. Thus this provision is explicitly extended to apply at sub-federal levels of government, although the conditionality of "like circumstances" does proscribe this extension to some degree. There is also no mention in this agreement of formally similar or identical treatment or of inherent disadvantages. So, there is somewhat more ambiguity in this agreement about the scope and interpretation of the national treatment provision.

7.4.1.3 Transparency

The GATS provision on transparency requires prompt publication of all relevant measures of general application and all international agreements, to which the members are signatories, which have a bearing on the agreement. Where this is not possible, the information is to be made publicly available. In addition, members are to provide notification of the introduction of or changes to regulations and procedures which would affect their commitments and should also respond promptly to all requests from other members seeking information. There is also a requirement to establish inquiry points within two years, with some flexibility for developing country members. There is also scope to notify the Services Trade Council if measures are taken by the other member, which affect the operation of the agreement.

In the PTAs, for the most part, the GATS provision on transparency holds verbatim. Some of the PTAs, such as the China–Pakistan and the China–ASEAN agreements, specifically refer to the GATS Article III on transparency and note that this provision of the GATS is incorporated in and forms an integral part of the PTA. Others such as the India–Korea and the India–Singapore PTAs repeat the clauses of the GATS under the transparency article. However, there are instances where the PTAs make specific points which do not appear in the GATS provision. For example, the Japan–Philippines EPA mentions the application of transparency to licensing and qualification procedures through an enquiry point, where the latter would be notified to the other party by a diplomatic note as soon as the agreement enters into force. Furthermore, there is a clause which specifies that a public list has to be provided of all existing measures, at all levels of government in both Japan and the Philippines, falling within the scope of the PTA's services chapter, and which are inconsistent with the market access and national treatment provisions, whether or not these are included in the specific commitments. It also specifies that this list would need to provide information on the sector or subsector, the nature of the inconsistency, the legal source or authority of the measure, and a description of the measure, with provision for an annual review of this list. Thus, in effect, the transparency requirement in the JPEPA is more specific about certain measures, namely those pertaining to movement of natural persons (licensing and qualification-related procedures) which is a sensitive issue for Japan and a major negotiating issue in this particular agreement. The institutional requirement is also more stringent as the nature of the listing. Thus it is evident that on issues that are particularly important in a PTA, members may go beyond the GATS provisions on transparency to address their specific interests and insist on more binding obligations.

The US–Korea agreement is again different in nomenclature and content. The article on transparency in the services chapter is called "transparency in developing and applying regulations" where regulations are explicitly noted as including those establishing or applying to licensing authorization or criteria at different levels of government. The provisions under this article in the US–Korea agreement appear to be weaker than those under the GATS. For instance, one clause requires each party to establish or maintain appropriate mechanisms for responding to enquiries, although there is no specific mention of contact points or any institutional directions for what might constitute such appropriate mechanisms. Thus more leeway is provided to the two parties. A second clause notes that if a country does not provide advance notice of or opportunity for comment on regulations proposed for adoption, then "to the extent possible" it will address the reasons for not doing so. The latter is a very openly worded clause as it not only allows countries the scope not to provide information in advance, but also does not mandate the country to provide the reasons for not informing the other party, leaving this dependent upon the feasibility of doing so. The third clause of this transparency provision calls for reasonable time to be allowed between publication of final regulations and their implementation. This is also absent from the GATS. There is also reference to a separate chapter on transparency and consistency with provisions under that chapter. Hence, the US–Korea agreement is on the whole much more ambiguous about what is meant by transparency, how this is to be ensured, and how much flexibility countries can retain in this regard. In contrast, the other PTAs either repeat the scope and intent of the GATS transparency provision or go a bit further as in the case of JPEPA.

7.4.1.4 Market access

This discipline governs the extent of, and conditions for, entry of foreign service suppliers into other markets under the GATS. The market access provision in the GATS is conditional upon the limitations inscribed in the member countries' commitment schedules. Hence, unless otherwise inscribed in the commitments, members are not permitted to restrict entry based on limitations on the number of foreign service suppliers, the total value of their transactions, the total quantity of service output, the number of natural persons employed in a certain sector, on the type of legal entity, or on the extent of participation by foreign capital.

In most of the PTAs, the content of this discipline is identical to that found under the GATS, including the various limitations whose use is prohibited unless specifically included in the commitments undertaken. However, there are some noteworthy differences in content in the case of three of the selected PTAs. The US–Korea agreement does not include limitations on participation of foreign capital in terms of maximum foreign equity limits or total value of foreign investment in its list of proscribed market access measures, while retaining all the others. The two agreements involving Japan have additional notes with regard to the movement of capital where the latter is an essential part of the service and where the country has taken a market access commitment for the supply of this service through mode 1 or mode 3. In such a case, the party cannot put restrictions on the movement of capital. Thus, both these PTAs make it harder for the parties to inscribe limitations on cross-border movement of capital when this is integral to entering the other market in a particular service sector and when that service sector is covered by a market access commitment. Another additional note present in both the PTAs that involve Japan states that limitations on inputs for the supply of a service are not covered even if limitations on the total number of service operations or on the total quantity of services output, expressed in terms of numerical limits or quotas or economic needs test requirements, are not permitted. This is an interesting exclusion to the extent that it has a particular bearing on movement of natural persons. It implies that although the parties may not be able to restrict the number of operations, the number of foreign service suppliers required to conduct these operations can still be restricted. Thus seemingly innocuous notes in some PTAs may allow scope for maintaining limitations that are of significance to their partner countries.

7.4.1.5 Domestic regulation

In view of the importance of domestic regulations in governing services trade and investment flows, the GATS article on domestic regulation requires members to ensure that all such measures in sectors where members have undertaken specific commitments are to be administered in a reasonable, objective, and impartial manner. Further, the provision also calls for judicial or administrative mechanisms for review and remedy, but in a manner consistent with member countries' legal systems. Additional conditions are also specified with respect to transparency, objectivity, and necessity of the measures.

The PTAs are broadly in line with the aforementioned domestic regulatory principles and often repeat the same clauses. But, again, there is some variation on specific issues added in the PTAs but which are not present in the GATs text. In the India–Singapore and India–Korea PTAs, for instance, there is a specific mention of joint review of the results of the negotiations on disciplines pertaining to qualification and licensing requirements and procedures and technical standards with a view to their incorporation into the services chapter of this PTA. The clause requiring parties to ensure that such requirements and procedures do not nullify or impair their specific commitments is made contingent on the incorporation of the disciplines developed in this regard under the WTO. Hence, clearly this PTA not only uses the GATS as a reference for domestic regulatory principles but also looks ahead at prospective developments in the GATS for their inclusion in the PTA text. The India–Sri Lanka agreement is similar in this regard. The US–Korea and the China–ASEAN agreements also incorporate the possibility of taking into account the results of similar negotiations. The Japan–Singapore PTA, however, does not include such a forward-looking clause, linking itself to developments under the GATS on this discipline.

The China–Pakistan FTA, while mostly similar to the GATS in its provision on domestic regulation, has an additional clause which is not found in any of the other PTAs. This clause requires the parties to consult periodically to determine the feasibility of removing any remaining nationality requirements for licensing and certification of each other's service suppliers. Thus, the specific issue of domestic regulations which link provision of a service to nationality is given importance in this PTA. The China–ASEAN agreement similarly includes additional detailed clauses. There is, for example, a sub-clause which requires competent authorities to identify all additional information in the case of an incomplete application and to remedy any deficiencies, to provide scope for resubmission of an application.

There is also deviation from the GATS with regard to the inclusion of additional conditionalities such as in the US–Korea agreement. In this agreement, one of the clauses on domestic regulation states: "while recognizing the right to regulate and to introduce new regulations for meeting national policy objectives", while noting that qualification requirements and procedures, technical standards, and licensing requirements are not to constitute unnecessary barriers to services trade. This makes the provision somewhat more nuanced and flexible by specifying the need for domestic regulations to meet national objectives.

While the clauses included under the domestic regulation discipline are more or less the same in the PTAs as under the GATS, in the Japan–Singapore PTA the specific reference to commitments regarding professional services and provision of adequate procedures to verify the competence of professionals, which is present in the GATS, is missing. Thus the scope is narrower in this PTA than in the GATS in that the parties are not mandated to ensure such procedures even where commitments have been taken.

There is also deviation with regard to the nomenclature used in this provision. In the Japan–Philippines agreement there is no discipline termed "domestic regulation". However, if one examines the content of the corresponding provision in this PTA, the domestic regulation discipline appears in the form of a provision termed "authorization, licensing or qualifications" wherein the regulations pertaining to authorization, licensing, and qualification of service suppliers are covered. The principles are the same in terms of ensuring objectivity, transparency, being no more burdensome than required, and not constituting disguised restrictions, but the scope is considerably narrower than that under the GATS. No generally applicable domestic regulatory measures with a bearing on trade in services are covered, only the narrow subset of domestic regulations pertaining to qualification and licensing issues.

Thus compared to other disciplines, in the case of domestic regulation, one finds much more variation across the PTAs in relation to the GATS. There are additional clauses and sub-clauses, or conditional statements included within the clauses, or outright exclusions from the scope of the provision. But the underlying principles of objectivity, transparency, and impartial review, continue to apply.

7.4.1.6 Mutual recognition

Mutual recognition is another discipline where one finds some variation among the PTAs and also in comparison with the GATS. The GATS gives countries the right to choose whether to accord recognition to the supplier of the other country and the manner in which to accord recognition, whether by harmonization, or by mutual agreement, or autonomously. It also calls upon members to provide adequate opportunity to other members to negotiate entry into such mutual arrangements on recognition or negotiate comparable ones with other countries. Thus, there is intent to extend the benefits of recognition to more members. Further, the standards and criteria used for according recognition are not to be applied in a discriminatory manner across members or to be a disguised restriction on services trade. Wherever appropriate, multilateral criteria and international standards are to be used in granting recognition. The Council for Trade in Services is to be informed about any mutual arrangements.

The discipline on recognition takes very different forms under the selected PTAs, all of which, except the Japan–Singapore agreement, contain this provision. While these PTAs replicate the GATS clauses regarding according recognition autonomously, or through mutual arrangement, or through harmonization, and of providing opportunity to other parties, several go further by specifically calling upon the two parties to enter into negotiations on recognition. The China–ASEAN PTA, for instance, includes a specific paragraph which says that two or more parties may enter into, or encourage their relevant competent bodies to enter into negotiations on recognition of qualification and licensing requirements and procedures in order to meet their respective standards or criteria for authorization, licensing or certification. Likewise, the China–Pakistan agreement asks both sides to facilitate the development of mutual recognition arrangements among professional or regulatory bodies via discussions and exchange of information on focal points to be appointed.

A similar degree of specificity with regard to launching discussions and with regard to specific sectors and services is found in the India–Singapore CECA. The latter calls upon the parties to ensure that their respective professional bodies (in accounting and auditing, architecture, medicine, dentistry and nursing) negotiate and conclude within one year of the agreement's entry into force, arrangements for mutual recognition of qualifications and experience, including the details of the extent and scope of this recognition. In other regulated sectors, if a request is made for discussions, then the parties would encourage their relevant professional bodies to enter into negotiations. However, delays or failures to conclude such arrangements are not to be regarded as a breach of obligations and thus would not be subject to dispute settlement, with continual review of progress. Furthermore, disputes arising out of or under such arrangements will not be covered under the dispute settlement mechanism of this PTA. The specific mention of entry into negotiations for achieving mutual recognition and with additional specificity regarding the sectors for consideration takes this PTA further than the equivalent provision under the GATS. However, there is no clear time-bound nature to the conclusion of these negotiations in so far as delays or failure to conclude are not to be deemed a breach of obligations and the dispute settlement mechanism is not applicable. The India–Korea CEPA similarly excludes the application of dispute settlement provisions in case of failure or delay in negotiating such arrangements. Thus, while being specific with regard to sectors, the provisions are rather soft in terms of implementation and timelines.

There is, however, one clause which is missing in all these PTAs, although present in the GATS. This is the reference to international standards. There is also no reference to according adequate opportunity to extend the arrangements reached between the two parties to third countries or that the criteria or standards agreed upon would not be applied in a discriminatory manner to suppliers of other countries. Thus, while the PTAs go a little further than the GATS in some respects, they are also weaker with regard to extending achievements outside the PTA and thus potentially may provide scope for trade diversion.

7.4.1.7 Other provisions – government procurement, emergency safeguards, subsidies

As noted above, provisions on issues such as government procurement, emergency safeguards, and subsidies are not commonly found in the PTAs. Where these disciplines are found, generally, they either replicate those found in the GATS text, take a more nuanced and weaker form, or are explicitly specified as being excluded from the scope of the services chapter. It is also worth pointing out that some of these disciplines are covered in the form of chapters in the PTAs rather than as disciplines within the services chapters.

Government procurement The GATS discipline on government procurement states that the articles on MFN treatment, market access, and national treatment do not apply to laws, regulations or requirements governing the procurement by governmental agencies of services purchased for governmental purposes and not for commercial resale or for the use in supply of services for commercial sale. The discipline also calls for multilateral negotiations on government procurement of services within two years of the GATS' entry into force.

Among the selected PTAs, three contain disciplines on government procurement within the services chapter. The India–Singapore and India–Sri Lanka PTAs, which have provisions on government procurement duplicate the GATS in terms of the scope of the agreement with regard to government procurement but do not make any mention of continuing future negotiations in this area. However, even where there is no separate discipline on government procurement in the PTAs, there is reference to the matter in the provision on scope and coverage in their services chapters, wherein it is noted that the measures discussed in the chapter would not apply to government procurement, without any conditions. Hence, the carve-out for government procurement is stronger in the PTAs than under the GATS to the extent that the exclusion is unqualified and there is also no mention of future discussions on this issue. However, as highlighted earlier, some of the PTAs also contain a separate government procurement chapter which is more detailed (as will be discussed later). Thus, in general, as in the multilateral context, there has been little progress on government procurement in the regional context.

Subsidies The GATS discipline on subsidies is rather open-ended and embryonic in nature. It only calls for members to recognize that subsidies could, under certain circumstances, distort trade in services and that member countries should try and develop multilateral disciplines to avoid such effects and negotiate the feasibility of countervailing procedures. In addition, the discipline also takes note of the role subsidies can play in development and accords developing countries flexibility in this regard. The discipline also calls for exchange of information on subsidies and allows members to request consultations if adversely affected by subsidies.

Four of the selected PTAs have disciplines on subsidies. A striking aspect of this discipline in the PTAs is that it is even weaker than that found under the GATS. The subsidies provision in the China–ASEAN PTA, for example, states that the agreement *does not* apply to subsidies or grants provided by either party or to conditions related to the receipt of such subsidies or grants. Moreover, this exclusion is specified as being independent of whether such subsidies or grants are offered only to domestic services, consumers, and suppliers, which makes it a strong carve-out. However, as in the case of the GATS, the PTA provision also mentions that, if such measures are seen as distorting trade, then consultations may be sought and, as specified in the GATS, the PTA also requires members to exchange information on subsidies relating to trade in services and to review their treatment when disciplines are developed in the WTO. Thus, the PTA ties this discipline to developments under the GATS.

The India–Korea, India–Singapore, and India–Sri Lanka PTAs similarly carve out subsidies from the scope of the services chapter. The subsidies provisions in these PTAs again refer to developments in multilateral negotiations on subsidies and information exchange. But these agreements go a step further in that they also outline what is meant by information exchange between the two parties. The provision specifies that this information would pertain to laws and regulations under which the measure is introduced, the form of the measure, the policy objective and purpose of the measure, the dates and duration of the programme and time limits, and the eligibility requirements and criteria applied. Such detail is not provided under the GATS. Moreover, the provision also states that dispute settlement-related provisions will not apply to any such discussions. Thus, as in the case of government procurement, there is little development of the subsidies discipline under PTAs, barring some clarification on the content of information exchange.

Emergency safeguard measures Emergency safeguard measures is another area where the GATS discipline remains embryonic, calling for multilateral negotiations on this issue based on non-discrimination and stating that the results of such discussions are not to enter into force within three years from the entry into force of the GATS. However, this provision also permits countries to declare their intent to modify or withdraw their specific commitments within a year if it is not possible to wait for three years. However, the latter provision would not apply after three years. Hence, the GATS does not permit countries to respond to surges in imports by using safeguard measures.

In the PTAs, one finds considerable variation in wording and intent for this discipline. While the China–Pakistan FTA contains a verbatim repetition of the GATS provision on emergency safeguard measures, the others are quite different. The China–ASEAN PTA, for instance, does not go so far as the GATS regarding the possible withdrawal or modification of commitments. Instead it calls for the parties to discuss such measures as may be adversely affecting their services trade. It requires that any such measures be undertaken through mutual agreement, and that due consideration be given by the other party in such circumstances. Hence, the wording is more nuanced. The India–Korea and India–Singapore PTAs prohibit both parties from taking safeguard action or from initiating or continuing with any safeguard investigation against services and service suppliers. However, in the India–Sri Lanka agreement, India's stance is different, permitting safeguard measures to be taken for a period of six months with an initial period of three months. There is also reference to the GATT Agreement on Safeguards requiring identification of domestic industry which produces like or directly competitive services. The provision, however, does not seem to be operationally feasible or meaningful as a three- or six-month time frame is unlikely to be sufficient for the domestic service to recover and because identification of like services or estimation of injury caused is likely to be very difficult in the case of services. Thus, ESMs are clearly a sensitive issue, with some countries providing scope for discussions in this area, others excluding outright the possibility of such measures, and yet others including them in a manner that may not be useful.[8]

7.4.1.8 Additional provisions in PTAs

There are several common provisions found in the sample of selected PTAs which are not found in the GATS. These include provisions on services-investment linkages, for sub-committees on services trade, on cooperation, and others. A few of these are highlighted below.

Sub-committee on trade in services Two of the PTAs contain provisions for the establishment of a sub-committee on trade in services. The India–Sri Lanka CEPA calls for the setting up of such a sub-committee to review commitments to enable further liberalization, to review the implementation and operation of the services trade chapter, and the implementation of MRAs. However, no details are provided regarding the structure and composition of the members of such a body or its functioning, barring mention that there should be representatives with the required expertise

[8] In several PTAs which do not contain a provision on safeguard measures in the services chapter, such a provision is found in the chapter on investment, as discussed later.

and an inaugural meeting within a year of entry into force of the chapter on services. No such provision is present in the other two PTAs involving India in this sample. This may reflect India's existing experience with Sri Lanka with regard to the India–Sri Lanka Free Trade Agreement and the recognition that institutional mechanisms can help in operationalizing this agreement, or possibly concerns on the part of Sri Lanka regarding competition in services from Indian suppliers. But it is worth noting that the provision is rather vague and does not give any operational framework or guidelines for such an institutional mechanism.

The JPEPA contains a similar provision for setting up an institutional mechanism for the effective implementation and operation of the services trade chapter. Again, the provision calls for a review of commitments to enable progressive liberalization, exchange of information on domestic laws and regulations, and discussion of issues related to services trade. But further details, for example, in terms of concrete timelines, as to how this mechanism would actually function, and who the members would be, are not provided.

The China–Pakistan agreement likewise calls for the setting up of a Committee on Trade in Services to review commitments relating to measures affecting services trade and to review the implementation and operation of this agreement. Specific mention is made of the need to review and discuss the provisions on mutual recognition and emergency safeguard measures, to report the outcome of the discussions to the Free Trade Commission, and to carry out other (unspecified) functions. Issues such as recognition and safeguards are thus clearly recognized as focus areas for this committee. However, once again, there is no detail on how this committee should be constituted, how it would operate, and the operational framework is left open to further discussions.

Hence, in all cases, while the inclusion of a provision for the establishment of a committee or sub-committee on services trade indicates the need to set up institutional structures to oversee liberalization and proper implementation of the PTAs, there is little operational or substantive content to this discipline. It is also worth noting that the N–N PTAs do not include such a provision, possibly because institutional structures are in place on both sides.

Services-investment linkages There is a provision on services-investment linkages in the three PTAs involving India. The provision specifies that certain articles of the chapter on investment (those relating to minimum standards of treatment, transfers, expropriation and compensation, losses and compensation, subrogation, special formalities and information requirements, access to administrative and judicial procedures, dispute settlement, and entry into force, duration, and termination) would apply to measures affecting the supply of a service through commercial presence, if these measures relate to investment. This application would be independent of whether the service sector has been scheduled or not in the specific commitments. It is further specified that certain provisions of the investment chapter would apply to the supply of financial services through commercial presence to the extent that such measures relate to investment, again independent of whether the service concerned has been committed or not. Hence, certain disciplines outlined in the investment chapter (discussed in detail below) are seen as overarching. By explicitly noting this linkage, the investment-related regulatory framework that would be applicable to services trade through commercial presence is specified.

Cooperation The two PTAs involving China contain this additional provision. The wording is the same in both cases. The provision requires the parties to strengthen cooperation efforts in services, including in sectors not covered by existing cooperation arrangements. The discipline calls for the countries to discuss and mutually agree on the sectors covered and to develop cooperation programmes to improve their domestic capacities, efficiencies, and competitiveness. The basic intent here is capacity building and gradual expansion of sectors for liberalization. There is, however, no specificity in this provision regarding what the institutional mechanisms would be, the time frames, scope, or how outcomes are to be incorporated into the commitment framework and future negotiations. Thus, though there is intent, there is no clarity on the framework.

Other provisions There are a few provisions which are quite distinctive and are found in one of the PTAs. For instance, the US–Korea agreement contains an article on local presence, wherein it is specified that neither party can require a service supplier of the other country to establish or maintain a representative office or any form of enterprise or to be a resident in its country as a condition for cross-border supply. This means that local presence conditions cannot be attached to commitments in mode 1. There is also a provision on non-conforming measures which specifies that the market access, national treatment, MFN, and local presence provisions would not apply to any existing, continued or renewed, or amended non-conforming measures that are maintained at the central, regional, or local levels of government as laid out in its Annex on Government Procurement. So, in effect, the carve-out for government-provided services is extended to government-procured services that fall within certain threshold values.

While most of the PTAs make reference to third parties in that any subsequent agreements or recognition granted to the latter by one of the parties are to be extended to the other party, only one of the PTAs in this sample includes a provision for service suppliers of non-members. The Japan–Singapore PTA contains an article which requires each member to accord treatment granted under the services chapter to a third-country service supplier, provided this supplier is constituted under the laws of either member and provides the service through commercial presence, and has substantive business operations in either of the member countries. What this implies is that there would not be any differential treatment between member and non-member service providers with regard to supply through commercial presence subject to certain terms and conditions being met. This is important as it reflects an open regionalism, permitting third countries to benefit from the services chapter's provisions, if they are operating in a substantive way in one of the member countries. Thus there is scope for extension of bilateral preferences to third country suppliers. However, this does not appear to be a common provision across PTAs.

7.4.1.9 Inferences from an analysis of key disciplines

Although this is a small sample, the above analysis of the content of some key, as well as additional, provisions contained in the services text of these agreements provides some interesting insights regarding the scope, intent, and value addition seen in these PTAs. Some of the main inferences drawn from this analysis are highlighted below.

- Often the services disciplines in the PTAs are more loosely worded and more ambiguous than the GATS, even though one would expect PTAs to go beyond the GATS and to be more specific and detailed in their key provisions. They may also be more restrictive than the GATS in that they include additional clauses which provide scope for retaining or introducing limitations or provide some flexibility to allow members to not fulfil certain obligations which are otherwise mandated in the GATS text.
- There is considerable benchmarking of the PTA services disciplines to those found in the GATS. There is also explicit linking of some PTA provisions to future developments in GATS disciplines in some unfinished areas such as domestic regulation, subsidies, safeguards, and government procurement.
- The few areas where there is most deviation in wording or where additional detail or specificity is present in the PTAs (often supplemented with additional coverage under separate chapters) is

on issues such as qualification and licensing procedures, recognition, financial services, government services, and government procurement.

- The PTAs tend to be more cognizant than the GATS of federal and sub-federal application or carve-out of measures, by highlighting the different levels of government in the context of several services provisions, in addition to the initial reference excluding services provided in the exercise of governmental authority at all levels of government from the scope of the services text.
- By and large, the PTAs are not specific about extending preferences between the members to third parties or providing non-members scope to obtain similar treatment. Thus, open regionalism is not a feature of most PTAs.
- The PTAs do not go beyond the GATS with regard to institutional frameworks and capacity building. While some do contain provisions calling for such mechanisms to be developed or for capacity building through cooperation, nothing concrete is outlined. There is intent, but no formal development of guidelines and operating procedures in the PTAs.
- Issues which are sensitive under the GATS are also sensitive under the PTAs and thus either carved out or dealt with in separate chapters.
- There is some recognition of the cross-cutting nature of issues such as investment and government procurement in the PTAs, as evident from the cross-referencing to other chapters or parts of the agreement in certain provisions within the services chapters. This kind of cross-linkage is not present explicitly in the GATS text.
- By and large, the scope of the disciplines is the same as that found in the GATS, excepting some additional provisions.
- There are a few identifiable patterns that emerge along the developed–developing country dimension. The South–South PTAs tend to include cooperation-type disciplines whereas these are not found in North–North agreements. Establishment of institutional mechanisms is discussed in North–South and South–South agreements but not in North–North agreements. Thus, capacity building and formalization of institutional mechanisms appears to be more of a concern in PTAs involving developing countries than for developed countries, as would be expected.
- There is more of a chapter-based coverage of sensitive issues in North–North than in North–South agreements.
- Issues of recognition and qualification appear to be more important in North–South than in North–North agreements, probably

reflecting the export interest of developing countries in the movement of natural persons and developed country sensitivities in this mode.

Overall, the PTAs do not seem to go beyond the GATS with regard to rule making. They are forward looking only to the extent that they anticipate developments in the GATS negotiations. Specificity and detail are often lacking and there is little discussion of concrete operating structures and procedures.

7.4.2 Content of Important Chapters and Annexes: Some Insights

As highlighted earlier, several issues are covered under separate chapters and annexes. The following discussion examines the scope and intent of the provisions in these chapters and compares these to annexes on similar issues under the GATS. It also tries to find out whether and in what manner the nature of the countries involved in a PTA influences the nature of these chapters and annexes. The discussion also highlights additional areas which are covered by the PTAs through chapters that are not found in the GATS, and once again whether this added scope is related to the nature of the countries involved in the agreement.

7.4.2.1 Investment

Almost all the PTAs have a chapter on investment. This is the area where the texts are the most detailed, with the scope, definitions, and measures described extensively. There are numerous provisions in the investment chapters. These provisions fall into three categories, (i) those pertaining to treatment of investors from member countries of the agreement and terms and conditions to be accorded to them; (ii) circumstances when exceptions or derogations to the terms and conditions are justified; (iii) judicial, administrative, and institutional requirements and procedures which would enable member countries to resolve investment-related disputes and ensure implementation of the investment-related provisions in these agreements. The first set of provisions includes disciplines such as minimum standards of treatment, national treatment, repatriation, and expropriation. The second includes disciplines such as restrictions to safeguard the balance of payments, denial of benefits, measures in the public interest, and general as well as security exceptions. The third includes disciplines such as disclosure of information, special formalities and information requirements, transparency, review of commitments, investment disputes, and on the entry into force and operation of the agreement. A few PTAs also include a provision to establish a sub-committee on investment for reviewing the implementation and operation of the investment chapter, although by and large there is not much reference to institutional issues other than the arbitration-related aspect of investor disputes.

The detail is greatest on issues of scope and application, such as what is covered by the investment chapter provisions, which kinds of investors are covered, what kinds of transfers would be covered by the provisions on repatriation, what kinds of exceptions can be taken in the case of expropriation, under what conditions members can invoke restrictions to safeguard their interests, and what the procedures would be for resolving investment disputes in terms of the obligations of the parties and the arbitration and institutional frameworks.

A distinction can be made with regard to the agreements involving developed country partners. In such cases, the investment chapter is particularly detailed with additional annexes on certain provisions such as expropriation and investor–state dispute settlement. The developed country agreements also make an important departure by linking the investment provisions to environment, labour, and movement of natural persons. The Japan–Philippines agreement for instance, notes that parties would not encourage investments by investors of the other party by relaxing environmental or labour regulations, and if such derogations are made, then consultations can be sought with the other party. The JPEPA notes specifically what is meant by "labour laws" in this context. The US–Korea agreement similarly contains a clause on investment and the environment, but here the provision is weaker and merely states that the investment activity would be undertaken in a manner that is sensitive to environmental concerns. The latter agreement also contains provisions linking investment to management, noting that neither party can impose nationality conditions for appointment to senior management positions, while it also states that the members to the agreement can require the majority of the board of directors of an enterprise covered by the investment provisions to be of a particular nationality. Such a clause is also found in the India–Korea and India–Singapore agreements. Hence, there is clear recognition of the links between investment and other parts of the agreement in the North–South agreements.

As investment is perhaps the most important mode of supply in services trade, the elaboration of important provisions on investment is significant and indicates that the PTAs could potentially help evolve investment disciplines which can shape the GATS as well as WTO architecture on this issue. The investment chapters further highlight the cross-cutting nature of disciplines in this area and thus indicate the cross-linkages between services investment and other sectors subject to investment disciplines.

7.4.2.2 Movement of Natural Persons

Compared to the GATS, the PTAs go further in evolving disciplines concerning the movement of natural persons (MNP). They provide greater detail on the scope of the MNP provisions, explicitly noting the different categories of natural persons and what they cover, and also by clearly linking MNP to other regulatory issues by including additional provisions within the chapter on MNP. This is in contrast to the GATS Annex on MNP which is quite ambiguous. The only detail that is present in the GATS Annex regarding the scope of MNP is that the agreement excludes citizenship, residency, or employment on a permanent basis from the scope of the measures applying to natural persons.

The three PTAs involving India contain the most detailed chapters on MNP. They outline in detail the definition of the different categories of natural persons, i.e. contractual service suppliers, business visitors, independent professionals, and intra-corporate transferees. The three agreements with India also lay down the terms and conditions for entry and stay of these different categories, such as specifying the period for which entry would be granted for a single visit and the maximum period of stay allowed, exempting natural persons from making social security contributions in the other country, specifying the documentation and administrative requirements for different kinds of natural persons, and even outlining the conditions applicable to spouses and dependants. The India–Korea agreement also lists the occupations under the professional category which are covered by the MNP provisions under this agreement. India's interest in accessing partner country markets through mode 4 is evident from the kind of substantive discussion present in the MNP chapter in all its agreements.

A similar approach is found in the JPEPA. The latter also contains provisions regarding the scope and coverage of natural persons, restrictions that may not be imposed, and the requirements and procedures for entry and stay of a natural person. The terms and conditions for temporary entry and stay are not as clearly laid down in the JPEPA as they are in the above-mentioned PTAs involving India. An interesting aspect of the MNP chapter of JPEPA, however, is that it includes a provision on mutual recognition, which is identical to the mutual recognition article found in the services chapter of most PTAs and also in the GATS. By incorporating this provision into the MNP chapter, the agreement clearly establishes the link which exists between mutual recognition and MNP. Thus, as in the case of investment, the cross-linkage between this mode and other parts of the agreement is clearly recognized in the PTAs. An interesting feature of the MNP chapter in JPEPA is that in addition to the usual categories of short-term business visitors, intra-corporate transferees (ICTs), and professionals working on contracts, there is an additional category of investors and one for nurses or certified caregivers, reflecting the significance of these categories to the two parties.

The US–Korea FTA likewise incorporates many of the issues relating to MNP in a separate annex to its chapter on cross-border supply of services. There is an annex on professional services which calls for the establishment of a Professional Services Working Group to exchange information on standards and criteria for the licensing and certification of professional service suppliers, and to undertake discussions to frame mutual recognition agreements and model procedures for licensing and certification, with a review every three years. It also contains an appendix which specifies three professional services sectors, namely, engineering, architectural, and veterinary services, for mutual recognition and temporary licensing. This annex also notes that information will be provided on standards and criteria for licensing and certification, on concerned regulatory bodies, and calls for the establishment of a working group.

Institutional mechanisms are important in the MNP chapters. Like the US–Korea annex which refers to the setting up of a Working Group on Professional Services, the JPEPA includes a provision for establishing a sub-committee on MNP. The functions of this proposed sub-committee are also outlined. There are also other institutional references in the MNP chapters, such as to provisions regarding regulatory transparency, i.e. providing contact points to supply information and facilitating the exchange of information, as well as articles pertaining to settlement of disputes concerning MNP. However, the PTAs do not further clarify institutional details in terms of operating guidelines, time frames, and the constitution of the proposed committees or working groups.

Overall, as in the case of investment, the PTAs go further than the GATS in developing rules and in defining the scope of measures affecting MNP. Moreover, it is in the North–South PTAs involving potential supplier countries such as India and the Philippines, where such chapters tend to be more substantive in nature, which clearly reflect the interest on the part of member countries in trading through this mode of supply and likely sensitivities to imports through this mode on the other side.

7.4.2.3 Government procurement

As highlighted earlier, this discipline is not present in most of the PTAs under discussion. Furthermore, only three of the PTAs (US–Korea, Japan–Philippines, and Japan–Singapore) in this sample have chapters on government procurement, clearly indicating the sensitive nature of this issue. However, the PTAs which do cover government procurement in some detail move considerably beyond the equivalent GATS provision, although there is also considerable variation across the PTAs which include a chapter on this subject, in terms of the content, coverage, and institutional details.

The JPEPA includes the basic principles of government procurement, such as according national treatment, ensuring transparency of measures, fair and effective implementation, and consistency of measures used by the parties with international principles. An important element of this chapter is the institutional dimension of future negotiations on this subject, with the establishment of a sub-committee with specified functions and time frames (though not very specific or detailed). Thus there is a progressive nature to this chapter, with negotiations and development of institutional mechanisms in future, while the focus remains on the governing principles that would guide the use of government procurement policies. In contrast to the JPEPA, the US–Korea FTA contains a very elaborate government procurement chapter, which not only outlines scope and coverage and general principles in the use of such policies, but also introduces new areas such as use of electronic means, valuation, conditions of participation, digital products, time frames, and tendering specifications. Construction services are separately addressed in terms of threshold contract value, highlighting the importance of this sector in the US's government-funded programmes as well as Korea's competitive construction services sector. The government procurement chapter in the US–Korea FTA goes further by including an annex for different central level government entities in the two countries.

Overall, the extent of detail and reference annexes highlights the importance of this issue for the US in particular, as well as offering an appreciation of the new modalities for government procurement that have emerged. It is also worth noting that, while South Korea has a detailed government procurement chapter in its PTA with the US, this is absent in its PTA with India, indicating a difference in negotiating interests, strategies, and bargaining power depending on the partner country.

7.4.2.4 Financial services

Financial services is an area where again one sees some improvements in rule making compared to the GATS. Financial services are covered by a separate annex in the GATS. This annex focuses on issues of definition and scope as well as basic regulatory principles such as the flexibility of member countries in applying prudential regulations and recognizing similar measures taken by other member countries. But the annex does not go further than outlining these general principles. The PTAs, while addressing similar regulatory issues, go beyond the GATS with regard to outlining institutional and judicial elements and at times link financial services to other chapters, such as those on investment, cross-border delivery of services, and dispute settlement, recognizing the importance of this sector and its linkages with many other aspects of the agreement.

In the Japan–Singapore PTA there is an annex on financial services, which includes provisions on domestic regulation, recognition, and dispute settlement, along the lines of the GATS. However, there is also a separate provision for "new financial services" and the manner in which these services are provided. These new services would be subject to licensing, institutional and juridical requirements, as other financial services on a non-discriminatory basis. The inclusion of new financial services reflects the forward-looking aspect of this annex in recognizing the growing tradability of services and the emergence of new sub-domains within this sector.

The India–Korea PTA similarly reflects anticipation of emerging financial services. Its annex on financial services specifies that the specific commitments undertaken and the principles of non-discrimination, flexibility in applying prudential regulations, and transparency would also apply to new financial services. Moreover, each party is to allow the other party to supply new financial services where it allows its own financial institutions to do so.

The US–Korea FTA is once again the most detailed in this area. The chapter on financial services in this agreement contains provisions for cross-border trade and national treatment of financial services, while giving flexibility to partners to not accord national treatment and to require registration for some cross-border financial services suppliers. The chapter also includes a provision for new financial services, to allow them access while also giving countries the flexibility to determine the institutional and juridical form by which new financial services are supplied and to require authorization (to be granted within a reasonable period of time) for their supply. There are also detailed provisions on transparency in terms of providing information on regulations and status of applications, and also a separate provision on self-regulated organizations, a feature that is not found in any of the financial services chapters or annexes. The agreement also calls for a financial services committee to supervise implementation, consultations, dispute settlement and investment disputes in this sector, thus reflecting the importance of developing institutional mechanisms.

In some agreements, financial services are referred to in the context of the investment chapter provisions on dispute settlement mechanisms as well as safeguard measures. For instance, in the JPEPA, the safeguard provision in the investment chapter refers to balance of payments problems created by cross-border capital transactions. It also specifies that prudential measures for financial services can be maintained or introduced in conformity with the provisions of the investment chapter, indicating the cross-cutting nature of the investment provisions as well as the special nature of the financial services sector in terms of its bearing on macroeconomic stability.

One also finds PTAs such as the China–Pakistan agreement where there is no separate annex on financial services and it is specified that the GATS annex in this area (and all other areas where GATS annexes exist) would apply to the PTA, unless otherwise agreed. Moreover, the substantive content of these annexes is specified as being integral to this agreement. Hence, some agreements still use the GATS as their benchmark and there is no further development of disciplines or institutional mechanisms.

7.4.2.5 Telecommunications

The annex on telecommunication services in the GATS, like the financial services annex, lays down various regulatory principles such as those of transparency and provision of access to and use of public telecom transport networks and services. It also outlines permissible conditions and criteria for imposing restrictions regarding such access and use. The PTAs contain several provisions which echo the same principles, such as those of fair competition, transparency, allowing interconnection to public networks, and public availability of procedures and conditions. There are some deviations, however.

The telecom annex in the Japan–Singapore agreement, for instance, allows for asymmetric regulation, with each member being given flexibility to determine the appropriate level of regulations in accordance with its own rules and frameworks, so as to ensure fair competition. It also mentions that universal service obligations are not be viewed as anti-competitive measures so long as measures relating to these are transparent and applied in a non-discriminatory manner. Allocation of scarce resources is to be done in a transparent and non-discriminatory manner, but parties are not required to provide information on such allocation if this is for government purposes. Thus there is some customization of the principles to fit the partners' institutional and regulatory frameworks and discretionary scope is provided to address public policy objectives.

The India–Korea PTA contains a detailed annex on telecom services, which goes deeper than the GATS. While the GATS framework only specifies that negotiations shall be entered into on a voluntary basis aiming for progressive liberalization of trade in telecom transport networks and services, the PTA annex calls for integrated liberalization. Several aspects of this annex are different from the telecom annex found in the GATS. For example, the PTA annex excludes cable or broadcast distribution of radio or TV programming, reflecting the sensitivities associated with audiovisual services and the treatment of this area in a separate chapter of this agreement. Some additional provisions in this chapter relate to providing reasonable and non-discriminatory terms and conditions for access to and use of public telecommunication services for movement of information and ensuring the security and confidentiality of messages and protecting the privacy of personal data of end-users. There is also a separate section on the conduct of major suppliers which includes articles on access to infrastructure, anti-competitive safeguards, interconnection, resolution of interconnection disputes, role of independent regulatory bodies, and principles for licensing, allocation and use of scarce telecom resources. The dispute and appeal procedures are outlined in some detail in the agreement. It is interesting that the PTA also makes note of the precedence of the provisions of the telecom services chapter over other chapters in the agreement if there is any inconsistency in provisions. Thus, the regulatory principles of the telecom services chapter prevail; this would potentially be most relevant in cross-cutting areas such as dispute resolution, transparency, and investment.

Overall, a comparison of the PTA chapters on telecom services with the GATS annex on telecom services reveals that, while the broad principles of transparency and non-discrimination continue to hold in the PTAs, the latter tend to be more detailed, better defined in terms of the scope of their provisions, and also more precise on matters such as resolution of disputes or conditions when access and use of public telecom services networks can be restricted in the public or private interest. There is, however, relatively less elaboration or progress on the institutional side.

7.4.2.6 Other issues

As highlighted earlier, several of the selected PTAs contain chapters on new issues such as e-commerce, information and communication technology, and audiovisual services. One area where there is notable progress relative to the GATS is in e-commerce. There is considerable detail on scope, definitions, and principles guiding the application of measures in this area. The India–Singapore agreement and the US–Korea agreement are good examples in this regard.

The chapters on e-commerce in both these agreements are quite similar in that they recognize the economic growth and trade opportunities provided by e-commerce, the importance of avoiding barriers to the use and development of this mode of supply, and the applicability of the WTO agreement to measures affecting e-commerce. Issues such as electronic signatures, authentification, online consumer protection, paperless trading, principles on access and use of the Internet for e-commerce, and protection of personal information are covered in the US–Korea PTA. The India–Singapore agreement highlights the importance of national treatment and transparency in the application of measures in this area. Both agreements further make an exception for government procurement and measures affecting broadcasting, cable casting, and video-on-demand, again reflecting the sensitivities associated with the issues of government procurement and audiovisual services.

The other area where there is some advancement relative to the GATS is in audiovisual services. Some of the PTAs contain a separate chapter on audiovisual services. The India–Korea CEPA contains a short chapter on audiovisual co-production, which covers films, videos, broadcasting, animation, and digital devices and other forms of distribution, including new and emerging ones. While there is little substantive content in terms of concrete regulatory principles and mechanisms laid down and the focus is more on scope and intent, this chapter does identify this sector as important for intensifying cultural and economic relations and the principle of national treatment for any co-production in terms of benefits and government support provided, in line with the rules and regulations of each member. The chapter also calls for discussions between competent authorities in the two countries.[9]

Some PTAs also contain cooperation chapters which specifically note the need for facilitating cooperation and information exchange as well as capacity building in areas such as higher education, energy and environment, science and technology, human resource development, tourism, and transport services. The need for cooperation in financial services is also highlighted in the PTAs involving Japan, with reference to capital markets, prudential regulations, and the setting up of working groups. The India–Korea PTA is a case in point, which covers a wide range of issues and services where cooperation is to be undertaken. However, on the whole, the cooperation chapters tend to be general and are not particularly detailed. They are mostly indicative of their recognition of certain issues or sectors as important for expanding bilateral relations and read more as general expressions of intent to hold future discussions and to engage in capacity-building efforts.

---

[9] The US–Korea agreement also has an annex on express delivery services which asks the parties to maintain the existing level of market openness, to prevent revenues derived from monopoly postal services from being used to confer an advantage on domestic or other competitors' suppliers of express delivery services. However, the two sides can adopt or maintain measures outside the scope of the chapter or measures in their schedule pertaining to transport services.

7.4.2.7 Inferences from an analysis of key chapters and annexes

Several important insights can be obtained from a review of the scope and substantive content of the chapters and annexes on specific sectors and issues in the selected PTAs. There are several cross-cutting issues on which the PTAs move significantly beyond the GATS. There are others where there is some progress in terms of outlining the way forward but without complementary information on mechanisms and procedures.

- The area where most progress is visible is investment, particularly with regard to terms and conditions, investors' rights, and arbitration issues. Investment is also related to other issues such as environment and labour and to important sectors such as financial services. These disciplines provide a possible reference for GATS negotiations on investment-related matters.
- There is also notable progress in the area of MNP relative to the GATS. Again, the extent of detail and specification of various categories of service suppliers, albeit based on the GATS discussions in this area, but also customized to suit the interests of PTA partner countries, with listing of professional categories and occupations of interest, provide a useful reference for the GATS negotiations in this area.
- There has perhaps been less movement in areas such as government procurement than for investment and MNP issues. However, where government procurement is covered through additional chapters, the provision of details on institutional requirements and the outlining of the scope of such measures is a step forward from the GATS' rather loosely worded, embryonic provision on government procurement.
- In their treatment of specific services such as financial or telecom services, the PTAs largely benchmark themselves to the GATS by upholding the same regulatory principles of transparency and non-discrimination as well as providing some flexibilities for imposing regulations that meet certain kinds of objectives. However, once again they go further than the GATS in outlining institutional and judicial processes and requirements, by highlighting linkages to other parts of the agreements, and also introducing references to new and emerging segments into the ambit of future negotiations in these sectors.
- The PTAs also cover a wider range of issues and sectors, many of an emergent nature, through their additional chapters and annexes. By incorporating areas such as energy, the environment, ICT, and e-commerce, they clearly reflect a more forward-looking and

dynamic approach, with obvious implications for the scope of services negotiations under these agreements.

7.5 SCOPE AND DEPTH OF COMMITMENTS IN ASIA'S SERVICES PTAS

The preceding discussion has highlighted the areas in which the PTA disciplines on services have gone beyond the GATS and where they have relied on the GATS as a reference document, and have almost identical content. The following discussion examines how much further countries have gone in their PTAs in terms of undertaking liberalization commitments in services relative to their services commitments under the GATS. The analysis looks at both the scope and depth of the commitments undertaken in terms of the sectoral and subsectoral coverage as well as the modal profile of the commitments undertaken in the PTAs vis-à-vis those under the GATS. Such an analysis is possible given that all six PTAs where there are scheduled commitments adopt a positive list approach.[10] The analysis also tries to identify patterns with regard to the nature of liberalization undertaken for specific services and modes of supply and looks at patterns with regard to the level of development, the type of PTA (developed–developed, developing–developing, and developed–developing) and the countries concerned. An attempt is also made to assess if countries have indicated a greater willingness to liberalize over time as reflected in the nature and scope of the commitments they have undertaken in recent versus earlier PTAs.

7.5.1 Sectoral and Sub-sectoral Coverage

The first level of analysis is to compare the number of service sectors scheduled by countries for liberalization under their PTAs with the number of service sectors they have scheduled under the GATS. This comparison should provide a broad indication of their willingness to negotiate under PTAs vis-à-vis the GATS. Table 7.5 summarizes the number of services scheduled by each of the countries in the sample of agreements under consideration in this chapter, in the GATS and in their PTAs.

---

[10] The PTAs under consideration for analysing the scope and depth of services liberalization commitments include the India–Singapore, India–Korea, Japan–Philippines, Japan–Singapore, China–ASEAN, and China–Pakistan agreements. The US–Korea and India–Sri Lanka PTAs do not have scheduled commitments as of date and are thus excluded from this analysis.

Table 7.5 Number of service sectors scheduled in the GATS and in selected PTAs

Country	GATS	India–Korea	India–Singapore	Japan–Singapore	Japan–Philippines	China–ASEAN	China–Pakistan
Pakistan	6						11
India	6	11	9				
Philippines	4				9	5	
Indonesia	1					6	
China	9					5	11
Thailand	10					4	
Malaysia	8					8	
Korea	8	10					
Singapore	6		11	11		8	
Japan	10			11	10		

Source: Based on an examination of the countries' GATS schedules and their commitments under the selected PTAs.

It is evident from Table 7.5 that in most cases countries have scheduled a larger number of services sectors in their PTAs than under the GATS. In several cases, the number of services scheduled has increased several fold to cover all 11 possible service sectors (excluding other services). For instance, both India and Pakistan have increased the number of service sectors scheduled from six under the GATS to 11 under the China–Pakistan PTA and the India–Korea PTA, respectively. The Philippines has increased its scheduling coverage from four under the GATS to nine under the JPEPA. Overall, countries have moved towards near universal coverage of service sectors in their scheduling process.

The China–ASEAN PTA, however, presents a mixed picture. While some countries such as Singapore and Indonesia have increased the number of services scheduled under this PTA vis-à-vis their sectoral coverage under the GATS, some, such as Thailand, have significantly reduced the scope of their commitments. Even China has scheduled fewer sectors under this PTA than under the China–Pakistan PTA. Certain countries, for example, Singapore, have shown less willingness to negotiate sectors in the China–ASEAN PTA than in their other PTAs. Hence, under the China–ASEAN PTA, countries have shown less willingness on both sides to schedule sectors for negotiations, not only compared with the GATS but also compared with other agreements they have signed. The latter is also to some extent reflected in the much weaker nature of provisions in this agreement, as highlighted in the preceding section. But for all the other PTAs, countries have improved the scope of liberalization commitments.

An examination of the sub-sectoral scope for commitments similarly highlights the willingness of countries to negotiate a larger number of service activities within certain individual service sectors under the PTAs compared with that under the GATS. This applies to almost all the countries covered in this sample of agreements and holds across almost all the PTAs, excepting the China–ASEAN agreement.

Available data on country commitments reveal a number of interesting patterns across different service sectors. For instance, business services have seen the greatest increase in the number of subsectors in which commitments have been made for almost all countries and across almost all PTAs (excepting the China–ASEAN PTA). The number of business service subsectors committed by India has increased from eight under the GATS to 39 under the India–Singapore agreement and to 34 under the India–Korea agreement. The Philippines has likewise increased its subsectoral commitments in this sector from zero under the GATS to 18 under JPEPA and Pakistan has increased the scope of its business services commitments from ten under the GATS to 23 under the China–Pakistan agreement. Even developed countries such as Japan, Singapore, and Korea have significantly increased the number of business service activities for which commitments have been made under their PTAs relative to their commitments under the GATS, from 35 to 50 for Korea under the India–Korea agreement, from 23 to 55 and 49 for Singapore under the Japan–Singapore and India–Singapore agreements, respectively, and from 28 to 65 and 47 for Japan under the Japan–Singapore agreement and JPEPA, respectively. For sectors other than business services there is no clearly identifiable sector where one sees a consistent improvement in the scope of subsectoral commitments. In some cases communication and transport services have seen improvements in scope, albeit to varying degrees.

In general, the developed countries in the sample show a greater willingness to commit in more service activities, the number of subsectors in which commitments have been made also being much greater than for developing countries. Among the developing countries in this sample, India stands out, as the scope of its subsectoral commitments has increased significantly in both the India–Korea and India–Singapore agreements and this improvement is seen across almost all services. While the Philippines and Pakistan have also shown willingness to commit more services under their PTAs, the number of service subsectors in which they have made commitments tends to be much lower than that for India, across nearly all services. India's greater proactiveness in scheduling more service sectors and subsectors probably reflects its keen interest in negotiating services given its comparative advantage in the service sector.

One also finds that country-specific considerations are reflected in the scope of commitments. For example, India has made commitments in eight subsectors under construction services in its agreement with Singapore, up from one under the GATS. However, it has committed only two subsectors under its agreement with Korea, probably reflecting South Korea's competitiveness in construction services and the greater sensitivity of this sector in the context of India's negotiations with Korea. Thus, sector and country-specific concerns are evident in the subsectoral pattern of commitments. Further, services such as health, education, environment, and distribution, where there is less scheduling under the GATS, exhibit a similar pattern under the PTAs. There is at best a marginal increase in the number of subsectors where commitments have been made in such services, indicating that these remain sensitive on public policy and social grounds even under PTAs. It is also interesting to note that some services, such as financial services, have also seen a decrease in the number of subsectors in which commitments have been made by almost all the developing countries. This is particularly so for the ASEAN countries which have significantly reduced the number of financial services where commitments have been made to zero under the China–ASEAN agreement, possibly reflecting the cautious approach to this sector following the 1997 Asian crisis, and the absence of any separate provisions on financial services under this agreement.[11]

Table 7.6 offers a summary depiction of the trends depicted above for four selected services, namely, business, financial, communication, and construction services, by agreement. The reason for presenting the information in this manner is to enable analysis across four dimensions, i.e. to see how the commitment pattern varies: (a) across the four selected services; (b) across the different PTAs; (c) for the same country across its different PTAs, and; (d) between the two partners for a given PTA.

Table 7.6 clearly shows that, with the exception of the China–ASEAN PTA, in general there has been an improvement in the scope of

---

[11] It would be worth examining whether the PTAs which have stronger regulatory provisions for the financial services, such as through additional chapters and annexes in this area, also tend to be associated with more subsectors having commitments in this sector, i.e. how the strength of the PTA framework and provisions influences countries' willingness to commit, especially in sensitive areas like financial services.

Table 7.6 *Number of subsectors in which commitments have been made in four services under the GATS and in selected PTAs*

PTA Name	Country	Business Services		Financial Services		Communication Services		Construction Services	
		GATS	PTA	GATS	PTA	GATS	PTA	GATS	PTA
India–Korea	India	8	34	10	20	11	16	1	2
CEPA	Korea	35	50	22	24	26	19	7	1
India–Singapore	India	8	39	10	18	11	14	1	8
CECA	Singapore	23	49	17	17	5	8	0	8
Japan–Singapore	Japan	28	47	0	0	15	20	8	16
CECA	Singapore	23	55	17	17	5	14	0	8
Japan–Philippines	Japan	28	65	0	16	15	21	8	5
EPA	Philippines	0	18	35	17	5	21	0	0
China–Pakistan	China	22	31	13	19	11	13	5	8
FTA	Pakistan	10	23	16	16	11	15	2	6
China–ASEAN	China	22	14	13	0	11	0	5	8
FTA	Indonesia	13	0	23	0	26	0	6	11
	Malaysia	29	7	23	2	5	2	7	7
	Philippines	0	4	35	0	5	13	0	1
	Singapore	23	17	17	17	5	5	0	0
	Thailand	23	4	15	0	5	0	3	0

Source: Author's calculations based on country's GATS commitments available at the WTO website (www.wto.org) and text documents of countries' PTAs.

commitments, particularly in business services. The developed countries in this sample are more extensive in the scope of their commitments relative to the developing countries. India has signalled stronger liberalization intent in its PTAs than the other developing countries in this sample. Individual country interests, sensitivities (in particular services), and partner country advantages and specifics seem to play a role in determining how extensive the commitments are and in which services they are made, as countries do not necessarily show a similar willingness to commit across their various PTAs. There is also some backtracking or status quo maintained relative to the GATS in the financial services sector. The China–ASEAN agreement clearly stands out as an aberration, with commitments in many fewer subsectors on both sides, perhaps reflecting partner-specific concerns and the fact that this is a weaker agreement in terms of its framework and provisions than the other PTAs under discussion.

While the above data provide a good idea of countries' willingness to negotiate, they only capture the absolute number of services subsectors. However, since the maximum possible number of subsectors varies considerably between different services, one also needs to consider the percentage of total possible subsectors in which commitments have been made in each sector, across the different PTAs. Table 7.7 provides this overview for the same four selected services.

Table 7.7 highlights the same patterns discussed earlier, with the greatest increase in the share of commitments in all possible subsectors being in business services, with a mixed pattern for other services. However, one also finds that a significant percentage of commitments in the feasible set of subsectors has been made under the PTAs across several other services. Moreover, in some PTAs, the share exceeds 100%, indicating the expansion of the sector to include additional subsectors relative to the GATS (even in cases where the share of commitments under the GATS exceeds 100%). The latter implies that PTAs are often more detailed than the GATS in terms of listing more services sub-categories and explicitly including new services (as also highlighted earlier in the context of new financial services being explicitly mentioned in the services chapters of several agreements). Once again, however, the China–ASEAN agreement clearly shows backtracking relative to the share of services in which commitments were made under the GATS.

7.5.2 Correlating Scope of Liberalization with Stage of Development

There is also a clear positive correlation between the level of development of countries and the scope of their sectoral and subsectoral commitments, both under the GATS and under their PTAs. Figures 7.1 to 7.4 illustrate

Table 7.7 Share of total possible subsectors in which commitments have been made in the GATS and in selected PTAs (%)

PTA Name	Country	Business Services		Financial Services		Communication Services		Construction Services	
		GATS	PTA	GATS	PTA	GATS	PTA	GATS	PTA
India–Korea	India	17.39	73.91	58.82	117.65	45.83	66.67	20.00	40.00
CEPA	Korea	76.09	108.70	129.41	141.18	108.33	79.17	140.00	20.00
India–Singapore	India	17.39	84.78	58.82	105.88	45.83	58.33	20.00	160.00
CECA	Singapore	50.00	106.52	100.00	100.00	20.83	33.33	0.00	160.00
Japan–Singapore	Japan	60.87	102.17	0.00	0.00	62.50	83.33	160.00	320.00
CECA	Singapore	50.00	119.57	100.00	100.00	20.83	58.33	0.00	160.00
Japan–Philippines	Japan	60.87	141.30	0.00	94.12	62.50	87.50	160.00	100.00
EPA	Philippines	0.00	39.13	205.88	100.00	20.83	87.50	0.00	0.00
China–Pakistan	China	47.83	67.39	76.47	111.76	45.83	54.17	100.00	160.00
FTA	Pakistan	21.74	50.00	94.12	94.12	45.83	62.50	40.00	120.00
China–ASEAN	China	47.83	30.43	76.47	0.00	45.83	0.00	100.00	160.00
FTA	Indonesia	28.26	0.00	135.29	0.00	108.33	0.00	120.00	220.00
	Malaysia	63.04	15.22	135.29	11.76	20.83	8.33	140.00	140.00
	Philippines	0.00	8.70	205.88	0.00	20.83	54.17	0.00	20.00
	Singapore	50.00	36.96	100.00	100.00	20.83	20.83	0.00	0.00
	Thailand	50.00	8.70	88.24	0.00	20.83	0.00	60.00	0.00

Note: A share of more than 100% indicates that the sector has been subclassified in more detail than is given in the GATS sectoral classification list. This is true even in the case of the GATS commitments made by countries where various service activities which have been grouped together under a particular service subsector under the GATS have been listed separately by countries in their commitments.

Source: Author's calculations based on countries' GATS commitments available at the WTO website (www.wto.org) and text documents of country's PTAs.

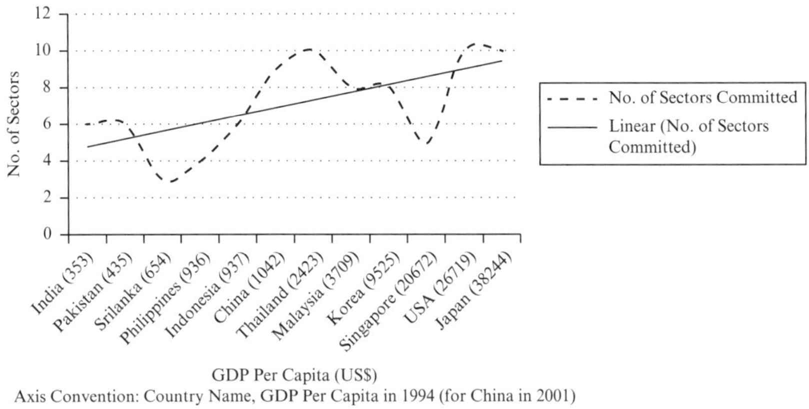

Source: Based on countries' GATS commitments available at the WTO website (www.wto.org) and GDP per capita data from http://data.worldbank.org/indicator/NY.GDP.MKTP.CD.

Figure 7.1 Number of sectors in which commitments were made under the GATS and GDP per capita

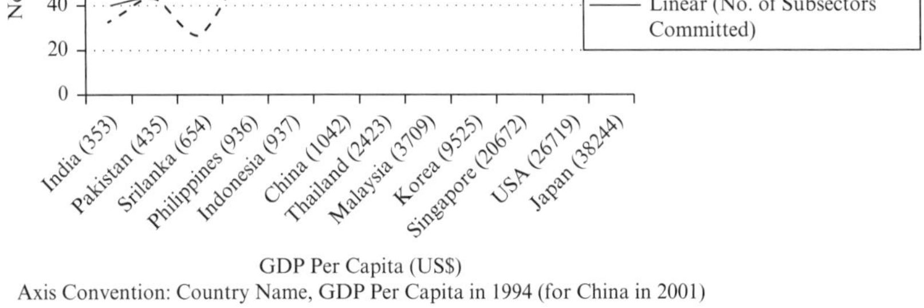

Source: Based on analysis of countries' schedules of commitments under the selected PTAs and GDP per capita data from http://data.worldbank.org/indicator/NY.GDP.MKTP.CD.

Figure 7.2 Number of subsectors in which commitments were made under the GATS and GDP per capita

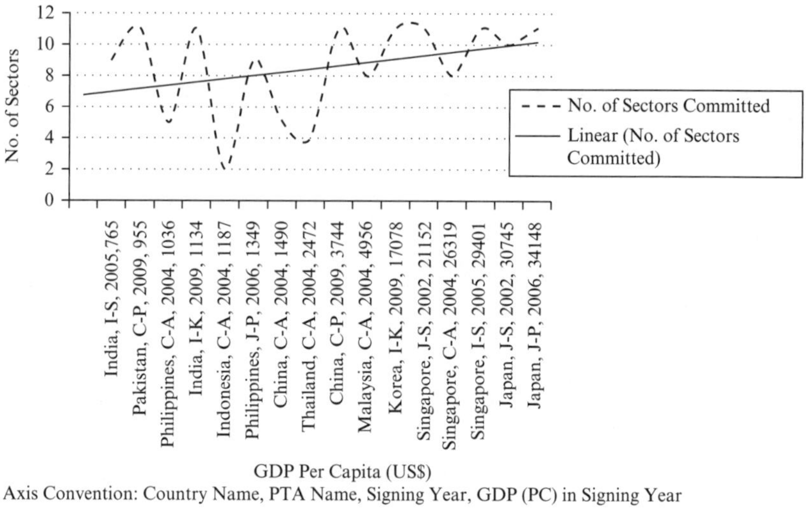

Source: Based on analysis of countries' schedules of commitments under the selected PTAs and GDP per capita data from http://data.worldbank.org/indicator/NY.GDP.MKTP.CD.

Figure 7.3 Number of sectors in which commitments were made under selected PTAs and GDP per capita

this positive relationship. The figures for gross domestic product (GDP) per capita are taken for the year when commitments were undertaken, under the GATS and under the PTAs for each country. The trend line that best fits the actual number of sectors and subsectors in which commitments were made by the sample of countries in the multilateral and bilateral/regional context is positively sloped, indicating that the more advanced countries tend to commit in more sectors and subsectors.

One interesting feature that emerges, however, is that countries have not tended to progressively improve in any significant way on the scope of their commitments by scheduling a much larger number of sectors or subsectors under subsequent PTAs. Thus, while relative to the GATS, the scope tends to improve, relative to earlier PTAs, the scope increased slightly in some cases or is almost the same in later PTAs. This reconfirms the fact that, while countries are willing to offer more under bilateral agreements, they still tend to customize the scope and nature of their liberalization commitments to take into account their interests and sensitivities with different trading partners.

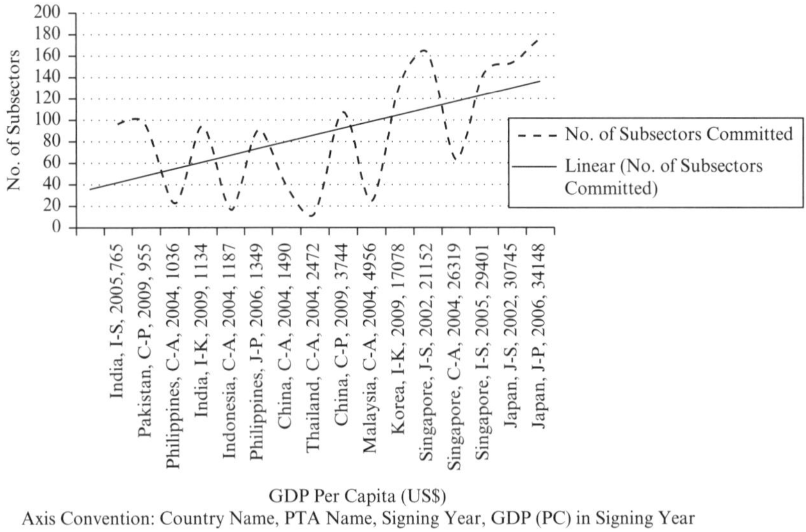

Source: Based on analysis of countries' schedules of commitments under the selected PTAs and GDP per capita data from http://data.worldbank.org/indicator/NY.GDP.MKTP.CD.

Figure 7.4 Number of subsectors in which commitments were made under selected PTAs and GDP per capita

7.5.3 Modal Features of Liberalization Commitments

Another dimension for analysing the nature of liberalization undertaken in the PTAs relative to the GATS is in terms of the modal distribution, i.e. whether countries exhibit similar willingness to liberalize certain modes of supply over others in their PTAs, and what kinds of restrictions they tend to maintain under PTAs compared to the GATS. Such an analysis permits one to go beyond the scope of country commitments to understand the depth of these commitments under PTAs relative to the GATS.

An analysis of the mode-wise nature of commitments made by countries in the selected services highlights several interesting facts. The first is that, contrary to expectations, countries have not necessarily improved upon their modal commitments in terms of increasing the share of commitments which are unrestricted. In several cases, the share of modes 1, 2, and 3 commitments which are unrestricted has actually decreased under the PTAs relative to the GATS. This is particularly so under the China–ASEAN PTA, which not only exhibits reduced scope of commitments (with sectors scheduled under the GATS not scheduled under the PTAs) but also GATS-minus commitments. Even developed countries such as Japan and Singapore have made more restrictive modes 1 and 2 commitments in some of the selected services relative to their commitments in the GATS. This GATS-minus nature of commitments is most evident in the communication services sector. To the extent that there is improvement, this is most visible for mode 3 where countries have made a larger share of their commitments in this mode unrestricted than under the GATS.

The second feature of the mode-wise commitments is that among the countries in this sample, India tends to show the greatest improvement in the depth of its commitments, with a significant increase in the share of unrestricted commitments across modes 1, 2, and 3 for all the selected services except communication services. The improvement is greatest for business services and for modes 1 and 2. In comparison, the other developing countries in the sample do not show such an improvement; some even show a significant decline in the share of unrestricted commitments. Improvements in developed country commitments are found mainly in financial services.

A third noteworthy feature is that, although the modal nature of commitments for a given country tends to be similar across different services, at times it does vary. For instance, Japan has scheduled partial mode 3 commitments in financial services under the Japan–Singapore PTA while, under JPEPA, all its mode 3 commitments are unrestricted. Hence, there appears to be some customization of the commitments in line with the strengths of the partner country and associated sectoral sensitivities, in the extent of liberalization undertaken.

Thus, while the range of services under negotiation may be larger under the PTAs, the extent of liberalization is not necessarily greater. In many cases, the commitments are more restrictive than in the GATS. Business services generally see greater improvement than other services, both in scope (as discussed earlier) and in depth of commitments.

A country-wise examination of the modal distribution of commitments further reveals that, for a given country, the extent of liberalization relative to the GATS varies across services and also across PTAs. Broadly, three categories of countries emerge: the first consisting of countries such as India and the Philippines which have made more liberal commitments; the second consisting of countries such as Japan, Singapore, and Korea which have exhibited more as well as less liberalization; and the third category consisting of countries such as China which have tended to go below their GATS commitments. For example, India has scheduled services such as education, transport, environmental services under its PTAs, with 100% unrestricted commitments across modes 1–3, while these services were not scheduled under the GATS. The Philippines has scheduled a larger number of services under its PTAs and the share of its unrestricted commitments has increased in all services, excepting financial services. Overall, there is a GATS+ nature to the PTA commitments made by both these countries. The picture is quite different for Korea, Singapore, and Japan whose commitments show a mix of improvement and backtracking on the GATS. On the other hand, China's commitments in its PTA with ASEAN and with Pakistan fall below those under the GATS for many services. Some services which China has scheduled under the GATS have not been scheduled under its PTAs and the share of its unrestricted commitments has also declined in several services. There is less scope and less depth in China's PTA commitments, possibly reflecting the fact that China was compelled to make extensive commitments under the WTO as part of its accession process, while similar considerations may be at work under its PTAs.

Overall, the country-wise analysis does not reveal any clear pattern between the modal distribution of commitments and the development status of the countries forming the PTAs. Some developing countries, like India, appear to be more proactive in their liberalization intent than other developing countries. Some developed countries appear to be less willing to commit under PTAs than under the GATS in certain services. Hence, it appears that PTAs may be governed by their own strategic dynamics among the partner countries and that the GATS need not serve as a reference point in terms of signalling willingness to liberalize sectors under the PTAs. The tradeoffs in PTAs may be different from those under the GATS, resulting in differences in the scope and depth of liberalization undertaken.

A quick examination of the PTA commitments with autonomous policies in selected services for some of the countries in this sample further suggests that countries have liberalized more unilaterally. In some services, countries have opened up to 100% FDI, while they have made partial commitments in mode 3 under the PTAs. This is true for both developed and developing countries. Moreover, in terms of the depth of the commitments made, the PTA commitments tend to be more restrictive than the unilateral policies for FDI. Overall, one finds that the scope and degree of liberalization is greatest at the autonomous level, followed by liberalization under PTAs, with the least liberalization being undertaken at the multilateral level. Hence, in effect, what matters most is the liberalization undertaken unilaterally as PTAs either bind the status quo or fall short of binding the status quo.

7.5.4 Mode 4 Commitments and Provisions

A key feature of several Asian PTAs has been the inclusion of provisions pertaining to the movement of natural persons. For example, the Asia-Pacific Economic Cooperation grouping, ASEAN, the India–Singapore CECA, the India–Korea CEPA, the recently concluded India–Japan CEPA and India–Malaysia CECA, Japan's FTAs with Thailand, Indonesia, Singapore, and the Philippines; and China's FTAs with ASEAN, Singapore, and New Zealand all contain labour mobility provisions aimed at opening up selected sectors or occupations and to help member countries alleviate labour market shortages. Table 7.8 highlights the nature of labour mobility provisions in some intra-Asian PTAs.

As is evident from Table 7.8, for the most part, Asian PTAs focus on highly skilled workers and on selected sectors. They mostly cover categories that are closely related to investment flows or where there are labour shortages in one of the partner countries. The approach to labour mobility is mainly as a complement to goods and capital market integration and to facilitate trade and investment flows among partner countries.

A review of the mode 4 outcomes under some of the Asian PTAs suggests that countries have been better able to secure their market access interests, for skilled service suppliers or specific occupational categories under these agreements, than under the GATS although, operationally, there have been difficulties in making progress on regulatory issues such as mutual recognition and outcomes have not necessarily materialized to the extent anticipated. The case of three of the selected PTAs is highlighted here.

India–Singapore CECA (IS–CECA) Under this PTA, both countries have committed to go beyond their WTO commitments in mode 4 and to liberalize norms for temporary entry for four categories of service providers, namely, business visitors, short-term service suppliers, professionals and ICTs (defined as personnel from businesses operating in both countries who need to move between establishments in the two countries). This liberalization has taken the form of increased duration of stay, facilitating repeat entry, liberalizing the terms and conditions for visa renewals and extensions, and lifting various entry restrictions. For example, the commitments made by Singapore enable these selected categories of service providers to provide services for a period ranging from two months in the case of business visitors to as much as eight years for ICTs, without being subject to quantitative restrictions, economic needs and labour market tests and social security contribution requirements. Short-term service suppliers who provide a specific service are allowed to stay up to three months, with a possible extension of another three months. ICTs can apply for a visa of up to two years, with possible extensions of up to three years at one time, for a maximum of eight years. Business visitors can get temporary visas for engaging in business-related activities for up to two

Table 7.8 Labour mobility provisions in selected Asian RTAs[12]

Agreement/ Scheme	Country/Region Covered	Type	Labour Mobility Provisions	Coverage
APEC Business Travel Card Programme	Australia, Brunei, Chile, China, Hong Kong, Indonesia, Japan, Korea, Malaysia, Mexico, New Zealand, PNG, Peru, the Philippines, Singapore, Chinese Taipei, Thailand and Vietnam; US and Canada (transitional members)		Facilitates the entry of business visitors to the region from the participating economies in APEC – Valid for three years and permits multiple short-term business visits for two or three months each	Highly skilled
Japan–Philippines Economic Partnership Agreement	Japan and Philippines	EPA	– About 400 to 500 Philippine nurses and caregivers will be allowed to work in Japan annually on condition that they pass Japanese qualifying exams	Semi-skilled
Japan–Thailand Free Trade Agreement	Japan and Thailand	FTA	– Japan will accept Thai nurses and caregivers on condition that Thai caregivers will be required to obtain Japanese qualifications	Semi-skilled
Japan–Indonesia Economic Partnership Agreement	Japan and Philippines	EPA	– Japan will accept 400 nurses and 600 careworkers subject to meeting some conditions regarding graduation from higher education institutions and completion of vocational training – The government will issue special visas for	Semi-skilled

12 See Chanda and Sasidaran (2011), Table 6.

Table 7.8 (continued)

Agreement/ Scheme	Country/Region Covered	Type	Labour Mobility Provisions	Coverage
			up to three years to Indonesian nurses and four-year visas to careworkers	
India–Singapore Comprehensive Economic Cooperation Agreement	India and Singapore	CECA	– Easing of visa restrictions for a list of 127 professionals, covering a variety of sectors – Short-term service suppliers, intra-corporate transferees, and business visitors	Highly skilled
India–Korea Comprehensive Economic Partnership Agreement	India and Republic of Korea	CEPA	– Temporary movement of professional workers such as computer programmers and engineers etc.	Highly skilled
Japan–Singapore Free Trade Agreement	Japan and Singapore	FTA	– Chapter on Movement of Business Persons covering four major categories of business persons – business visitors, intra-corporate transferees, engineers and investors	Highly skilled
China–Singapore Free Trade Agreement	China and Singapore	FTA	– Facilitates temporary entry of business persons for three categories – business visitors, intra-corporate transferees and contractual service suppliers	Highly skilled

Source: Compiled from the original texts and documents of the trade agreements listed in the external trade and commerce ministries of the various countries discussed.

months, with the provision of extension by another month. National treatment has also been accorded to each other's service suppliers. From the Indian perspective, one of the most important outcomes has been the easing of visa restrictions for professionals in 127 occupations spanning a wide range of sectors (e.g. IT, medicine, engineering, nursing, accountancy, and university lecturers), subject to the successful conclusion of MRAs in these professions. Professionals in these selected sectors and occupations have been allowed to apply for a multiple entry visa of up to one year.

Another important aspect addressed by the IS–CECA is that of wage parity. The agreement permits the allowances paid in India and Singapore to be added to the basic pay of Indian professionals in order to meet the salary equivalence requirement for market entry into Singapore, thereby facilitating the entry of Indian professionals into Singapore. Earlier, failure to demonstrate equivalence of salary with professionals based in Singapore had led to denial of visas. Both countries have also committed to simplify procedures and expedite the granting of visas. Professional bodies such as the Institute of Chartered Accountants of India (ICAI) or the Medical Council of India (MCI) are expected to provide adequate procedures to verify the competence of professionals of the other country, determine the requirements met, evaluate the licences or certifications granted in that sector, and work out the exact intent and scope of recognition. Broad agreement has also been reached to accord mutual recognition for degrees issued by specified universities and technical education boards of both countries. India has also called for the recognition of qualifications of capable professionals from second-grade Indian institutions, in reciprocity for the concessions made by India in the goods sector, in order to better leverage its advantage as a source of English-speaking qualified workers for export to Singapore. Overall, the IS-CECA tries to facilitate the movement of business visitors and professionals between the two countries, without the hassle of going through the regular visa application process. By targeting selected sectors and occupations, it aims to build on the complementarity in supply of and demand for skilled service providers between India and Singapore, respectively.

To date, however, the outcome on mode 4 is not very encouraging. Market entry into Singapore by professionals from second-line colleges and institutions in India (an area where India had expected gains) has not been facilitated as Singaporean authorities have not been very forthcoming in recognizing the degrees of second-rung professional institutions in India. According to the Indian authorities, it remains difficult even for students from good Indian universities to be considered qualified by Singaporean authorities, let alone those from second-tier institutions. The main problem has been the failure to conclude negotiations on MRAs and to come to an understanding on the equivalence of qualifications and the list of accepted institutions and boards. According to the IS–CECA provisions, professional bodies in the five aforementioned initial target sectors should have completed this work within one year after the agreement came into force, by August 2006. However, even as the pact entered its second phase, this matter had not been resolved. The main challenge has been the inability to find a way to get the educational qualifications of capable professionals from second-grade institutions in India to be accepted by Singaporean authorities. Indian officials have attributed this failure to the lack of initiative on the part of Indian professional bodies such as the MCI, the Nursing Council and the ICAI. There have also been problems on the Singaporean side as some Singaporean institutions have asked their Indian counterparts to amend laws and regulations so as to conform to standards acceptable to them.

In part, the failure to take forward the process of mutual recognition can be attributed to the lack of strict timelines and enforcement mechanisms for the implementation of MRAs under the IS–CECA. Although the agreement had set a deadline of one year following its entry into force, to conclude MRAs in selected occupations, its provisions also state that *failure or delay to do so would not be regarded as a breach of obligations* under the agreement and *would not be subject to dispute settlement procedures*. In addition, disputes arising out of or under such arrangements are not covered under the dispute settlement mechanism of this agreement. Thus, the absence of clear timelines for the conclusion of these negotiations, the fact that there are no penalties and no strict enforcement mechanism in case of delays or failure to conclude recognition arrangements, and the inapplicability of dispute settlement mechanisms, to a great extent undermine the value of the agreement's provisions on recognition. Hence, the provisions for mode 4 remain as best endeavour clauses. They are soft on implementation, ambiguous on institutional issues, and open-ended on deliverables.

Following the recent review of the IS–CECA, it has been proposed that in order to realize the potential gains under this agreement, the Indian government should work hand in hand with professional bodies to facilitate the establishment of MRAs in services. In particular, it should take up the issue of recognition of qualifications from second-grade Indian institutions as a matter of reciprocity and to make the conclusion of the MRAs time bound.

India–Korea CEPA Like the IS–CECA, the IK–CEPA, which came into force in January 2010, aims to facilitate access for contractual service suppliers, business visitors, ICTs, and independent professionals and similarly identifies a selected list of professions for easier entry.[13] Some noteworthy provisions under this agreement include access by contractual service suppliers and independent professionals in the Korean market for up to one year, admission for up to two years for ICTs without being subject to any numerical quotas or labour market tests and stays of up to three months for business visitors. The agreement also makes a very significant extension in its coverage of MNP by including work permits and authorization for *dependants* of professionals, contractual service suppliers, and ICTs. The two countries have also identified a list of 163 professions, mostly involving IT professionals, engineers across a range of sectors (construction, automobile, marine, telecommunications, etc.), consultants in various fields, and English-language teachers who would qualify for easier entry into each other's markets. Once again, there is an attempt to customize the coverage to include occupations that are mutually relevant and address skill gaps in the labour market.

The IK-CEPA has also provided the basis for signing a Social Security Agreement (SSA) between the two countries. The SSA is meant to be for the benefit of employees and employers having cross-border operations in the two countries, as it enables them to avoid double payment of social security contributions. Under the SSA, for the purpose of meeting eligibility requirements, the period of service rendered by an employee in both the countries is to be added under the respective social security schemes, subject to certain conditions. The SSA is linked to the chapter on MNP under the IK–CEPA in that its provisions are applicable to all categories of workers covered by the agreement, excepting independent professionals.[14] Hence, as with the issue of recognition, this CEPA has laid the foundation for discussions on an important complementary regulatory issue such as social security taxes.

Philippines–Japan EPA (PJEPA) An important element of the PJEPA is the movement of Filipino professionals to Japan. Under the agreement, Filipino nationals are to be permitted to practise their profession in Japan, subject to certain conditions. The professions covered include: legal, accounting and taxation, architectural and engineering, computer and related, advertising and management consulting, translation and interpretation, services incidental to agriculture, audiovisual, higher education,

---

13 http://commerce.nic.in/trade/INDIA%20KOREA%20CEPA%202009.pdf.

14 http://www.kpmg.com/IN/en/WhatWeDo/Tax/FlashNews/KPMG-Flash-News-Social-Security-Agreement-between-India-and-Republic-of-Korea.pdf.

tourism and travel, entertainment (theatre and live bands) and maritime transport services. One of the most important areas of negotiation has been the movement of Filipino nurses and caregivers, given Japan's ageing population and the decline in the availability of domestic caregivers and nurses and the Philippines' keen interest in obtaining access for its nurses and caregivers in the Japanese market.

There is a specific provision covering the entry of Filipino health and care personnel into Japan, subject to certain terms and conditions being fulfilled. Filipino nurses and careworkers can practice their profession in Japan provided they meet certain requirements. These include passing the Philippine licensure exam and having a minimum of three years of work experience, undergoing skills and language training for six months in Japan and passing the Japanese nursing examination which is written in Nihonggo, with a maximum of three attempts. Filipino careworkers must finish a four-year college course and must be a certified caregiver in the Philippines. They must undergo skills and language training for six months in Japan and must pass the Japanese national exam written in Nihonggo for caregivers. The duration of stay is specified for each type of health worker, with limits on extensions and maximum length of stay. A Filipino nurse can stay for a maximum of two years in Japan, while a caregiver can stay up to three years. For those natural persons engaged in training in certified training facilities, permission to stay is granted for the period necessary for the completion of training. On the Filipino side, practice of all professions remains limited to nationals unless allowed by law.

Training or contractual arrangements with certified establishments are an important component of the entry and stay provisions. Coverage is limited to natural persons of the Philippines who supply services as nurses or certified careworkers or related activities on the basis of a contract with public or private organizations in Japan or on the basis of admission to public or private training facilities. The provisions further clarify that entry and temporary stay for a specified period, as given in the agreement, would be granted to a natural person of the Philippines, "who is designated and notified to the government of Japan by the government of the Philippines in accordance with the Implementing Agreement, and who enters into Japan on the dates specified by the Government of Japan" and who engages in specified activities during his temporary stay in Japan. These specified activities include obtaining qualifications as a nurse under Japanese law, undertaking a training course including Japanese language training as referred to in the Implementing Agreement for six months, and acquiring required knowledge and skills at a hospital. It is further specified that such activities are to be conducted on the basis of a personal contract with a public or private organization in Japan, which establishes a hospital under Japanese laws and regulations, and notified to the Philippines government by the Japanese government or a competent authority in Japan. Likewise, temporary entry and stay is permitted for Filipino caregivers in Japan for the purposes of obtaining qualification as a certified careworker under Japanese laws and regulations, with similarly specified conditions regarding the nature of this training. It is also specified that the training, whether in hospitals or caregiving facilities, or under public, private, or personal contracts, must satisfy the conditions notified by the Japanese government to the Filipino government. Home country certification is required for consideration as a natural person in Japan.

While the terms and conditions with regard to eligibility, duration of stay, and activities permitted are laid down in the agreement, the agreement fails to address some important aspects of health worker mobility between the two countries. Although training is an important component, there is no clarity about who is to bear the cost of training. There is also no mechanism specified regarding the process by which workers are recruited and placed or to regulate the specified terms and conditions. At present, an elaborate recruitment and deployment mechanism is already in operation between the two countries for health workers, but the PJEPA neither institutionalizes the existing arrangements nor specifies measures to regulate them. The mechanisms for placing Filipinos at Japanese hospitals are still unclear. Hence, there is a basic framework but procedural modalities are yet to be worked out.

The outcome, to date, is not very promising. As yet no nurses or caregivers have gone from the Philippines to Japan under this bilateral provision since the matter is still pending approval by the Philippines Senate. However, there is evidence that Filipino nurses and caregivers have already been recruited and have entered Japan or are being trained to work in Japan, in anticipation of the eventual approval of the agreement.

7.5.5 Recent Developments in Asian PTAs

The preceding discussion has highlighted only a very small subset of PTAs within Asia. However, as the PTA scenario is very dynamic, no discussion can do justice to the developments and outcomes that are taking place every year with new PTAs being announced and concluded, new rounds of negotiations being launched and reviews being undertaken of existing PTAs. Some of the most noteworthy developments in Asian PTAs warrant a quick mention.

India, one of the countries discussed in this chapter, has concluded two more significant PTAs with its Asian partners. The first is the India–Japan Comprehensive Economic Partnership Agreement which became operational in August 2011, seven years after negotiations were begun. It is India's first broad-based bilateral agreement with an industrialized country and has been termed more comprehensive than the earlier ones, given the wide range of issues it covers. It has been hailed for the opportunities it could provide for Indian service providers in sectors such as architectural and computer-related services as Japan has gone beyond the offers it has made in the ongoing Doha Round negotiations. Like the agreements with Korea and Singapore, this agreement too covers the categories of business visitors, ICTs, contractual service suppliers and independent professionals, which are pertinent to India, and also extends to areas that are tailored to address skill gaps in the Japanese market and supply capacity in the Indian market.[15] Japan has further agreed to consider opening its market for Indian nurses and caregivers. As part of this agreement, the two countries have also agreed to enter into negotiations on a social security agreement and to conclude the same within three years.

India has also concluded a PTA with Malaysia which could potentially facilitate the temporary movement of business people, including contractual service suppliers and independent professionals in various services, including accounting, engineering, architecture, medical, dental, nursing, consulting and IT. The agreement is also expected to boost cross-border investment between the two countries. A special category of installers and servicers, which refers to persons who install or service machinery and/or equipment, has also been included, subject to certain conditions on remuneration and nature of engagement.[16] Overall, India has received significant concessions from Malaysia in mode 4, through longer duration visas, easier renewal of visas, relaxation of criteria such as economic needs tests and inclusion of additional service supplier categories. There is also a

---

[15] For example, it involves special commitments by Japan on entry and temporary stay for Indian instructors of yoga, cuisine, Indian classical music and dance and the English language. The agreement also envisages cooperation among professionals in a range of services such as accounting, research and development, market research and management consulting.

[16] The entry terms and conditions have been liberalized. Business visitors from India are permitted to stay up to 90 days and can obtain a multiple entry visa of up to five years validity. ICTs are permitted to stay up to ten years in the case of senior managers and up to five years in the case of specialists. Contractual service suppliers and professionals from both countries are allowed to stay up to one year. Installers have been permitted to stay up to three months in either country. See http://www.indianhighcommission.com.my/pdf/Presentation%20by%20Dato%27%20Dr.%20Rebecca%20Sta%20Maria,%20Secretary%20General,%20Ministry%20of%20International%20Trade%20and%20Industry.pdf and http://commerce.nic.in/trade/IMCECA/Annex%209-1%20Movement%20of%20Natural%20Person.pdf.

strategic dimension to this PTA in that it gives India access to the ASEAN services market through the bilateral route, given the delay in including services in India's free trade agreement with ASEAN.

Another noteworthy recent development in the region is the Trans-Pacific Partnership (TPP), which would link the US with Australia, Brunei, Chile, Malaysia, New Zealand, Peru, Singapore, and Vietnam on a wide range of issues, with a few others looking to join the agreement. There is also a parallel Asian track which includes a major cluster of agreements that centre on the ASEAN negotiations among China, Japan, and Korea. The potential gains from services and investment liberalization from the Trans-Pacific and Asian track agreements are estimated to be large.

There are thus a growing number of bilateral, plurilateral, and regional agreements that are being forged, within Asia and between key countries in Asia and countries in other regions. The picture is quite complicated given the complex web of rules, provisions, and commitments under these broad agreements. Hence, given such a dynamic scenario, it is difficult to assess to what extent the inferences drawn from the earlier analysis of existing PTAs would remain valid. Nevertheless, some broad patterns are certainly evident.

7.6 CONCLUDING THOUGHTS

The analysis of the eight selected Asian PTAs offers several useful insights. The analysis suggests that the real value of PTAs may not lie in extending services liberalization. Although the PTAs do extend the scope of commitments in terms of the number of sectors and subsectors in which commitments are made by the countries, they do not for the most part involve more liberal commitments within subsectors and in the various modes. While some additional liberalization may be offered, particularly in mode 3, this is not uniformly true and similar restrictions continue to apply under the multilateral and the preferential commitments. Further, liberalization under PTAs still tends to fall short of the autonomous liberalization undertaken. Hence, the Asian PTAs do not necessarily enable deeper liberalization within sectors and modes.

The analysis also reveals that there is no significant improvement over the GATS in terms of the architecture of the services chapter and the provisions therein. Many PTAs almost mirror the services provisions of the GATS, while a few include additional provisions, refer to additional issues, elaborate further on the scope of certain provisions, and draw linkages with other parts of the PTA texts. However, there is no significant development in terms of the content of key disciplines or in terms of strengthening of institutional mechanisms in the services chapters. They are stronger on intent than on substantive content.

However, the real improvement is in terms of the overall architecture of the agreement, i.e. the additional chapters and annexes which go into considerable detail on a variety of cross-cutting issues and sectors that impinge on services trade. In particular, cross-cutting issues of investment and mobility of persons are covered in considerable detail relative to the GATS, along with references to institutional mechanisms for operationalizing the provisions such as through elaborate dispute settlement mechanisms. The additional annexes cover many sectors and new age issues which are absent from the GATS, including coverage of certain services which have proven difficult to liberalize under the WTO. Hence, the value of the PTAs is more in terms of (a) making progress in important areas such as investment and labour mobility; (b) developing disciplines and frameworks not necessarily specific to services but in a variety of other areas which have a bearing on services; and (c) enabling the coverage of new issues. Moreover, the differences that exist between PTAs with regard to the provisions which have a direct or indirect bearing on services suggest that such agreements enable countries to negotiate strategically and to frame the PTA texts and commitments in a manner that addresses specific interests and sensitivities associated with different partner countries.

Some broad generalizations can also be made about the nature of countries involved and the nature of the PTA texts and commitments. In general, the scope of commitments is greater for developed countries under the GATS and under the PTAs. However, developing countries tend to show more expansion in scope under PTAs relative to the GATS, partly because they have scheduled fewer sectors and subsectors than have developed countries under the GATS. Some developing countries such as India emerge as being significantly more proactive in their liberalization stance and their willingness to negotiate more comprehensively through additional annexes and extra detail in areas of strategic interest such as movement of natural persons. But overall, there is no consistent pattern with regard to the typology of PTAs either in terms of the nature of commitments or in terms of their modal distribution. Where some distinction can be made among the various kinds of PTAs is in terms of the framework and issues covered through additional chapters and annexes. North–North agreements tend to cover some of the more difficult issues such as government procurement, while North–South agreements have a focus on issues such as recognition of qualifications which relate to the importance of mode 4 in North–South services trade. South–South agreements tend to focus on institutional cooperation and establishment of mechanisms, reflecting the need to strengthen capacity and institution building in these countries. But there is sufficient diversity even among the various types of PTAs and all North–North or North–South, or South–South agreements do not follow a uniform pattern, indicating that the negotiating dynamics vary by partner countries.

REFERENCES

Abeysinghe, S., "Structure and Content of the Draft Services Chapter of India-Sri Lanka CEPA: To What Extent does it Go Beyond GATS in Promoting Transparency, Credibility and Liberalization of Services?," Master's thesis, World Trade Institute, September 30, 2010

ADB Asia Regional Integration Data Center Database for FTAs, http://aric.adb.org/FTAbyCountryAll.php

Adlung, R. and P. Morrison, "Less than the GATS: Negative Preferences in Regional Services Agreements", mimeo, November 27, 2009

ASEAN Secretariat, China-ASEAN Free Trade Agreement, http://www.aseansec.org/16646.htm

Board of Investment Sri Lanka, www.boi.lk

Board of Investment Pakistan, www.pakboi.gov.pk

Carzaniga, A., "A Warmer Welcome? Access for Natural Persons under PTAs", in J. Marchetti and M. Roy (eds.), *Opening Markets for Trade in Services: Countries and Sectors in Bilateral and WTO Negotiations*, Cambridge, Cambridge University Press, 2008, pp. 61–112

Centre for Trade and Development, "Barriers to Foreign Direct Investment in Services, in South Asia", http://www.centad.org/relatedinfo21.asp

Chanda, R. and G. Sasidaran (2011), "Managing Migration in Asia: Role of Interstate Cooperation", in Randall Hansen, Jeanette Money, and Jobst Koehler (eds.), *Migration, Nation States, and International Cooperation*, London: Routledge Press, pp. 170–210

China Banking Regulatory Commission, Background Information for the Regulations of the People's Republic of China on Administration of Foreign-funded Banks, http://www.cbrc.gov.cn/chinese/home/jsp/docView.jsp?docID=2869

Dee, P. and J. Gali, "The Trade and Investment Effects of Preferential Trading Arrangements", prepared for the Fourteenth Annual East Asian Seminar on Economics, Taipei, September 2003

Department of Industrial Policy and Promotion, Government of India, "Consolidated FDI Policy 2010", http://dipp.gov.in/FDI_Circular/FDI_Circular_02of2010.pdf

Economic Times, "Services Gains Seen as India, Malaysia Enter Pact Today", February 18, 2011, http://articles.economictimes.indiatimes.com/2011-02-18/news/28615298_1_mustapa-mohamed-bilateral-trade-negative-list

Fink, C. and M. Molinuevo, "East Asian FTAs in Services: Roaring Tigers or Timid Pandas", East Asia and Pacific Region, Report No. 40175, The World Bank, 2007

Government of India, Ministry of Commerce, India-Korea Comprehensive Economic Partnership Agreement, http://commerce.nic.in/trade/INDIA%20KOREA%20CEPA%202009.pdf

Government of India, Ministry of Commerce, India-Singapore Comprehensive Economic Cooperation Agreement, http://commerce.nic.in/ceca/toc.htm

Government of Singapore, Information Kit on the India-Singapore CECA, http://www.fta.gov.sg/ceca/ceca_india_infokit.pdf

Government of Japan, Japan-Singapore Economic Partnership Agreement, http://www.mofa.go.jp/region/asia-paci/singapore/jsepa.html

Government of Japan, Japan-Philippines Economic Partnership Agreement, http://www.mofa.go.jp/region/asia-paci/philippine/epa0609/main.pdf

Government of Pakistan, China-Pakistan Agreement on Trade in Services, http://www.commerce.gov.pk/PCFTA-S/Agreement.PDF

Government of India, Ministry of Commerce, India-Sri Lanka Comprehensive Economic Partnership Agreement, http://commerce.nic.in/trade/international_ta_current_details.asp#b22

Government of India, Ministry of Commerce, India-Malaysia Comprehensive Economic Cooperation Agreement, http://commerce.nic.in/trade/IMCECA/Chapter%2009%20MNP.pdf and http://commerce.nic.in/trade/IMCECA/Annex%209–1%20Movement%20of%20Natural%20Person.pdf

Gopalan, S. and R. Rajan, "Financial Sector De-Regulation in Emerging Asia: Focus on Foreign Bank Entry", *Journal of World Investment and Trade*, 14(12), 2010 http://www.freewebs.com/rrajan1/bankentry.pdf

KPMG, "Social Security Agreement between India and Korea Comes into Effect", KPMG Flash News, KPMG India, 2011, http://www.kpmg.com/IN/en/WhatWeDo/Tax/FlashNews/KPMG-Flash-News-Social-Security-Agreement-between-India-and-Republic-of-Korea.pdf

Marchetti, J. and M. Roy, "Services Liberalization in the WTO and in PTAs", in J. Marchetti and M. Roy (eds.), *Opening Markets for Trade in Services: Countries and Sectors in Bilateral and WTO Negotiations*, Cambridge, Cambridge University Press, 2008, pp. 61–112

Mattoo, A. and P. Sauvé, "The Preferential Liberalization of Services Trade", NCCR Trade Regulation Working Paper 2010/13, http://www.wti.org/research/publication/?tx_nccr_pi1%5Bshow%5D=97&cHash=309ad4541e97e8a7b3b3dd02dff099d5

Mattoo, A. and P. Sauvé, "Regionalism in Services Trade", *A Handbook of International Trade in Services*, New York, Oxford University Press, 2008

Ministry of International Trade and Industry, "Malaysia-India Comprehensive Economic Cooperation Agreement (CECA): Opportunities for Business", presentation by Secretary General, November 21, 2011, http://www.indianhighcommission.com.my/pdf/Presentation%20by%20Dato%27%20Dr.%20Rebecca%20Sta%20Maria,%20Secretary%20General,%20Ministry%20of%20International%20Trade%20and%20Industry.pdf

Nag, B. and D. De, "Services in Regional Trade Agreements: Implications for India", MPRA, Munich, September 2008, http://mpra.ub.uni-muenchen.de/15871

Roy, M., J. Marchetti and H. Lim, "Services Liberalization in the New Generation of PTAs: How Much Further than the GATS", *World Trade Review*, 6(2), 2007, pp. 1455–93

Thangavelu, S. and S. Abe, "Singapore, India and Japan in the Framework of FTA/EPA Arrangement", Centre for Contemporary Asian Studies, Doshisha University, CCAS Working Paper No. 6, May 2007

UN-ESCAP Trade Agreements database, http://www.unescap.org/tid/aptiad/agg_db.aspx

UN-ESCAP, "Trade in Telecommunications Services Experiences of Australia, Japan and Singapore under WTO Agreements", http://www.unescap.org/tid/mtg/ituwtoesc_s52.pdf

Ure, J., "FDI in Telecommunications Services in Asia", Kyoto, 2004, http://www.tif.trpc.com.hk/papers/2004/fdi_asia_telecoms.pdf

USTR, US-Korea Free Trade Agreement, http://www.ustr.gov/trade-agreements/free-trade-agreements/korus-fta

Wignaraja, G. and D. Lazaro, "North-South vs. South-South Asian FTAs: Trends, Compatibilities, and Ways Forward", UNU-CRIS Working Papers, W-2010/3, 2010

World Bank database, http://data.worldbank.org/indicator/NY.GDP.MKTP.CD

WTO, Individual country GATS commitments, www.wto.org

WTO, Trade Policy Review: Singapore, http://www.philexport.ph/policy/wto/businessbriefingvol9_tpr_singapore.pdf

WTO, RTA Database, http://rtais.wto.org/UI/PublicMaintainRTAHome.aspx

Yukyong Yeo, Department of Social and Public Administration, City University of Hong Kong, "Regulatory Politics in China's Telecommunications Service Industry", June 2008, http://regulation.upf.edu/utrecht-08-papers/yyeo.pdf

8. Services trade in South Asia: the India–Sri Lanka CEPA

A.P.C. Subhashini Abeysinghe

8.1 INTRODUCTION

Regional agreements on trade in services are different from those on trade in goods. Agreements on liberalisation of trade in services mainly deal with "behind the border" regulatory barriers, whereas those on liberalisation of trade in goods deal mainly with "at the border barriers" such as tariffs. Another key difference is that the definition of trade in services is much broader than that of goods. Given the importance of proximity of services suppliers (be they juridical persons or natural persons) and consumers, the definition of trade in services encompasses both investments (commercial presence) and movement of people. Hence, the architecture and content of regional agreements in trade in services is significantly different from that of trade in goods.

The architecture of an agreement refers to rules and disciplines and the method of liberalisation of trade in services. The content refers to the actual liberalisation commitments made. The architecture and content of existing regional agreements show significant variations.[1] The two fundamental approaches towards regional services agreements have been the GATS-type/hybrid list approach and the NAFTA-type/negative list approach. The Asian countries have generally tended to adopt the GATS-type approach, while countries in the Western hemisphere have adopted the NAFTA-type approach. Nevertheless the two approaches have not been mutually exclusive, with each agreement showing variations and certain features of both approaches. The variations in the architecture of these agreements impact on the level of liberalisation and also determine the transparency and credibility of the liberalisation commitments.

Trade in services can be promoted mainly by enhancing transparency of the trading regime, by enhancing credibility through legally binding

[1] Fink and Molinuevo (2007), p iv.

commitments and by further liberalisation of restrictions that prevent trade. The objective of this chapter is to evaluate the architecture and content of the India–Sri Lanka CEPA to discover to what extent it goes beyond GATS in terms of transparency, credibility and liberalisation of the services sector and whether the choice of architecture and content of the agreement will lead to promotion of trade in services between the two countries. The chapter also compares the India–Sri Lanka Comprehensive Economic Partnership Agreement (CEPA) with three other agreements on services involving India and other South Asian countries – the South Asian Agreement on Trade in Services (SATIS), the India–Singapore CECA and the India–Korea CEPA – and highlights similarities and differences between these agreements, with the objective of identifying a future regional approach towards liberalisation of services in Sri Lanka in particular and South Asia in general.

Sri Lanka is a latecomer to the regional integration process in services. The India–Sri Lanka CEPA proposed in 2002 is the first agreement negotiated by Sri Lanka to include services.[2] The negotiations have had a bumpy ride from the very beginning and in the process have missed several deadlines. Resistance to the signing of the agreement has come from Sri Lanka, where various interest groups, ranging from domestic industrialists and professional associations to leftist political parties have been lobbying against it.

Sri Lanka already has an agreement with India dealing with trade in goods. Relative to the country's other three regional agreements (the South Asian Free Trade Area (SAFTA[3]), the Asia Pacific Trade Agreement (APTA[4]) and the Sri Lanka–Pakistan FTA) the India–Sri Lanka FTA is hailed as a success.[5] Total trade between the two countries accounted for 22% of Sri Lanka's total trade, with imports accounting for 17% of total imports and exports accounting for 5% of total exports of Sri Lanka at last count. Trade in services and investment between the two countries have been growing and India became one of the top five investors in Sri Lanka in recent years. Although a sectoral breakdown of

---

[2] In addition to a chapter on services, the CEPA includes chapters dealing with trade in goods, movement of natural persons, investment, air services, customs, technical barriers to trade (TBT) and sanitary and phytosanitary measures (SPS), economic cooperation and dispute settlement.

[3] Member countries of SAFTA are Sri Lanka, India, Pakistan, Bangladesh, Nepal, Bhutan and the Maldives.

[4] Member countries of APTA are Sri Lanka, India, China, Bangladesh and the Republic of Korea.

[5] Kelegama and Mukherji (2007).

Indian investments is not available, the Indian presence is dominant in services sectors such as banking, telecommunications, advertising, education, tourism and IT. India is the preferred investment destination of Sri Lankan businesses investing abroad.[6] Many services suppliers already have a commercial presence in India in sectors such as logistics, hotels and retailing. The Mode 2[7] supply of services is also prominent between the two countries; Sri Lanka's Mode 2 exports are mainly in sectors such as port services, ship repair services, tourism and aviation, whereas India's Mode 2 exports are mainly in tourism, health and higher education. From an economic point of view, an agreement in services would be helpful in cementing and assisting expansion of existing regional dynamics between the two countries. However, whether the proposed architecture and content of the agreement would in fact promote further expansion of trade in services between the two countries is a critical question which this chapter aims to address.

The main focus is on the India–Sri Lanka CEPA because, at the bilateral level, the level of ambition and depth of liberalisation is likely to be far greater than at the regional level. Sri Lanka has already signed a services agreement in the SAARC context – the South Agreement on Trade in Services (SATIS), which was signed by the SAARC countries[8] in April 2010. However, within SAARC, the schedule of commitments has yet to be developed; hence the content of the agreement regarding the extent of liberalisation cannot be analysed. Further, the experience with SAARC in liberalising trade in goods has been disappointing, and compared to the progress in SAARC, Sri Lanka has been able to move faster at the bilateral level, especially with India. Given the complexity, regulatory intensity and political sensitivity associated with services liberalisation, SAARC is likely to progress poorly in this area. The India–Sri Lanka CEPA's draft conditional offers in services are available to allow an analysis of the content of the agreement and an assessment of the level of liberalisation.[9]

The chapter will mainly follow the methodology used by Fink and Molinuevo[10] to assess the key features of the architecture of the agreement and to measure the extent of liberalisation. The chapter does not,

---

[6] The Ceylon Chamber of Commerce (2008).

[7] For a definition of the four modes of service supply, refer to Section 8.6.

[8] SAARC countries comprise India, Sri Lanka, Pakistan, Bangladesh, Nepal, Bhutan, the Maldives and Afghanistan.

[9] However, it must be noted that, being draft conditional offers, the analysis only gives an indication of the extent of liberalisation and not the actual level that will be achieved.

[10] Fink and Molinuevo (2007).

however, elaborate on the dispute settlement mechanism in the India–Sri Lanka CEPA since the focus is mainly on services-specific rules. Fink and Molinuevo assess the architecture of the regional agreements by comparing how they differ from GATS architecture and whether these differences lead to greater transparency, credibility and liberalisation of services at the regional level than at the multilateral level. The content or the extent of liberalisation is assessed by comparing the services schedules at the regional level with the services schedules of each country at the multilateral level.[11]

The chapter is structured as follows. Section 8.2 analyses the key general obligations and disciplines of the India–Sri Lanka CEPA: scheduling approach, national treatment, market access, most favoured nation treatment, domestic regulation, subsidies, and emergency safeguard measures, which encompass rules that apply horizontally to all commitments as well as the sub-committee on trade in services. Section 8.3 specifically looks at rules of origin in services adopted by the India–Sri Lanka CEPA and how these will determine competition and efficiency in the domestic market and potential for market access. Section 8.4 is devoted to disciplines governing movement of natural persons and Section 8.5 looks at disciplines on commercial presence or the investment in services. Section 8.6 analyses the extent of liberalisation. All the sections make an assessment of how far the regional commitments go beyond the GATS commitments and at the impact of the choice of architecture on transparency, credibility and extent of liberalisation. Each section also compares provisions of the India–Sri Lanka CEPA with SATIS, the India–Singapore CECA and the India–Korea CEPA to identify similarities and differences between these agreements. Section 8.7 concludes by analysing the policy implications of the architectural choices and extent of liberalisation of Sri Lanka and what it means for future liberalisation efforts.

8.2 GENERAL OBLIGATIONS AND DISCIPLINES

This section highlights the similarities and differences between the key obligations in the India–Sri Lanka CEPA and those of the GATS, SATIS, India–Singapore CECA and India–Korea CEPA. The objective is to assess how far the obligations in the India–Sri Lanka CEPA go beyond GATS, and how the India–Sri Lanka CEPA differs from other agreements

---

[11] The methodology developed by Fink and Molinuevo in assessing the extent of liberalisation is given in detail in Section 8.6.

in the region and to what extent the key provisions assist in promoting trade in services by enhancing transparency, credibility and liberalisation of the services sector. The general obligations and disciplines refer to the rules that provide the foundation for services liberalisation. The key obligations discussed in this section include the scheduling approach chosen, which has a significant influence on the overall architecture of an agreement, national treatment (NT), market access, most favoured nation treatment (MFN), domestic regulations, subsidies and emergency safeguard measures (ESM) and one institutional aspect of the agreement: the Sub-Committee on Trade in Services.

8.2.1 Scheduling Approach

There are two main approaches taken by countries in scheduling liberalisation commitments – the GATS-type hybrid list approach and the NAFTA-type negative list approach. The GATS-type agreements are not pure positive list agreements; they are hybrid agreements where sectors and sub-sectors are selected on a positive list basis. The liberalisation commitments in each sector, however, are undertaken either on a positive list or a negative list basis. More frequently, Mode 3 commercial presence commitments take a negative list approach and Mode 4 commitments on movement of natural persons take a positive list approach.[12]

In GATS-type hybrid list agreements, countries list only the sectors and sub-sectors for which they make liberalisation commitments. They are under no obligation to provide information on non-conforming measures in sectors where commitments have not been made. In NAFTA-type negative list agreements all the sectors and non-conforming measures that are not specified in the list of reservations and non-conforming measures (negative list), have to be liberalised.

The choice of architecture depends largely on the negotiating partner.[13] However, agreements signed by Asian countries have a bias towards GATS-type positive listing, whereas agreements signed by countries in North America and countries of the Western hemisphere follow the NAFTA-type negative listing.[14] Table 8.1 summarises the scheduling approach taken by the India–Sri Lanka CEPA and compares it with SATIS, the India–Singapore CECA and the India–Korea CEPA.

---

[12] Where a commitment is listed as "none except" that is a negative listing and where a commitment is made as "unbound except" that is a positive listing (Fink and Molinuevo, 2007, p 12).

[13] Ochiai et al. (2007), p. 4.

[14] Ibid., p. 4.

Table 8.1 Scheduling approach

Agreement	Listing of sectors	Listing of level of openness
India–Sri Lanka CEPA	Positive	Hybrid
SATIS	Positive	To be seen, since schedules are not yet negotiated; expected to be hybrid
India–Singapore CECA	Positive	Hybrid
India–Korea CEPA	Positive	Hybrid

Table 8.2 Sectoral carve-outs

Agreement	Carve-out(s)
India–Sri Lanka CEPA	Article 3.a – Services supplied in the exercise of government authority Separate chapter on air services (Chapter 6), best endeavour provisions for bilateral negotiations
SATIS	Article 3.2 – Government procurement, services supplied in the exercise of government authority, transportation and non-transportation air services including domestic and international services, related services (e.g. ground handling) except aircraft repair and maintenance, selling and marketing of air transport services and computerised reservation systems
India–Singapore CECA	Same as in India – Sri Lanka CEPA
India–Korea CEPA	Same as in SATIS

Both India and Sri Lanka seem to be following the example set by other Asian countries in negotiating services agreements by adopting a GATS-type hybrid list approach to scheduling. However, the choice of scheduling approach is not the main determinant of the extent of liberalisation in services sectors. One of the main determinants is sectoral reservations or sectoral carve-outs whereby certain sectors are exempt from the scope of the agreement.[15] Sectoral carve-outs are generally outlined in the article giving the scope and coverage of the agreement. Table 8.2 summarises the sectoral carve-outs of the India–Sri Lanka CEPA together with those of the SATIS, India–Singapore and India–Korea agreements.

15 Fink and Molinuevo (2007), p. 9.

The India–Sri Lanka CEPA carves out services supplied in the exercise of government authority, following the architecture of GATS. This exemption is found in almost all the regional services agreements. The countries seem to find the same difficulties and sensitivities faced in liberalising air transport services at the multilateral level at the regional level too, leading to that sector being carved out from the agreements as well.

Although the India–Sri Lanka CEPA has not carved out air transport services entirely from the scope of the agreement, the chapter on air services is a stand-alone chapter which has no relation to the chapter on services, and is largely a best endeavour provision which encourages negotiations at the bilateral level. Hence, the agreement does not go beyond GATS in air transport services. In the India–Singapore CECA, the air transport services are covered in a separate chapter in a similar manner.

Both the India–Korea CEPA and SATIS specifically carve out government procurement from the scope of the services disciplines. This is an area where disciplines at the multilateral level remain underdeveloped. The India–Sri Lanka CEPA does not carve out government procurement, but repeats the provisions in GATS Article XIII by exempting application of market access and national treatment disciplines to government procurement. The GATS calls for future multilateral negotiations on government procurement. The India–Sri Lanka CEPA can be said to fall short of GATS in this respect by not making any reference to future multilateral negotiations and also by not providing any room for future negotiations in the regional context.

The India–Sri Lanka CEPA does not provide for automatic binding of future new services and services that are currently not technologically feasible but could become so in future. There is a best endeavour clause for possible inclusion of such services unilaterally or at the request of the other party. The same best endeavour provision is found in both the India–Singapore and India–Korea agreements. In SATIS, there is reference only to services which are not technically or technologically feasible but not to other new services.

The India–Sri Lanka CEPA, having chosen the GATS-type hybrid listing approach, has retained a high degree of policy flexibility and the following sections will discuss whether this flexibility has undermined the transparency, credibility and extent of liberalisation provided for in the agreement.

8.2.2 National Treatment

The principle of national treatment (NT) ensures that foreign services and services suppliers do not receive less favourable treatment than the domestic like services and services suppliers in service sectors where a party has undertaken specific liberalisation commitments in its schedule of commitments. All services agreements have provisions on NT but not all agreements provide NT on an unconditional basis. However, GATS-type and NAFTA-type agreements follow different approaches in providing for NT. The NAFTA-type agreement "applies NT to any measure of a party with respect to any service sectors or sub-sectors *unless* they are expressly listed in that party's schedule ('negative list' approach), the national treatment obligation in the GATS *only* applies in sectors inscribed in Members' schedule and subject to any conditions and qualifications set out therein ('positive/negative list' approach)".[16]

The reach of the NT obligation depends crucially on whether foreign and domestic services suppliers are considered "like". In NAFTA, the services suppliers are to be treated not less favourably in "like circumstances", whereas in GATS "like services suppliers and services" are to be treated not less favourably. The wording will have important legal implications when it comes to dispute settlement.[17]

The NT provision in the services chapter of the India–Sri Lanka CEPA refers to like services and services suppliers, and this has been the practice in SATIS, the India–Singapore CECA and the India–Korea CEPA. Further, NT in all these agreements follows the GATS approach and is applicable only to sector-specific commitments and subject to conditions and limitations scheduled in the NT column of the Schedule of Services. In all three bilateral agreements, India–Sri Lanka, India–Singapore and India–Korea, there are two additional paragraphs inserted into the NT provisions in GATS Article XVII. One refers to subsequent establishment, acquisition and expansion of investments by a services supplier that is duly organised under the law of a party, which is owned by service suppliers of the other party, being considered as an investment of the other party under the services chapter. The second additional paragraph applies to the NT at the regional and local level for like service suppliers. It states that the services suppliers of the other party be treated no less favourably than the most favourable treatment accorded at that regional or local level to like service suppliers of the party of which it forms a part.

The second article has been inserted, most likely taking into consideration the federal structure of India, where State governments can impose their own rules and regulations governing services which may treat services suppliers within that State more favourably than like services

16 Ortino (2007), p. 17.
17 Ibid.

suppliers from the rest of India as well as those from abroad. The NT provision in the India–Sri Lanka CEPA is as narrow as that of GATS; it limits its applicability to specific commitments and retains flexibility to maintain existing discriminatory treatment by scheduling these in the schedule of commitments.

8.2.3 Market Access

The market access (MA) provisions govern the entry of services and services suppliers of the other party into the market of a party. These could be discriminatory or non-discriminatory. GATS Article XVI on market access lists four types of market access restrictions which cannot be maintained or adopted unless specified in the schedule of commitments: quantitative restrictions, restrictions on type of legal entity, restrictions on foreign equity and restrictions on number of natural persons that can be employed.[18] The GATS-type regional agreements list MA restrictions in the market access column of the services schedule, whereas NAFTA-type agreements do not have a specific provision on market access but include a similar provision addressing "quantitative restrictions" and the list of non-conforming and future measures would list these restrictions.[19]

Similar to NT provisions, even market access provisions in regional services agreements are not applied across the board; they are applicable only to the extent of limitations listed in the schedule of commitments or the list of reservations. The MA provisions in the India–Sri Lanka CEPA mirror GATS Article XVI. The same approach is adopted by the other three agreements.

8.2.4 Most Favoured Nation Treatment

MFN treatment in bilateral and regional agreements differs from the MFN treatment provisions in GATS. These agreements are permissible deviations from the GATS/WTO principle of MFN treatment, which allows countries to grant preferential treatment on a regional or bilateral basis, without having to extend such treatment to other WTO members.

The MFN provisions in bilateral agreements are about extending subsequent preferential treatment, granted at a future date to non-parties, to parties to the agreement. In addition to the above, if the agreement involves more than two countries, the MFN provision also has an article

---

18 Ortino (2007), p. 19, Fink and Molinuevo (2007), p. 22.

19 Ortino (2007), p. 20.

which requires members to the agreement to extend preferences granted to one member to all other members to the RTA.

A binding MFN provision will reduce trade diversion and, by extending concessions to non-parties, it increases competition in the domestic market. Therefore, from an economic efficiency point of view it has a positive impact. However, one objective of negotiating trade agreements is to get preferential access, which is not available to other non-parties. The objective is to exclude competition to some extent and to have a captured market. Hence, from a market access point of view this is negative for parties that negotiate an agreement. Having many binding MFN provisions in bilateral agreements hence reduces the bargaining position of the negotiating country.[20]

The MFN provision of the India–Sri Lanka CEPA is a soft provision, which calls for each party to give consideration to a request made by the other party for the incorporation of treatment no less favourable than that accorded to the non-party. The agreement seems to follow the same trend adopted by India in the other two bilateral agreements, with Singapore and Korea, and SATIS has the same provision. In addition, SATIS has a binding provision for MFN treatment to all parties involved in the agreement, which requires that the preferences extended to one party be extended to all Parties to the agreement. However, this is subject to Article 22.b, which is on special and differential treatment accorded to least developed countries (LDCs) in the region. Where a non-LDC extends special concessions to LDCs, they are not required to extend such concessions to other non-LDCs on an MFN basis.

However, the significance of the MFN provision depends on two criteria; first, whether the commitments are in fact preferential, compared to the unilateral level of liberalisation and, secondly, the probability of backtracking unilateral liberalisation. If the concessions go beyond unilateral liberalisation, then legally binding MFN provisions play a critical role in enhancing efficiency and reducing trade diversion. However, if the concessions are at status quo, then services suppliers from a non-party also face the same limitations as a party in entering the market; hence competition in the market is secured. If the probability of backtracking unilateral liberalisation is high, then even if concessions are at status quo, they still play a key role in enhancing credibility for services suppliers. If the probability is low, then binding MFN provisions do not play a significant role. In Section 8.6, the discussion on the extent of liberalisation will shed light on the significance of the MFN provision in the India–Sri Lanka CEPA.

---

20 Fink and Molinuevo (2007), p. 23.

8.2.5 Domestic regulation

Domestic regulation is an area where GATS disciplines are incomplete and a mandate exists for future negotiations. Domestic regulations in GATS deal with impartial, objective and reasonable administration of domestic regulations, establishing practicable, judicial, arbitral or administrative tribunals, adopting international standards where applicable and where domestic regulations are necessary and do not constitute an unnecessary obstacle to trade which will nullify or impair the concessions granted. GATS provisions on domestic regulation apply only to sectors where specific commitments are undertaken and are ranked as one of the weakest elements in the agreement.[21] In theory it is said that, when foreign regulatory preferences are similar and regulatory institutions are broadly compatible, regulatory convergence and policy harmonisation costs will be smaller, and this is more likely to happen among countries that are "closer" in physical, linguistic, cultural or historical terms.[22] However, in practice, the existing FTAs have failed to make much progress in the area of domestic regulation.[23]

The India–Sri Lanka CEPA simply replicates the exact provisions in Article VI of the GATS with a provision for future review of the disciplines subject to developments in the GATS negotiations on rule making. The same trend is observed in SATIS and in the India–Singapore and India–Korea agreements. In addition to horizontal rules on domestic regulation, trade disciplines may also establish regulatory disciplines for specific service sectors. WTO members have established regulatory rules under the GATS in financial services, accountancy services and telecommunications services. For example the India–Singapore agreement has developed separate disciplines on electronic commerce. However, the India–Sri Lanka CEPA does not have any sectoral disciplines.

8.2.6 Subsidies and Emergency Safeguard Measures

The disciplines on subsidies in services have not been developed in the multilateral context, nor has there been much progress in this area in the regional context. The GATS-type regional agreements generally replicate provisions in GATS Article XV on subsidies calling for future develop-

21 Mattoo and Sauvé (2003), p. 1.
22 Mattoo and Sauvé (2010), p. 31.
23 Fink and Molinuevo (2007), pp. 45–7.

ments on subsidies, whereas NAFTA-type agreements tend to exclude subsidy practices from the coverage of the agreement.[24]

The India–Sri Lanka CEPA has carved out subsidies from the scope of the services chapter, stating that the disciplines of the services chapter do not apply to subsidies. The agreement provides room for revision of subsidy disciplines subject to the developments in the multilateral context. Furthermore, the article on subsidies explicitly states that the dispute settlement mechanism does not apply to subsidies. In line with GATS Article XV, which refers to exchange of information on subsidies, the India–Sri Lanka CEPA outlines in detail the kind of information to be shared. The India–Singapore CECA, the India–Korea CEPA and SATIS also include similar provisions.

GATS does not provide for emergency safeguard measures (ESM) by which WTO members can temporarily depart from their commitments in response to an unanticipated surge in services imports with harmful effects on domestic service suppliers. Article X of GATS on ESM merely calls for future development of disciplines related to safeguards in services. The findings of empirical studies on existing regional services agreements reveal that the "governments confront the same conceptual challenges, data limitations, feasibility challenges and political sensitivities in developing safeguard measures at the regional level as they do on the multilateral front".[25]

As can be seen from Table 8.3, India has departed from its stance of

Table 8.3 Provisions on emergency safeguard measures

Agreement	Safeguard measures
India–Sri Lanka CEPA	Article 14 – serious injury (guided by Article 4 of Agreement on Safeguards), initially 3 months, and extension for another 3 months – maximum 6 months
SATIS	Article 15 – reference to GATS provision – sympathetic consideration in the event of adverse impact
India–Singapore CECA	Article 7.14 – neither party shall take safeguard action against services and service suppliers of the other party from the date of entry into force of this agreement. Neither party shall initiate or continue any safeguard investigations in respect of services and service suppliers of the other party. Provisions on safeguards will be reviewed based on GATS negotiation outcome
India–Korea CEPA	Article 6.11 – same as in India–Singapore CECA

24 Sauvé and Mattoo (2004), p. 36.
25 Mattoo and Sauvé (2010), p. 36.

not allowing for safeguard actions in its regional agreements by providing room for such measures. The provision on ESM in the India–Sri Lanka CEPA, however, lacks clarity and raises strong doubts as to its operational feasibility. The safeguard measures can be taken for a period of six months (with an initial period of three months), which is likely to be too short to allow any breathing space for domestic services suppliers if they are really being injured as the result of a surge. The chapter on trade in goods in the India–Sri Lanka CEPA provides for preferential safeguard measures for a duration of two years (with an initial period of one year). The GATT Agreement on Safeguards provides for safeguard measures to be put in place for a maximum of eight years, with an initial period of four years.

The ESM in the India–Sri Lanka CEPA makes reference to Article 4 of the GATT Agreement on Safeguards. Once again the practicality of applying Article 4 of the Agreement on Safeguards to services is questionable. For example, identifying domestic industry that produces like or directly competitive services will be a major challenge. Also, the lack of data will pose major problems in measuring the increase in imports and injury to domestic industry.

It is most likely that Sri Lanka wanted to have a provision for ESM to make the agreement politically feasible. Given the fears among domestic services suppliers of a surge in Indian services and services suppliers, it would have been more difficult to sell an agreement without such a provision back home. India is likely to have agreed to the provision in the clear knowledge that it was very unlikely to be used.

8.2.7 Sub-Committee on Trade in Services

The India–Sri Lanka CEPA has provided in Article 25 for the establishment of a Sub-Committee on Trade in Services to review commitments with the objective of further liberalisation, and to review the implementation and operation of the Chapter on Trade in Services as well as effective implementation of mutual recognition agreements. The composition of the sub-committee is rather vague, the article merely refers to representatives with necessary expertise and there is no reference to number of representatives or to the term that each representative will serve on the committee. It does not allow for regular meetings, only for ad hoc meetings.

The Sub-Committee on Trade in Services appears only in the India–Sri Lanka CEPA; there is no such provision in the India–Singapore CECA, the India–Korea CEPA or SATIS. This is a proposal by Sri Lanka, and is likely to have emerged from Sri Lanka's experience with the implementation of the India–Sri Lanka Free Trade Agreement. The practical difficulties of market access in relation to liberalisation commitments only surface when businesses try to make use of the concessions to enter the other party's market; the problems related to the implementation of services commitments are likely to be greater than in the goods sector, because of regulatory intensity in the services sector. Hence, having an institutional mechanism to meet regularly and discuss implementation issues will help with the speedy resolution of such matters and facilitate the smooth functioning of the agreement.

The general obligations and disciplines of the India–Sri Lanka CEPA are very similar to the provisions in GATS. The agreement fails to make any progress in areas where GATS has an unfinished agenda: government procurement, subsidies and domestic regulation. The only minor innovation is the adoption of safeguard measures, yet the operational feasibility and commercial significance of the provision are highly doubtful.

8.3 RULES OF ORIGIN

Rules of origin (ROO) ensure that services and services suppliers from non-parties do not free-ride on the concessions granted to parties, and that only services and services suppliers from parties to the agreement benefit from the concessions. This section discusses the special features of ROO in services as well as the costs and benefits of adopting liberal ROO, with specific reference to the India–Sri Lanka CEPA.

Defining ROO of services is different from and more complex than for goods. Services being intangible, it is difficult or nearly impossible to measure domestic value addition, a common criterion used in trade in goods agreements. The change in harmonized system (HS) classification is also impossible in services, since services have no highly developed classification system like that for goods, and transformation of services is not as clear as in the case of goods to distinguish processing. Further complications arise due to services being traded through commercial presence and movement of persons and not only across the border as in the case of goods.

Generally, for services supplied across the border, the ROO are determined by whether the service is supplied from the territory of a partner country or not. If the service is supplied from the territory of a non-party, then the concessions are denied. In terms of commercial presence, some regional agreements extend concessions only to services suppliers or juridical persons owned and controlled by the partner country. This follows the definition of juridical person given in GATS Article XXVIII (n). Agreements adopting liberal rules extend benefits to third party service suppliers that fulfil the two criteria of being established in one of the FTA parties and showing substantive business operations. ROO for natural persons supplying services are extended to nationals of a partner country, and in some agreements, to nationals and to permanent residents.

Generally the ROO in services can be found in the definition of what constitutes a "service of another party" and "services suppliers of another party" and in the article dealing with denial of benefits, modelled following the structure of Article XXVII of GATS. As in GATS Article XXVII (b), regional agreements have special ROO for maritime transport services, where concessions are denied if it is established that the service is supplied: by a vessel registered under the laws of a non-party, and by a person who operates and/or uses the vessel in whole or in part but who is of a non-party. Table 8.4 summarises the denial of benefit clauses in the India–Sri Lanka CEPA in comparison with the India–Singapore CECA, the India–Korea CEPA and SATIS.

According to Fink and Molinuevo, the substantive business rule does not apply for party-owned and controlled companies in the India–Singapore CECA.[26] However, the article on scope and coverage states that the provisions in the chapter on services do not apply to shell companies located in the territory of either party with negligible business operations, indicating that the substantive rule applies even for party-owned companies. The same will be true for the India–Sri Lanka CEPA. However, since the India–Korea CECA does not make reference to shell companies, it is most likely that juridical persons of a party to that agreement do not have to meet the substantive business criteria to be eligible for concessions. Furthermore, the India–Sri Lanka CEPA, the India–Korea CECA and the India–Singapore CECA discourage their own firms, which are commercially present in the territory of the other party, from re-exporting back to the home country through Modes 1 and 2.

The agreements do not provide a definition of what constitutes "substantive business operations". Although one may argue that, for the sake of transparency and predictability, it is desirable to have a definition of substantive business operations, one could counter-argue that, given the diverse nature of services, it may not be realistic or rational to adopt a single criterion on substantial business operations applicable to all services sectors and sub-sectors.

The India–Singapore and the India–Korea agreements' definition of natural persons covers both nationals and permanent residents; however, the chapter on MNP applies only to nationals. Given that in both agreements India's Mode 4 horizontal commitments in its schedule of com-

[26] Fink and Molinuevo (2007).

Table 8.4 Criteria for the denial of benefits (what is ineligible for preferential treatment)

Agreement	Origin of service suppliers in the form of juridical persons
India–Sri Lanka CEPA	Modes 1 and 2 – if the service is supplied from the territory of a non-party or by a service provider owned or controlled by the denying party, without real and continuous business operations Mode 3 – if the service is being provided by a juridical person that is owned or controlled by persons that have no real and continuous business activities or no substantive business operations in the territory of the other party The chapter on trade in services does not apply to a shell company, which is any legal entity falling within the definition of "juridical person" in this chapter, which is established and located in the territory of either party with negligible or nil business operations or with no real and continuous business activities carried out in the territory of either party Juridical person means: owned – more than 50% of equity interest; controlled – power to name a majority of directors; affiliated
SATIS	Modes 1 and 2 – if the service is supplied from the territory of a non-party (no ownership or substantive business operations requirement) Mode 3 – if the services are supplied by an enterprise owned or controlled by a non-party and that has no substantive business operations in the territory of the party. Special concessions to LDCs not extended to non-LDC owned and controlled juridical persons, in the territory of LDCs with no substantive business operations in the territory of the LDC
India–Singapore CECA	Same as in India–Sri Lanka CEPA
India–Korea CEPA	Concessions denied to service provider of the other party where the party establishes that the service is being provided by a juridical person that is owned or controlled by persons of a non-party or of the denying party and that has no real and continuous business activities or no substantive business operations in the territory of the other party (applicable to all modes of supply), definition of juridical person same as in India–Sri Lanka, no reference to shell company which can be taken to indicate that the substantive business operations rule does not apply to party-owned juridical persons

mitments state "Unbound except as indicated in the chapter on MNP", although the definition covers both nationals and permanent residents, in effect the commitments made in Mode 4 only apply to nationals of a party.

From the point of view of economic efficiency, liberal rules of origin minimise trade diversion effects and promote entry of the most efficient service providers. Particularly in sectors where sunk costs, network externalities and economies of scale play an important role, having liberal rules will prevent a country being inundated by a less efficient services supplier from the partner country. The first-mover advantage of a less efficient supplier from a partner country in such services sectors (e.g. telecommunications or transport) will generate longer-term deadweight losses that cannot be reversed by sequential liberalisation, since the entry costs for a new player will be higher and this may deter entry of other efficient services suppliers into the market.[27]

With respect to such services sectors, if the rules of origin are not liberal, it is important to bind status quo policies and ensure their credibility to encourage establishment of the most efficient services supplier regardless of whether that supplier is from a partner country or a non-party. In other words, instead of sequential liberalisation, the best policy is to have simultaneous liberalisation by all countries.

Liberal ROO are important for countries with a higher share of non-party presence in their services sector. If the rules are too strict, most of the services suppliers in such countries will be prevented from accessing the partner country market because they will not be eligible for concessions.[28] Also, if a small country aims to become more attractive for investments from third countries as a result of regional integration and an expanded market, restrictive ROO could make it less attractive. It is important to note, however, that regional agreements are only one factor in determining the attractiveness of a destination for foreign investment.

However, liberal ROO undermine the bargaining advantage that FTAs offer relative to multilateral negotiations because the objective of preferential access is to have a captive market and discourage competition from third countries.[29] An economic argument favouring strict ROO is that they allow services suppliers to face limited competition from regional suppliers, and thereby learn and mature in order to face competition from the rest of the world. This is the infant industry argument for services.

---

27 Mattoo and Sauvé (2010), p. 40.
28 Fink and Molinuevo (2007), p. 41.
29 Ibid., p. 37.

Other factors that favour adoption of restrictive ROO are fear of free-riding by third parties, and fear of domestic services suppliers of import competition. Moreover, countries that have services suppliers who are regionally dominant, but globally not competitive, would also favour restrictive ROO.[30]

From Sri Lanka's perspective, adopting restrictive ROO could be disadvantageous from both a competition and an efficiency point of view as well as in terms of potential access to the Indian market. Sri Lanka is a small market economy; hence allowing services suppliers from one country preferential entry could allow less efficient suppliers in sectors where sunk costs, network externalities and economies of scale matter to enter the market and establish themselves, leading to long-term deadweight losses. In terms of market access, there is a high level of foreign presence in the Sri Lankan services sector and it is growing. Since Sri Lankan services suppliers are still not globally competitive in most sectors, partnerships with foreign firms could enhance their ability to enter the Indian market (e.g. Mode 3).[31] Hence, strict ROO are likely to prevent Sri Lankan companies from exploiting the market access opportunities that arise out of the India–Sri Lanka CEPA. India is a large market, therefore the market size is not an issue in attracting investments into India. However, for Sri Lanka, if the expectations are to make regional agreements an attraction to foreign investors from non-parties, strict ROO are a disadvantage. From India's perspective, having a large number of regionally competitive (but not necessarily globally competitive) services providers, adopting restrictive ROO benefits India in terms of securing a captive market in partner countries.

The above considerations become relevant, however, only if the liberalisation goes beyond the unilateral level and only if there is a higher probability of backtracking on unilateral liberalisation. If the commitments are below or at status quo and if the probability of backtracking on unilateral liberalisation is low, then whether ROO are liberal or restrictive is immaterial, because parties and non-parties face the same MA and NT conditions. Whether the ROO are critical in determining market access and deadweight losses associated with preferential access to less efficient suppliers has to be evaluated against liberalisation commitments made by the two countries in the India–Sri Lanka CEPA. To the extent that they are below or at status quo, the significance of ROO in the agreement will be small.

---

30 Mattoo and Sauvé (2010), p. 40.
31 The Ceylon Chamber of Commerce (2008).

8.4 INVESTMENT IN SERVICES

Given the need for physical proximity of services suppliers and consumers in the provision of services, the definition of trade in services incorporates investment in services, which is generally referred to as commercial presence. This section seeks to evaluate the investment provisions of the India–Sri Lanka CEPA to assess the extent to which these go beyond those of GATS and what impact such deviations will have on transparency, credibility and the extent of liberalisation of services.

Investment is an area where regional services agreements have gone well beyond GATS. The investment protection provisions in GATS are very weak, whereas the recent wave of regional agreements contain stronger provisions for investor protection which are similar to those contained in bilateral investment treaties (BITs). NAFTA-type agreements cover investments in both services and non-services in one schedule and disciplines in one chapter. Furthermore, NAFTA-type agreements typically provide disciplines for both pre- and post-establishment matters. GATS-type agreements generally provide for dual coverage, where liberalisation commitments and disciplines related to services are covered by the chapter on trade in services and investment disciplines are covered in the chapter on investment. The disciplines on investment chapter that are incorporated into the commercial presence in services chapter only deal with post-establishment matters.

The India–Sri Lanka CEPA provides for dual coverage of services, as do the India–Singapore and India–Korea agreements. Since SAARC does not have an agreement on investment, SATIS strictly follows the GATS model and provides for weaker disciplines on investment protection. In the instances of dual coverage, the link between the investment chapter and the services chapter is important in terms of transparency and clarity. Table 8.5 summarises the investment provisions in the India–Sri Lanka CEPA in comparison with those of the India–Singapore CECA and the India–Korea CEPA. The last amendment to the India–Sri Lanka CEPA investment text, made in July 2008, takes a different approach in linking the services chapter to the investment chapter by stating that "in the event of any inconsistency between this Chapter and another Chapter, *this Chapter* shall prevail to the extent of the inconsistency", whereas in the India–Singapore CECA and the India–Korea CEPA it states that the "*other chapter*" shall prevail to the extent of the inconsistency.

Investment in services and performance requirements The Agreement on Trade Related Investment Measures (TRIMS) is a GATT agreement

Table 8.5 Key investment provisions

Agreement	Key provisions
India–Sri Lanka CEPA	***Coverage***: Dual ***Services definition***: GATS definition ***Investment chapter definition***: Broad, including movable and immovable property, shares, stocks, IPRs, business concessions ***Investment services linkage given in services chapter***: Applicable to services provided through commercial presence to the extent they relate to an investment ***Investment services linkage given in investment chapter***: In the event of any inconsistency between this chapter and another chapter, this chapter shall prevail to the extent of the inconsistency ***Provisions in investment chapter applicable to services supplied through commercial presence***: Compensation for losses, expropriation, repatriation, subrogation, measures in the public interest, special formalities and information requirements, access to courts of justice, senior management and board of directors, other obligations, investment disputes, prohibition of performance requirements ***Applicability of investor–state arbitration***: Applicable, *mutatis mutandis*, to measures affecting the supply of a service by a service supplier of a party through commercial presence in the territory of the other party, only to the extent that they relate to an investment and an obligation under the chapter on investment
India–Singapore CECA	Same as in India–Sri Lanka CEPA except: the services investment linkage in the investment chapter states that in the event of any inconsistency between this chapter and another chapter, the other chapter shall prevail to the extent of the inconsistency
India–Korea CEPA	Same as in India–Singapore CECA except: the article on performance requirements in the investment chapter is not applicable to the services chapter and investor–state arbitration is applicable in the services chapter solely for claims that a party has breached Article 10.12 (Expropriation and Compensation)

and, at the multilateral level, rules on performance requirements are not applicable to GATS.[32] Hence, there is nothing in GATS to prevent a member from imposing performance requirements with respect to investments in services, the only requirement being that they be scheduled

32 Zampetti and Sauvé (2007), p. 253.

under restrictions and limitations to the extent they affect MA and NT provisions. However, it is interesting to note that both the India–Sri Lanka CEPA and the India–Singapore CECA extends TRIMS coverage to services investments. However, the India–Korea CEPA limits provisions on performance requirements to the investment chapter and does not extend it to cover services investments. By extending coverage of TRIMS to services, Sri Lanka and India have shown willingness to give up policy flexibility or policy space that is available in the multilateral context at the regional level.

In the chapter on investment in both the India–Sri Lanka CEPA and the India–Singapore and India–Korea agreements, the ROO are more liberal than those applied in the services chapter, providing only for the substantive business operations requirement without requiring ownership. Furthermore, national treatment provisions refer to "investments in like circumstances" as compared to the definition of national treatment in services chapter, which refers to "like services and services suppliers". However, none of the agreements extends the national treatment provisions or ROO provisions (denial of benefits clauses) in the investment chapter to the services chapter. Dual coverage of investment has both advantages and disadvantages. The advantage is that it allows for formulation of services-specific disciplines in the services chapter, for example, market access and domestic regulation. The disadvantage is that it reduces transparency, especially where the provisions overlap and if there are inconsistencies.[33] The India–Sri Lanka CEPA has provisions on how to deal with inconsistencies, making the agreement transparent despite dual coverage. Moreover, it goes beyond GATS by extending investment protection to services supplied through commercial presence and by incorporating TRIMS provisions into the services chapter.

8.5 MOVEMENT OF NATURAL PERSONS

This section looks at the provisions in the India–Sri Lanka CEPA on movement of natural persons (MNP) across borders and at mutual recognition to assess how these differ from the provisions in GATS. A comparison is made with similar provisions in SATIS, and in the India–Singapore and India–Korea agreements to see whether the characteristics of the Sri Lanka–India CEPA show a pattern that is likely to be repeated in future services agreements of Sri Lanka with South Asia. To sum up, the chapter

---

[33] Fink and Molinuevo (2007).

seeks to assess to what extent the provisions of the MNP chapter will influence transparency, credibility and the extent of liberalisation in Mode 4 commitments.

MNP is an important mode of supply of services across borders given that the provision of many services requires the physical proximity of suppliers and consumers. A good example is the necessity of the presence of a surgeon to perform surgery. Liberalisation of MNP is a highly politically sensitive area, since it directly affects the employment and salary structure of a country. Hence countries have been cautious in making commitments in Mode 4 at both the multilateral and regional levels.

The WTO does not have disciplines on labour mobility; it is only dealt with as a mode of trading services under the GATS. The disciplines in GATS have been formulated to accommodate the political sensitivities associated with liberalisation of MNP. This is done by carving out entry to the labour market and permanent migration from the scope of MNP and by restricting the scope to temporary movement. Furthermore, it does not prevent WTO members from regulating the entry of natural persons provided that regulations are not applied in such a manner as to nullify or impair the benefits accruing from specific commitments made by WTO members. Hence, discriminatory visa arrangements are not regarded as nullifying or impairing benefits under a specific commitment. The level of actual liberalisation of movement of persons under GATS depends on each individual member's schedule of commitments.

In the context of the India–Sri Lanka CEPA, the imbalance between the two economies in terms of labour and skill availability makes this issue extra sensitive. It is not only a matter of the sheer size of the Indian labour pool, which was estimated to be 748 million in 2010 compared with 13 million in Sri Lanka, but also the structure that makes Sri Lankans fear opening up Mode 4 to India. Sri Lanka's labour force (persons aged 15–59) is expected to decline from 63% in 2010 to 59% by 2025. In contrast, India's labour force is growing fast; it is forecast to increase from 62% in 2010 to 65% by 2025. Furthermore, the population in India is young compared with that in Sri Lanka; in 2010 the median age of a Sri Lankan was estimated to be 31 years compared with 25 years in India.[34] From an economic point of view, Sri Lanka is likely to face labour and skill shortages in the future and India is likely to be in an ideal position to fill this shortage. However, from a political perspective, this makes liberalising Mode 4 all the more difficult, for fear of a surge of Indians

---

34 UN population database, http://esa.un.org/unpp/, accessed 6 September 2010.

into Sri Lanka. Lack of a proper monitoring mechanism to ensure that the movement of labour is in fact "temporary", and will not be permanent makes countries like Sri Lanka even more cautious about making liberal commitments in Mode 4.

The India–Sri Lanka CEPA feature GATS-style carve-out regarding access to the employment market of contracting parties, permanent migration and the regulation of entry of natural persons, where these fall outside the scope of the agreement. The same carve-out can be observed in SATIS, the India–Singapore CECA and the India–Korea CEPA.

Most regional agreements have a separate chapter dealing with MNP as do the India–Sri Lanka CEPA, the India–Singapore and India–Korea agreements, but SATIS does not. Having a separate chapter dealing with MNP can be considered as going beyond GATS, because this chapter deals with movement of people in general, related to both services and investment, not restricted to services alone. However, this leads to dual coverage of MNP in the chapter on MNP and in the services and investment schedules; hence, it is important to clarify the link between the two. The India–Sri Lanka CEPA states that the obligations of the chapter on MNP only apply to the sectors where specific commitments are undertaken and subject to any terms and conditions, reservations and limitations it has scheduled. Hence, to understand the actual market access for natural persons, the provisions in the chapter on MNP should be read together with the schedule of services commitments of each country. The chapter on MNP deals with facilitation of entry; actual right to entry to provide a service depends on whether a commitment has been made in Mode 4 in the schedule of services.

Generally the chapter on MNP can be considered the horizontal provision for Mode 4 applicable to all specific commitments. This is further clarified by the cross-reference given in the horizontal section of the schedule of commitments. A common insertion found in regional services agreements is "unbound except as indicated in the chapter on MNP" in the market access (MA) column, which is generally taken to apply to both the MA and NT columns.

In the case of the Sri Lanka–India CEPA draft conditional offer, this cross-reference is made only in the NT column. Scheduling guidelines of the agreement state that if a certain limitation is applicable to both the MA and NT columns, the limitation will be scheduled in both columns. However, there is only a limited reference to business visitors in the MA column. Unless this is a typographical error, from a legal point of view, it would mean that the only provision in the chapter on MNP that is applicable to MA is that dealing with business visitors; all others are subject to general Sri Lankan laws on immigration, consumer laws, and other relevant laws and regulations as indicated in the MA column, and the full chapter on MNP applies only with respect to NT.

Although GATS covers movement of persons at all skill levels, like most other countries, India in its GATS commitments has taken a horizontal commitment limiting movement of persons to a few highly skilled categories; business visitors, intra-corporate transferees and professionals. In contrast, Sri Lanka has not restricted movement of persons to specific skill categories under GATS, but has stated that MNP will be subject to Sri Lanka's laws on immigration, consumer laws, and other relevant laws and regulations.

The chapter on MNP in the India–Sri Lanka CEPA limits coverage to specific skill categories; business visitors, contractual service suppliers, intra-corporate transferees (limited to managers, executives and specialists) and independent professionals. India, by undertaking to cover contractual service suppliers under MNP (which were not covered under its GATS commitments), has gone beyond its GATS commitments. Hence, all Mode 4 commitments in India's schedule under the India–Sri Lanka CEPA amount to an improvement over GATS. India has gone further in its commitments in MNP in the India–Singapore CECA and the India–Korea CEPA, by not restricting the scope to specific skill categories but extending coverage to all services suppliers, services sellers, sellers of goods, investors and employees of investors. Since SATIS does not have a separate chapter on MNP, it can be said that the framework agreement on services does include all skill categories. However, the fact that the chapter on MNP covers all skill categories is no guarantee that the countries concerned will make commitments in all skill categories. They can and do limit labour mobility to highly skilled categories in their schedule of commitments. Since Sri Lanka did not limit its horizontal commitments in GATS to specific skill categories, if its intention in the India–Sri Lanka CEPA is to do so, it can be considered a GATS-minus provision for Sri Lanka.[35]

The India–Sri Lanka CEPA has adopted the GATS definition of Mode 4 which is supply of a service "by a service supplier of a party through the presence of natural persons of that party in the territory of the other party". SATIS, the India–Singapore CECA and the India–Korea CEPA also adopt the same definition. This definition only covers independent service providers, the self-employed and foreign individuals employed

[35] However, since Sri Lanka has not linked the MA column of the schedule of commitments with the MNP chapter, it is not clear whether the country intends to bind its MA through the chapter on MNP or leave it as it has done under GATS.

by foreign companies. It does not cover individuals employed by domestic companies. For example, according to the definition, this does not cover an Indian naval architect employed by the Colombo Dock Yard. According to Chaudhuri, "in so far as foreigners seeking employment with host country firms can be deemed to be accessing the labour market of a country, they would seem to fall outside the scope of the GATS"[36] (because the agreement specifically carves out access to the employment market of contracting parties).

Mode 4 temporary movements can be considered an ideal avenue for local companies to source highly skilled service suppliers from India at a lower cost and as an avenue to meet skill shortages experienced in the country. This will enhance quality and price of services supplied in the local market. However, if the definition does not extend to cover local firms hiring natural persons of the other party, this is not possible. It is obvious from Sri Lanka's schedule of commitments that some of its commitments on Mode 4 were made based on requests by local companies to meet their skill needs by recruiting Indian nationals (e.g. ship repair services – naval architects). Hence, it is important to clarify the scope of the provision since GATS is not clear on that; CEPA should strive to explicate this issue. It seems that juridical persons of one party may be able to engage the services of independent professionals of the other party, according to the definition of independent professionals in the chapter on MNP. However, since the chapter on MNP is subject to the schedule of specific commitments, which in turn is subject to the definition of the four modes of supply, there is legal ambiguity in this area. Given the political sensitivity in Sri Lanka with respect to MNP and strong resistance by professional associations and labour unions to making commitments on MNP, extending scope to allow local companies to recruit Indian nationals (which may be defined as giving access to the employment market of Sri Lanka) may further reduce the political feasibility of concluding the agreement.

8.5.1 Mutual Recognition of Professional Qualifications

Article VII of GATS dealing with recognition covers all services suppliers and is not limited to professional services. However, most regional agreements show a bias towards mutual recognition of professional services. The liberalisation of Mode 4 plays a critical role in the supply of professional services as well as services provided by other skilled persons, although, increasingly, technological developments have made it possible to supply

---

[36] Chaudhury et al. (2004), p. 6.

such services cross-border (Mode 1). Even Mode 3 liberalisation of services would become more meaningful if coupled with Mode 4 liberalisation.[37]

In professional services, removal of entry barriers alone will not guarantee market access. Non-recognition of professional qualifications acquired in the partner country, or a mandatory requirement to obtain local qualifications, could pose a significant barrier to entry, because re-qualifying can be costly in terms of both time and money.

Professional standards are established to address the market failure of information asymmetry. Unlike in goods, the quality of the service delivered by a professional cannot be discerned prior to consumption. Hence, it is necessary to have standards to protect the interests of the public and to ensure the quality of the services provided. However, there may be instances where the requirements are not at all related to the quality of the services provided (e.g. the requirement of citizenship), but which may pose a significant barrier to entry.

The GATS, like the GATT, does not specifically require the use of international standards. It generally provides weaker incentives for the use of such standards than the SPS or the TBT Agreements, and does not provide a presumption of compliance as to the latter two agreements. This problem is exacerbated by the absence of widely accepted international standards in services, unlike in goods. It is unlikely that meaningful standards for most services will be developed any time soon.[38] Furthermore, the MRAs in GATS are exempt from MFN treatment, and provide for members to afford adequate opportunity to other interested parties to negotiate comparable agreements.

The India–Sri Lanka CEPA makes no reference to use of international standards and, similar to GATS Article VII, exempts recognition agreements from MFN treatment with the same condition of affording adequate opportunity for other non-parties to enter into similar agreements. Furthermore, the India–Sri Lanka CEPA, while not specifically restricting MRAs to professional services, by making specific reference to professional services categories, shows a bias towards providing recognition to professional services. Table 8.6 summarises the provisions on recognition in the India–Sri Lanka CEPA in comparison with those of SATIS, the India–Singapore CECA and the India–Korea CEPA. All four agreements follow a similar trend with minor variations.

---

[37] Although Mode 3 liberalisation can occur without Mode 4 liberalisation, by recruiting local professionals (the quality, cost and availability, however, are important considerations).

[38] Mattoo and Sauvé (2010), p. 33 and Sauvé and Mattoo (2004), p. 33.

Table 8.6 Summary of provisions on mutual recognition of professional qualifications

India–Sri Lanka CEPA	Soft, non-binding provision Priority sectors identified; accounting, auditing, architecture, medical (doctors), dental, advertising Non-binding time period of 12 months to conclude MRAs Dispute settlement mechanism does not apply Soft law MFN provision – in the event that qualification of a non-party is recognised, accord adequate opportunity upon request to negotiate access to such an agreement
SATIS	Same provisions as above, except priority sectors not identified, time period not stipulated, simply says within a reasonable time and encourages development of regional standards
India–Singapore CECA	Same as in India–Sri Lanka CEPA, except in priority sectors identified advertising is dropped and nursing included
India–Korea CEPA	Same as in India–Sri Lanka CEPA, except priority sectors not identified

The formulation of domestic regulation and standards does not fall within the ambit of trade agreements. Domestic regulations and standards play a role in regional agreements only to the extent that their implementation impacts on trade.[39] The impact matters in a trade agreement where it creates an unnecessary obstacle to trade, and is enacted in a manner to nullify or impair the concessions granted. Nothing in a trade agreement prevents the right of a country to regulate or set standards to meet legitimate policy objectives.

The popular belief is that FTAs offer a fertile forum for directly facilitating the recognition of professional qualifications, given the small number of players involved and possible similarities in qualification systems. However, in practice "there are only a few examples of successful operative MRAs in services trade".[40] Furthermore, the timetables stipulated in agreements to conclude MRAs are rarely adhered to.[41]

There is little enthusiasm among Sri Lankan professionals to work in India. Compared to the millions of graduates churned out of universities

---

39 Mattoo and Sauvé (2010), p. 34.

40 Ibid.

41 Ibid., p. 37.

in India each year, Sri Lanka produces only a few thousand annually[42] and these professionals are keen to work in the West, in countries such as the UK, the USA, Canada and Australia.[43] On the other hand, the Sri Lankan professional sector is very apprehensive about opening up the Sri Lankan market to Indian professionals. Hence, the lack of market access interest, coupled with Sri Lanka's apprehension about allowing entry to Indian professionals, is likely to delay progress in signing MRAs.

The architecture of the chapter on MNP in the India–Sri Lanka CEPA clearly shows that the same difficulties faced by countries in liberalising MNP at the multilateral level are also felt at the regional level. The disciplines governing MNP in the Sri Lanka–India CEPA fall short of GATS, by restricting its scope to specific skill categories, and this will have a negative impact on the extent of liberalisation commitments made. In terms of recognition, although the agreement goes beyond GATS by identifying priority sectors where MRAs will be signed, and stipulating time periods, the effectiveness of these provisions, given their non-binding best endeavour nature, is highly doubtful and such non-legally binding provisions offer little credibility with regard to actual progress. In terms of transparency, Sri Lanka's schedule of commitments lacks clarity on the relationship between the chapter on MNP and the horizontal commitments made in the schedule. The next chapter on the extent of liberalisation clearly demonstrates that having separate disciplines dealing with MNP has not ultimately led to significant improvement of Mode 4 commitments at the regional level, compared with that of GATS.

8.6 EXTENT OF LIBERALISATION

This section deals with the degree of liberalisation that can be expected from the India–Sri Lanka CEPA services chapter. The following analysis is based on the draft conditional offers of the two countries as at June 2008. These draft schedules were in the final stages, since they were tabled at the 12th round of negotiations, just before the deal was to be concluded in August 2008. Hence they can be considered as a fair guide to the actual liberalisation that would have been achieved eventually.

The degree of liberalisation is compared with the GATS schedules of

---

42 Number of students enrolled in universities and colleges in India is estimated at 160 million (National Sample Survey, India, 2003/04) compared with 12,000 students enrolled in universities in Sri Lanka (University Grants Commission, Sri Lanka, 2001).

43 The Ceylon Chamber of Commerce (2008).

each country. The methodology adopted to assess the extent of liberalisation is that of Fink and Molinuevo.[44]

The GATS services classification list has 12 main sectors and 154 sub-sectors. The liberalisation commitments are made in these 154 sub-sectors according to the four modes of supply. This leads to 616 entries in total for a country schedule. Following the methodology of Fink and Molinuevo, the 616 entries of each country schedule were classified into the following four categories:

(i) Sub-sectors and modes for which only a GATS commitment exists or CEPA does not offer any improvement (GATS only);
(ii) Sub-sectors and modes for which a partial GATS commitment exists and CEPA eliminates one or more remaining trade-restrictive measures (CEPA improvement);
(iii) Sub-sectors and modes for which no GATS commitment is available, but a CEPA commitment is made (CEPA new sectors); and
(iv) Sub-sectors and modes for which neither a GATS nor a CEPA commitment exists (unbound).

The first three categories are further broken down in terms of whether the offer made is a partial or a full commitment. Partial commitment refers to a commitment made with some limitations or restrictions, whereas a full commitment is made without any limitations or restrictions. Further, horizontal commitments are also treated as limitations or restrictions scheduled under each sector, since these are applicable to all committed sectors. Hence, even if a sector-specific commitment says "None" under Mode 3 for example, if there are horizontal restrictions on Mode 3, it will be taken as a partial commitment. In analysing sectoral commitments, the degree of liberalisation is assessed against the 12 main services sectors. The percentages given in each sector are relative to the number of sub-sectors in each main services sector, which ranges from 46 in business services to three in distribution services.

India has simply submitted its Doha revised offer as its conditional offer to Sri Lanka. Hence, when comparing Mode 4 commitments of India in the CEPA context, it was supposed that India's horizontal commitment on Mode 4 would read "unbound except as per the commitments in the Chapter on MNP". This is a fair assumption given that this has been the practice of India in its agreements with Singapore and Korea. Sri Lanka's draft conditional offer under CEPA makes very limited reference in the

44 Fink and Molinuevo (2007).

horizontal section to the chapter on MNP in its market access column, only referring to business visitors. Otherwise, the market access column repeats what is inscribed in its GATS schedule. There is an entry in the national treatment column that it is unbound except for what is provided in the chapter on MNP. However, since the schedule of commitments in CEPA (Article 7.2) says that if a measure affects both MA and NT it will be inscribed in both columns, this cannot be taken to apply to MA as well. This could very well be a typographical error.

The methodology of Fink and Molinuevo has several limitations; first, it does not capture the actual degree of liberalisation. The extent of liberalisation is assessed against GATS commitments. Hence this approach does not capture the extent of liberalisation in comparison with the actual unilateral liberalisation of each country. Second, all minor and major improvements are given the same weight, for example a foreign equity relaxation from 0% to 25% and from 0% to 75% are both given equal weight and simply recorded as a CEPA improvement, without making any judgement on the depth of improvement. Third, in identifying whether a commitment is partial or full, a distinction is not made regarding MA and NT; even if there is a restriction in either of the columns, it is listed as a partial commitment.

In terms of sectors covered in the India–Sri Lanka CEPA, Sri Lanka has increased the number of sub-sectors committed from 21 in GATS to 40 in CEPA (out of 154 sub-sectors), which in percentage terms is an increase from 14% to 26%. The number of sub-sectors covered by India has increased from 37 out of 154 sub-sectors in GATS to 88 in CEPA. This is a percentage increase from 24% to 57%.

As shown in Table 8.7, of 616 entries, which include all the sub-sectors by four modes of supply, 79% of the services sectors remain unbound by Sri Lanka, meaning that Sri Lanka has not undertaken any commitments in these sectors and modes of supply. Another 6% continue to be GATS-only commitments. The CEPA has led to the additional liberalisation of only 16% of sectors and modes of supply, where 4% is the improvement

Table 8.7 India–Sri Lanka CEPA: draft commitments of Sri Lanka and India

	Unbound	GATS only		CEPA improvement		CEPA new sectors		Total
		Partial	Full	Partial	Full	Partial	Full	
Sri Lanka	79	5	1	3	1	5	7	100
India	51	1	1	12	5	16	14	100

over the existing commitments under GATS and 12% represents new commitments. Moreover, half of the commitments that go beyond GATS are partial commitments.

In contrast, India's conditional offer is much more liberal, with unbound sectors and modes amounting to 51% of the total, GATS-only commitments accounting for only 2% and commitments that go beyond GATS of 47%, with improvements over existing commitments being 17% and new commitments 30%. Nearly 60% of the commitments of India that go beyond GATS, however, are partial commitments.

Sri Lanka's commitments have gone beyond GATS in communication services, financial services, tourism and travel services and health-related social services as indicated in Table 8.8. The first three services categories reflect the high level of unilateral liberalisation of these sectors. The CEPA has gone beyond GATS also in terms of business services and transport

Table 8.8 India–Sri Lanka CEPA: sector-wise draft commitments of Sri Lanka (%)

Sectors	Unbound	GATS Only		CEPA Improvement		CEPA New Sectors		Total
		Partial	Full	Partial	Full	Partial	Full	
Business services	88	0	0	0	0	6	7	100
Communication services	52	4	7	4	1	9	22	100
Construction and related engineering services	100	0	0	0	0	0	0	100
Distribution services	100	0	0	0	0	0	0	100
Educational services	100	0	0	0	0	0	0	100
Environment services	100	0	0	0	0	0	0	100
Financial services	46	31	0	21	3	0	0	100
Health-related and social services	63	0	0	0	0	25	13	100
Tourism and travel-related services	50	19	6	0	25	0	0	100
Recreational, cultural and sporting services	100	0	0	0	0	0	0	100
Transport services	92	0	0	0	0	4	4	100
Other services not included elsewhere	100	0	0	0	0	0	0	100

services. Sri Lanka has undertaken new commitments in health, communications, business and transport services. In contrast, new commitments in financial and tourism-related services are nil, reflecting the already liberal commitments the country has undertaken in these sectors at the multilateral level. Sri Lanka has not taken any commitments in construction, distribution, education, environment and recreational services.

India has undertaken commitments in all the main sectors (except other services) as shown in Table 8.9, although the degree of commitment varies from sector to sector. For example, in the construction sector, India has taken commitments in all sub-sectors and all modes of supply, whereas in education, health and transport services, over 75% of the sub-sectors and modes remain unbound. Among all the sectors in which India has taken commitments that go beyond GATS, most noteworthy are construction (100%), tourism (75%), business (68%) and financial (54%) services.

Table 8.9 India–Sri Lanka CEPA: the sector-wise draft commitments of India

Sectors	Unbound	GATS Only		CEPA Improvement		CEPA New Sectors		Total
		Partial	Full	Partial	Full	Partial	Full	
Business services	32	0	0	9	8	27	24	100
Communication services	58	3	5	20	10	2	1	100
Construction and related engineering services	0	0	0	10	10	40	40	100
Distribution services	60	0	0	0	0	20	20	100
Educational services	80	0	0	0	0	15	5	100
Environment services	50	0	0	0	0	25	25	100
Financial services	41	4	0	44	0	6	4	100
Health-related and social services	75	0	0	19	6	0	0	100
Tourism and travel related services	25	0	0	25	25	13	13	100
Recreational, cultural and sporting services	63	0	0	0	0	25	13	100
Transport services	76	0	0	0	0	14	10	100
Other services not included elsewhere	100	0	0	0	0	0	0	100

Among these, in construction 80% and in business 52% are new commitments. The other two sectors where a significant percentage of new commitments has been taken are environment and distribution services.

Table 8.10 shows Sri Lanka's commitments by modes of supply. The largest share of full commitments of Sri Lanka is taken in Modes 1 and 2. Sri Lanka has not taken any full commitments in Mode 4. However, most of the commitments that go beyond GATS are in Mode 4, largely reflecting the very shallow commitments the country had taken in GATS in Mode 4. This is followed by Modes 3, 2 and 1. Over 75% of all modes remain unbound.

Commitments taken by India by mode show a similar trend as can be seen in Table 8.11, with most of the full commitments taken in Modes 1 and 2. India also has not undertaken any full commitments in Mode 4 and full commitments in Mode 3 amounts to only 1%. Almost all new full commitments are undertaken in Modes 1 and 2 and the new commitments in Modes 3 and 4 are all partial.

Table 8.10 India–Sri Lanka CEPA: mode-wise draft commitments of Sri Lanka

Mode of Supply	Unbound	GATS Only		CEPA Improvement		CEPA New Sectors		Total
		Partial	Full	Partial	Full	Partial	Full	
Mode 1	82	3	3	0	1	1	10	100
Mode 2	81	1	3	1	1	0	12	100
Mode 3	75	8	0	3	2	7	5	100
Mode 4	75	6	0	8	0	10	0	100
Total	78	5	2	3	1	5	7	100

Table 8.11 India–Sri Lanka CEPA: mode-wise draft commitments of India

Mode of Supply	Unbound	GATS Only		CEPA Improvement		CEPA New Sectors		Total
		Partial	Full	Partial	Full	Partial	Full	
Mode 1	62	1	3	1	6	3	23	100
Mode 2	55	1	0	1	14	1	30	100
Mode 3	45	2	0	22	0	30	1	100
Mode 4	44	0	0	24	0	32	0	100
Total	51	1	1	12	5	16	14	100

Table 8.12 Overall comparison of commitments of India in RTAs

India's commitments	Unbound	GATS only		CEPA improvement		CEPA new sectors		Total
		Partial	Full	Partial	Full	Partial	Full	
India–Sri Lanka	51	1	1	12	5	16	14	100
India–Singapore	57	3	1	9	5	14	10	100
India–Korea	50	1	1	11	5	18	14	100

8.6.1 Comparing India's offer to Sri Lanka with India's offer to Singapore and Korea

India's revised conditional offer to Sri Lanka is more liberal than its offer to Singapore. However, the offer of India to Korea is slightly better than its offer to Sri Lanka, which means India's offer to Korea goes beyond India's Doha revised offer.

As shown in Table 8.12, only 38% of sub-sectors and modes of supply go beyond GATS in India's schedule of commitments under the India–Singapore CECA, compared with 47% in the India–Sri Lanka CEPA and 48% in the India–Korea CEPA. India has undertaken new commitments in 24% of sub-sectors and modes in the India–Singapore CECA compared with 30% in the India–Sri Lanka and 32% in the India–Korea agreements. Of the total commitments made in the India–Singapore CECA 16% are full commitments compared with 20% in each for the India–Sri Lanka and India–Korea agreements.

India has made some form of commitment in all main sectors (other than other services not listed elsewhere) in both the India–Sri Lanka and the India–Korea agreements, whereas in the India–Singapore agreement, India has undertaken no commitments in education and environment services. The three sectors where India has undertaken most liberal commitments (more than 50% commitment) are business services, financial services and tourism and travel-related services. The three sectors where India has been most reluctant to make commitments (over 75% unbound) are transport services, education services and health and social-related services (see Tables 8.13 and 8.14).

The India–Singapore CECA is India's first services agreement, and the India–Sri Lanka CEPA was to be the second, and the India–Korea CEPA the third. From the level of commitments in each agreement, India seems to be willing to be more liberal and more confident with each agreement. Furthermore, unlike in the case of the India–Sri Lanka CEPA, where Sri Lanka has reciprocated with very shallow liberalisation commitments,

Table 8.13 India's commitments under the India–Singapore CECA

Sector	Unbound	GATS Only		CEPA Improvement		CEPA New Sectors		Total
		Partial	Full	Partial	Full	Partial	Full	
Business services	36	0	0	8	9	28	19	100
Communication services	58	7	5	14	9	4	2	100
Construction and related engineering services	0	0	0	10	10	40	40	100
Distribution services	70	0	0	0	0	10	20	100
Educational services	100	0	0	0	0	0	0	100
Environment services	100	0	0	0	0	0	0	100
Financial services	43	19	0	28	0	7	3	100
Health-related and social services	75	0	0	25	0	0	0	100
Tourism and travel-related services	50	0	0	25	25	0	0	100
Recreational, cultural and sporting services	50	0	0	0	0	25	25	100
Transport services	84	0	0	0	0	10	6	100
Other services not included elsewhere	100	0	0	0	0	0	0	100
Total	57	3	1	9	5	14	10	100

both Singapore and Korea, being countries with more experience in services agreements as well as relatively more liberal and well-developed services sectors, the reciprocal commitments India has received were much more significant.

Fink and Molinuevo's methodology does not assess bilateral commitments against unilateral commitments. This is a more complex task given the difficulties of obtaining information on actual regulatory and other barriers to entry in the services sectors of a country, and falls beyond the scope of this chapter. However, without going into the specificities, it is interesting to note briefly and at a broader policy level whether the

Table 8.14 India's commitments under the India–Korea CEPA

Sector	Unbound	GATS Only		CEPA Improvement		CEPA New Sectors		Total
		Partial	Full	Partial	Full	Partial	Full	
Business services	27	0	0	9	9	30	26	100
Communication services	58	3	5	20	10	2	1	100
Construction and related engineering services	0	0	0	10	10	40	40	100
Distribution services	60	0	0	0	0	20	20	100
Educational services	80	0	0	0	0	15	5	100
Environment services	50	0	0	0	0	25	25	100
Financial services	41	4	0	38	0	13	3	100
Health-related and social services	75	0	0	19	6	0	0	100
Tourism and travel-related services	31	0	0	25	25	13	6	100
Recreational, cultural and sporting services	56	0	0	0	0	25	19	100
Transport services	76	0	0	0	0	14	9	100
Other services not included elsewhere	100	0	0	0	0	0	0	100
Total	50	1	1	11	5	18	14	100

bilateral offers of India and Sri Lanka are likely to go beyond the status quo, to remain at the status quo or to fall below the status quo. Analysis of India's revised Doha offer states that it is far-reaching and the commitments reflect bindings at an autonomous level.[45] However, it is important to note that the offer was made by India in 2005 and, depending on the degree of unilateral liberalisation which has taken place in India since

[45] UNDP (2009), p. 33.

then, the revised Doha offer may not be reflective of the current *status quo*. Further, India is a country that is very cautious in taking liberalisation commitments at the multilateral level, and generally retains a high degree of policy space by binding below the status quo, as is clear from the tariff bindings of India under GATT[46] and the services commitments of India under GATS. Hence, the revised Doha offer, being an offer made by India at the multilateral level, will not go beyond the status quo and may very well fall below the status quo. India's revised Doha offer is a conditional offer which is still under negotiation and, once the Doha Round is concluded, may become India's new GATS schedule of commitments. Hence, by offering the revised Doha offer to Sri Lanka, India is making a pre-commitment eventually to multilateralise its liberalisation commitments made at the bilateral level.

Sri Lanka, in sectors where it has taken commitments, largely reflects status quo policies and in one sector (motion picture projection services) Sri Lanka has granted preferential access in the form of quotas allocated specifically for India. There are sectors where Sri Lanka has undertaken commitments below the status quo, for example in convention services, by requiring joint ventures to supply services through commercial presence, and there are many sectors which are open to foreign investments (e.g. construction, IT and education[47]), where Sri Lanka has not undertaken any commitments.

The unilateral and reciprocal (bilateral or regional) liberalisation of services takes place simultaneously. In the India–Sri Lanka CEPA, there is no upward ratcheting mechanism where autonomous liberalisation is automatically bound at the bilateral level. Hence, to the extent that services sectors undergo faster unilateral liberalisation, the commitments made at the bilateral level become outdated and of little commercial and economic value. This of course depends on the success of rounds of progressive liberalisation provided for in the agreement, scheduled to take place once in three years, and to what extent countries will be willing to legally bind the autonomous liberalisation undertaken at these negotiation rounds.

Although it is beyond the scope of this chapter, it is important to note the difference between actual liberalisation and effective liberalisation at the bilateral level from a market access point of view. Actual liberalisa-

---

[46] For example, the simple average bound rate of India in agriculture at the WTO is 114.2, compared with the simple average applied rate of 32.2, and the non-agriculture bound rate is 34.7, compared with the simple average applied rate of 10.1 (Source: WTO, World Tariff Profiles 2009, p. 93).

[47] Board of Investment, Sri Lanka, www.boi.lk/2009,

tion is actual commitments made; effective liberalisation is how much the actual concessions in fact reflect trade potential: whether they cover sectors that are currently traded which can be further expanded and new sectors with potential to be traded if the existing restrictions are removed. It is the effective liberalisation that will eventually lead to expansion of trade in services between parties to an agreement. If the preferences are granted in sectors with few or no offensive interests, then even though a large number of sectors are committed, this will not lead to increased trade in services between countries. This is especially relevant in the case of a country like Sri Lanka which has offensive interests only in a handful of sectors, the exclusion of which can undermine its potential to export services to India.

The India–Sri Lanka CEPA draft commitments fall below the status quo by not taking commitments in sectors which are unilaterally liberalised (even though this is partial); it largely reflects the status quo in sectors where commitments are taken. The same is true of Sri Lanka; where commitments are undertaken, the status quo is bound, but commitments have not been taken in a number of sectors where unilateral liberalisation has taken place. Hence, in the India–Sri Lanka CEPA, the reciprocal liberalisation efforts are likely to be more a reflection of unilateral liberalisation already undertaken by the two countries, rather than a driver of the liberalisation process in these countries. Sri Lanka's commitments are shallow even at bilateral level and this is clearly an indication that bilateral agreements will not be instrumental in promoting liberalisation of the services sector in the country. Even though India's commitments show a relatively high degree of improvement over its current GATS commitments, this may very well be because the comparison is being made from a very low base, given that India's commitments in GATS were very shallow.

8.7 CONCLUSION

This chapter sets out to evaluate the architecture and content of the India–Sri Lanka CEPA as compared with GATS to see whether the CEPA has been able to craft stronger disciplines than those of GATS, which will promote trade at the regional level by enhancing transparency, credibility and liberalisation and whether commitments made at the regional level show more ambition than the commitments made in GATS. The chapter also makes an assessment of other agreements in the region – SATIS, the India–Singapore CECA and the India–Korea CEPA – to see whether the India–Sri Lanka CEPA is demonstrating what can be regarded as the likely regional approach that will be adopted by Sri Lanka and the other South Asian countries in future regional agreements in services.

The architecture of the India–Sri Lanka CEPA is very similar to that of GATS and has not progressed much beyond GATS in formulating stronger disciplines governing trade in services. The agreement is further proof of the cautious and defensive attitude of Sri Lanka in particular and of South Asian countries in general towards regional integration. The agreement has made hardly any progress beyond GATS in areas where multilateral disciplines are still underdeveloped: government procurement, domestic regulation and subsidies. Although the India–Sri Lanka CEPA has made a weak effort at creating emergency safeguard measures, at least compared with the other three agreements which do not have safeguards, the operational feasibility of this provision is highly doubtful. The India–Sri Lanka CEPA has moved beyond GATS in terms of services supplied through commercial presence by extending investment protection to investors in services and by bringing in TRIMS provisions to GATS. In terms of movement of people, however, CEPA provisions fall short of GATS by limiting scope to specific skill categories.

The services liberalisation commitments made in the India–Sri Lanka CEPA show that, in terms of liberalisation, both India and Sri Lanka have moved beyond GATS. However, it is important to note that both countries had taken rather shallow commitments in GATS; hence, the significant improvement is partly because it is assessed against a lower baseline. The agreement, however, faces the same difficulties faced at the multilateral level in making commitments in air services and services supplied in the exercise of government authority; hence these are carved out from the scope of the services chapter.

In terms of specific commitments, India's offer is much more liberal than that of Sri Lanka. This reflects the high level of offensive interest of India and the progress India is making in unilateral liberalisation of its services sector. Sri Lanka's shallow commitments indicate that its defensive interests against India far outweigh its limited offensive interests. The commitments are largely binding of status quo policies; however, both countries have refrained from taking commitments in a number of sectors where autonomous liberalisation has taken place, using the flexibility provided in the GATS approach to bind below the status quo.

The agreement has adopted restrictive ROO, reflecting the defensive approach adopted by the countries towards liberalisation of services. However, given that the commitments made are largely binding at an autonomous level of liberalisation and that the instances of backtracking of liberalisation undertaken by the two countries in the past have been rare, ROO are unlikely to be a critical element that determines actual liberalisation and market access. The other three agreements – SATIS, the India–Singapore CECA and the India–Korea CEPA – also follow the GATS architecture and vary little from that of the India–Sri Lanka CEPA. India's improved offer at each successive agreement it signs reflects the progress the country has made in unilateral liberalisation of its services sector.

The architecture and content of the India–Sri Lanka CEPA, with its in-built flexible GATS-type approach with a very high degree of policy flexibility, offer little promise that the agreement will ultimately lead to deeper and wider liberalisation of services trade between the two countries. It is most likely that the liberalisation of trade in services in the two countries will happen unilaterally and the commitments made bilaterally or regionally will at best reflect status quo policies, rather than actual preferential access. Given the regulatory intensity and political sensitivity of the services liberalisation process, and the fact that the agreement has already met with many protectionist pressures, it is doubtful whether much progress will be achieved by the two countries in the future rounds of progressive liberalisation. However, given the regional dynamics, and the unilateral liberalisation and the growth in services exports that is taking place, the trade in services between the two countries and in the region will continue to grow.

Retaining policy flexibility in regional services agreements is not necessarily a bad thing because in countries like Sri Lanka the cost of compiling regulations on all services sectors is high and in many sectors regulations are still lacking or in the process of being developed. Further, services liberalisation is politically, socially and culturally a highly sensitive subject. Hence, careful evaluation of the costs and benefits of liberalising particular sectors at the regional level and sequencing liberalisation can be of benefit. However, the agreement can be used to fast track the enactment of sound regulations, to encourage stocktaking of existing regulations and also to enhance transparency further by obliging countries to share information on non-conforming measures. Moreover, the India–Sri Lanka CEPA could enhance credibility by compelling the parties to bind status quo policies. Nevertheless, given the flexibility of the scheduling approach taken and the absence of political will to lock in reforms, liberalise services, enhance competition and expand trade in services at the regional level, the likelihood of this happening is doubtful.

The India–Sri Lanka CEPA is likely to be the format for future Sri Lankan services agreements and, given that the CEPA follows the same format as other regional agreements, it is likely to be the format for future services agreements of other South Asian countries as well. Although there could be variations depending on the negotiating partner, Sri Lanka and the rest of South Asia are likely to continue to adopt a cautious and defensive approach towards regional integration and liberalisation of services at the bilateral and regional levels. The services trade between India and Sri Lanka as well as within South Asia will continue to grow. However, it will not be due to reciprocal agreements in the region, but will be the result of regional dynamics and autonomous liberalisation.

REFERENCES

Chaudhuri, S., Mattoo, A. and Self, R., "Moving People to Deliver Services: How Can the WTO Help?" World Bank Policy Research Working Paper 3238, March 2004

Fink, C. and Molinuevo, M., "East Asian Free Trade Agreements in Services: Roaring Tigers or Timid Pandas?" The World Bank, June 2007

Kelegama, S. and Mukherji, Indra Nath, "India – Sri Lanka Bilateral Free Trade Agreement: Six Year Performance and Beyond", Research and Information Systems for Developing Countries, RIS-DP No. 119, February 2007

Kulkarni, P. and Choudary, B., "Trade in Services and India's Preferential Agreements", in Chanda, R. (ed.), *Trade in Services and India: Prospects and Strategies*, Centre for Trade and Development, New Delhi: Wiley-India, December, 2006, pp. 359–405

Mattoo, A. and Sauvé, P., "The Preferential Liberalization of Services Trade", NCCR, Working Paper No. 2010/13, May 2010

Mattoo, A. and Sauvé, P., "Domestic Regulation and Trade in Services: Looking Ahead", The World Bank, 2003

Ministry of Commerce and Industry (India), "Investing in India, Foreign Direct Investment Policy and Procedure", Department of Industrial Policy and Promotion, 2010

Nikomborirak, D. and Stephenson, S., "Liberalization of Trade in Services: East Asia and the Western Hemisphere, Regional Trading Arrangements: Stocktake and Next Steps", Trade Policy Forum, Bangkok, 12–13 June 2001

Ochiai, R., Dee, P. and Findlay, C., "Services in Free Trade Agreements", RIETI Discussion Paper Series 07-E-015, March 2007

Ortino, F., "Regional Trade Agreements and Trade in Services", 2007, available at: http://ssrn.com/abstract=995781

Sauvé, P. and Mattoo, A., "Regionalism in Services Trade", A teaching module prepared for the World Bank Institute, The World Bank, First Revision, April 2004

Stephenson, S.M., "Approaches to Liberalizing Services", The World Bank, 1999

The Ceylon Chamber of Commerce, "Survey on Services Exports between Sri Lanka and Pakistan: Potential for a Bilateral Agreement", September 2008

UNDP, "Policy Space and Investment Rules under GATS: Select Asian Experience", Asia Pacific Trade and Investment Initiative, UNDP Regional Centre for Asia Pacific, Colombo Office, 2009

World Trade Organization, *Sri Lanka's Draft Consolidated Schedule of Specific Commitments*, S/DCS/W/LKA, 24 January 2003

World Trade Organization, *Communication from India, Draft Consolidated Schedule of Specific Commitments*, S/DCS/W/IND, 2 April 2003
World Trade Organization, *India: Revised Offer*, TN/S/O/IND/Rev.1, 24 August 2005
World Trade Organization, World Tariff Profiles 2009, available at www.wto.org
Zampetti, A.B. and Sauvé, P., "International Investment", in Guzman, A.T. and Sykes, A.O. (eds.), *Research Handbook in International Economic Law*, Cheltenham, UK and Northampton, MA, USA: Edward Elgar Publishing Limited, 2007, pp. 211–71

APPENDIX: ABBREVIATIONS

APTA	Asia Pacific Trade Agreement
BIT	Bilateral Investment Treaty
CECA	Comprehensive Economic Cooperation Agreement
CEPA	Comprehensive Economic Partnership Agreement
ESM	Emergency Safeguard Measures
FTA	Free Trade Agreement
GATS	General Agreement on Trade in Services
GATT	General Agreement on Tariffs and Trade
LDCs	Least Developed Countries
MA	Market Access
MFN	Most Favoured Nation Treatment
MNP	Movement of Natural Persons
MRA	Mutual Recognition Agreement
NAFTA	North American Free Trade Agreement
NT	National Treatment
ROO	Rules of Origin
RTA	Regional Trade Agreement
SAARC	South Asian Association for Regional Cooperation
SAFTA	South Asian Free Trade Area
SATIS	SAARC Agreement on Trade in Services
SPS	Sanitary and Phytosanitary
TBT	Technical Barriers to Trade
TRIMs	Trade Related Investment Measures
WTO	World Trade Organization

9. Much ado about nothing much? Australian PTAs in services

Malcolm Bosworth and Ray Trewin*

9.1 INTRODUCTION

The importance of enhancing services productivity in improving the Australian economy's efficiency and performance is widely acknowledged. Trade liberalization in services is seen as an important means to this end. It is therefore worth assessing the extent to which Australia's acceleration into Preferential Trade Agreements (PTAs), all of which have included services, have contributed to liberalization. In Australia and internationally, PTAs may have gone up to or even beyond GATS commitments in some areas, and hence appear more liberalizing 'on paper'. However, the relevant question remains whether they have actually significantly opened services and increased trade and investment beyond what has been achieved unilaterally. If not, what has been their real liberalization value? Have they led to better regulations and performance, such as generating more or improved Mutual Recognition Agreements (MRAs), and achieved more open trade in professional services? Have regional public goods, such as joint institutions, been formed off or through PTAs and led to better performance and regional integration? Could well-performing regulations and institutions have been introduced without the significant additional cost and complication of entering PTAs?

These issues were recently addressed by the Australian Productivity Commission (PC) in the government-commissioned public study on Bilateral and Regional Trade Agreements (PC 2010). This watershed study offered a major opportunity to reflect on Australia's experience with PTAs, including in services. The Study led to the last Government's April 2011 Trade Policy Statement, which signaled reinvigorating and returning

* The authors would like to gratefully acknowledge useful comments provided by Rudolf Adlung, Dale Honeck, Bernard Hoekman, Sebastian Saez and Andrew McCredie.

Australian trade policy, including for services, to the unilateral economic policy roots of the reform period of the 1980s and 1990s to help reverse the slide in Australian productivity growth over the past decade (DFAT 2011).[1]

Services are by far the largest component of the Australian economy, accounting for some 70% of GDP and employment. Total services exports stood at around $89 billion in 2008–09, 1.7 times greater than suggested on the basis of the level of cross-border services exports; embodied services in merchandise exports were estimated at about $35 billion (ITS Global 2010). These were primarily in property and business services, transport and storage, wholesale trade, and mining services; key "carrier" exports are in minerals. Australian overseas subsidiaries (including joint ventures) deliver substantial services, with estimated sales of over $100 billion annually (ITS Global 2010). For every percentage point increase in the intensity of intermediate services used in production, embodied services exports are estimated to rise by at least $1 billion annually. This highlights the critical link services have to Australian competitiveness.

This chapter argues that Australian PTAs have delivered little significant actual services trade liberalization, and may have obstructed it. Moreover, on the few occasions where they have changed measures, their economic value is questionable at best, leading to discriminatory measures and/or changes that have not been adequately assessed economically, instead being "negotiated outcomes". The chapter also explains recent trade policy developments in Australia, and explains why a return to unilateralism offers far more liberalization potential than the pursuit of PTAs.

The chapter is structured as follows. Section 9.2 looks at the economics of services trade liberalization, including why unilateralism matters most. Section 9.3 examines Australia's PTAs, and the increasing role played in Australian trade policy. Section 9.4 discusses liberalizing services trade through PTAs, including their inherent limitations relative to other trade liberalization approaches and the associated problems of

---

[1] Since writing this chapter, the Australian Labor Government was replaced at the September 2013 elections by the Liberal Coalition Government. While it is still too early to properly appraise the new Government's trade policy directions, evidence suggests so far that it is intending to follow the previous Government's priorities, especially in wanting to quickly conclude outstanding PTAs with Korea (concluded in December 2013), Japan and China (Robb 2013). Despite the optimism expressed in this chapter that the previous Labor Government would deliver a return to unilateral trade policy settings, this did not eventuate. The same challenges remain for the new Government and only time will tell if it is successful.

piecemeal reform in services. Section 9.5 draws on Australia's experience with using PTAs in services. Section 9.6 highlights the essential role that transparency coupled with unilateralism must play in advancing meaningful and sustainable trade-related reforms, especially in services where barriers tend to be behind the border. Section 9.7 examines recent developments in Australian trade policy likely to impact on PTAs in services and liberalization more generally. Section 9.8 concludes the chapter.

9.2 ECONOMICS OF SERVICES TRADE LIBERALIZATION

The Australian economy derived significant benefits from the trade and investment liberalization that began in the mid-1980s (Box 9.1).[2] These unilateral, comprehensive microeconomic and related structural reforms, which reduced domestic trade barriers without the need for any specific international engagement, improved substantially Australia's economic efficiency and performance (Banks 2010a). Despite short-term structural and related adjustment costs, the longer-term economic benefits were so pronounced that both major political parties embraced liberalization, albeit with different priorities and timetables. The economy is now much more flexible and globally integrated, with international price signals transmitted domestically to more efficiently allocate resources primarily by non-interventionist market forces.

While the unilateral domestic reforms remain incomplete and require more comprehensive efforts, the Australian economy is now far more open. It still has major trade and investment obstacles and other areas in need of structural reform. One major concern is that the traditionally successful unilateral reform program has largely stalled and is under threat, including from recent trade policy developments that have placed too much emphasis on achieving negotiated liberalization, either in Geneva or more especially in regional capitals. The decline in unilateral reform focus started from 2000 has been well documented by the PC and others (PC 2010). This policy reversal reflected a misconception, also held by the Department of Foreign Affairs and Trade (DFAT), that Australia had gone far enough on the domestic trade liberalization agenda and should not liberalize too much ahead of its APEC trading partners, but rather wait

---

[2] These reversed Australia's highly protectionist "inward-looking" post-war policies.

BOX 9.1 TWO DECADES OF AUSTRALIAN REFORM

The 1980s and 1990s saw the Australian economy transformed from a closed, non-competitive and inefficient economy to a relatively open and internationally competitive country. Such reforms were applied comprehensively across all sectors, including services.

Capital markets — floating of the Australian dollar in 1983, progressive removal of foreign exchange controls and capital rationing (through interest rate controls) from the early 1980s and allowing foreign-owned banks to compete.

Infrastructure — airlines, coastal shipping, telecommunications and the waterfront partially deregulated and restructured from the late 1980s.

Commercialization, corporatization and privatization initiatives for government business enterprises progressively implemented from the late 1980s, e.g. Commonwealth Bank, introduction of Optus telecommunications and partial privatization of Telstra as well as Qantas.

Human services — competitive tendering and contracting out, performance-based funding and user charges introduced in the late 1980s, along with administrative reforms in health, education, community services from the 1990s.

'National Competition Policy'(NCP) reforms — further broad-ranging reforms to essential service industries (e.g. energy and road transport), government businesses and anti-competitive regulation commenced by all Australian governments through a coordinated national program in 1995.

Overview of the NCP Reforms

General

- anti-competitive conduct provisions in Trade Practices Act extended to unincorporated enterprises and government businesses.

- structural reforms to public monopolies and other government businesses, including separating regulatory from commercial functions; reviewing merits of separating natural monopoly from potentially contestable service elements; and/or separating contestable elements into smaller independent businesses.
- competitive neutrality requirements adopted for public monopolies, involving the adoption of corporatized governance structures for significant government enterprises; the imposition of similar commercial and regulatory obligations to those faced by competing private businesses; and the establishment of independent mechanisms for handling complaints that these requirements have been breached.
- creation of independent authorities to set, administer or oversee prices for monopoly service providers.
- introduction of a national regime providing third-party access on reasonable terms and conditions to essential infrastructure services with natural monopoly characteristics.
- Legislation Review Program to assess if regulatory restrictions on competition are in the public interest and, if not, what changes are required, including in areas of the professions and occupations, retail trading, transport, communications, and insurance, superannuation, child care, gambling; and planning and development services.

Sector-specific

Electricity: various structural, governance, regulatory and pricing reforms to introduce greater competition into generation and retailing, and establishing a National Electricity Market in the eastern states.

Gas: similar suite of reforms to facilitate more competitive supply arrangements and greater retail competition.

Road transport: heavy vehicle charges and a uniform approach to regulating heavy vehicles implemented to improve efficiency of the road freight sector, enhance road safety and reduce the transactions costs of regulation.

Water: various reforms to achieve a more efficient and sustainable water sector, including institutional, pricing and investment measures, and arrangements implemented to allow for permanent trading of water allocations.

Estimated economic benefits

Major elements of NCP have potentially generated a net benefit equivalent to 5.5% of GDP, and the observed productivity and price changes in key infrastructure sectors in the 1990s – to which NCP and related reforms have directly contributed – have increased Australia's GDP by 2.5%, or $20 billion (excluding any "dynamic" efficiency gains from more competitive markets).

Source: Banks (2010a), and PC (2005).

until their voluntary reforms caught up. The new belief seemed to be that it was more beneficial to re-direct Australian trade policy towards negotiating PTAs as a means of opening up foreign markets. Australia's demonstrably successful approach of Unilateral Liberalization Domestically, Open Regionalism in Asia, Multilateralism Abroad (ULDORAMA) was "dead" (Garnaut 2003).

Australia no longer relies primarily on unilateral reforms and instead has regressed by embracing the PTA "frenzy". Owing to the revival of flawed mercantilist thinking linked to negotiated forms of liberalization, especially through discriminatory bilateral/regional trade agreements, to focus trade policy on its external rather than the domestic dimensions, DFAT has adopted completely the wrong perspective and now become the problem rather than the solution in achieving effective trade policy (Trebeck 2009).[3]

The potential gains to national welfare in Australia and elsewhere from non-preferentially reforming barriers to services trade via increased competition encouraging firms to reduce costs and expand output in competitive areas using resources most efficiently are well known, including from quantitative studies with and without dynamic productivity gains (Box 9.2).

[3] Trebeck suggests relocating trade policy responsibility to the Treasury to enable the economy wide arguments and interests to receive fuller and more rigorous assessment.

BOX 9.2 POTENTIAL GAINS FROM SERVICES TRADE LIBERALIZATION

Services liberalization covers barriers affecting all four modes of supply that are used to trade services, namely cross-border trade (Mode 1), consumption abroad (Mode 2), commercial presence (Mode 3) and temporary movement of people (Mode 4). Studies have estimated the potential gains from (non-preferential) reductions in services barriers to be:

Allocative efficiency: removing distortions in the use and movement of resources allows them to shift to the most productive areas, thus increasing welfare.

Changes in the return to capital endowments: increasing the return on capital from freer FDI movements raises real world gross product.

Increases in product variety: consumers benefit from greater choice.

Global services liberalization is estimated to raise services activity in Asian economies, especially China (by 33%), while services sectors would decline slightly in relative terms in a number of other countries (e.g. Australia, Canada, New Zealand, and the United States), due partly to their low trade barriers and the expected services expansion in the newly opened Asian countries (Dee and Hanslow 2000).

Another study estimated that complete liberalization (i.e. removal of national treatment restrictions and market access barriers in financial services and telecommunications) would raise world real GNP by about 0.1% for each sector (Verikios and Zhang 2001). Most of the telecommunications gain came from removing restrictions on market access, while the opposite was the case in financial services.

A recent DFAT-commissioned study projected that world production (in dollar terms) would rise by 0.4% above the baseline after 15 years (i.e. by 2025); 0.20% and 0.90% in developed and developing countries, respectively, if all trade barriers in services delivered cross-border and by commercial presence (estimated to supply some 85% of international services trade) were liberalized overnight (CIE 2010). Australian GDP was projected to rise above the global average (0.81%). The study included dynamic productivity gains from services trade liberalization via greater import competition, learning-by-doing in export markets, and FDI-related technology transfers. Most gains were found to come from removing barriers to commercial presence.

Source: PC (2010).

9.2.1 Unilateralism Matters Most

A country benefits most from its own trade-related liberalization, not from trading partners reducing their trade barriers. Reducing barriers to trade and investment benefits countries by improving resource allocation and efficiency from access to lower import prices and increased availability of capital, labor and knowledge, thus enhancing competitiveness and productivity (PC 2010, p. 196).

In terms of liberalization and economic benefits to Australia, the PC resoundingly rejected PTAs in favor of unilateralism supported to the extent possible by multilateralism (PC 2010). The potential advantages of unilateralism are especially apparent in services given that they are typically protected by complex behind-the-border regulatory measures (e.g. regulations and institutional arrangements restricting competition) that generally cannot be liberalized by PTAs. Expecting governments to significantly liberalize measures in PTAs (and multilaterally) is wishful thinking, which also fails to appreciate how essential unilateralism is to implementing sound reforms. Trade policy is not trade negotiations nor are policy measures something best determined by negotiations. Thus, trade negotiators generally do not negotiate actual policy measures, and play a minor role in liberalization, a preferable result given the non-economic outcomes such negotiations would in all likelihood deliver.[4] Growth-promoting policies do not depend upon trade negotiations, but rather on governments adopting sound unilateral outcomes as part of their ongoing microeconomic reform programs.

Most gains from trade liberalization are better achieved through unilateral reforms (PC 2010). Substantive trade liberalization generally involves tackling domestic constraints that can only be effectively achieved unilater-

[4] The main exception is outside services, namely tariffs, whereby PTAs negotiate applied discriminatory rates, unlike in the WTO where MFN bindings are negotiated.

ally. Most trade liberalization, including in services, has and is occurring unilaterally, in recognition that the reforming country benefits most.[5] Providing preferential access may on occasions be welfare-enhancing but it will almost always be welfare-limiting (if not welfare-reducing) compared with unilateral MFN liberalization. Strengthening these domestic outcomes offers the best prospects for advancing services liberalization, which must form an essential part of improving any economy's competitiveness and productivity.

Unilateral reforms, correctly implemented using sound and transparent economic analysis, also have the advantage of empowering all governments, no matter how small or weak, to control their trade-related economic policies without having to involve other countries, including world powers.[6] The basis of autonomous liberalization is domestic transparency – generally the exact opposite of what PTA negotiations involve, at least in Australia where they undergo relatively little public scrutiny and only when they have been concluded.

9.2.2 Rent-creating versus Cost-increasing Barriers

Trade costs in services largely relate to regulatory measures that either create entry barriers or increase the cost burdens facing firms, in addition to geographical, cultural, and institutional differences (Miroudot et al. 2010). Some services barriers primarily increase costs of suppliers by raising the real resource cost of producing a given quantity of output (i.e. reduce price-cost margins). Many of these barriers arise from broad competition policy settings that non-discriminate in a trade sense, whereas others may discriminate, such as foreign businesses and professionals having to incur retraining and accreditation costs to operate across borders. Other barriers to services trade (e.g. quantitative restrictions) artificially restrict supply and primarily create rents (i.e. raise price-cost margins). Lowering these barriers, whether preferentially or non-preferentially, may have limited economic welfare gains compared with reducing cost-raising barriers. This is because, while reducing rent-creating barriers will improve allocative efficiency by re-allocating resources to more productive uses, removing

---

[5] Well over two-thirds of actual global tariff reductions in the past few decades came from unilateral reforms.

[6] While in the field of international diplomacy the term unilateralism often conjures up negative outcomes, in the trade area it is synonymous with autonomous liberalization, which will invariably be in the country's own best economic interests. Members unilaterally liberalizing on a non-discriminatory basis also offer the best means of reducing the proliferation of PTAs and strengthening the multilateral system as well as global integration.

cost-raising barriers effectively lifts productivity, both releasing resources to other uses and also enabling the affected sector to cut costs, and possibly to expand. Such measures would benefit domestic and foreign-service providers. Thus, the welfare gains from removing measures that generate real costs are likely to greatly exceed those from abolishing measures that generate rents to domestic agents (Francois and Hoekman 2010, Dee 2009).

Identifying which services trade barriers are rent-creating or cost-raising is difficult, largely due to them operating "behind-the-border" and embedded in complex domestic regulatory legislation, often aimed at meeting legitimate social and economic objectives, but also open to misuse as protectionist measures. For example, prudential controls help maintain an efficient and well-functioning financial sector, regulation of natural monopolies constrains market power abuse, and licensing or accreditation requirements on standards protect consumers by overcoming asymmetric information. Service barriers can have both rent-creating and cost-raising impacts (e.g. non-discriminatory market access barriers that create a domestic monopoly by prohibiting both domestic and foreign entrants). Hence, assessing the impact of trade restrictions on services trade and ensuring those offering the greatest economic benefits are reformed first are so complex that such reform should not be relegated to the whimsical outcomes of trade negotiations (even assuming they are capable of delivering actual reforms).

9.3 AUSTRALIA'S PTA POLICY RELATIVE TO OTHER TRADE LIBERALIZATION APPROACHES

Australia's past unilateral trade-related reforms have secured the greatest economic gains irrespective of the actions of other countries (Box 9.3). It liberalized trade in goods independently of the WTO and, while claiming credit for its autonomous reforms, has still not removed ceiling bindings to fully "lock" in tariff reductions.[7] This unilateral liberalization approach

---

[7] This last aspect most likely reflects the preference of trade negotiators to maintain "negotiating coin" for future multilateral rounds that base reductions on bound rather than applied tariff levels, as well as governments wishing to maintain policy space to raise tariffs. As argued in this chapter and the PC (2010), this "negotiating coin" argument for keeping protection, either multilaterally or bilaterally/regionally, is economically flawed. If having "negotiating coin" was the key to the success of trade agreements, the Doha Round should have been a raging success given that all governments seem to have built up large reserves of it over the past decade (Banks 2013).

BOX 9.3 ECONOMIC GAINS TO AUSTRALIA FROM UNILATERAL TRADE-RELATED REFORMS

The economic reforms of the 1980s and 1990s included floating of the currency, financial market deregulation, public enterprise reform, introduction of competition policy and reduction of trade barriers and industry protection. They greatly enhanced Australian economy's resilience and flexibility by exposing it to international competition, and thus helped insulate the country from regional economic downturns (e.g. the 1990s Asian Financial Crisis, and more recently the Global Financial Crisis). Trade liberalization, an integral part, alone increased GDP by an estimated 2.5 to 3.5%, and drove wider economic reform (CIE 2009). Opening the economy to trade by reducing tariff and non-tariff barriers is estimated to have made Australian households better off in real terms by on average A$3,900 annually. While reform imposed painful adjustments in some manufacturing activities, almost all were better off in the long run, along with the economy, in terms of lower unemployment, low inflation, rising incomes, higher wealth levels, and greater stability.

The above estimates exclude benefits from services liberalization. However, the potential economic gains to all countries, including Australia, are thought to be even greater. It has been estimated, for example, that comprehensive overnight liberalization of Mode 1 and Mode 3 barriers would generate global cumulative GDP gains of over A$5.3 trillion from 2011–25 (in present value terms) (CIE 2010). While both developed and developing countries would benefit, the latter would gain most, with average GDP growth of 0.9 % versus 0.2% in 2025, respectively. The study suggested that Mode 3 services liberalization potentially delivered greater economic gains than Mode 1 liberalization: the phased liberalization by developing countries of Mode 3 equity barriers would raise global cumulative GDP gains from 2011–25 by A$1.2 trillion (in present value terms).

While the study did not quantify the gains to Australia from unilaterally liberalizing its services barriers (a major oversight), these are expected to be significant. For example, while the real Australian prices of previously highly protected goods have fallen substantially (e.g. by as much as 50% for clothing, footwear and motor vehicles) since 1985 following trade liberalization and greater competition, they have risen by 15% for haircuts, 17% for house rents, and by a staggering 68% for dental care (DFAT 2011).

from the 1980s was strongly resisted by many vested interests, including the then Trade Department and Minister, arguing that Australia should only liberalize as part of the multilateral negotiations to ensure it received reciprocal market access abroad and got something in return for making "concessions". The Department's traditional trade policy advice was that since the GATT excluded agriculture, the multilateral system inadequately addressed Australian trade interests in obtaining market access abroad in these products, and it should make minimal commitments in Geneva. This policy opposition was a major obstacle to the success of Australia's unilateral reforms, and their successful adoption and subsequent opening was in spite of, and not because of, WTO membership and the Trade Department.

Australia's unilateralism, based on domestic transparency, greatly diminished the relevance of multilateral bindings to prevent policy backsliding. By domestically exposing protectionism as poor public policy and changing public perceptions on the economic costs of protection, Australia's ongoing commitment to transparent unilateralism became the best means of preventing policy reversal. After all, if reductions in protection are seen as good policy to improve economic efficiency, raising import barriers is likely also to be viewed as bad and economically costly policy.

Services liberalization largely extended this unilateral approach. As goods markets were opened to import competition, manufacturers increasingly saw the need to access efficient services at world prices to compete. Similarly, technology improvements made many traditionally non-traded services internationally traded.[8] Thus, economists and politicians began shifting attention to services as inputs, to improve the competitiveness not only of manufacturers but also of services. This growing interest in services culminated in the GATS being negotiated in the WTO and to the subsequent proliferation of PTAs as so-called "new-age" or "third wave" agreements.

9.3.1 Australia's PTAs

While Australia initially resisted PTAs, favoring instead multilateralism as a distant second-best alternative to unilateralism, it joined the global preferential fray by negotiating its first PTA in 2003 with Singapore (apart from the longstanding agreement with New Zealand (ANZCERTA) that formalized many expanding economic connections as both countries unilaterally reformed). Further PTAs followed. The need to liberalize services

---

[8] Services only began being highlighted in the international trade policy agenda in the 1980s (Francois and Hoekman 2010).

internationally was seen as a major policy driver for PTAs, even though it was generally acknowledged that successfully liberalizing services trade required substantial doses of unilateralism to tackle domestic regulations, as was being highlighted in the shallow outcomes of the GATS negotiations of the Uruguay Round and the offers in the Doha Round.[9]

The shift towards PTAs coincided with a more subtle and negative development in Australian trade policy. As the practical emphasis veered back towards negotiated, especially preferential, forms of liberalization, Australian trade policy began to focus more on these avenues at the expense of unilateralism. Its move to PTAs reflected a breakdown in Australia's commitment to open and transparent processes that supported unilateralism, and corrupted domestic policy setting and processes (Garnaut 2010a and 2010b).[10] Reversing the associated domestic deterioration in the climate of opinion about the benefits of trade liberalization requires challenging the enhanced legitimacy of conceptions of narrowly defined reciprocity, and re-establishing the role of independent, transparent policy analysis (Garnaut 2003).

Australia's PTAs follow the international convention of being deceptively called Free Trade Agreements (FTAs). In addition to an FTA with Singapore (SAFTA), Australia has FTAs with ASEAN (with New Zealand, AANZFTA), Chile (ACFTA), Korea, Thailand (TAFTA) and the United States (AUSFTA). It is negotiating PTAs, some well advanced, with China, GCC, Indonesia, Japan, Malaysia, Pacific Islands (PACER), India, and the Trans-Pacific countries of Brunei, Canada, Chile, Japan, Malaysia, Mexico, New Zealand, Peru, Singapore, the United States and Vietnam (TPP). While Australia has no service-specific PTAs, all PTAs include services, using either a positive or negative list approach (Box 9.4). Key common provisions on services in these "third wave" PTAs is

---

[9] It is widely accepted that the GATS negotiations of the Uruguay Round resulted in no actual significant liberalization, and that this outcome would not be changed by the Doha offers (Gootiiz and Mattoo 2009). The current multilateral and regional approach to services trade liberalization is not working; services offers on the table in the Doha Round contain "not one iota" of genuine liberalization in the form of new market access, and some members are still unprepared to bind current levels of liberalization (PECC 2011). Thus, the frequent claim that GATS is an effective "standstill" agreement is exaggerated.

[10] The stalling of Australia's unilateral trade liberalization was compounded by the ascendancy of narrow conceptions of "reciprocity" with trading partners, and by the policy-making processes behind the Cabinet decision in December 2000 to seek an FTA with the United States; no public service assessment or preferably independent transparent analysis was conducted on its economic effects, and it was subsequently justified by highly constrained consultancies (Garnaut 2003).

BOX 9.4 AUSTRALIA'S PTAS

SAFTA: provisions on market access, national treatment and transparency, negative list approach (substantially more exemptions than ANZCERTA); key Australian outcomes professional residency requirements, removal of some quantitative restrictions (e.g. number of wholesale bank licenses in Singapore for Australian banks), and framework for developing MRAs; air transport carved out; range of investor protections (e.g. national treatment, transparency, expropriation and nationalization, compensation for losses and transfer of investors' funds), including investor-state dispute settlement.

AUSFTA: national treatment to each other, no local presence requirements, market access provisions, MFN treatment, negative list (substantially more exemptions than ANCERTA but less than SAFTA); framework for developing MRAs (including Working Group on Professional Services); in investment, provides for national treatment, MFN treatment and a minimum standard of treatment in accordance with customary international law, no investor-state dispute settlement, higher screening thresholds for US investors.

TAFTA: positive list (less comprehensive commitments than SAFTA or AUSFTA), further negotiations within three years (not yet held); Australia granted very limited Mode 4 concessions for Thai chefs and masseurs, largely as trade-off for Thai agricultural concessions (Bosworth and Trewin 2009); in investment, provides for national treatment, MFN treatment, expropriation, compensation for losses and transfers, and investor-state dispute settlement; Australia allowed majority ownership – up to 60%, or in some cases 100%, up from 49.9% – for various business types (e.g. mining and construction).

ACFTA: provisions on market access, national treatment, local presence, MFN treatment, negative list with ratchet mechanism; in investment, provides for national treatment, MFN treatment, minimum standard of treatment in accordance with customary international law, and transfers, treatment in case of strife and expropriation; investor-state dispute settlement.

AANZFTA: positive list and no automatic MFN provision, but scope for consultation of more favorable treatment is extended to another party; reviewed within three years to progressively extend commitments; in investment, covers post-establishment elements and investor protection through national treatment, fair and equitable treatment and full protection and security (in line with customary international law), non-discriminatory treatment for investors who suffer losses due to armed conflict, civil strife or states of emergency, free transfer of funds, and compensation for expropriation or nationalization and transparency; investor-state dispute settlement, except between Australia and New Zealand; work program aimed at including pre-establishment market access issues (e.g. foreign equity limits) within five years.

Source: PC 2010.

the coverage of national treatment; mutual recognition of selected professional qualifications; relaxed restrictions on commercial presence by foreign-service providers; and to varying degrees attempts to harmonize regulatory frameworks (PC 2010).

Australian policy has been to seek comprehensive PTAs. In services trade and investment, PTAs appear mainly motivated to limit foreign discrimination against Australian exporters rather than to gain preferential access; to include arrangements for developing mutual recognition of standards and professional qualifications; and to provide for the temporary movement of employees and business people to work in partner countries (DFAT 2010a). However, the distinction between limiting foreign discrimination rather than gaining preferential access is operationally unclear since negotiating former outcomes in a particular market also provides Australian exporters preferential access over non-preferential world suppliers.[11] Australia's key negotiating objectives have indeed in practice been to obtain, and to the extent possible retain, preference margins for Australian exporters, and to use services trade and investment liberalization as vehicles for achieving priority business objectives regarding behind-the-border regulatory barriers (ASR 2008). However, to the extent that Australian PTAs in practice do not engage in actual liberalization at

[11] Such an objective would imply only negotiating in PTAs what Australia has committed to multilaterally in the GATS. However, this would make PTA negotiations redundant and is clearly not the case.

home or in its trading partners but rather focus on negotiating only "on paper" commitments, they fail to achieve this objective, and instead end up becoming more "gloss" than substance.

Australia has sought a number of goals in pursuing PTAs, including on services (DFAT 2010a):

- bind existing market access levels (e.g. ANZCERTA, SAFTA, AUSFTA, ACI-FTA, and AANZFTA (restricted));
- negotiate new market access in sectors of priority commercial interest (e.g. ANZCERTA and ACFTA);
- embed MFN commitments to ensure benefits are offered to future PTA partners (e.g. ANZCERTA, AUSFTA, and ACFTA);
- improve regulatory transparency;
- promote the adoption of good-governance disciplines on domestic regulation (standards, licensing, recognition of qualifications);
- seek commitments to treat service investors as at least equal to investors in goods;
- include separate chapters on sectors of particular interest (e.g. telecommunications, financial services, education, and movement of natural persons); and
- adopt a ratchet mechanism to lock in future autonomous liberalization by partners (e.g. ACFTA).

Australia's PTA patchwork already shows the signs of potentially inefficient and trade-damaging overlapping agreements (the so-called "spaghetti" or "noodle" bowl effect). Australia's six PTAs cover 13 trading partners, with multiple memberships. Singapore, Thailand and Indonesia are covered by two PTAs. Nine PTAs are currently being negotiated, covering some 20 trading partners plus the Pacific Island economies (e.g. Papua New Guinea and Fiji).[12] When negotiated, New Zealand and Singapore will each be members of three Australian PTAs, while Malaysia, Brunei, Chile, US and Vietnam will each be members of two Australian PTAs (Figure 9.1).[13] There are no signs that Australia is attempting to rationalize its PTAs and/or to remove duplication; indeed quite the opposite.

Such a complex web of PTAs is arguably likely to be an inefficient and

---

[12] The only PTA currently being negotiated by Australia not mentioned in the Trade Policy Statement was PACER.

[13] This already growing complex network of Australian PTAs is only a small subset of the Asian Pacific "noodle bowl" which would of course include "third party" agreements.

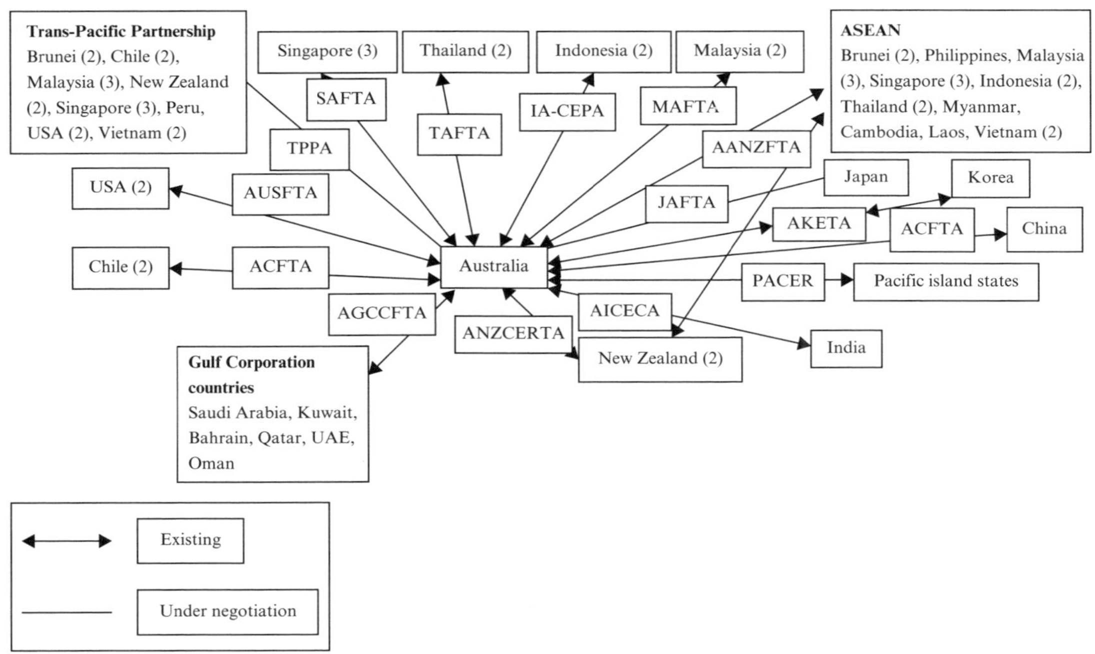

(number) Refers to the number of separate PTAs Australia has or will have with that country e.g. Singapore (3) means Australia has or will have three separate PTAs with Singapore, namely SAFTA, AANZFTA and TPP

Figure 9.1 Australia's overlapping PTAs in services

cumbersome trading outcome for Australia. It contradicts the goal of establishing a transparent, predictable trading regime free of government intervention that would generate welfare-enhancing trade for Australia. The private sector's very mixed views on the desirability and usefulness of PTAs reflects mainly individual business vested interests, when it is the economy-wide or national interest that is relevant. Australia's peak services group, the Australian Services Roundtable (ASR), believes Australia's inefficient bilateral PTAs must be significantly redesigned (Box 9.5).

While from a trade negotiations perspective, Australian PTAs appear to be and are politically sold as major achievements, such outcomes are more apparent than real. They are highly duplicative, including of multilateral rules and obligations, and have added little to Australian "on paper" commitments, and even less in practice to reforms in terms of actual or "on-the-ground" liberalization (Table 9.1). Indeed, PTAs have generally done little more than re-hash WTO commitments on all sides, and have been misleadingly portrayed as substantive. This WTO re-hash is totally unnecessary given that all parties to Australian PTAs are also WTO members. Such PTAs would be more transparent and less deceptive if they included only those differences negotiated in the PTA, leaving out each parties' WTO commitments. In this way, seemingly substantive and comprehensive PTAs would in most cases become "wafer-thin" and their lack of achievement would more easily be seen.[14] Moreover, many PTA provisions affecting foreign investment in services repeat, but generally fall well short of, those found in respective Bilateral Investment Treaties (BITs).[15] PTAs (like GATS) should also include actual measures so that the commitments can be compared with the existing situation, thereby improving transparency and indicating the extent of "binding overhang" and any areas where actual liberalization has occurred as a result.

---

[14] PTAs also duplicate many other existing provisions. For example, the minimum standard of treatment and conditions on expropriation for foreign investors included in AUSFTA are intended to reflect customary international law and partly correspond to provisions in both the Australian and US Constitutions (Mitchell and Voon 2009).

[15] A country's BITs affecting trade in services, as defined in the GATS (i.e. including investment), must be applied on an MFN basis unless it has taken out an MFN exemption for these treaties under GATS, which most, including Australia, have not. BITs generally cover a far wider range of sectors than scheduled under the GATS, and often contain greater obligations (e.g. compensation in the case of expropriation); nevertheless no WTO member, including Australia, has notified its BITs to the WTO as a measure deemed to significantly affect trade in scheduled services as would be required under GATS Article III(3) (Adlung and Molinuevo 2008).

BOX 9.5 ASR CRITICAL OF AUSTRALIAN PTAS IN SERVICES AND WELCOMES RECENT UNILATERAL TRADE POLICY RE-FOCUS

Services have played a prominent role in Australia's PTAs. However, in PTAs with developing country partners, services and investment liberalization are not proving much easier to negotiate one-on-one than they are in the multilateral context. In every PTA, services and investment aspects have been exceedingly difficult. This is because services markets typically have very high levels of government intervention, thus making trade and investment liberalization highly politically sensitive; most developing country governments are not displaying the will to undertake the necessary regulatory reforms.

The most constructive aspect of PTA negotiations with developing countries has been that it enables Australia to undertake a much deeper policy dialogue on services-related matters, including what constitutes regulatory best practice, than is otherwise possible with non-OECD trading partners (e.g. dialogue to facilitate regulatory cooperation and harmonization), carrying the promise of deeper economic and business integration over the medium term. Unfortunately, in the context of formal trade negotiation, this has not been Australia's apparent intention. The negotiating intention has been to obtain, and to the extent possible retain, a margin of preference for existing Australian exporting firms. Australia's negotiating mandates have been too narrowly focused on achieving small wins on market access, rather than on achieving deeper microeconomic reforms. Domestic regulatory issues have been largely off the agenda and not part and parcel of bilateral PTAs.

Consequently, Australia's PTA agenda has been of limited actual value in improving trade and investment in services. The most constructive outcomes have been to establish ongoing working groups and committees to examine possible regulatory harmonization or mutual recognition over time. To be effective, however, such panels/committees must have teeth. The value of PTAs lies simply in establishing a vehicle, which, though possibly of limited utility in itself, can nevertheless provide a platform to chip away at behind-the-border barriers, bring the domestic constituency on board over time, and hopefully in time facilitate a staged approach to regulatory reform.

The current suite of services trade negotiating mechanisms are unlikely to help reap the large potential economic gains to Australia from liberalizing services. To put it simply, they are not working multilaterally and, unless certain conditions apply as set out below, they are unlikely to work on a bilateral or regional basis either. WTO market access outcomes on services to date have been poor. Bilateral "WTO plus" outcomes are rare. To achieve the objective of "WTO plus" outcomes, Australia will need to drop a lot of old negotiating habits and develop a next generation tool kit. Interestingly, ASR has found a high degree of common ground on this matter with services export coalitions in our trading partners, whether they be from developed or developing economies.

There is a need to significantly redesign services trade and investment liberalization vehicles to reform behind-the-border regulatory barriers to doing business, specifically including current inefficient bilateral PTAs. ASR has little interest in pursuing them as currently constructed; a new suite of bilateral instruments is needed, focused on policy and regulatory microeconomic dialogue.

ASR believes the Government's recent Trade Policy Statement is a blueprint for needed productivity growth in Australia, and also sees trade policy as an indivisible part of overall economic policy. In particular, ASR endorses the Statement's emphasis on pursuing pro-competitive reform in its own right, especially in services. Such unilateral reform by Australia can demonstrate regional services policy leadership, particularly important as very high services barriers of many neighbors have proven difficult to lower through the WTO or PTAs.

Source: ASR 2008 and 2011.

It is generally acknowledged that Australia negotiates PTAs more for foreign policy than economic considerations. The Government uses PTAs as instruments to secure wider foreign policy and strategic objectives often unrelated to trade and commerce; AUSFTA, which was driven by politics and not economics as demonstrated by Australia's willingness to accept such poor outcomes in major interest areas like agriculture is the most obvious contemporary example (Capling 2008). AUSFTA had at least as much to do with broader foreign policy objectives than with pure trade and investment goals (Commonwealth of Australia 2004). Australia's

Table 9.1 Poor performance of Australian PTAs in achieving domestic services liberalization

PTA	Improvements	Comments
AANZFTA	Virtually none	Mainly re-hash of WTO commitments; added "unbound" Mode 4 in MA & NT; replaced a few "unbound due to non-feasibility" entries in Mode 1 with "none"; added a few already liberalized sectors; made GATS-minus commitments; and slightly improved access of employer-sponsored contractual serviced suppliers (Mode 4)
AUSFTA	Virtually none	Higher screening threshold given in sensitive services to US investors, GATS-minus commitments (Adlung and Morrison 2010)
SAFTA	Virtually none	Mainly re-hash of WTO commitments in a "NAFTA-styled" agreement (negative listing)
ACFTA	Virtually none	Mainly re-hash of WTO commitments in a "NAFTA-styled" agreement (negative listing)
TAFTA	Minimal	Mainly re-hash of WTO commitments; slightly liberalized temporary access by Thais to labor market without market testing, including for employer-sponsored contractual serviced suppliers, especially chefs; made some GATS-minus commitments; added a few already liberalized sectors; replaced a few "unbound due to non-feasibility" entries in Mode 1 with "none"; CA in MA & NT allowed in several banking services (little liberalizing impact) Added insurance relating to maritime shipping and commercial aviation, space launching and freight (including satellites) covering goods being transported, vehicles transporting the goods; and goods in international transit, and reinsurance and retrocession and the services auxiliary to insurance e.g. consultancy, actuarial, risk assessment and claim settlement services – cross-border supply as a principal, through an intermediary or as an intermediary is permitted. CA permitted. Otherwise all unbound.
ANZCERTA	Minimal	US higher screening threshold in sensitive sectors extended to New Zealand investors.

Source: Authors' assessments.

assessment on PTA negotiations necessarily has regard to a broad range of considerations, including commercial and strategic (DFAT 2010a). In any event, such non-economic outcomes are usually better achieved outside PTAs; the characterization of security and strategic goals as a central justification for a PTA causes concern, as the practical value of any such contribution from a PTA is often unclear and yet seems to dominate other considerations (PC 2010). For example, a bilateral defense or security agreement would usually be superior in meeting defense-related strategic goals.

Australia pursues both negative (e.g. AUSFTA and ANZCERTA) and positive lists in its services PTAs (e.g. AANZFTA). While no compelling conceptual reason exists as to why a negative list should be more liberalizing than a positive list (other than automatically subjecting new services to liberalizing commitments), Australian PTAs with negative lists generate more commitments. However, this may reflect the ambitions of the partners (e.g. the US) rather than the listing approach; positive listing seems to be associated with a more defensive or minimalist approach to commitments by partners. Notwithstanding, the US has a widespread tendency to use negative list reservations to exclude measures maintained at the sub-national level, raising skepticism of the self-proclaimed "gold standard" quality of US PTAs (Heydon and Woolcock 2009). Australian service providers have encountered instances under AUSFTA where the competent sub-national authorities have not implemented MRA mandates agreed nationally. MRA provisions, promoted as trade liberalizing in AUSFTA at least, thus had little practical effect, highlighting that such arrangements must include those state governments responsible for administering them to be effective.

While in practice positive list agreements would be unlikely to be more liberalizing than those with a negative list, Australia on balance should generally follow negative lists, where possible (PC 2010, ASR 2008).

9.4 LIBERALIZING SERVICES TRADE THROUGH PTAS

The extent to which PTAs can liberalize services trade critically depends on whether they can reduce the main types of barriers impeding services trade in a way that unambiguously improves national welfare. This mainly depends on the nature of the impact of the services barrier.

Evidence suggests that the biggest gains from reforming services barriers accrue from reducing non-discriminatory market access restrictions on competition affecting both foreign and domestic suppliers (Dee and

Findlay 2007a, ITS Global 2010). Discriminatory regulations that raise costs could include additional capital requirements for foreign insurance firms, or pricing regulations specifically targeting foreign insurance providers. The same rules could, however, also be non-discriminatory and raise costs for both foreign and domestic firms, thereby causing greater welfare losses. The next largest source of gains is likely to result from discriminatory market access restrictions that inhibit foreign access only. Market access barriers, especially non-discriminatory measures, are likely to exert large cost-escalation and rent-creating impacts, and should be liberalized first.[16] Usually entry barriers to domestic and foreign suppliers coexist, and significant barriers to foreign supply are usually associated with non-trivial barriers to domestic suppliers; it is rare to have significant barriers to foreign entry and/or operations without similar restrictions on domestic entrants (Dee 2009). Market access and regulation are interrelated, such that the key to sound policy reform is to increase market contestability by easing entry barriers for both domestic and foreign entrants.

In contrast, liberalizing national treatment measures discriminating against foreign suppliers, post-establishment, offers much smaller gains. This is because such measures have a much lower anti-competitive or protective impact since they affect competition between suppliers rather than preventing new suppliers from entering the market. Moreover, the expressed reason for having PTAs in services is to reduce or eliminate national treatment and not market access restrictions (GATS Article V).

Poor progress in even making liberalizing commitments (let alone liberalizing actual measures) in PTAs (and the WTO) is a problem for policy makers who would like them to support their domestic programs, but it seems they will be waiting "till the cows come home" (Drake-Brockman and Findlay 2011, Francois and Hoekman 2010). A far preferable course of action would be to build support for domestic unilateral reform rather than trying to side-step the fundamental problem through PTAs that focus on commitments rather than achieving actual liberalization, and can work against domestic reform by concentrating resources on trade negotiations, thereby undermining pursuit of actual on-the-ground unilateral reforms. Additionally, while it is often claimed that implementing liberalized commitments preferentially under PTAs helps pave the way for multilateralizing them in future, this is not supported by the Australian experience in

---

[16] For example, empirical studies indicate that the gains to the ASEAN region from unilaterally reforming non-discriminatory restrictions on competition in services in a group of East Asian economies exceeded those from forming an East Asian PTA and from a successful Doha Round by almost sixfold and threefold (Dee 2010).

those few instances where actual measures have been preferentially liberalized. Indeed, such preferential measures can be more difficult to extend on an MFN basis as certain lobby groups in both countries unite against such developments and related commitments become ripe to be used as "negotiating coin" in future PTAs. For example, Australia has refrained from extending the preferential FDI screening thresholds provided US investors unilaterally on an MFN basis, which would be the best outcome economically, but instead has decided to use these in PTA negotiations, having recently extended them to New Zealand.

Even in terms of commitments, it is important not to automatically conclude that a PTA with commitments that go "beyond the WTO" in "new" areas such as services trade and investment is necessarily a good outcome; precisely the opposite could well be the case (Drake-Brockman 2003). Exceeding WTO rules obviously does not necessarily mean progress or even greater trade openness (Mitchell and Voon 2009). PTAs are inefficient and largely inappropriate mechanisms for services and investment trade liberalization because they do not focus sufficiently on barriers to trade which are located behind-the-border (ASR 2011 and Box 9.5). History shows that few market opening reforms come from trade negotiations, which primarily arise within a domestic productivity agenda (ASR 2011 and Box 9.5). While there have been many new PTAs with improved services commitments, trade liberalization is mainly unilateral (Miroudot 2011). Significant market opening actually comes from within economies because of the associated benefits to the community (Kwan 2011). PTAs are the best excuse reform-weary governments have had for not doing what really matters, and for distracting reform-ready governments with limited regulatory reform capacity from the main game (Dee 2007).

9.4.1 PTA Limitations in Liberalizing Services Trade

Because of the nature of trade barriers to services, PTAs (and the WTO) are unlikely to be effective in reducing many non-discriminatory or even some discriminatory market access barriers. PTA negotiations tend to focus on the removal of national treatment barriers that explicitly discriminate against foreign suppliers. This is hardly surprising given that only provisions that discriminate against and between foreigners can be readily liberalized preferentially (Dee and Findlay 2007a, Dee 2009).[17]

---

[17] For measures to be preferably liberalized, they must be capable of easily being implemented in a way that can discriminate not only between domestic and foreign suppliers, but also by country of origin. Non-discriminatory market access

Discriminatory market access barriers are also likely to be downplayed in PTAs (e.g. foreign ownership limits).[18] Also, since the Government's main commercial motive for negotiating PTAs is to obtain preferential access for service exporters, discriminatory national treatment barriers that can readily favor them over suppliers from other countries will be targeted, especially given the "request-and-offer" modalities used to negotiate concessions (including in the WTO). PTAs focus mainly on issues between domestic and foreign suppliers, while the real reform issues are between incumbent and other domestic suppliers.

There seems no escaping the fact that significant services liberalization of the main trade restrictions can only be successfully tackled unilaterally because of the nature of the measures (i.e. embedded in domestic legislation and the difficulties of liberalizing preferentially). PTAs (and especially the WTO) may marginally help but are no substitutes for unilateralism. The politics of services reform differs from that of goods; additional foreign market access is not required as part of a big political bargain to offset the local resistance to reform in services, being largely about FDI, and when barriers are removed local activity can actually increase (Drake-Brockman and Findlay 2011). Furthermore, in many cases the service businesses themselves push for services reform to remove unnecessary and costly regulation or rules. Also, for PTAs, it's hard to define origin in a way to support discrimination since market failures are not linked to the origins of services. If problems of asymmetric information exist, for example with professional services where clients cannot sufficiently assess quality and demand licensing or accreditation requirements for suppliers, regulations should apply uniformly to domestic and foreign providers to ensure equal recognition of similar overseas qualifications and experience.[19]

Most services trade barriers likely to raise costs cannot be eliminated through bilateral negotiations and, for the most part, can be addressed only through domestic competition policy reforms; while negotiations can

---

limitations are thus poor fits for preferential liberalization, since it would require allowing domestic entry at the same time as permitting only foreign entry from preferential countries.

18 Maintaining discriminatory or preferential market access restrictions, such as different foreign equity limits, is likely to be fraught with implementation problems as foreign investors respond by shifting origin to become eligible for preferential access (assuming that PTAs have liberal "denial of benefits" clauses).

19 This is usually achieved by negotiating Mutual Recognition Agreements (MRAs), often as part of PTAs. However, when entrenched in PTAs, such MRAs can become a major source of discrimination between PTA members and non-members. MRAs would be better negotiated outside PTAs to enable any new country to more easily negotiate to join the MRA.

hope to eliminate some particularly restrictive regulations, for example, to agree on mutual recognition of some professional qualifications, they cannot enforce complex legislative changes, such as better competition policies (Elek 2010).

Most significant policy reforms in services have been domestically driven, with PTAs offering limited scope to reform services, partly also due to a lack of domestic constituencies focusing on self-liberalization rather than mercantilism efforts concentrating on obtaining greater access abroad. Achieving domestic reform of services markets through external trade agreements, including the WTO, has proven difficult in practice (Francois and Hoekman 2010). At best, negotiated forms of liberalization, including PTAs, have resulted in commitments "on paper" without generating actual liberalization of measures, and this is certainly the case in Australia (Tables 9.1 and 9.2, Bosworth and Trewin 2009).[20] While the trade negotiating community claim binding such measures via "on paper" commitments to be major achievements, their value, especially in services, is largely overstated. This is especially so when commitments contain significant "binding overhang" to provide substantial policy space to de-liberalize. Unfortunately, while perhaps of academic interest, much of the research documenting so-called services liberalization under PTAs (and the WTO) has overly focused on countries' scheduled commitments, which are known to contain significant binding overhang and/or to have contributed little to actual or "on-the-ground" liberalization, and thereby have been of limited policy value (Fink and Molinuevo 2007, Roy et al. 2006, Marchetti and Roy 2008, Mattoo and Sauve 2010, Sauve and Shingal 2011).[21] The domestic politics of trade in services may make it difficult to achieve real liberalization in PTAs (or WTO) as opposed to international codification of measures already approved domestically (Van Grasstek 2011). There has also been a marked inclination among governments to dress up issues in PTAs which do not fundamentally free up markets – because eliminating the barriers needed is too hard – and instead to focus on issues which may please constituents but have little impact (ITS Global 2011).

Of real value to policy makers and the proper benchmark by which to evaluate the liberalizing impact of PTAs (and the GATS) is to assess the

[20] Even applying the Fink and Molinuevo (2007) analysis to TAFTA found only small improvements over Australian and Thai GATS commitments, themselves second-rate (Bosworth and Trewin 2009).

[21] This largely reflects the ease of conducting such analysis due to the availability of PTA (and GATS) commitment databases across countries, while no such comprehensive or easily accessible databases exist on actual liberalization.

Table 9.2 Australian GATS commitments compared with SAFTA and TAFTA

Sector/service	Comparison
SAFTA	
Horizontal section	Mode 4 horizontal commitments significantly improve on GATS; many of these reflected in Doha offers which are potentially nearly as liberalizing as SAFTA, certain of which (e.g. rights for permanent residents) may still be more liberalizing than Doha offers.
Business	SAFTA on legal services probably more liberalizing than Doha offer; in most other areas, it and Doha offers appear comparable.
Communications	SAFTA appears slightly more liberalizing than the Doha offer.
Construction	Likely that SAFTA and Doha offer comparable, although significance of the "other construction services" sector unknown.
Distribution	Additional Doha offer appears roughly comparable to SAFTA.
Financial	SAFTA, including chapter on financial services rules, seems more liberalizing than Doha offer.
Education	SAFTA reservations probably mean it does not go meaningfully beyond GATS.
Environmental	SAFTA appears more liberalizing than Doha offer.
Health & Social	No Doha offer, SAFTA same as GATS (only commitments in podiatry and chiropody).
Tourism	SAFTA appears marginally beyond GATS (no new Doha offers).
Transportation	Although Doha offer potentially considerably more liberalizing than GATS, the same SAFTA reservations would likely apply to GATS so that SAFTA's negative list approach likely more liberalizing overall than Doha offer.
Recreational, cultural & sporting	No Doha offer and SAFTA same as GATS.
TAFTA	
Horizontal section	TAFTA notable for Mode 4 provisions on temporary entry of qualified Thai chefs and agreement to work toward similar provisions for qualified massage therapists. In nearly all other areas, access limited to senior executives and or managers/specialists.
Business	Doha Round offer potentially more generous than TAFTA (e.g. legal services).
Communications	Doha offer potentially more generous than TAFTA.

Table 9.2 (continued)

Sector/service	Comparison
TAFTA	
Construction	Doha offer potentially more generous than TAFTA, which has same commitments as GATS.
Distribution	Doha offer potentially more generous than TAFTA, which has same commitments as GATS.
Financial	Doha offer potentially more generous than TAFTA, in which GATS+ commitments reflect only partly Doha offer.
Education	TAFTA commitments, tied to traditional Thai specialties, more interesting than Doha offer, which is same as GATS.
Environmental	Doha Round offer essentially same as TAFTA.
Health & Social	No Doha offer, TAFTA same as GATS.
Tourism	No Doha offer, TAFTA same as GATS.
Transportation	Doha Round potentially considerably more generous than TAFTA.
Recreational, cultural & sporting	No Doha offer, TAFTA same as GATS.

Source: Trewin, Bosworth et al. 2008.

extent to which they actually reform measures. In this respect, the picture both in Australia and elsewhere is bleak, and the extent to which PTAs (and the GATS) "lock in" past unilateral reforms is overstated.[22] Usually when a country's PTA commitments exceed those in the WTO, it is primarily through new rather than improved existing bindings, when arguably the latter is more likely to imply real liberalization (Dee 2009). Similarly, comparing a country's PTA and GATS commitments misleadingly avoids the main policy question, namely to what extent have PTAs liberalized "on-the-ground" more than GATS (Box 9.6).

Analysis based on commitments cannot therefore measure the extent to

[22] Working with countries' schedule of commitments therefore creates an overly rosy picture of the extent to which PTAs (and the GATS) have actually liberalized measures, thereby potentially misleading policy makers and governments. For example, a country scheduling a new sub-sector "unbound" in its positive list is often seen as liberalizing, even though in reality nothing has changed, even in terms of bindings. Similarly, adding new service sub-sectors to the list with partial or full commitments is seen as liberalizing, even though policy measures have not changed.

BOX 9.6 AUSFTA COMMITMENTS

Many parts of the agreement codify the status quo, and in some cases even the bindings are not new, with Australia already having the same promises under GATS to the US and all other WTO Members.

Because AUSFTA commitments on national treatment and market access are based on a negative list and not a positive list as for the GATS, the services chapter may potentially offer more than the status quo, particularly for sectors unlisted by one or both countries within the WTO. While in principle the same applies to chapter 13 on financial services, in practice it is primarily a status quo chapter. Similarly, since the investment chapter of AUSFTA uses a negative list for national treatment commitments compared with a positive list in GATS, it may potentially offer more than the status quo, particularly for sectors unlisted by one or both countries within the WTO.

However, importantly, AUSFTA commitments do not necessarily imply that there were significant barriers present in these areas being removed; in most cases there were not. This confirms the Government's claim that the main Australian benefit on investment and cross-border services trade were US promises not to apply new discriminatory measures (i.e. standstill provisions), rather than rolling back any existing measures. Hence, the promises will not cost either party commercially and have resulted in minimal liberalization of Australian or US measures.

Intellectual property

AUSFTA required Australia to extend copyright protection by 20 years, from the life of the author plus 50 years, to the life of the author plus 70 years. The economic benefit to Australia is the additional works created from the extra incentive to authors. However, the cost to Australia, as a net importer of copyright material, is the additional royalties that must be paid to copyright holders of existing works. The net cost to Australia is that it could eventually pay 25% more annually in net royalty payments, not just to US copyright holders, but to all copyright holders, since this provision is not preferential. This could amount to up to A$88 million annually, or up to A$700 million in net present value terms. This is a pure transfer overseas, and hence a pure cost to Australia.

Source: Dee (2004).

which PTAs achieve actual liberalization, nor assess the degree to which any liberalizing commitments would increase trade. Indeed, such analysis can badly mislead. For example, a country with open trade policies and few commitments would be found to be far less liberal than a country with substantial trade restrictions but many more scheduled commitments. Such erroneous comparisons and assessment would also apply at individual sub-sector and across-mode comparisons. It is not commitments that matter but actual policy measures. It is far better for a country to have open trade and investment regimes in reality and poor commitments than to have restricted regimes and liberal commitments. Often this fundamental distinction is lost as trade policy becomes confused with trade negotiations, and the impression often created that commitments matter as much as actual measures, and that trade negotiations are actually setting trade measures and policy.[23]

How much discipline PTAs impose, whether in terms of policy changes "on paper" or in terms of actual implementation, is little studied, making it difficult to argue that in practice specific agreements live up to what theory "predicts" they will achieve as a lock-in device and adding reform credibility (Francois and Hoekman 2010). PTAs appear to have wider coverage than the GATS but their contribution with respect to actual policy change and implementation is difficult to assess (Drake-Brockman and Findlay 2011). Most PTAs (like the WTO) have not achieved significant additional services liberalization, and while PTAs can be useful "laboratories" for cooperation on specific sectors or policies, including mutual recognition and the adoption of common standards, "most services policy reforms tend to be implemented unilaterally. . . there is not much compelling evidence that PTAs are going significantly beyond already applied services policies" (Hoekman 2008). Even where PTAs significantly improve on GATS offers, they only "sometimes" lead to real market liberalization (Roy et al. 2006). Trade agreements do not appear to have played much of a role, if any, in generating significant policy reforms (Francois and Hoekman 2010). This is certainly true of Australian PTAs.

An OECD study found that PTAs had reduced services trade barriers much less than for goods, primarily due to the nature of the restrictive measures; unilateral non-discriminatory policy reforms matter most in services markets, and are the effective basis for anything that happens

[23] Blurring this distinction seems often to be intentional, especially among trade and officials and governments. It provides them with ammunition to give the impression that they are doing a lot of trade reform when in fact the reality is far different, a potentially dangerous development that can backfire and undermine genuine efforts to unilaterally reform.

within regional arrangements or multilaterally (Miroudot et al. 2010). In other words, unilateralism operates effectively in liberalizing services without multilateralism or regionalism, but without unilateralism these negotiated forms of liberalization have little impact.

9.4.2 Problems of piecemeal reforms

At a broad level, all economic reforms tend to be piecemeal. This reflects reality – governments cannot possibly reform everything simultaneously, so that priorities and sequencing are essential. At a micro-level, however, reforms should be as comprehensive as possible to minimize risks of "second-best" outcomes from piecemeal reforms that may worsen, not improve, economic welfare. Comprehensive reforms also have other advantages, such as "watering down" any adverse effects on certain groups as positives help offset any negatives.

In trade, for example, it is widely accepted that the most efficient means of tariff reform is general across-the-board MFN reductions to reduce the level and disparity in rates rather than piecemeal cuts, especially since lowering tariffs on inputs without also reducing high output tariffs can worsen resource-use efficiency by raising already high effective rates of assistance.

Problems of piecemeal trade reform are accentuated in services. This is because services barriers are usually enshrined "behind-the-border" in a maze of domestic regulatory legislation that is designed to meet an uncertain mix of desirable and non-desirable (protectionist) goals. Disentangling this web is complex. The prevalence of domestic regulation complicates and constrains the use of reciprocity negotiations for services because of the difficulty in designing multilateral rules and national commitments in a way that clearly separates or distinguishes between measures that protect by preventing entry, create rents for incumbents by raising prices, or needlessly raise costs, from those having good domestic efficiency or social equity rationale relating to quality and performance; marginal *quid pro quo* changes to domestic regulatory policies may not necessarily enhance welfare (Francois and Hoekman 2010). There is no internationally accepted best framework for regulating services, such that unique differences between countries are likely not only to exist, but to be desirable. Many PTAs, including for example AUSFTA, are negotiated so hurriedly that it is difficult to believe that their domestic economic implications could have been properly considered.[24]

---

[24] For example, negotiating time for the US's PTAs between 1984 and 2005 varied between nine and 38 months (Ferrantino 2006).

Intellectual property, which also affects services and investment, is a case in point. The most economic appropriate degree of intellectual property protection is far from clear and, in any event, when IP is increasing at an accelerating rate, would likely differ between intellectual-property-exporting and intellectual-property-importing countries. Creeping strengthening of intellectual property protection, pushed hard in its FTAs by the US as one of the world's major exporters of intellectual property, risks upsetting the delicate balance between providing sufficient monopoly conditions as an incentive for innovation and creativity, and preventing anti-competitive conduct and ensuring access to new products and technologies (Mitchell and Voon 2009, Fink and Reichenmiller 2005, Mercurio 2006).[25] Intellectual property protection became a sensitive issue in AUSFTA, where Australia agreed to meet US requests to strengthen its intellectual property protection (e.g. extending the term of copyright protection by an additional 20 years, to bring Australia into closer conformity with the US), seemingly against Australia's national interest (Box 9.5).[26]

It is also claimed that some of the AUSFTA patent provisions that exceeded TRIPS may raise Australian drug prices and unnecessarily delay introduction of generic drugs (Drahos et al. 2004, Mercurio 2005, Mitchell and Voon 2009). AUSFTA, unlike TRIPS, also banned parallel imports of patented products, thereby removing the possibility of allowing them if found to be in Australia's best economic interests.

Australia should not seek to include intellectual property provisions in PTAs as an ordinary matter of course, and should only include such provisions after an economic assessment of the impacts, including on consumers, in Australia and partner countries (PC 2010).[27] Moreover, intellectual property protection should arguably be outside the scope of PTAs (and the WTO) as they generally restrict competition rather than liberalizing trade (Correa 2006).

---

[25] Since the WTO TRIPS Agreement has no general MFN exemption for PTAs, WTO members who provide any stronger intellectual property protection preferentially must generally extend these provisions to all (Mitchell and Voon 2009).

[26] This decision reportedly involved the input of the Australian Prime Minister at the time, and reversed an earlier government decision to accept the recommendation of the Intellectual Property and Review Committee not to extend the term of copyright protection (Mitchell and Voon 2009).

[27] PTA provisions that are in Australia's national interest should be extended to other countries willing to settle high-quality, trade-creating agreements unlike those that are not in the national interest, such as extending the duration of foreign copyright in a PTA that does not offer obvious economic benefits to Australia (Emerson 2010).

Governments, for good reason, are therefore hesitant in negotiating service barriers (either preferentially or non-preferentially) that could constrain their ability to design and implement regulatory norms that maximize national welfare; "standard" mercantilist bargaining may not do much to support significant exchange of liberalization commitments as countries are reluctant to make commitments in trade agreements or to expand on existing ones (Francois and Hoekman 2010). Indeed, negotiating "behind-the-border" regulatory services measures as the basis for setting domestic policy would be undesirable and would likely lead to sub-optimal measures, as other countries demand reforms that are not in the country's own best economic interests; such reform is best done unilaterally away from the negotiating arena (Dee and Findlay 2007a). Since services are highly differentiated, removing all discrimination against all foreigners multilaterally may not ensure that the full benefits from opening service markets will be realized as domestic service suppliers will remain "too pricey" if still penalized by domestic regulatory distortions (Dee 2009).[28]

One area where piecemeal trade reforms in services through PTAs can worsen members' economic welfare relates to the scope for preference-induced trade diversion. The frequent claim that such negative effects are unlikely when liberalizing trade barriers in services, since there is no foregone tariff revenue, is incorrect. Preferential rent-creating measures can divert rents both overseas and between trading partners and thus have similar economic effects to the redistribution of tariff revenue (Dee and Findlay 2007b). For example, allowing foreign equity by a firm from a PTA partner in a domestic monopoly protected by non-discriminatory market access barriers would have negligible efficiency effects, and would reduce economic welfare by transferring rents overseas. Similarly, PTAs diverting investment in services from more efficient suppliers in non-PTA countries to investors in PTA partners may transfer rents between countries and reduce the economic welfare of the host economy. Welfare losses from allowing preferential foreign ownership of a domestic monopolist can be ongoing, especially for services with high sunk costs, where first-mover advantages can be significant, such that the economic costs of preferentially attracting an inefficient supplier can be long lasting (Mattoo and Fink 2002, Bosworth and Trewin 2009). In other words, access liberalization (i.e.

---

[28] These outcomes may be substantial (Dee 2007). Maintaining such regulatory impediments on domestic suppliers while opening to foreign competition may actually worsen resource allocation by causing the already too small sector to shrink further (Dee 2009, Dee, Hardin and Holmes 2000).

abolition of quotas on the number of participants) should be accompanied by equity liberalization (i.e. allowing greater foreign equity).

Preferential liberalization of services will not necessarily enhance welfare, and where it does the effects will be small relative to non-preferential unilateral liberalization. Most economists and policy makers would agree that global unilateral liberalization or multilateral trade liberalization on an MFN basis is the ultimate objective, and that anything else, such as PTAs, reflects a "second best" policy choice (CIE 2010). While trade agreements are best limited to removing discriminatory policies, in practice the "benign neglect" of domestic regulation implies no assurances that liberalization will increase national welfare or raise export opportunities for firms; trade negotiators are not concerned with the adequacy of national regulation and enforcement institutions, or the need for international regulatory cooperation where there are regulatory externalities (Hoekman and Mattoo 2011).

9.5 AUSTRALIA'S EXPERIENCE WITH PTAS ON SERVICES

The economic benefits of Australian PTAs, all of which cover services, have generally been oversold (PC 2010). They have only modestly increased Australia's national income, with only limited impacts on reducing trade barriers and meeting other policy objectives. Australia would have been better served in sustaining strong economic performance as a multilaterally free trading economy, strongly focused on removing impediments to domestic economic efficiency, than by contributing to the scramble for FTAs, even in an increasingly fractured international trade environment (Garnaut 2003).

PTAs covering services have been supported in Australia for two main reasons. First, they are seen as a means for Australia to open overseas markets to advantage exporters (offensive), or to prevent them being disadvantaged by diversion to exporters in third markets with preferential access (defensive). Second, PTAs are seen as a means of liberalizing Australia's barriers to services trade and of "locking in" domestic reforms. While domestic liberalization produces most economic gains to Australia, the first reason usually attracts most attention from trade negotiators and other PTA supporters. While appearing separate reasons, they are really intertwined since PTAs inadequately opening Australia's services market are also unlikely to successfully open export markets, and vice versa. This is an inevitable outcome given the mercantilism approach to trade negotiations, whereby all governments negotiate by trying to gain maximum concessions from trading partners while giving as little market opening in return as possible.

Many services influencing the international competitiveness of Australian businesses are associated with significant network externalities (e.g. transport services; electricity, gas and water, postal services and telecommunications). However, as already indicated, these are the least suited to negotiated liberalization, including preferentially. PTAs are not well-suited to addressing "behind-the-border" barriers (e.g. good governance, competition policy and domestic regulations more broadly); these can be better achieved through bilateral cooperative and regional mechanisms, such as those of APEC (Treasury 2010).

9.5.1 Impact on Overseas Liberalization

Australia's PTAs, which cover services, have had only limited success in reducing barriers and opening up new opportunities, and are instead more likely to bind existing levels of openness (DFAT 2010a). However, research on Australian PTAs has shown that even though they may in some cases have gone beyond other countries' multilateral commitments, they have resulted in negligible actual liberalization. While it is generally acknowledged that the GATS – with few exceptions, such as in telecommunications and commitments of certain countries negotiating WTO accession – has performed little actual liberalization, PTAs suffer to a greater degree from the same weaknesses (Bosworth and Trewin 2009). PTA developments in the Asia-Pacific region, where unilateral liberalization abroad had benefited Australia substantially through regional growth and export demand, marked the end of unilateralism, and removed the political basis driving such reforms (Garnaut 2010b). Since APEC's Bogor objectives of free and open trade and investment by 2020 (developed economies) and 2010 (developing economies) are expressed in non-discriminatory terms, the focus on PTAs of APEC economies and the associated drift away from unilateralism have threatened these goals.

The value of international legal bindings is overstated, especially in services, where substantial "binding overhang" exists and sectoral coverage of bound commitments is low. Bindings per se do not prevent de-liberalization but rather the best insurance against backsliding, although imperfect, are successful unilateral reforms themselves by establishing market and economic conditions that make such backsliding poor economic policy. Australia generally refrained from introducing protectionist measures in response to the Global Financial Crisis, even though it could have under its PTA (and WTO) commitments. It did so for unilateral economic reasons, believing that to unwind, even temporarily, its successful trade and investment liberalization policies would only "shoot itself in the foot". The nature of services barriers also makes many of them politically and economically irreversible once liberalized (e.g. Mode 3 liberalization allowing foreign entities to become established domestically). According to ASR, its members place no significant value on reducing binding overhang in trade agreements, a view supported by the Global Services Coalition.[29]

Policy reforms based on sound domestic unilateral economic analysis are likely to be more sustainable than those introduced simply to meet international commitments.[30] For a start, they are self-enforcing and do not rely on other trading partners taking dispute settlement action, which they may not be in a position to do given a lack of knowledge of the measures being adopted, or may simply choose not to challenge for other, including broader political and commercial, reasons. Moreover, any such challenges can become protracted and complex, thus making dispute settlement a poor enforcer against bad, especially "temporary", economic policies. Relying on dispute settlement challenges by trading partners to avoid policy backsliding also suffers from the fundamental weakness that good trade legal decisions (including within the WTO) are not necessarily good economic policy outcomes, and can lead a country losing such cases to implement equally bad or even worse trade policies that are legally consistent.[31]

---

[29] Personal email from ASR, 22 June 2011.

[30] If the domestic unilateral support to maintain open measures is lost then it is implausible to think that internationally bound legal commitments, either in PTAs or the GATS, will prevent policy backsliding. At best it will only encourage governments to think imaginatively to develop restrictive measures that are consistent with international commitments, which may be more distorting and non-transparent than the inconsistent measures. Moreover, in the case of PTAs, it is also likely to encourage countries to target restrictive measures against non-preferential trading nations, thus increasing discrimination. It has been estimated, for example, that crisis import restrictions taken in response to the Global Financial Crisis significantly reduced affected trade flows by 5% from border measures and 7% from "behind-the-border" measures, such as unconventional types of protectionism like non-tariff barriers, discriminatory purchasing policies, bailouts, and domestic subsidies (Henn and McDonald 2011). Negotiated commitments, including in PTAs, do not seem to have put a brake on the re-introduction of protectionist measures, and it certainly does not follow that these commitments effectively prevented more backsliding. It seems incongruous to believe that PTAs which played a negligible role in liberalization to begin with could somehow effectively prevent de-liberalization.

[31] Of course, unilateralism policy making should be a major pre-requisite to any government's decision to defend a dispute settlement case. There is little or no value in a government legally defending a trade restrictive policy if it is a bad measure economically, and hence once established it would be better to unilaterally reform it.

Substantial "binding overhang" exists in service commitments, both multilaterally and within PTAs, especially in positive list agreements. For example, services trade in APEC economies is freer than reflected in GATS and PTA commitments (DFAT 2010b). Services commitments in the GATS and PTAs of ASEAN members are also well known to lag actual practice considerably (Stephenson and Nikomborirak 2002). Hence plenty of room exists to introduce more restrictive measures, and there is no hard evidence that "binding overhang" has been substantially reduced under PTAs.[32] Moreover, there is no formula approach (as for tariffs) to ensure "binding overhang" is reduced over time; indeed it may increase if countries' commitments lag their unilateral trade liberalization measures.

The significant "binding overhang" is due to most services liberalization being undertaken unilaterally (Hoekman and Mattoo 2011).[33] The GATS bindings, on average 2.3 times more restrictive than currently applied policies, allow more than a doubling of average restrictiveness levels without breaching commitments.[34] While some PTAs have wider sectoral coverage of services, they do not appear, with a few exceptions, to have induced significant market opening (Hoekman and Mattoo 2011). Alarmingly, and surprisingly, evidence also suggests that many PTAs have less than GATS commitments (i.e. are "GATS-minus"), thus creating non-WTO compatible systems of trade agreements.[35] Australian PTAs contain a few of these (Table 9.1).[36] Moreover, many commitments in PTAs are no better specified than in the GATS, such that they are virtually impossible to interpret.

The PC received little specific evidence in its Study of the private sector significantly benefiting from export openings in services from PTAs, apart from the legal profession. The evidence suggested this resulted more from

---

[32] Even substantially reducing "binding overhang" could be largely redundant if significant binding overhang remains to allow backsliding. Some bindings are so much lower than what is applied that even large changes would have no impact.

[33] Based on a new World Bank database on services trade barriers of 93 economies covering the five sectors of financial services (banking and insurance), telecommunications, retail distribution, transportation, and professional services.

[34] While Doha offers were found to improve GATS commitments by about 10%, offers still remained on average twice as restrictive as actual policies.

[35] OECD research of 56 PTAs in services found that some 80% had some form of GATS-minus commitments in either their horizontal or sectoral sections (Adlung and Morrison 2010).

[36] The motivation for negotiating "GATS-minus" commitments is unclear. It may simply be oversight and/or incompetence on the part of negotiators, facilitated by interpretation problems of relevant GATS provisions and commitments due to inadequate wording and understanding. However, it seems highly likely that in many cases it is intentional (Adlung and Morrison 2010).

direct dialogue between the professions of negotiating countries driven by the need for unilateral reforms to become internationally competitive rather than MRAs within PTAs. Australia's PTA agenda has been of limited actual value in improving the business environment for enhanced trade and investment in services (ASR 2011 and Box 9.5). The much used mantra that bindings on services in PTAs (and the WTO) significantly encourage FDI by reducing uncertainty and promoting investor confidence is difficult to believe, and unsupported empirically. The risks to Australia of including investor-state dispute settlement (ISDS) clauses, present in almost all of Australia's PTAs with the notable exception of AUSFTA, were found by the PC to outweigh the possible benefits, and that such provisions granting foreign investors in Australia greater substantive or procedural rights than enjoyed by Australian investors should be excluded from PTAs (PC 2010).

Other evidence indicated that, while some Australian firms had benefited from PTAs, they: (a) were generally skeptical of the extent of these benefits, and saw them as at best marginal; (b) did not appear to have significantly improved market access to promoted PTA partners, even though they saw them as good places to do business when choosing markets; (c) were disappointed as high business expectations and optimism at the time of negotiating PTAs dissipated quickly as achievements dwindled, and (d) had been helped far more by "practical trade facilitation measures" (e.g. Export Market Development Grants) (PC 2010).

This limited use by business of the opportunities from Australia's PTAs also reflected that the main factors relevant to decisions on doing businesses overseas (e.g. domestic regulations, infrastructure) were outside their scope. Other approaches were seen as more cost-effective (e.g. separate MRAs, bilateral investment treaties, and less diversion-prone open regionalism, such as APEC, which has led to the introduction of cost-effective initiatives that facilitate trade, such as the APEC Business Travel Card). While reforms to services in PTAs may cover barriers in a range of services industries, the benefits obtained depend in large measure on the subsequent uptake of opportunities by business, which in turn will depend largely on the extent to which the services barriers addressed in the PTAs are important for facilitating commerce (PC 2010). The experience is that, in PTAs with developing country partners, services and investment liberalization is not proving any easier to negotiate one-on-one than in the multilateral context, and that there is little interest in further pursuing PTAs as currently constructed, with calls instead for a new suite of bilateral instruments focused on policy and regulatory microeconomic dialogue (ASR Box 4, Drake-Brockman 2003).

MRAs in PTAs can lead to arrangements that are indeed preferential, not MFN-like (Heydon 2010). In professional services, the removal of barriers to export has been best achieved through direct negotiation with stakeholders in the relevant jurisdictions rather than through PTAs which are weak in this area, with arrangements using terms like "enhance cooperation in terms of mutual recognition (ASEAN AFAS)" (PC 2010).[37] Singapore, for example, imports medical skills using lists of acceptable qualifications, developed by its professional medical bodies completely outside of PTAs and, while shared standards reduce trade costs, this may be achieved by countries unilaterally adopting recognized international standards (Dee 2007). Opening is not the same as having common standards which may not make sense in some situations, for example when the PTA partners are at quite different stages of development. Substantial trade facilitation may be required before common standards and associated aspects can be meaningfully introduced. Thus unilateral reforms to implement good domestic policies are essential to services becoming internationally competitive (Bosworth and Trewin 2009).

It is frequently argued that Australia must negotiate PTAs for defensive reasons to ensure that exporters do not face exports being diverted from third markets by non-Australian exporters receiving preferential access. However, it does not automatically follow that PTAs designed to protect defensive interests should be pursued; like all trade agreements they should first be subject to an assessment of their likely national benefits to ensure that the gains from securing access for one or a few sectors are not outweighed by losses in others (PC 2010). For example, while a PTA that opens up an export market for Australia's less efficient services benefits those exporters, this would be inconsistent with Australia's national welfare if more efficient services did not achieve the same opening. Also, the potential negative impacts upon Australia from not being involved in PTAs with major trading partners can be ameliorated by unilateral (trade and broader domestic) reforms to improve competitiveness (PC 2010). Australian unilateral trade-related reforms best safeguard export interests by permanently improving competitiveness of all exporters to all countries, including to new and emerging markets and for new services. Moreover, unilateral reforms have the added benefit of improving competitiveness of domestic firms competing with imports and of goods with embodied services.

---

[37] While PTAs may on occasion weakly direct industry groups to engage in negotiating PTAs, as indicated elsewhere in this chapter, MRAs are best left out of the PTA negotiations to minimize potential discrimination.

9.5.2 Impact on Domestic Liberalization

Australian PTAs have not significantly advanced Australia's services liberalization, and in a few significant cases have resulted in Australia preferentially liberalizing measures when non-discriminatory unilateral liberalization was required (PC 2010, and Table 9.1). The main case was preferentially providing US investors higher investment screening thresholds under AUSFTA.[38] Despite being granted from 2005, these have not been either multilaterally extended in Doha offers or applied unilaterally, but have been subject to negotiations with China and Japan under PTA negotiations. Preferential thresholds make no economic sense and risk diverting investment to less efficient US investors that detracts from Australian welfare, thus making it highly ambiguous whether these PTA developments are in Australia's economic interests. Doubt exists as to the practical significance of these higher thresholds given Australia's liberal FDI regime and that the screening thresholds have only stopped FDI projects a few times on national interest grounds, which questions why such measures were negotiated; another example of insignificant outcomes being negotiated in PTAs while meaningful policy measures (such as unilaterally increasing or preferably removing these thresholds) are put aside. Alternatively, if higher thresholds are significantly beneficial to US investors it means that the welfare-reducing risks for Australia are greater. While Australia should multilateralize these PTA preferences, in reality this has not happened as they have become "negotiating coin" in future PTAs. Australia has recently extended the higher US investment screening thresholds preferentially to New Zealand as well, in return for its investors' receiving higher thresholds.[39]

The need for unilateral reforms, especially in services, while allowing governments to maintain sovereignty and control over policy, requires improved transparency in domestic policy making and its likely effects. Domestic institutions that highlight the economy-wide impacts of policy decisions would help (PC 2010).

Indeed, Australia moving from traditional unilateral liberalization to

---

[38] Foreigners must in advance notify if acquiring an interest of 15% or more in an Australian business valued above A$231 million or for US investors A$1,005 million, except in the prescribed sensitive sectors of mainly media; telecommunications; and transport (including airports, port facilities, rail infrastructure, international and domestic aviation and shipping services provided within, or to and from, Australia).

[39] ANZCERTA contained no investment provisions until the Investment Protocol was signed under the ANZCERTA umbrella in February 2011.

a bilateral agreement opens up the possibility that domestic gains from its own liberalization may be eroded by imports being diverted to a higher-cost source. Australia's traditional non-discriminatory approach to protection and its (unilateral) liberalization has to date largely ensured that we used the lowest-cost sources of imports – as well as having the benefits of administrative simplicity and avoidance of international frictions (Banks 2010a).

9.5.3 Joint Feasibility Studies on Gains from PTAs Found Wanting

The effects of Australia's PTAs, including on investment and services, were likely to have been small, and their economic benefits to Australia oversold (PC 2010). Overselling started with DFAT's commissioning of "independent" joint feasibility studies on proposed Australian PTAs to quantify, using economic modeling, the economic benefits to both countries. The PC criticized this broad institutional mechanism formed out of PTA negotiations. Such ex ante studies lacked transparency and tended to highlight "outer envelope guestimates" based on complete liberalization, which bore little resemblance to what was eventually negotiated. Most of these studies did not cover all the costs (many of which are hard or impossible to reliably quantify) and lacked objectivity. While done by credible "independent" economic consultants, their highly constraining commissioning and oversight by DFAT compromised the consultants' objectivity and tarnished the results. The risks are heightened given that the mere commissioning of such a study itself usually signals the trade minister's and government's support for the PTA. There has been no case of a proposed Australian PTA being abandoned, especially based on an ex ante study finding insufficient economic benefits. No study, not even those involving little trade or facing barriers that have never been or likely to be overcome in a trade agreement, have shown anything but extreme "outer" envelope positive estimates of the economic benefits.[40] The approach used to conduct feasibility studies for most Australian PTAs produced overly optimistic expectations of their likely economic effects, and provided an inadequate basis for assessing their merits (PC 2010).

Moreover, Australian taxpayers have had to incur the cost of "absurdly hypothetical" computable general equilibrium studies on the gains from so-called free trade agreements (Emerson 2010). These studies, commissioned

---

[40] A renowned Australian economist said at the time that a DFAT-commissioned modeling study quantifying the economic benefits of AUSFTA "did not even pass the laugh test" (Garnaut 2004).

by advocates of particular bilateral trade deals, will inevitably report enormous potential gains to both countries; modelers are handed the assumptions by government officials and produce the results sought in a process best described as an expensive farce designed to hoodwink the public (Emerson 2010). More independent modeling of the impact of PTAs, such as that undertaken by Dee for an Australian Senate inquiry into PTAs, has been useful in raising public concerns about the overselling of the benefits of Australian PTAs (Dee 2004).

9.5.4 Impact on Regional Integration

Apart from with Chile and the US, Australia's PTAs are regionally focused, especially within Asia and New Zealand. However, PTAs, being discriminatory, are likely to work against regional integration, especially whenever the region is defined more broadly than the PTA, or when there are several PTAs within the region. The old adage that "who you do not invite for dinner can be just as important as who you do" suggests PTAs can work against regional integration. Empirical evidence suggests that larger regional and non-preferential agreements have had a greater trade-creating impact (for both members and non-members) and thus have greater potential to contribute to broader regional integration, such as the APEC (PC 2010). Moreover, Australia's economic success relies on obtaining the most efficient integration, whether regional or global. There is no reason for policy to favor one over the other.

Integration differs from liberalization, and the later should be the focus of trade policy since it is what primarily generates economic benefits to Australia. Integration is the by-product. Non-discriminatory liberalization will itself promote the most efficient degree and form of integration Australia should have with its trading partners, which will differ across products, partners and regions. Discriminatory liberalization to promote pre-determined degrees and forms of integration with certain selected trading partners, based on Government's views, will create inefficient integration from Australia's economic perspective. Unless regional integration is defined or interpreted to mean a customs union or economic union, the term has no practical meaning for setting Australian trade policy. But Australia's PTA negotiations are not predicated as such, so that talking about integration in the context of its PTAs makes little economic sense. Moreover, the term "integration" has greater policy relevance at the global rather than the regional level since efficiency, specialization and pursuing comparative advantage are global issues requiring global supply chains. Regional integration at the expense of global integration would be a poor trade-off for Australia.

There is little compelling evidence that PTAs have helped Australia integrate regionally. Indeed, by selecting certain Asian neighbors to participate in PTAs, we have explicitly ranked our relationships, such that politically we may have diverted attention away from other Asian neighbors. Just as important, there is no indication from the Asian perspective that such PTAs have fostered their regional integration, including with Australia. Trade policy in Asia is currently very unbalanced, relying too much on weak and partial FTAs which will not liberalize where it matters and thus not be a driving force for regional or global integration (Bosworth and Trewin 2009). With few exceptions, Asian FTAs are too 'trade-light' to change existing national practice in a liberalizing or trade-facilitating direction (e.g. in respect of professions via MRAs). Clearly, they have not proved to be a force for regional integration; nevertheless, as Sally (2010) argues, PTA proponents claim that they are stepping-stones to wider regional-integration initiatives. The barriers that exist today, and the treatment of sensitive sectors, will continue to prove a stumbling block for PTAs to yield regional integration, and it is pie-in-the-sky ("psychedelic cloud-nine politics") to expect very large group cooperation to produce a strong, clean, comprehensive PTA in Asia, at least not for a long time to come. As Sally (2010) also states, it will take Herculean policy making to account for the many differences spread across so many bilateral and plurilateral PTAs, and fold them into a sensible regional PTA. Rather the result is likely to be a very low common denominator – another trade-light PTA, adding to (not subtracting from) an expanding noodle bowl and distracting attention from further unilateral liberalization and domestic reforms . . . That will probably hinder, not help, the cause of regional economic integration, with the emerging hub-and-spoke pattern of dirty PTAs threatening to contribute to regional disintegration (Sally 2008 and 2010).

9.6 ADVANCING SERVICES LIBERALIZATION

Unilateral reform is the most direct means for reducing Australia's trade and investment barriers; pursuit of PTAs can create incentives to delay unilateral reforms and entail administrative and compliance costs (PC 2010). The PC recommended Australia examine further unilateral reductions in trade and investment barriers as a priority rather than pursuing liberalization through PTAs, and not delay such beneficial reforms in order to retain "negotiating coin" (PC 2010). PTAs are not a substitute for properly designed strategies for economic reform. However, they are limited in the policy changes they can drive to encourage and stimulate programs to address "behind-the-border" barriers to facilitate a more open and transparent business environment (BCA 2010).

Of particular significance since PTAs are often associated with the pursuit of non-economic objectives, such as strategic alliances, these objectives can typically be addressed more effectively by other means; PTAs are generally not the ideal means for advancing non-economic interests in their own right (PC 2010). Governments should only use PTAs for non-economic purposes if they know the alternatives to be more costly, and have a clear notion of what is an unacceptable price to pay for achieving these non-economic goals.[41]

Because the big gains in services are from reforming non-discriminatory, anti-competitive measures affecting both domestic and foreign suppliers, services reforms are best handled domestically where the political economy considerations principally pit incumbents against new entrants, and not domestic versus foreign (Dee and Findlay 2007a and 2007b). The main risks to reform are to focus too much on national treatment, which typically happens in both regional and multilateral trade negotiations (Dee and Findlay 2007a and 2007b). The steps in sensible unilateral reform are: (i) transparency, (ii) review and evaluation, and (iii) domestic reform (Dee and Findlay 2007a and 2007b).

9.6.1 The Value of Domestic Transparency in Reforming Services

Transparency is a vital first step in any trade-related reforms. Even knowing the full array of a country's trade-related barriers, including at the state or provincial level, is a major achievement, let alone analyzing their effects and disentangling these from protectionism and legitimate outcomes.

Governments should be encouraged to develop institutions which highlight the economy-wide impacts of policy decisions (ANZBLE 2010). Since protectionism results from decisions taken by governments at home, for domestic reasons, any response must therefore begin at home, and bring into public view the domestic consequences of those decisions by creating domestic transparency arrangements in individual countries to provide public information about the economy-wide costs of domestic protection to counter the powerful influence protected domestic interests exercise over national trade policies. Australia is one of very few developed countries to have substantially liberalized its industry protection regime unilaterally, outside the conventional concession-swapping milieu favored by other countries (Banks 2010b). The PC has been an important

---

[41] On a similar point it is also worth bearing in mind that WTO-plus PTAs are not necessarily better, such as in their coverage of core labor standards and overly strict IPR protection (Heydon 2010).

part of the institutional architecture for regulatory reform in Australia and provides a model with many features that could usefully be emulated overseas (OECD 2010).[42] The WTO has also noted the important contribution the PC and its predecessors have made to domestic transparency and Australian trade-related reforms (WTO 2007). Developing countries would also seem to have much to gain from greater domestic transparency in trade-related policy formulation, especially linked into the institutional policy-setting framework as in Australia (independently funded think-tanks with sufficient policy formulation input may also play an effective role, especially where public institutions can be starved of funds or commissioned inquiries to avoid domestic transparency of sensitive issues). Institutions and processes within government played a crucial role in the Australian reform successes, with virtually every major reform in the past Reform Era preceded by public review processes that were commissioned by but conducted at arm's length from government (Banks 2010b). Since unilateralism is fundamental to setting trade policy, including liberalizing services, improving domestic transparency and associated institutional arrangements is essential. Without it, review and domestic trade reform is unlikely to be complete – transparency is the key.

9.7 AUSTRALIA'S "BACK TO THE FUTURE" TRADE POLICY, INCLUDING ON SERVICES

In response to the 2010 PC Study, the previous Government released through the Minister of Trade a new Trade Policy Statement in April 2011, urging for a return to past successful unilateral reforms and less reliance on traditional PTAs (DFAT 2011).[43] Significantly, the Government accepted almost all of the PC's recommendations (Box 9.7 and Appendix 9.1).

Consistent with the fundamental objective of trade policy to increase

---

[42] While few, if any countries, have replicated the PC, New Zealand established its own Productivity Commission in early 2011.

[43] This followed an earlier visionary address by Trade Minister Emerson to the Lowy Institute (Emerson 2010). He was previously Microeconomic and Trade Policy Adviser to then Prime Minister Hawke. The Government's Statement rejected entirely the minority opinion of the external Associate Commissioner appointed for the Study, an experienced trade lawyer and former US Trade negotiator and Deputy Director of the WTO. The minority opinion disagreed with most of the PC's recommendations, supporting analysis and findings, and was carefully considered by the PC in reaching its conclusions and recommendations (PC 2010). The minority opinion was very sympathetic to DFAT's support of PTAs as contained in its two submissions to the Study.

BOX 9.7 PC STUDY ON THE IMPACT OF BILATERAL AND REGIONAL TRADE AGREEMENTS (BRTAS) ON TRADE AND INVESTMENT BARRIERS AND AUSTRALIA'S TRADE AND ECONOMIC PERFORMANCE

The terms of reference required the PC to:

- examine the evidence that BRTAs have contributed to reducing trade and investment barriers, and to what extent they are suited to tackling them, including in the context of the proliferation of BRTAs between other countries;
- examine the evidence that BRTAs have safeguarded against the introduction of new barriers, and the potential for trade discrimination against Australian businesses without full engagement in the evolving network of BRTAs;
- consider the role of BRTAs in lending support to the international trading system and the WTO;
- analyze the potential for BRTAs to facilitate global economic adjustment and to promote regional integration;
- assess the impact of BRTAs on Australia's trade and economic performance, in particular on trade flows, unilateral reform, behind-the-border barriers, investment returns and productivity growth;
- assess the scope for Australia's BRTAs to reduce trade and investment barriers of trading partners or to promote their structural reform and productivity growth, and consider options for doing so; and
- assess if BRTAs can evolve to deliver extra benefits, including via review provisions and built-in agendas.

The study was made within the context that, while it is widely acknowledged that the benefits of trade liberalization are greatest if it is undertaken multilaterally, the Doha Round has proven elusive, with many countries seeking more quickly realizable outcomes through BRTAs. Many countries have also used them to promote broader economic integration and serve foreign policy and strategic interests. BRTAs have thus emerged as part of the global policy landscape. The WTO estimates that close to 400 free trade agreements will be in force globally by 2010. Their proliferation poses many challenges for Australia and for the global trading system, including the risk of trade diversion depending on their nature. Non-parties can be disadvantaged by preferences offered under BRTAs.

The Australian Government is committed to reinforcing the primacy of the multilateral trading system and resisting any rise in global protectionist measures. Australia has pursued BRTAs intended to support the multilateral trading system, while also enhancing commercial opportunities between Australian and overseas businesses along with Australia's broader economic, foreign and security policy interests. Australia has signed a number of BRTAs and is in the process of negotiating, or considering, several others.

Against this background, the PC was requested to advise on the effectiveness of BRTAs in responding to national and global economic and trade developments, and in contributing to efforts to boost Australia's engagement in the region and evolving regional economic architecture.

Source: PC (2010).

national prosperity, the Statement re-set Australian trade policy based on five guiding principles, namely unilateralism; non-discrimination; separation; transparency; and the grand unifying principle of trade policy as an indivisible part of overall economic reform (Box 9.8). The Statement also indicated that Australia in future would no longer seek the inclusion of investor-state dispute resolution procedures in PTAs with developing countries, and that the Government would not support PTA provisions that constrained Australia's ability to regulate legitimately on social, environmental or other similar important public policy matters.

While in parts the commendable Statement is unclear, and even contradictory, it sees PTAs as a continuing priority, provided they meet the WTO benchmarks or are "high quality, truly liberalizing trade deals that support global trade liberalization", which will be offered to all of its trading partners (DFAT 2011).[44] However, the operational meaning of

---

[44] Since the Trade Policy Statement was released, the Government announced the launching of FTA negotiations with India in May based on achieving a

BOX 9.8 PRINCIPLES GUIDING AUSTRALIA'S TRADE POLICY

Unilateralism: Pursue pro-competitive economic reform in its own right by further opening the economy to trade and investment and avoid adopting a bargaining-chip approach of refusing to liberalize unless trade partners offer similar openings as a *quid pro quo*. In PTAs, negotiations will be assessed according to national interest, excluding considerations of how Australia had to give up, or "pay", by way of domestic economic reform. Presumably such an assessment of national interest from PTAs will be based on what actual liberalizing impact the PTA will have both in Australia and in the trading partner, and not simply on the basis of "on paper" commitments which may result in no economic gains.

Non-discrimination: Will help address the proliferation of PTAs which have MFN treatment more the exception than the rule; non-discriminatory trade agreements offer better long-run returns for Australia. Future PTAs will not insist on entrenching preferential treatment, just an opportunity to compete on level terms.

Separation: Clearly separate trade and foreign policies, which had deliberately become entangled since the late 1990s. This would presumably mean dispensing with so-called "economic diplomacy".[45] Australia will consider negotiating a PTA with any country genuinely interested in reducing its trade barriers and will only sign it if it is demonstrably in Australia's national interest. It will not allow foreign policy or geo-political considerations to dictate to parties and on the content of trade deals.

Transparency: Rather than possibly misleading decision makers and the public by modeling hypothetical PTAs based on assumptions of full liberalization, including on services and

high-quality, truly liberalizing trade deal that supported the multilateral trading system (Emerson 2011).

[45] Separation of political from economic diplomacy has been increasingly made more difficult by having trade and foreign affairs handled by the one department (DFAT), even though with two ministers.

investment, only final or actual arrangements negotiated will be modeled, and be independently peer reviewed.[46]

Indivisibility of trade policy and economic reform: Trade policy and microeconomic policy are as one; the best trade policy is domestic economic reform – a productivity-raising, competitiveness-enhancing microeconomic reform program supported by responsible fiscal policy.

Source: DFAT 2011.

this is unknown. It should imply ensuring that any future PTAs in services are genuinely liberalizing both in Australia and overseas with respect to liberalizing actual measures restricting trade in services, and that simply achieving more commitments "on paper", especially with substantial binding overhang, would fail the test. The benchmark in deciding whether a PTA is "truly liberalizing" should not be commitments in other PTAs (or the WTO), but rather whether it is liberalizing "on-the-ground". Moreover, previous trade ministers have echoed similar views, yet in reality the PTAs concluded by Australia have fallen well short of these standards. Of greater government priority than concluding new PTAs would be to ensure that current PTAs are improved to satisfy these standards.[47] However, this in itself is likely to threaten additional economic risks of setting domestic policies affecting services based not on sound unilateral microeconomic outcomes but rather on negotiating expediencies.

---

[46] However, there is some confusion between this statement in the text of the Trade Policy Statement and the Summary of the Government's Responses to the PC Recommendations included in the Statement (Appendix 9.1). The Summary indicates that the Government only partly agreed with the PC's recommendations on economic modeling, stating that while an assessment of the benefits of any proposed PTA should be transparent and credible, over-reliance on highly abstract quantitative analysis can be very misleading. It also rejected the PC recommendation that the Government should commission and publish an independent and transparent assessment of the final text of the agreement at the conclusion of negotiations but before an agreement is signed, stating instead, the obvious, that quantitative analysis can be highly misleading, with modeling conclusions heavily dependent on simplifying assumptions.

[47] The Australian Treasury also recently expressed policy concerns over Australia's growing PTA proliferation, including in services. It highlighted that PTAs were not meeting Australian needs, their proliferation had not built support for multilateralism, and that they had delivered only modest preferential market access outcomes at the cost of reduced policy reform flexibility (Treasury 2010).

Re-focusing Australian trade policy on unilateralism will be enormously challenging as the Government steers its negotiating agenda on a middle course of championing the multilateral system while seeking to negotiate high-quality, truly liberalizing sectoral, bilateral and regional trade deals that do not detract from multilateralism. Restoring Australia's trade reform culture and integrity of the policy-setting processes based on independent transparent analysis and transparency will be essential (Garnaut 2010a and Garnaut 2010b). PTAs are arguably the most non-transparent aspect of Australian trade policy. The PC plays no role in their negotiation, evaluation or assessment, and its recent study was the first requested by the Government, some seven years after it adopted the policy of concluding PTAs. It is unbelievable that the PC was not first consulted on this policy change, the most significant departure in Australian trade policy in the past two decades. Decisions on ratification of PTAs will continue to be made in the political arena by the Joint Standing Committee on Treaties, which is only usually after the Treaty has been signed when it is too late to make changes (Mitchell and Voon 2009).[48]

Australian trade departments and minister, as elsewhere, are not generally major players or advocates for unilateral reforms. Instead they tend to be preoccupied, given their mandate and responsibilities, with the external dimensions of trade policy, namely trade negotiations in Geneva and especially regional capitals, given the proliferation of PTAs, including on services. Trade departments are paradoxically often major obstacles to liberalization in many countries, especially developing countries. Thus, an essential step in promoting unilateral reforms, especially in services, is to develop a strong domestic reform base that enables trade policy to be mainstreamed into domestic economic policy, including in services. This is unlikely to happen while trade departments, inherently mercantilist by design and nature and strong supporters of negotiated liberalization, are left to set trade policy.[49] Setting trade policy to reflect domestic considerations requires strong policy input from departments responsible for

---

48 In Australia the executive branch of government negotiates and enters international treaties which the legislative branch then implements by enacting the needed legislation to "transform" the treaty provisions into domestic law.

49 Negotiated liberalization, whether preferential or multilateral, is the "bread and butter" of trade officials (and ministers) and hence is likely to be their preoccupation rather than non-negotiated (unilateral) liberalization, which may not be seen to be in their own self-interest. Also, trade departments rarely have the economic expertise required to lead a domestic agenda based on unilateral economic trade-related reform, and hence should not be expected to play a major, but rather a facilitating, role.

domestic economic policy, such as reinvigorating the Treasury's resolve to champion microeconomic, including trade-related reforms and gaining strong support from top political leaders, underpinned by domestic transparency. This is despite recent assurances from DFAT and others that Australia's PTAs are among the world's most comprehensive, being at least as comprehensive as those negotiated between other industrialized countries and, on average, much more comprehensive than those negotiated between developing countries in terms of coverage of sectors, commitments and rules (Mortimer 2008). While this may be so, they have been no more successful in promoting real liberalization.[50]

Steering a strong unilateral reform agenda, including in services, as called for in the Trade Policy Statement, will require the Government to re-focus efforts on microeconomic impediments currently undermining productivity growth. Matching the Statement's objectives with actual policy reforms will necessitate a unilateral reform agenda being developed and implemented. However, this has not emerged yet, and so it remains very unclear as to the previous Government's unilateral reform priorities. Indeed, as time passes it seems that the Statement's call for a return to unilateralism and a re-balancing of trade policies away from discrimination has had little, if any, impact (see footnote 2).

9.7.1 The Trans-Pacific Partnership Agreement (TPP)

According to its 2011 Trade Policy Statement, the Government will continue to champion the Asia Pacific Economic Cooperation (APEC) as a proven effective grouping for trade liberalization in the region. It supports the longer-term aspiration by APEC members to form a Free Trade Area of the Asia-Pacific (FTAAP) among themselves, which the Government sees as a logical extension of APEC's Bogor Goals. The Government's highest regional trade negotiation priority is the conclusion of the TPPA, as one possible, and the most advanced, pathway to a FTAAP.

However, the FTAAP is not a "logical extension" of APECs Bogor Goals; it is hard to see how forming a discriminatory APEC trade bloc will serve these non-discriminatory goals. Indeed, the Government's claim ignores the advice of its independent advisor that Australia "should give weight, in prioritizing and negotiating agreements, to non-preferential

---

[50] However, the generally acknowledged failure of Australia's PTAs to promote genuine liberalization, especially in services, and the PC's report, along with the Government's Policy Response, clearly indicates the emptiness, and indeed irrelevance, of such claims.

arrangements such as APEC, and to non-preferential provisions within other agreements (PC 2010). Initially, Australia as the instigator of APEC, along with some other members, fought hard to ensure that it would not become a myopic trade bloc that discriminated against and sought to divert economic activity away from others. Its shining light was "open regionalism" based on "concerted unilateralism" – members acting voluntarily and unilaterally to reduce trade and investment obstacles on a most favored nation (MFN) basis to grant non-APEC economies the same access. The Bogor Goals reinforced APEC, with members agreeing to voluntarily achieve "free and open trade and investment" by 2010 (developed) and 2020 (developing). Despite its weaknesses, including falling well short on meeting these goals for developed economies, APEC was contributing significantly to non-discriminatory regional trade and investment. The US, reluctant to embrace unilateralism, insisting instead on reciprocal trade deals, always favored a discriminatory APEC FTA trade bloc that would exclude non-APEC economies from any access benefits.

Two decades on, the US is getting its way in APEC as most economies, including Australia, jettison the MFN principle and rush to form discriminatory FTAs. APEC is now being subtly recast as an FTA trade bloc, the FTAAP, along traditional US lines. The TPPA between the APEC economies of Australia, Brunei, Chile, Malaysia, New Zealand, Peru, Singapore, US, Vietnam and probably Canada, Japan and Mexico might be the first installment. However, some APEC economies, most notably China, one of the world's cheapest suppliers, may never join the TPPA, as many of the provisions insisted upon by the main TPPA driver, the US, make such membership increasingly difficult; hence what such a discriminatory agreement will be worth in a liberalizing sense is highly questionable (Bhagwati 2012). Australia should oppose the TPPA/FTAAP for the same reasons it initially rejected APEC preferentialism. While the TPP/FTAAP may suit the US's political and trade agenda, it is not in the economic interests of the region, APEC or Australia.

First, the TPP/FTAAP would be retreating to discrimination. The FTA label is deceptive. FTAs are really "Preferential Trade Agreements" and have about as much in common with free trade as a thoroughbred race horse has with a donkey.

Second, Australia and the APEC region already have a growing noodle bowl of overlapping FTAs, and the TPP would simply compound this mess, for example it would be Australia's third FTA involving Singapore.

Third, it would further demean the non-discriminatory Bogor Goals, already fudged to support discrimination.

Just how pursuing the TPP/FTAAP could ever be reconciled with the previous Government's five praiseworthy guiding principles of its Trade Policy Statement for setting Australian trade policy is a mystery.

9.8 CONCLUSIONS

Australia's pre-occupation with PTAs in the past decade has come at a substantial economic cost to the economy (PC 2010). PTAs in services have disappointed in achieving both economic and non-economic objectives. They have not been truly liberalizing, either in Australia or in trading partners, being concerned with negotiating commitments "on paper" rather than policy reforms "on-the-ground". Trade policy is not the same as trade negotiations, and these do not generally set trade measures; these are generally a "side-show" to policy formulation which can easily become the "main show", as is the case in Australia. While it is commonly suggested that PTAs may provide a useful focal point for countries to strengthen institutions and adopt legal reform, international evidence of this happening is weak. Australian PTAs have certainly not led to such outcomes, either in Australia or in its partners to such agreements.

On the non-economic front (e.g. strategic alliances or other foreign policy matters), such objectives can be better met outside PTAs. In services, they have not led to better regulations, regional public goods like joint institutions or better performance, such as in relation to MRAs. They have been associated with derailing Australia's highly successful unilateral approach to trade-related reforms based on sound domestic transparency and economic analysis, led by the PC (and its predecessors) and other domestic economic reform departments, especially the Treasury. The re-ascendancy of DFAT as the main setter of trade policy has seen a strong move away from unilateralism to negotiated forms of trade liberalization, especially PTAs, given the almost certain failure of the Doha multilateral negotiations. It is thus vital for Australia's productivity growth, which has suffered in recent years due largely to lack of essential microeconomic, including trade-related reforms, especially affecting services, to get back on track and to focus renewed attention on unilateralism. This is the only effective means of reforming services given their complex nature as barriers to trade that are usually embedded in domestic regulation. PTAs are even less well-equipped than the WTO to reforming the service barriers that really matter when it comes to achieving improvements in national welfare, namely market access barriers that raise costs and rents, thus also distorting resource-use efficiency as well as effectively reducing productivity, rather than discriminatory national treatment measures which are mainly the concern of trade negotiators.

Summing up, PTAs in services have to date been a major distraction from what really matters: reforming Australia's barriers to trade in services, which as for goods is the main source of economic gains to the country, as opposed to bargaining to have other trading partners open their markets. Australian PTAs (and the GATS) have achieved little in contributing to real liberalization, which is just as well since such negotiated actual outcomes would more than likely result in inefficient measures, such as discriminatory ones, or in regulations that may not be welfare-enhancing for Australia. Because of the complexity of reforming services trade barriers, it is unrealistic (and undesirable) for such policies to be set at the negotiating table.

Australia's trade policy should return to unilateralism and non-discrimination as the main reform approaches, which will probably have implications for Australia's reliance on PTAs, including in services. This unfortunately involves "re-inventing the wheel" and developing again a domestic appetite for unilaterally reforming Australia's barriers to imported services, and ensuring that negotiated forms of liberalization, especially PTAs, do not divert or delay them by holding back "negotiating coin". However, uncertainty still surrounds the role to be played by PTAs in Australian trade policy and, as time passes, reform efforts have not yet matched the rhetoric. Australia will still negotiate PTAs that are "high quality, truly liberalizing" of trade, but similar past policy objectives failed to crystallize as Australian PTAs clearly failed the test. The correct interpretation of this test should be actual liberalization of measures, and not simply so-called liberalized commitments "on paper", especially if they contain substantial binding overhang.

Trade policy in Australia is very unbalanced, relying too much on weak and partial "trade-light" PTAs which have not liberalized where it matters. Such agreements have thus not been a driving force in regional or global integration. This is despite repeated assurances by trade officials and others with vested interests in saying so that Australia's PTAs are of world-best standard and among the most comprehensive. A return to a focus on unilateral liberalization, hopefully supported by a more active multilateral system, is required to advance trade in services liberalization and reforms. PTAs should be recognized for what they are – failures to achieve genuine liberalization and a distraction for policy makers and governments from what really counts. PTAs are not an end in themselves, nor a means to what the real end should be in all countries, namely promoting unilateral trade-related reforms as part of transparent and evidence-based microeconomic or structural policies. Based on sound economic reasoning and the Australian experience, PTAs cannot genuinely liberalize services trade. They generate outcomes that reflect mainly negotiating expediencies rather than what would be sound economic reform (e.g. enhanced discrimination or non-transparent changes that may not correctly reflect the national economic interest). At a time when Australian PTA activity is at its highest, Australia's unilateral commitment is at its lowest. Unilateralism is always likely to be undermined as long as PTAs "rule the policy roost", which is also likely to contribute to ensuring a doomed Doha outcome that is beyond rescue – a true prediction even if many cannot accept it, which still is true despite the meek Bali outcomes in December 2013.

REFERENCES

Adlung, R. and M. Molinuevo (2008), "Bilateralism in Services Trade: Is there Fire Behind the (BIT-) Smoke?", Staff Working Paper ERSD-2008–1, WTO, Geneva, January.

Adlung, R. and P. Morrison (2010), "Less than the GATS: 'Negative Preferences' in Regional Services Agreements", *Journal of International Economic Law*, 13(4): 1103–43.

Australian and New Zealand Business Leaders and Economists (ANZBLE) (2010), "Joint Submission to the Productivity Commission's Study on Bilateral and Regional Trade Agreements", No. 5, Canberra, 4 February.

Australian Services Roundtable (ASR) (2008), "Securing Australia's Place in the Global Economy", Submission to the Mortimer Review of Export Policies and Programs, Canberra, July.

Australian Services Roundtable (ASR) (2011), "Trade Review is Blueprint for Needed Productivity Growth", Media Release, Canberra, 12 April.

Banks, G. (2013), "Forward" in M. Adams, N. Brown and R. Wicks, "Trading Nation, advancing Australia's interests in world markets", UNSW Press, Sydney.

Banks, G. (2010a), "An Economy-wide View: Speeches on Structural Reform", Productivity Commission, Melbourne, March.

Banks, G. (2010b), "Successful Reform: Past Lessons, Future Challenges", Keynote address given by the chairman of the Productivity Commission to the Annual Forecasting Conference of the Australian Business Economists, Sydney, 8 December, available at: http://www.pc.gov.au/__data/assets/pdf_file/0018/104229/successful-reform.pdf.

Bhagwati, J.N. (2012), "America's Threat to Trans-Pacific trade", East Asia Forum, 10 January.

Bosworth, M. and R. Trewin (2009), "The Domestic Dynamics of Preferential Services Liberalization: The Experience of Australia and Thailand", in J. Marchetti and M. Roy (eds.), *Opening Markets for Trade in Services: Countries and Sectors in Bilateral and WTO Negotiations*, Cambridge: Cambridge University Press, pp. 663–66.

Business Council of Australia (BCA) (2010), "Submission to the Productivity Commission's Study on Bilateral and Regional Trade Agreements", No. 41, Canberra, 8 April.

Capling, A. (2008), "Preferential Trade Agreements as Instruments of Foreign Policy: An Australia-Japan Free Trade Agreement and its Implications for the Asia Pacific Region', *The Pacific Review*, 21(1): 27–43.
CIE (2000), "Economic Benefits from an AFTA-CER Free Trade Area", Report prepared for the Department of Foreign Affairs and Trade, Canberra.
CIE (2004), "Economic Analysis of AUSFTA: Impact of the Bilateral Free Trade Area", Report prepared for the Department of Foreign Affairs and Trade.
CIE (2009), "Benefits of Trade and Trade Liberalisation", Report prepared for the Department of Foreign Affairs and Trade, Canberra and Sydney, May.
CIE (2010), "Quantifying the Benefits of Services Trade Liberalisation", Report prepared for the Department of Foreign Affairs and Trade, Canberra and Sydney, June.
Clogstoun, R., M. Bosworth and R. Trewin (2006), "Would Emergency Safeguard Measures Work for Services?", *Asia-Pacific Economic Literature*, 20(2).
Commonwealth of Australia (2004), "Senate Select Committee on the Free Trade Agreement between Australia and the United States of America: Final Report", August, Canberra.
Correa, C.M. (2006), "Implications of Bilateral Free Trade Agreements on Access to Medicines", *Bulletin of the World Health Organization*, 84(5).
Deardorf, A., R. Stern and J. Whalley (2007), "Reviving the Doha Round: The Agenda for the Developing Countries" chapter 2 in "Monitoring Trade Policy: A New Agenda for Reviving the Doha Round", Trade Policy Monitoring Paper 1, Trade Policy Monitoring Centre, Keil Institute and Centre for Economic Policy Research, 31 May.
Dee, P. (2004), "The Australia-US Free Trade Agreement: An Assessment", Paper prepared for the Senate Select Committee on the Free Trade Agreement between Australia and the USA, June, Canberra.
Dee, P. (2007), "East Asian Economic Integration and its Impact on Future Growth", *World*
Economy, 30(3): 405–23.
Dee, P. (2009), "What Behind-the-border Reforms in Services and Investment are Best Done Through Trade Agreements?", April, Canberra.
Dee, P. (2010), "Deepening East Asian Integration in Services", ERIA Policy Brief No. 2010–01, October, available at: http://www.eria.org/pdf/ERIA-PB-2010–01.pdf.
Dee, P. and C. Findlay (2007a), "Services: A 'Deal-Maker' in the Doha Round?", chapter 3 in "Monitoring Trade Policy: A New Agenda for Reviving the Doha Round", Trade Policy Monitoring Paper 1, Trade Policy Monitoring Centre, Keil Institute and Centre for Economic Policy Research, 31 May.
Dee, P. and C. Findlay (2007b), "Services in PTAs – Donuts or Holes", April, Canberra.
Dee, P. and K. Hanslow (2000), "Multilateral Liberalization of Services Trade", Productivity Commission Staff Research Paper, Canberra.
Dee, P., A. Hardin and L. Holmes (2000). 'Issues in the Application of CGE Models to Services Trade Liberalization", in C. Findlay and T. Warren (eds.), *Impediments to Trade in Services: Measurement and Policy Implications*, London and New York: Routledge, pp. 267–86.
Department of Foreign Affairs and Trade (DFAT) (2010a), "Submission to the Productivity Commission's Study on Bilateral and Regional Trade Agreements", No. 53, Canberra, April.

Department of Foreign Affairs and Trade (DFAT) (2010b), APEC 2010 Bogor Goals, Canberra, available at: http://www.dfat.gov.au/publications/trade/APEC-2010-Bogor-Goals.pdf.
Department of Foreign Affairs and Trade (DFAT) (2011), "Gillard Government Trade Policy Statement: Trading our Way to More Jobs and Prosperity", Canberra, April.
Drahos, P., B. Lokuge, T.A. Faunce, M. Goddard and D. Henry (2004), "Pharmaceuticals, Intellectual Property and Free Trade: The Case of the US – Australia Free Trade Agreement", *Prometheus*, 22(3): 243–57.
Drake-Brockman, J. (2003), "Bilateral Approaches to Services Trade and Investment Liberalization – WTO Plus or WTO Minus?", Paper delivered at the Conference of Economists, Canberra, 31 September.
Drake-Brockman, J. and C. Findlay (2011), "Waiting till the Cows Come Home: New Routes to Services Reform", 24 January, Canberra, available at: http://www.eastasiaforum.org/2011/01/24/waiting-till-the-cows-come-home-new-routes-to-services-reform/#more-16777.
Elek, A. (2010), "Submission to the Productivity Commission's Study on Bilateral and Regional Trade Agreements", No. 44, Australian National University, Canberra, April.
Emerson, C. (2010), "The Future of Trade Policy in an Uncertain World", Address to the Lowy Institute, 10 December, Sydney, available at: http://www.lowyinstitute.org/Publication.asp?pid=1476.
Emerson, C. (2011), "Australia and India Launch Free Trade Negotiations", Media Release, Canberra, 12 May.
Ferrantino, M. J. (2006), "Policy Anchors: Do Free Trade Agreements And WTO Accessions Serve as Vehicles for Developing-Country Policy Reform?", Working Paper, U.S. International Trade Commission, Washington DC, April.
Fink, C. and M. Molinuevo (2007), "East Asian Free Trade Agreements in Services: Roaring Tigers or Timid Pandas?", East Asia and Pacific Region, Report No. 40175, World Bank, Washington, DC.
Fink, C., and P. Reichenmiller (2005), "Tightening TRIPS: The Intellectual Property Provisions of Recent US Trade Agreements", World Bank Trade Note No. 20, Washington, DC, 2 February.
Francois, J. and B. Hoekman (2010), "Services Trade and Policy", *Journal of Economic Literature*, 48(3) (September): 642–92.
Garnaut, R. (2003), "Requiem for ULDORAMA: A Plain But Useful Life", Canberra, available at: http://www.rossgarnaut.com.au/Documents/Requiem%20for%20Uldorama%20%20CEDA%20Forum,%205%20June%202003.pdf.
Garnaut, R. (2004), "Ross Garnaut says Government's FTA report laughable", AM Transcript, Canberra, 4 May, available at: http://www.abc.net.au/am/content/2004/s1100916.htm.
Garnaut, R. (2010a), "Video Presentation at Session Three: Trade Agreements for Better or Worse: Policy Conclusions", HC Coombs Policy Forum, An opportunity for national consultation on the Draft Report of the Productivity Commission on Bilateral and Regional Trade Agreements, Crawford School of Economics and Government, ANU, Canberra, 13 September.
Garnaut, R. (2010b), "2010 Hamer Oration" The University of Melbourne, Melbourne, 5 August [available at: http://images.theage.com.au/file/2010/08/06/1754673/garnautspeech.pdf].

Gootiiz, S. and A. Mattoo (2009), "Services in Doha: What's on the Table?," *Journal of World Trade*, 43(5): 1013–30.
Henn, C. and B. McDonald (2011), "Protectionist Responses to the Crisis: Damage Observed in Product Level Trade", IMF Working Paper No. WP/11/139, June, Washington, DC, available at: http://www.imf.org/external/pubs/cat/longres.aspx?sk=24975.0.
Heydon, K. (2010), "Submission to the Productivity Commission's Study on Bilateral and Regional Trade Agreements", No. 65, Canberra, July.
Heydon, K. and S. Woolcock (2009), *The Rise of Bilateralism: Comparing American European, and Asian Approaches to Preferential Trade Agreements*, Tokyo: United Nations University Press.
Hoekman, B. (2008), "The General Agreement on Trade in Services: Doomed to Fail? Does it Matter?", Washington, DC, October.
Hoekman, B. and A. Mattoo (2011), "Services Trade Liberalization and Regulatory Reform", Policy Research Working Paper 5517, World Bank, Washington, DC, January.
ITS Global (2010), "Services International Linkages", November, Melbourne, available at: http://www.dfat.gov.au/publications/trade/Services-International-Linkages.pdf.
ITS Global (2011), "Making the Trans Pacific Partnerhsip (TPP) a 21st century trade agreement", ASEAN+3 Trade Reporter, June, Melbourne.
Kwan, M. (2011), "Opening Address at PECC-ADBI Conference on Regional Trade in Services", Director-General of Hong Kong Trade and Industry Department, Hong Kong, China, 2 June.
Marchetti, J. and M. Roy (2008), "Services Liberalization in the WTO and in PTAs", in J. Marchetti and M. Roy (eds.), *Opening Markets for Trade in Services: Countries and Sectors in Bilateral and WTO Negotiations*, Cambridge: Cambridge University Press, pp. 61–112.
Mattoo, A. and C. Fink (2002), "Regional Agreements and Trade in Services", World Bank Policy Research Working Paper No. 2852, June, Washington, DC, available at: http://papers.ssrn.com/sol3/papers.cfm?abstract_id=636216.
Mattoo, A. and P. Sauvé (2010), "The Preferential Liberalization of Services Trade",
NCCR Working Paper No. 2010/13 (May), Bern: World Trade Institute.
Mercurio, B. (2005), "The Impact of the Australia-United States Free Trade Agreement on the Provision of Health Services in Australia", *Whittier Law Review*, 26(4).
Mercurio, B. (2006), "TRIPS-Plus Provisions in FTAs: Recent Trends", in L. Bartels and F. Ortino (eds.), *Regional Trade Agreements and the WTO Legal System*, Oxford: Oxford University Press.
Miroudot, S. (2011), "Global Value Chains and Trade in Services", presentation at the ADBI-UNESCAP/ARNeT International Conference on Selected Outstanding Issues in Services, Trade, and Development, Manila, 3–5 May.
Miroudot, S., J. Sauvage, and B. Shepherd (2010), "Measuring the Cost of International Trade in Services", GEM Working Paper, October 2010, Sciences-Po, Paris.
Mitchell, A., and T. Voon (2009), "Australia-United States Free Trade Agreement", in S. Lester and B. Mercurio (eds.), *Bilateral and Regional Trade Agreements: Case Studies*, Cambridge: Cambridge University Press, pp. 6–43.
Mortimer, D. (2008), "Review of Export Policies and Programs", Canberra.

OECD (2010), "Reviews of Regulatory Reform in Australia: Towards a Seamless National Economy", Paris.
Pacific Economic Cooperation Council (PECC) (2011), "Statement to APEC Ministers Responsible for Trade", Dr. Charles E. Morrison, Co-chair, Big Sky, Montana, 18–19 May.
Productivity Commission (PC) (2005), "Review of National Competition Policy Reforms", Inquiry Report No. 3, 28 February, Canberra.
Productivity Commission (PC) (2010), "Bilateral and Regional Trade Agreements", Final Research Report, November.
Roy, M., J. Marchetti, and H. Lim (2006), "Services Liberalization in the New Generation of Preferential Trade Agreements (PTAs): How Much Further than the GATS?", Economic Research and Statistics Division Staff Working Paper, World Trade Organization, Geneva.
Sally, R. (2008), "New Frontiers in Free Trade: Globalizations Future and Asia's Rising Role", Cato Institute, Washington, DC.
Sally, R. (2010), "Regional Economic Integration in Asia: The Track Record and Prospects", ECIPE Occasional Paper, No. 2/2010, Brussels.
Sauve, P. and A. Shingal (2011), "Reflections on the Preferential Liberalization of Services Trade", NCCR Working Paper No. 2011/05, 9 March.
Stephenson, S. and D. Nikomborirak (2002), "Regional Liberalization of Services", in S. Stephenson, C. Findlay and S. Yi (eds.), *Services Trade Liberalization and Facilitation*, Canberra: Asia Pacific Press, The Australian National University.
Robb, A. (2013), "Positioning Australia for Asia's surge", Minister for Trade and Investment, in "PwC Melbourne InstituteAsialink Index", Melbourne.
Treasury Department (2010), Incoming Government Brief – Red Book – Part 3 revised, 24 September, Canberra, available at: http://www.treasury.gov.au/contentitem.asp?ContentID=1875&NavID=.
Trebeck, D. (2009), "The Getting of Wisdom or Grumpy Old Policy Analysts?", Paper presented to the AGM of the Australian Agricultural and Resource Economics Society, ACT Branch, 8 July, Canberra.
Trewin, R., M. Bosworth, D. Narjoko, A. Mukherjee, A. Stoler, J. Redden, V. Donaldson, and G. Thomson (2008), "East Asian FTAs in Services: Facilitating Free Flow of Services in ASEAN?", Final Report, REPSF II Project No. 07/004, May.
Van Grasstek, C. (2011), "The Political Economy of Services in Regional Trade Agreements", OECD Trade Policy Working Papers, No. 112, available at:. http://dx.doi.org/10.1787/5kgdst6lc344-en.
Verikios, G. and X.-G. Zhang (2001), "Global Gains from Liberalizing Trade in Telecommunications and Financial Services", Productivity Commission Staff Research Paper, AusInfo, Canberra.
World Trade Organization (WTO) (2007), "Trade Policy Review of Australia", Geneva, 1 May.

APPENDIX: GOVERNMENT'S RESPONSES TO PC REPORT AFFECTING SERVICES

Recommendation

Government response

Recommendation 1: Should only pursue bilateral and regional trade agreements (BRTAs) where they are likely to:

- afford significant net economic benefits; and
- be more cost-effective than other options for reducing trade and investment barriers, including alternative forms of bilateral and regional action.

Agreed – consistent with the approach articulated in the Statement.

Recommendation 2: Should ensure that any BRTAs negotiated:

- as far as practicable, avoids discriminatory terms and conditions in favour of arrangements based on non-discriminatory (most-favoured-nation) provisions;
- does not preclude or prejudice similar arrangements with other trading partners; and
- does not establish treaty obligations that could inhibit or delay unilateral, plurilateral or multilateral reform.

Agreed – consistent with the approach articulated in the Statement.

Recommendation 3: Should not include matters in BRTAs that would serve to increase barriers to trade, raise costs or affect established social policies without a comprehensive review of the implications and available options for change.
Agreed – consistent with approach articulated in the Statement.

Recommendation 4: Should improve the scrutiny of the potential impacts of prospective trade agreements, and opportunities to reduce barriers to trade and investment more generally.

a) Should prepare a trade policy strategy which identifies impediments to trade and investment and available opportunities for liberalization, and includes a priority list of trading partners. This trade policy strategy should be reviewed by Cabinet on an annual basis, and be prepared before the pursuit of any further BRTAs. A public version of the Cabinet determined strategy should be released.
b) Before entering negotiations with any particular prospective partner, it should undertake a transparent analysis of the potential impacts of the options for advancing trade policy objectives with the partner. All quantitative analysis and modelling should be overseen by an independent body.

c) It should commission and publish an independent and transparent assessment of the final text of the agreement, at the conclusion of negotiations, but before an agreement is signed.

Agreed in part.
Recommendation 4(a): agreed.
Recommendation 4(b): agreed in part – an assessment of the benefits of a proposed free trade agreement should be transparent and credible. However, over-reliance on highly abstract quantitative analysis can be very misleading.
Recommendation 4(c): not agreed. Quantitative analysis can be highly misleading, with conclusions heavily dependent on simplifying assumptions used in modelling. Agreements will be presented for consideration by the Joint Standing Committee on Treaties before ratification.

Recommendation 5: If it is deemed that capacity building should be part of a trade agreement development process, the Australian Government should fund and deliver capacity building programs in a manner that minimizes potential (or perceived) conflicts of interest. Any such programs should not impose an obligation to negotiate a trade agreement.
Agreed.

Recommendation 6: To enhance transparency and public accountability and enable better decision making regarding the negotiation of trade agreements, the DFAT should publish estimates of the expenditure incurred in negotiating bilateral and regional trade agreements and multilateral trade agreements. These should include estimates for the costs of negotiating recent agreements.
Agreed.

Recommendation 7: Should examine the potential to further reduce existing Australian barriers to trade and investment through unilateral action as a priority over pursuing liberalization in the context of bilateral and regional trade agreements. The Government should not delay beneficial domestic trade liberalization and reform in order to retain 'negotiating coin'.
Agreed – consistent with the approach articulated in the Statement.

Recommendation 8: Should support worthwhile efforts to achieve multilateral liberalization. If meaningful progress within the WTO proves elusive, the Government should weigh up with like-minded countries the feasibility of appropriate broadly based agreements to advance reform.
Agreed – consistent with the approach articulated in the Statement.

Recommendation 9: Should lend support to initiatives directed at the establishment of domestic institutions in key trading countries to provide transparent information and advice on the community-wide impacts of trade, investment and associated policies.
Agreed – consistent with the approach articulated in the Statement.

Source: DFAT 2011.

PART III

Final thoughts

10. Reflections on the nature of preferences in services

Pierre Sauvé and Anirudh Shingal*

10.1 WHAT IS SPECIAL ABOUT SERVICES TRADE?

We consider first the salient features of services trade that distinguish it from trade in goods and have a bearing on the key issues under discussion in this chapter. For starters, and in marked contrast to goods trade, the bulk of services trade involves both trade and factor flows. There are four modes by which services can be supplied internationally and, unlike goods trade, trade in a broad range of services requires the physical proximity (and often simultaneous interaction) of the producer and the consumer for trade to materialize.[1] The characteristics depicted above in turn help explain the nature of restrictions imposed on services trade and thus the means of according preferential treatment on, *inter alia*, the value of services output, the number of service suppliers, the amount of foreign equity permitted, the type of legal structure required for market entry purposes, the technical standards, licensing and qualification requirements applied, as well as the conditions of eligibility for service sector subsidies.

Given the fact that domestic regulation and not border taxation measures in the form of tariffs constitutes the prime negotiating currency in services trade, there are strong grounds to believe that the classic means of estimating the welfare consequences of preferential market opening and distinguishing the trade-creating and trade-diverting properties of PTAs pioneered by Jacob Viner[2] is almost assuredly of lesser analytical relevance in the services field. Given that barriers to services trade are often prohibitive and their removal seldom revenue-generating, and the fact that trade in services is more often constrained by quantitative restrictions than by

* This chapter reproduces in full: Sauvé, Pierre and Anirudh Shingal (2011), "Reflections on the Preferential Liberalization of Services Trade", in Journal of World Trade, Vol. 45, No. 5, pp. 953–63.

[1] This is true of services delivered through Modes 2, 3 and 4.

[2] See Viner (1950).

overtly discriminatory practices, one may reasonably expect that determined efforts at dismantling service sector restrictions will result in lower costs of trade diversion than might be the norm in goods trade where border discrimination remains of paramount importance (in services trade, the border as a constraining device usually matters most for Mode 4 suppliers[3]).

An important caveat to the sanguine conclusion reached above flows from the work of Fink and Mattoo (2002), who noted that the sequence of liberalization may matter more in services than in goods trade. This is because location-specific sunk costs of production often assume considerable importance in several key service sectors, particularly those with infrastructural and/or network properties such as telecommunications, energy distribution, or transportation. In such sectors, even temporarily privileged access for an inferior supplier can translate into durable longer-term market advantages deterring future market contestability.

10.2 IMPLICIT PREFERENCE MARGINS: COUNTRY, SECTORAL AND MODAL PATTERNS

For a number of reasons rooted in the political economy of novelty, regulatory precaution, issue linkages and the greater overall difficulty of reciprocity-based bargaining, the liberalization of services trade under the WTO's General Agreement on Trade in Services (GATS) has yet to register meaningful advances. While the Doha Development Agenda (DDA) will almost certainly harvest some of the far-reaching advances made in opening service markets to competition since the curtain fell on the Uruguay Round, the fact remains that, in most countries, developed and developing, market opening in services has primarily proceeded along unilateral lines. This is especially true of the broad range of producer services (banking, insurance, telecoms, transportation, energy) where opening-up portends significant economy-wide benefits.

For instance, the average level of Mode 3 (commercial presence) access granted unilaterally via recent legislative changes in India is close to 70% in a number of key sectors, much higher than the 10% foreign equity ceiling embedded in India's initial (i.e. Uruguay Round) GATS commitments

---

[3] Mode 4 trade refers to the temporary admission of business people and professionals and other contract-based service suppliers engaged in the cross-border delivery of labour-based services.

and significantly higher than the 44.8% average level of foreign equity put forward in its latest conditional offer in the Doha Round (Gasiorek et al., 2007).

Beyond unilateral liberalization, a growing number of WTO Members have simultaneously turned to PTAs to deepen and quicken the pace of market opening in services markets. More often than not, and particularly when conducted along North-South lines and in agreements that resort to a negative list approach to scheduling market opening undertakings, PTA commitments in services tend to approximate and often lock-in the regulatory status quo flowing from recently enacted unilateral reforms.[4] The result is an increasing gap – indeed a growing implicit margin of preference – between the level of opening obtaining in the WTO and that stemming from preferential advances.

With only a few exceptions (e.g. NAFTA, ANZCERTA),[5] provisions on services trade brokered in PTAs prior to 2000 did not go significantly beyond what was negotiated in the GATS during the Uruguay Round (Hoekman and Sauvé, 1994; Hoekman, 2006). However, in the agreements notified to the WTO since 2000, preferential access accorded to countries in services trade has resulted in what at first sight could be likened to a significant dilution of MFN access privileges. Such a trend appears to hold true across country groupings, modes of supplying services and sectors.

Drawing on the work of Marchetti and Roy (2008), Table 10.1 below compares the average level of commitments scheduled under Modes 1 (cross-border supply) and 3 (commercial presence) by OECD and non-OECD countries under the Uruguay Round, such countries' most recent Doha Round (DDA) offers and their most liberalizing PTA commitments. While the average level of sub-sectors bound in the prevailing GATS schedules is rather low (24% for Mode 1 and 30% for Mode 3), the DDA offers made to date (these are arguably likely to be enhanced depending on the ultimate outcome of Doha Round talks on agriculture and non-agricultural market access) have not altered this landscape markedly.

The market opening value-added of PTAs, on the other hand, appears quite significant. For instance, Mode 1 access in PTAs is twice that in the DDA offers, while Mode 3 market access in PTAs is 1.67 times that in the

---

4 For a fuller discussion of recent trends in services liberalization and rule-making in PTAs, see Mattoo and Sauvé (2010).

5 NAFTA refers to the 1994 North American Free Trade Agreement linking Canada, the United States and Mexico; ANZCERTA is the 1987 Closer Economic Relations Trade Agreement between Australia and New Zealand.

Table 10.1 Comparing the level of services trade and investment liberalization across country groupings and modes of supply

	GATS	DDA Offer (0 to 100)	PTAs	GATS/PTA (%)	DDA/PTA (%)	Preference Margin (%)
Total score	27	34	63	43	54	56–57
Mode 1	24	30	59	41	51	49–59
Mode 3	30	38	67	45	57	43–55
OECD						
Mode 1	43	51	59	73	86	14–27
Mode 3	53	59	67	79	88	12–21
Non-OECD						
Mode 1	18	23	60	30	38	62–70
Mode 3	23	32	67	34	48	52–66

Source: Author calculations based on Marchetti and Roy (2008).

DDA offers. The figures of Marchetti and Roy (2008) suggest that there are significant margins of preference for the two modes of supply which together account for close to 80% of world services trade by value.

While preference margins between DDA offers and "best" PTA commitments are considerably lower for OECD countries (suggesting a higher propensity for the latter countries to lock-in the regulatory *status quo* in their multilateral commitments or offers), the gap is much starker in the case of non-OECD countries. For the latter, the level of bound Mode 1 access in PTAs is some 2.5 times greater than in their latest DDA offers, while Mode 3 access in PTAs is roughly twice that on offer in the DDA.

Much the same picture obtains at the sectoral level. On the basis of the most liberalizing commitments in PTAs in Modes 1 and 3 reviewed by Marchetti and Roy (2008), Table 10.2 compares services liberalization undertaken across the sectors listed in the Central Product Classification of the GATS. Using an index that ranks scheduled commitments on a scale from 1 to 100, Marchetti and Roy show how PTAs have gone beyond both GATS commitments and the latest DDA offers across the full range of service sectors. This includes both sectors that have attracted less commitments and DDA offers under the GATS – for example, postal-courier, distribution or environmental services – as well as those that have generally proven more attractive in a multilateral setting – such as computer or tourism services.

Interestingly, the two sectors with the lowest implicit preference margins are financial and telecommunication services, both of which

Table 10.2 Comparing the level of services trade liberalization across sectors

Sectors	GATS	DDA Offers (0 to 100)	PTAs	GATS/PTAs (%)	DDA/PTAs (%)	Preference Margin
Professional	30	39	67	45	58	42–55
Computer	55	74	93	59	80	20–41
Postal/Courier	14	20	53	26	38	62–74
Telecoms	51	58	80	64	73	28–36
Audio-visual	17	20	50	34	40	60–66
Construction	40	46	75	53	61	39–47
Distribution	32	41	76	42	54	46–58
Education	18	25	57	32	44	56–68
Environmental	20	30	62	32	48	52–68
Financial	36	40	53	68	75	25–32
Health	8	11	34	24	32	68–76
Tourism	51	61	83	61	73	27–39
Maritime	12	23	57	21	40	60–79
Rail	14	20	52	27	38	62–73
Road	16	18	56	29	32	68–71
Aux. Transport	21	24	58	36	41	59–64

Source: Author calculations based on Marchetti and Roy (2008).

were negotiated on a stand-alone, limited reciprocity, basis in the over-time negotiations that followed the completion of the Uruguay Round.[6] Both also happened to be priority sectors for dominant OECD countries (especially the United States and the European Union, whose negotiating leverage in the Uruguay Round's overtime negotiations between 1994 and 1997 was significant).

Meanwhile, the large margins of preference (i.e. the much greater level of PTA liberalization relative to the GATS or the latest DDA offer) that characterize sectors such as audio-visual, transport (all modes), health or education services need to be understood in the context of highly specific sectoral narratives. These defy easy generalizations. For instance, marked preferential progress in audio-visual services relates almost solely to the PTAs to which the United States is a party and the fact that, confronted

[6] The Uruguay Round's overtime negotiations in services also featured rapidly stillborn talks on maritime transport and Mode 4 trade, suggesting that sector- or modal-specific dynamics may, alongside constraints on reciprocal bargaining, play a key role in explaining the level of observed liberalization advances in services trade.

with "veto players"[7] in the WTO, the US has simply decided to assign greater prominence to PTA market opening efforts in the sector relative to the WTO.

In the case of transportation services, preferential advances most likely reflect gravity-related considerations as countries that share contiguous borders are significantly likelier to engage in deeper forms of trade-facilitating logistics cooperation across more transport modes than is feasible at the multilateral level. Seen this way, margins of preference in both of the above sectors may not shrink (i.e. be eroded) as much as in other sectors where genuine multilateral advances appear more feasible, such as in the area of environmental services.

10.3 MORE (OR LESS) THAN MEETS THE EYE? HOW "PREFERENTIAL" IS PREFERENTIAL LIBERALIZATION IN SERVICES TRADE?

Tables 10.1 and 10.2 above reveal a landscape of significant contrast in liberalization dynamics between multilateral and preferential (bilateral or regional) settings. Looking at the ever-present gulf between the latest DDA offers and PTAs, one might be tempted to draw sombre conclusions about the continuing relevance of the WTO as a meaningful theatre of services trade liberalization. Yet how alarmed should one be by the scale of the implicit margins of preference in services trade depicted above?

The very rationale behind a PTA is the quest for (positive) discrimination – granting to one's preferred partner what one may not be willing or prepared to accord to third country partners. Yet it may prove arduous, including in enforcement terms, if not impossible, to effect the opening of some services sectors or modes of supplying services on a preferential basis.

For a start, given that, as noted earlier, the very currency of services negotiations consists of domestic regulation,[8] the removal and/or reduction of most regulatory hurdles to market access and national treatment will tend *de facto* to proceed on a most favoured nation (MFN) treatment basis. In part, this may simply reflect practical feasibility considerations. In many regulatory settings, particularly in resource-poor environments, this may reflect weak enforcement capacity and indeed a recognition

7 A "veto player" is an individual or collective actor who has to agree to a change in the legislative (or negotiating) status quo. See Tsebelis (2002).

8 See Mattoo and Sauvé (2003).

that maintaining parallel regulatory regimes – one for insiders, another for third country suppliers – may result in undue regulatory compliance and/or enforcement costs. As an example, the number of partners in Indian accountancy firms is restricted to 20. If such a restriction were to be relaxed, it would be extremely difficult in practice to limit it to preferential suppliers. Similarly, much prudential regulation in financial markets or regulation targeting consumer or environmental protection concerns cannot meaningfully be applied in a preferential or discriminatory manner. In such cases, *de jure* preferential regulation (and hence access) becomes *de facto* MFN regulation and access.

One important caveat to the *de facto* multilateralization of regulatory concessions depicted above is that, even if all regulations ultimately apply to all suppliers, there may be first-mover advantages for the preferred partner in the form of incumbency advantages which could operate to the detriment of both suppliers from excluded countries and home country users or consumers. Preferential access to a services supplier could initially be in terms of market access, national treatment and/or regulatory requirements (e.g. licensing conditions). As noted earlier, these can translate into significant privileges in the domestic market once the foreign supplier has established a presence in it. As an example, one may think of a retail chain opening an outlet as part of a preferential agreement in a hitherto closed market. Such preferential market access could afford an incumbent significant advantages in terms of captive domestic clients and resources – access to land, labour, capital, entrepreneurship – and knowledge and use of the supply chain. These benefits may be sufficient to give it a competitive advantage even if it is inferior to more competitive suppliers from excluded countries. Such incumbency advantages could thus exert durably adverse welfare consequences relative to MFN-based liberalization under the GATS, leaving the host country stuck with weaker providers even when it subsequently liberalizes on an MFN basis.

The policy stance countries adopt with respect to service sector rules of origin (via so-called "denial of benefits" clauses) may offer an important means of addressing the risks described above.[9] As in goods trade, the restrictiveness of agreed rules of origin will determine the extent to which non-members can benefit from trade or investment preferences. The multilateral disciplines of the GATS, embedded in Article V.6, help to promote pro-competitive market outcomes by requiring that

---

[9] For a fuller discussion of the economics and law of rules of origin in services trade, see Beviglia-Zampetti and Sauvé (2006) and Miroudot et al. (2010).

North-North and North-South PTAs (over 60% of notified PTAs and, more importantly, among PTA partners whose aggregate share of world services trade is far greater) adopt the most liberal rule of origin – i.e. the substantial business operations test, whereby any third country investor carrying out substantial business activities in the territory of a party to a PTA must be treated like an investor from any PTA party. Under such circumstances, *de jure* PTA preferences become *de facto* multilateral commitments, a not insignificant development when one considers that Mode 3 is both the most important form of services trade (accounting for close to two-thirds of services trade) and, most importantly, that against which the greatest share of commitments (over 60%) are typically scheduled in all negotiating settings.

WTO disciplines are not, however, unambiguously virtuous, as GATS Article V.3(b) affords parties to South-South PTAs the right to adopt a more restrictive rule of origin and deny the benefits of integration to third country investors that are not owned or controlled by juridical persons of a PTA party. Many South-South PTAs – for instance MERCOSUR, ASEAN or the Andean Pact – have made use of the policy space on offer, with effects in terms of FDI attractiveness and overall developmental terms that are worthy of debate (to the extent that such restrictions are effectively enforced).

Thinking beyond Mode 3, it is unlikely that PTA partners may meaningfully enforce preferences applied to the growing volume of cross-border digital transactions (Mode 1 trade). Here again, feasibility issues suggest the convergence between *de jure* preferences and *de facto* multilateralized outcomes. Meanwhile, the question of rules of origin appears largely moot in regard to Mode 2 trade (consumption abroad), as few countries would seek to be overtly selective in discriminating in favour (or against) the consumption decisions of foreign consumers.

As a practical matter, it would appear that, as with goods trade, rules of origin in services trade assume importance only where the border matters as a tangible reality defining the possibility of market access. This is most obviously the case of Mode 4 trade, where service providers must physically cross a border in order to ply their trade internationally. Not surprisingly, rules of origin applied to Mode 4 suppliers rank among the most restrictive of all, with PTA benefits typically limited to citizens or permanent residents of PTA partners. However, it bears recalling that such restrictions affect a mode of supply that accounts for less than 5% of aggregate services trade.

10.4 MULTILATERALIZING SERVICES PREFERENCES

PTAs are here to stay and have become a mainstay of modern economic diplomacy. They offer a number of benefits, potential and real, that heighten their attractiveness to governments and business constituencies concerned by the liberalization and reform agendas in services markets. This includes their heightened expediency (relative to the WTO), the greater ease with which they allow negotiating agendas rich in behind-the-border challenges to be addressed and lead to trade-facilitating regulatory convergence, the scope they offer (with markedly contrasting take-up) for novel advances in rule-making, particularly in areas of WTO blockage, etc.

There is generally little debate over the fact that services PTAs offer economic welfare gains relative to the *status quo ex ante*. One cannot however deny that the gains from multilateral liberalization are likely to be larger as MFN-based competition is unbiased and the first-mover advantages of possibly second-best service providers are thwarted. To the extent that WTO Members undertake enhanced liberalizing commitments across a broad array of services sectors and modes of delivery at the end of the Doha Round, PTA-induced preferences will be automatically eroded, even if not fully. However, given lingering uncertainties on the ultimate fate of the DDA and the continued strong push towards PTAs of all types (North-North, North-South, South-South, bilateral, regional, trans-regional), the best alternative is perhaps to seek practical means of multilateralizing service sector preferences.

This chapter has argued that one may be generally sanguine that the potential downsides of preferential liberalization may be less ominous or feasible in services trade. This is so even as the margins of preference implicit in many recent PTAs appear significant when compared with existing GATS commitments or the (still very partial) signals emanating from DDA liberalization offers.

Preferences in services may be more theoretical than real for a number of reasons. This includes, first and foremost, practical concerns over the very enforceability of preferences rooted in what are often non-discriminatory domestic regulatory regimes. With regard to rules of origin, it is also a direct result of multilateral rule-design insofar as the most statistically meaningful sample of PTAs and PTA partners is concerned (i.e. PTAs with a partner from the North) in the predominant mode of supplying services (i.e. Mode 3).

In contemplating the scope that may exist to multilateralize preferential advances, greater use could be made of the disciplines on recognition found in GATS Article VII on Recognition.[10] Article VII.2 of GATS states that "members of a mutual recognition arrangement (MRA) shall provide adequate opportunity for other interested excluded countries to negotiate their accession to such an arrangement or to negotiate comparable arrangements". Article VII.4(b) further states that "such arrangements should be notified to the Council for Trade in Services well in advance of the start of negotiations to enable interested third parties to join these negotiations before they enter a substantive phase". Finally, Article VII.5 states that "wherever appropriate, recognition should be based on multilaterally agreed criteria".

Significantly, however, the above provisions have not enticed WTO Members to extend MRA benefits to third country suppliers to the extent that they have chosen to notify these under the "closed" integration provisions of Article V of the GATS which does not afford non-members an opportunity to accede to such an MRA. One means to multilateralize bilateral or plurilateral MRAs would be to make it mandatory for their members to notify them under Article VII of the GATS. An alternative would be to constrain eligibility for MRAs pursued under Article V solely to PTAs that share contiguous borders or a common geographical space, given that geographical proximity is more likely than not to be associated with higher levels of regulatory cooperation, including in matters of recognition and labour market cooperation. Under such rules, MRAs concluded among geographically distant countries (i.e. trans-regional PTAs) would need to be notified under the "open regionalism" provisions of Article VII.2 GATS.

Mattoo and Sauvé (2010) have suggested another possibility wherein PTA members could be required to pre-commit to future multilateral liberalization by signaling a precise time-frame over which preferential treatment would be progressively eroded and/or eliminated. An alternative to the above prescription would once again proceed along geographical proximity lines, by allowing parties to PTAs among contiguous or geographically proximate (i.e. forming a common geographical space) partners to dismantle preferences at a slightly lower pace. Such differentiated treatment could vary by level of development of PTA partners. It could,

---

[10] Recognition is the act of recognizing the education or experience of a foreign service provider for the purpose of meeting the domestic country's authorization, licensing or certification requirements and is especially important in the case of trade in professional services. Such recognition can be accorded autonomously or can be embedded in an arrangement or agreement with the interested country(ies) – the latter takes the form of a Mutual Recognition Agreement (MRA).

for instance, be limited solely to South-South PTAs in a manner analogous to the rule of origin provisions foreseen under Article V.3(b) GATS.

PTA rules of origin affecting Mode 4 suppliers should also be relaxed such that residents of a party (subject potentially to a six-month to one-year prior residency rule so as to avoid abuse), and not solely permanent residents or citizens, could enjoy temporary entry privileges within an integration area.

Finally, preferential services agreements adopting the most liberal denial of benefits provisions could be showcased as "best practice" agreements against which existing accords could be modified and/or future accords negotiated. Alternatively, WTO Members could be encouraged to agree to a set of voluntary best-practice/pro-multilateralization guidelines directed at those contemplating preferential liberalization and rule-making in services and against which existing accords could be modified and future accords negotiated.

REFERENCES

Beviglia-Zampetti, Americo and Pierre Sauvé (2006), "Rules of Origin for Services: Economic and Legal Considerations", in Estevadeordal, Antoni et al., eds., *The Origin of Goods: Rules of Origin in Regional Trade Agreements*, Oxford: Oxford University Press, pp. 114–45.

Fink, Carsten and Aaditya Mattoo (2002), "Regional Agreements and Trade in Services: Policy Issues", World Bank Policy Research Working Paper No. 2852 (June).

Gasiorek, Michael, Peter Holmes, Sherman Robinson, Jim Rollo and Anirudh Shingal (2007), "Qualitative Analysis of a Potential Free Trade Agreement between the European Union and India", the European Commission and CARIS, Department of Economics, University of Sussex, UK, (February), available at: http://trade.ec.europa.eu/doclib/docs/2007/june/tradoc_135101.pdf.

Hoekman, Bernard (2006), "Liberalizing Trade in Services: A Survey", World Bank Policy Research, Working Paper No. 4030.

Hoekman, Bernard and Pierre Sauvé (1994), "Regional and Multilateral Liberalization of Trade in Services: Complements or Substitutes?", *Journal of Common Market Studies*, 32, 283–317.

Marchetti, Juan and Martin Roy (2008), "Services Liberalization in the WTO and in PTAs", in Marchetti, J. and M. Roy, eds., *Opening Markets for Trade in Services: Countries and Sectors in Bilateral and WTO Negotiations*, Cambridge: Cambridge University Press, pp. 61–112.

Mattoo, Aaditya and Pierre Sauvé (2003), *Domestic Regulation and Services Trade Liberalization*, Washington, DC: Oxford University Press for the World Bank.

Mattoo, Aaditya and Pierre Sauvé (2010), "The Preferential Liberalization of Services Trade", NCCR Working Paper No. 2010/13 (May),

Bern: World Trade Institute, http://www.nccr- trade.org/publication/the-preferential-liberalization-of-services-trade-lessons-from-practice/.

Miroudot, Sébastien, Jehan Sauvage and Marie Sudreau (2010), "Multilateralising Regionalism: How Preferential are Services Commitments in Regional Trade Agreements?", OECD Trade Policy Working Paper No. 106 (December), Paris: OECD Trade and Agriculture Directorate, http://www.oecd/org/trade.

Tsebelis, George (2002), *Veto Players: How Political Institutions Work*, Princeton: Princeton University Press.

Viner, Jacob (1950), *The Customs Union Issue*, New York: Carnegie Endowment for International Peace.

11. A plurilateral agenda for services? Assessing the case for a Trade in Services Agreement (TISA)

Pierre Sauvé[1]

11.1 INTRODUCTION

On 15 February 2013, the European Commission formally proposed (in a submission to the European Council) opening negotiations on a new international agreement on trade in services. Initially called the International Services Agreement (ISA), the proposed plurilateral treaty currently involves a self-selected coalition of 23 WTO Members belonging to the so-called Really Good Friends of Services (RGFS) grouping.[2] It has since been re- named the Trade in Services Agreement (TISA). The RGFS aims for the agreement to comply with WTO rules so it can be "multilateralized" at a later stage.[3] The Commission's initiative[4] came on the heels of a similar process launched a few weeks earlier by the Obama administration in the United States.[5]

This chapter advances a set of conflicting thoughts on the proposed

[1] A preliminary version of this chapter was presented at the European Parliament's Committee on International Trade on 26 March 2013. The author is grateful for discussions with and comments from Sherry Stephenson, Jane Drake-Brockman, Rudolf Adlung, Stephen Woolcock, Guy de Jonquières, Malcolm Bosworth, Gary Hufbauer, Bernard Hoekman, Crawford Falconer and Pasquale de Micco. Email: pierre.sauve@wti.org.

[2] The RGFS grouping currently involved in the TISA talks includes the following WTO Members: Australia, Canada, Chile, Chinese Taipei, Colombia, Costa Rica, the European Union, Hong Kong, Iceland, Israel, Japan, Liechtenstein, Mexico, New Zealand, Norway, Pakistan, Panama, Paraguay, Peru, South Korea, Switzerland, Turkey and the United States. China and Uruguay have most recently made known their intention to join the TISA negotiations.

[3] See Hufbauer et al. (2012) for an early depiction of the plurilateral agreement's main aims.

[4] See European Commission (2013).

[5] See World Trade Report (2013).

TISA. Bruised veterans of services trade negotiations, including the author of these lines, are logically prone to applauding the sight of forward movement in an area of trade governance whose potential for growth and development, as a source of vibrant export growth and as a means of durably facilitating the entry of firms, big and small, into global value chains, mercifully no longer require much convincing. It was not always thus! This is so even as the full potential of services trade remains fiendishly difficult to harness in a negotiating setting, and particularly so at the multilateral level.

Still, based on the limited information available on the TISA negotiations to date, one may harbor a number of genuine doubts on the journey proposed, it's likely value-added and the potentially damaging collateral effects it could yet exert on the WTO's ongoing services negotiations under the General Agreement on Trade in Services (GATS) and, more broadly, on the centrality of the WTO as a locus of trade governance. Simply put: if TISA holds considerable promise as a potentially innovative preferential services trade agreement pursued under the aegis of Article V (Economic Integration) of the GATS, the prospects for its eventual incorporation into the WTO architecture seem significantly less compelling for reasons, both procedural and substantive, that this chapter aims to explore.

11.2 RECALLING THE STARTING POINT

As the GATS approaches its twentieth birthday, it bears recalling that it remains to this day the sole piece of the Uruguay Round jigsaw that has yet to be solved, with leftover negotiations pending in core areas of services rule-making such as subsidy or procurement disciplines, non-discriminatory regulatory conduct or emergency safeguard measures.

That the Uruguay Round is not yet completed in services even as the Doha Round languishes in the twelfth year of its own tortured journey says a lot both about the inherent complexity of services rule-making and the difficulty of harnessing the forces of reciprocity in markets subject to a dense layer of domestic regulation, the political economy of which is often dauntingly intractable.

The Uruguay Round's negotiating harvest in services was a mere (and meek) down payment, richer on rules (even if incomplete) than on market opening commitments. The GATS was and remains the product of a first encounter towards which protagonists displayed the natural collective caution typically associated with novel endeavors. Confronted with what was largely a blank page – a frightening sight for any policy official – early GATS negotiators had little choice but to tread lightly in what was essentially uncharted negotiating or rule-making terrain.

Yet, in a world that has witnessed a highly service-centric technological revolution of unprecedented magnitude since the curtain fell on the Uruguay Round, one can readily appreciate the unease that flows, most palpably in corporate circles, from playing services with yesterday's rulebook. That is, with the weak, incomplete, rules and the limited, regulatory precaution-laden, pre-internet, commitments of 1994.

In seeking the right epithet to characterize two and half decades' worth of efforts at prying open services markets, frustration probably ranks among the most apposite. The very currency of services negotiations consisting of domestic regulatory measures, dismantling the trade- and investment-impeding measures that lie chiefly behind borders, implies that services talks are wholly akin to negotiations on non-tariff barriers. This is in essence a slow, ponderous, process. Proof of the above can be seen from the relative ease with which WTO Members completed the 1996 International Technology Agreement (ITA), a critical mass, MFN-based, tariff-dismantling sectoral deal, compared with the continuing difficulties and definitional quagmires they have subsequently confronted in trying to dismantle the broad range of non-tariff measures inhibiting cross-border trade in IT products.

Meanwhile, those areas of services trade where the border retains crucial salience – transport and labor movement for instance – are precisely the ones where market opening gains have been least impressive, including in the generally more liberalization-friendly confines of preferential trade agreements (PTAs).

Frustration over the glacial pace of multilateral market opening and over the inability of services to gain adequate traction in the Doha Development Agenda (DDA) equation alongside agriculture and non-agricultural market access (NAMA) has prompted a large and growing number of WTO Members to turn to PTAs as the chief vehicle to advance their services agendas and harvest the proceeds of far-reaching unilateral liberalization. To date, 118 such agreements have been notified to the WTO, a number of which have achieved significant WTO+ and WTO-X[6] advances in the services field.[7] TISA looks set to become the latest, and most important, such agreement.

---

[6] The terms WTO+ and WTO-X were first coined by Horn et al. (2008) and refer to rules or market access commitments that go further than or involve a qualitative deepening over existing WTO rules or commitments (WTO+) or represent novel advances not yet found in the WTO (WTO-X).

[7] ACTA is the acronym for Anti-Counterfeiting Trade Agreement, which aimed unsuccessfully to establish an international legal framework for targeting counterfeit goods, generic medicines and copyright infringement on the internet.

11.3 TISA: A PLURILATERAL AGREEMENT OR AN ARTICLE V PTA?

A first question to raise in regard to TISA concerns its constitutional DNA. A negotiating process currently associating a coalition of 23 willing WTO Members (counting the EU-27 as one), TISA is unquestionably plurilateral in character. But it is plurilateral in the sense of the North American Free Trade Agreement (NAFTA) or of the Association of South-East Asian Nations' ASEAN Framework Agreement on Services (AFAS), not in that of the WTO-embedded Government Procurement Agreement (GPA). This, as it happens, is a non-trivial distinction.

The above distinction matters to the extent that TISA proponents have repeatedly affirmed the hope of seeing the Agreement's subsequent multilateralization or, alternatively, its anchoring in the WTO in the manner of the GPA. Yet the fact that the negotiations currently proceed:

(i) without the formal ascent of the broader WTO membership;
(ii) in Geneva but wholly outside the WTO's perimeter;
(iii) at arm's length from the WTO secretariat (despite the professed desire of TISA protagonists to see the WTO become the Agreement's ultimate custodian);
(iv) among the RGFS grouping but without currently allowing for third country (and WTO Secretariat) observership (i.e. as a closed club),

are all suggestive of a potentially difficult migratory journey.

Rather than opening the TISA doors wide and affording all WTO Members an opportunity to sit in and observe the negotiations in a transparent manner, determine where their interests lie in the deal on offer, allow those expressing a readiness to join (i.e. to move beyond mere observership towards active participation) the negotiations to contribute to shaping the Agreement's substantive texture and ultimately decide whether to opt-in or opt-out of the negotiated outcome, the TISA has to date operated as a closed club. That being the case, the recent history of trade multilateralism is strongly suggestive that this could be a major handicap from the perspective of any future WTO anchoring.

Indeed, for those old enough to have an institutional memory in these matters, such a process recalls the stillborn "Fu-Lung" Group, the

---

It would have created a new governing body outside existing intellectual property forums, such as the WIPO, the WTO or the UN. The Agreement's fate was sealed when the European Parliament voted overwhelmingly against its provisions in July 2012.

name of the Chinese restaurant in Geneva where secretive discussions on financial services among G-10 central bankers and finance ministries (comprising the G-7 nations as well as Australia, the Netherlands and Switzerland) took place in the Uruguay Round's early days and which eventually led to the drafting of the Understanding on Commitments in Financial Services to which not a single non-OECD country signed up by the Round's end.

The club mindset of TISA also recalls the failed quest for a "state of the art" Multilateral Agreement on Investment pursued in the mid-1990s at the Organisation for Economic Co-operation and Development (OECD), yet another "us against them/build it and they'll beg to join" construct whose all too predictable failure contributed in no small measure to the WTO's subsequent inability to complete its own legislative arsenal by embedding a comprehensive set of investment rules under the so-called "Singapore Issues" agenda. More recently still, the failure of ACTA[8] in the area of intellectual property enforcement shared a number of procedural similarities with TISA.

The longer the TISA negotiating process retains its current closed shop mindset, the weaker will be the agreement's perceived multilateral legitimacy and the dimmer its prospects for later WTO anchoring. Such procedural opaqueness paradoxically affords key reluctant players a ready-made excuse to justify their non participation in talks where genuine openness might help dampen conspiratorial instincts and prompt much needed proactive engagement on their part

Things look distinctively different if one looks at TISA as a WTO-sanctioned construct. At the end of the day, the most probable outcome will be to see TISA emerge as a preferential agreement on services proceeding on the basis of GATS Article V. Under WTO rules, WTO Members enjoy full rights to engage in PTA negotiations in services with the partner of their choice. Any such agreement need not raise any legitimacy concerns so long as it respects the legal strictures for WTO compatibility announced in GATS Article V, the provisions of which are reproduced in Appendix 11.1.

---

[8] This is not currently the case of TISA, whose negotiations, as noted above, do not associate the WTO Secretariat nor proceed under the WTO's auspices.

11.4 DETERMINING THE CRITICAL MASS THRESHOLD

A second major interrogation regarding the professed desire of the RGFS to see TISA multilateralized concerns the share of world commercial services trade the agreement could potentially cover. As Table 11.1 below reveals, the 23 countries currently party to the talks accounted for a combined 68.2 percent of world services trade in 2012.[9] Fully 91 percent of this total relates to the services trade of TISA participating countries from the OECD area, with the seven non-OECD countries associated to the talks providing the remaining 9 percent of covered trade. Hong Kong (China) and Chinese Taipei account together for close to nine-tenths (87 percent) of the non-OECD country share, with no other developing country RGFS accounting for more than 0.3 of world exports of commercial services.

It remains an open question whether the above numbers amount to a credible critical mass, an issue that once more does not arise in the context of an Article V services PTA. By comparison, the three critical mass agreements concluded in the WTO to date – the 1996 Information Technology Agreement, the Agreement on Basic Telecommunications and the Financial Services Agreement, the latter two completed in 1997 – were all reached with coverage ratios exceeding 90 percent of total trade in the respective sectors or issue areas at play.

The perception, largely corroborated by Table 11.1 data, that TISA, as currently configured, is chiefly an agreement for and by advanced industrialized nations, once again raises doubts over the smoothness of its possible subsequent multilateralization.

11.5 ARCHITECTURAL DIFFERENCES MATTER

The universe of agreements on trade in services is today almost equally divided between agreements that follow the negotiating modalities of the GATS, which are predicated on a hybrid approach,[10] to scheduling com-

[9] If a subset of WTO Members wished to conclude agreements whose benefits are not extended to all WTO Members, they would need to conclude preferential trade agreements that comply with the conditions laid down in Article V of the GATS or conclude recognition agreements that comply with the conditions set out in Article VII of the GATS.

[10] The hybrid approach to scheduling commitments under the GATS involves the positive choice of sectors, sub- sectors and modes of supply which WTO Members voluntarily choose to place in their schedules, combined with the nega-

Table 11.1 Share of TISA participants in world services trade

TISA Participant	Share of World Exports of Commercial Services Trade (%)
Australia	2.4
Canada	3.5
Chile	0.6
Chinese Taipei	2.1
Colombia	0.2
Costa Rica	0.2
European Union	36.4
Hong Kong, China	5.6
Iceland	0.1
Israel	1.2
Japan	6.6
Korea	4.3
Liechtenstein	0.02
Mexico	0.7
New Zealand	0.5
Norway	1.9
Pakistan	0.2
Panama	0.3
Paraguay	0.04
Peru	0.2
Switzerland	4.4
Turkey	1.8
United States of America	26.9
Share of world total	68.2
Of which: Share of OECD country TISA participants	*91.0*
Share of non-OECD country TISA participants	*9.0*

Source: WTO (2013).

mitments across four distinct modes of service supply and those, slightly more numerous today and which, following the 1994 North American Free Trade Agreement (NAFTA), turned the GATS upside down in pursuing a negative list approach to market opening. In the latter agreements, commitments relate to the preservation, in so-called "reservation

tive listing of limitations maintained in scheduled sectors, sub-sectors or modes of supply.

lists", of *existing* non-conforming (i.e. treaty-inconsistent) measures or the identification (in a separate reservation list) of sectors where scope for the introduction of *future non-conforming measures* can be maintained (the negative list equivalent of an "unbound" sectoral commitment in GATS-like agreements).

Significant experimentation in approaches to market opening has been pursued in recent years in the proliferating set of services PTAs, with combined approaches increasingly common – for instance a negative list approach for investment in services and a positive list approach for cross-border trade or other such variations.[11]

Despite the professed desire of TISA participants to craft an agreement that is compatible with the GATS so as to facilitate its eventual multilateralization, the TISA appears to be clearly departing from GATS practice by proposing to liberalize national treatment-inconsistent measures via a negative list approach, while maintaining a positive list approach for market access commitments. The likely rationale behind such segmentation could well lie in the fact that governments often find it easier to progressively liberalize discriminatory domestic regulations, which typically nonetheless allow for some (constrained) market contestability, than to dismantle quantitative restrictions limiting competition in services markets. The political economy of dismantling quota rents is indeed often more challenging given the political influence of those who hold such rents.

The adoption of such a novel approach to market opening would once more be perfectly feasible and uncontroversial in the context of an Article V agreement given the prevalence of PTA precedence. Its adoption in an agreement slated for subsequent multilateralization would, however, likely give rise to complex problems of legal coexistence and interpretation with regard to existing GATS commitments. This is so to the extent that, as currently holds, a large number of GATS provisions only apply if and when a specific commitment (on national treatment and market access) is scheduled.

Under TISA's proposed segmented approach to scheduling, a number of GATS disciplines – for instance on payments and transfers – would automatically apply to all measures affecting trade and investment in services that are left off the negative list of national treatment-inconsistent measures, but would only be applicable in sectors and modes of supply where positively listed market access commitments were scheduled. Such dualist treatment would appear devoid of any sensible policy rationale,

---

[11] For a fuller discussion of differing negotiating architectures in PTAs, see Mattoo and Sauvé (2011).

all the more so when one considers that the frequency of quantitative restrictions to services trade is typically greater than that of discriminatory measures.

Questions also arise as to the means under TISA to procure future regulatory immunity in respect of discriminatory measures, as the negative list approach to national treatment would solely lock in measures at their *existing* level of non-conformity and oblige signatories to accept that all future measures in the same sector or, more controversially still, in new (future) sectors be automatically bound at free. Such an outcome would in essence require that TISA replicate provisions, common to all negative list PTAs, allowing scope for parties to preserve the right to introduce new non-conforming measures in sectors with acute policy sensitivities. For the European Union, this would be the only means of accepting that TISA covers trade in sectors such as audio-visual, education or health services as the EU could then reserve such entire sectors from the Agreement's scope of coverage. The main policy lesson to be derived from the above discussion is a relatively simple one: the greater the architectural dissonance between TISA and the GATS, the harder the eventual normative migration to the WTO could prove to be.

Rather than pursue an approach to liberalization sure to sow greater confusion and give rise to heightened legal complexity (a likely major private sector turn-off), TISA proponents should rather consider forward-looking ways of remedying a number of the foundational weaknesses of the GATS in regard to scheduling commitments[12] by adopting practices that have been successfully pursued in a number of more recent PTAs, including by the EU in its Economic Partnership Agreement with CARIFORUM Member States.[13]

Were TISA participants genuinely concerned by TISA's subsequent multilateralization, the RGFS could seek to replicate the voluntary, bottom-up, approach to scheduling commitments of the GATS, but condition such an approach on two important qualitative improvements:

---

12 Arguably the greatest weakness of the GATS (and of PTAs predicated on the GATS approach) in respect of its market opening provisions is the fact that the Agreement allows parties to schedule commitments below the regulatory status quo, i.e. to maintain a gap between existing (applied) regulations and what appears in their GATS schedules. This in effect replicates the gap found under GATT between bound and applied tariffs in WTO Members' tariff schedules.

13 For a fuller discussion of the substantive provisions on services found in the EU-CARIFORUM Economic Partnership Agreement, see Sauvé and Ward (2009).

(i) the adoption of a new provision mandating that any commitment voluntarily scheduled lock in the regulatory status quo (i.e. that TISA signatories no longer bind less than the access flowing from *prevailing* regulatory regimes); and
(ii) the incorporation into TISA of country-specific annexes featuring *non-binding* negative lists of non-conforming measures, documenting, solely for transparency-promoting purposes, all treaty-inconsistent measures maintained by parties.

Such a dual approach would largely approximate the good governance and transparency-promoting properties of negative listing and ensure that TISA commitments relate to specific, existing, measures and no longer merely to a GATS-like standard of treatment that may be divorced from prevailing regulatory realities. The production of non-binding negative lists would allow members to conduct useful domestic audits of the optimality of their services regimes while also generating information that could usefully allow for a rank-ordering of measures based on their commercial and negotiating importance. Such an approach would thus generate information of considerable use to policy officials conducting periodic rounds of negotiations, allowing them to devise formula-based approaches to market opening in areas or sectors where the nature and incidence of policy restrictions appears convergent. The transparency gains flowing from such an approach would also yield commercially useful information for private sector users, who would be supplied a full mapping of regulatory restrictions likely to be encountered in foreign markets.

A further, if potentially more controversial, element to ponder in TISA's market opening arsenal could be the adoption of a so-called "ratchet clause", found today in a large number of PTAs (particularly in the Western Hemisphere) and through which unilateral liberalization measures enacted *between* negotiating rounds would automatically be bound at the new level of (lessened) non-conformity under TISA.

11.6 ADDRESSING SENSITIVE SECTORS AND MODES OF SUPPLY

Everybody has ghosts in their closet. For the United States, the maritime sector has historically proven impervious to services trade talks, followed more recently by Mode 4 trade (arguably in violation of Article V, which states that services PTAs should not exclude any mode of supply on an a priori basis).[14] For the EU and Canada, audio-visual services remain no-go zones in services trade, as are publicly funded health and education services in a large number of countries taking part in TISA talks.

Trade in air transport services offers another example of a sector largely immune from the forces of trade negotiating-induced liberalization. This is so despite the globally competitive nature of the industry, the continued need for airline consolidation and the lower cost of capital that a progressive lifting of onerous ownership restrictions would entail, as well as its central importance as a means of ferrying both goods and people (business people and tourists) to market.

The question naturally arises regarding those sectors in which TISA could generate the value-adding WTO+ and WTO-X commitments expected of its chief protagonists. A related question is the likelihood that TISA's political economy, particularly in the absence of large developing countries such as Brazil, India, Indonesia, South Africa or any number of leading ASEAN Member States, will be conducive to putting on the table what has largely stayed off it so far at the WTO and in many PTAs.

There are generally few signs suggesting a major shift in US attitudes towards maritime transport or Mode 4 liberalization,[15] nor would much hope appear to be warranted in the sudden ability of the EU or Canada to drop their long-standing reluctance to revisit the case for market opening in audio-visual or other services with notable public good characteristics. The above questions are equally germane with regard to the probable liberalization harvest of the proposed Transatlantic Trade and Investment Partnership (TTIP). Still, the TISA offers a platform for its participants to try as best they can to push the liberalization envelope in new directions; and the scope for binding commitments may have newly opened up as a result of recent autonomous liberalization, changes in market structures or novel advances in pro-competitive regulation. Sectors that come most prominently to mind in this regard include a wide range of environmental services, energy-related services as well as postal and courier services.

One area where TISA could usefully break new ground would be in testing out novel formula-based approaches to market opening, devising deeper à la carte liberalization packages using model schedules, collective requests to remove selected modal or sector- specific impediments such

[14] No PTA concluded by the United States since its bilateral agreement with Australia in 2004 has featured negotiated commitments on the temporary entry of service providers.

[15] It remains to be seen how the recent terrorist attack in Boston will, alongside continued concerns over white-collar outsourcing, impact ongoing discussions on immigration and temporary work permit reforms in the United States.

as foreign equity limitations or economic needs tests linked to licensing, as well as multi-sectoral clustering – for instance a TISA cluster on trade facilitation services combining transportation, distribution, customs brokerages and associated border management consulting services, warehousing, express delivery and logistics services. Another cluster where forward movement should be conceivable would relate to a package of IT-related business services (including selected professions with accompanying Mode 4), particularly with regard to Mode 1 trade, which could be packaged as the services complement to the WTO's Information Technology Agreement.

Should TISA delve more deeply into new sectors, notably those with network properties, such as waste disposal services, water and energy distribution or rail transportation, participating countries should explore the scope for developing new sets of pro-competitive regulatory disciplines first pioneered in the Uruguay Round's overtime talks on basic telecommunications.

Finally, there would seem every reason for TISA to take stock of the post-Uruguay Round revolution in digital trade and codify the latest set of trade-facilitating, pro-competitive, and net-neutral disciplines aimed at preserving transactional freedoms in cyberspace. This is a terrain that has already been mined extensively in chapters on digital trade in the PTAs of many TISA participants. Such precedents should, once again, facilitate TISA codification. However, in tackling the digital trade agenda, one should not underestimate the scope of a possible transatlantic divide on issues linked to data privacy and IP protection, both of which are salient in discussions of new disciplines on cross-border data flows.

11.7 RULE-MAKING ADVANCES IN TISA

The unfinished rule-making agenda of the GATS is by no means a multilateral monopoly. By and large, such an agenda has yet to be tackled meaningfully at the level of PTAs, with the notable, and commercially important, exception of government procurement in services.

Still, to the extent that a very large number of TISA participants have concluded PTAs in services with each other (see Table 11.2 below), significant (though by no means full) procurement liberalization in services has already been achieved. TISA offers scope for deepening this process, notably at the sub-federal level, but here again one needs to ponder the incentive for the US, Canada, Japan, Australia or any large individual EU Member with a federal political structure to open up this politically sensitive sector in return for reciprocal access to markets that are distinctly

Table 11.2 Existing and planned PTAs in services among TISA partners

TISA negotiating partner	Existing agreements with TISA partners	Agreements under negotiation with TISA partners
Australia (AU)	3 (CHL; NZ; US)	4 (JP; KO; MX; PE)
Canada (CA)	5 (CHL; CO; MX; PE; US)	6 (EU; IC; JP; KO; NO; CH)
Chile (CHL)	16 (AU; CA; CO; CR; EU; HK; IC; JP: KO; MX; NZ; NO; PAN; PE; CH; US)	0
Chinese Taipei (CHT)	1 (PAN)	0
Colombia (CO)	9 (CA; CHL; EU; IC; MX; NO; PE; CH; US)	0
Costa Rica (CR)	6 (CH; EU; MEX; PAN; PE; USA)	0
European Union (EU)	9 (CHL; CO; CR; ICL; KOR; MEX; NOR; PAN; PE)	4 (CA; ISL; JP; US)
Hong Kong China (HK)	5 (CHL; IC; NZ; NO; CH)	0
Iceland (IC)	8 (CHL; CO; EU; HK; KO; MX; NO; CH)	1 (CA)
Israel (ISL)	0	1 (EU)
Japan (JP)	4 (CHL; MX; PE; CH)	7 (AU; CA; CO; EU; KO; NZ; US)
Liechtenstein	8 (CHL; CO; EU; HK; KO; MX; NO; CH)	1 (CA)
Korea (KO)	8 (CHL; CO; EU; IC; NO; PE; CH; US)	5 (AU; CA; JP; MX; NZ)
Mexico (MX)	10 (CHL; CO; CR; EU; IC; JP; NO; PE; CH; US)	3 (AU; KO; NZ)
New Zealand (NZ)	3 (AU; CHL; HK)	5 (JP; KO; MX; PE; US)
Norway (NO)	8 (CHL; CO; EU; HK; IC; KO; MX; CH)	1 (CA)
Pakistan (PK)	0	0
Panama (PAN)	6 (CHL; CHT; CR; EU; PE; US)	0
Paraguay (PAR)	0	0
Peru (PE)	10 (CA; CHL; CO; CR; EU; JP; KO; MX; PAN; US)	2 (AU; NZ)
Switzerland (CH)	8 (CHL; CO; HKC; IC; JP; KO; MX; NO)	1 (CA)
Turkey (TU)	0	0
United States (US)	9 (AU; CA; CHL; CO; CR; KO; MX; PAN; PE)	3 (EU; JP; NZ)

Source: Author's calculations based on Marchetti and Roy (2013).

smaller in size and where market opening talks have already proceeded in most instances. Indeed, the issue of services procurement already is or will soon be at the core of ongoing bilateral negotiations between key TISA partners, notably the EU, Canada, the US, Australia and Japan (including under the TPP and the TTIP).

PTAs to date have shown a limited capacity to make headway beyond procurement on the unfinished agenda of the GATS. This reflects a clear (and recurring) revealed preference for regulatory inaction on issues such as subsidy disciplines or emergency safeguard measures, where many TISA participants remain deeply skeptical, including on feasibility grounds.

Some progress could however be expected on the issue of non-discriminatory domestic regulation, but more along the lines of DDA discussions on greater transparency than in the direction of the development of a full-blown necessity test for services.

The reluctance of large players such as the US, Canada and the EU to do for services what they have long done for goods trade under technical barriers to trade (TBT) and sanitary/phyto-sanitary (SPS) disciplines remains paradoxical, all the more so as the US and the EU, as the world's leading exporters of services, remain the most likely victims of needlessly burdensome or disproportionate regulatory conduct in foreign markets. Doubts can legitimately be expressed as to whether TISA could meaningfully break the above rule-making logjam, a rare instance where the quest for regulatory immunity trumps industry interests.

Meanwhile, it is worth recalling that some of TISA's strongest protagonists seem to attach an importance to regulatory transparency that is perhaps more rhetorical than real if the number of services measures notified under Article III.3 of the GATS is anything to go by. Since 2000, the US, the EU, Canada and Australia have collectively notified four new measures affecting their GATS commitments, as opposed to 60 each for Switzerland and China and 120 for Albania!

11.8 TENTATIVE CONCLUSIONS

It is possible to express genuine concerns about a negotiating process while still hoping it can garner useful forward-looking traction. This is very much the predicament one faces in looking at TISA.

The substantive merits of a proposed TISA would be easy to applaud if it the negotiations were presented for what they truly are more clearly from the outset: as the potentially largest GATS Article V PTA in services concluded to date. Meanwhile, and based on the limited information that has filtered out to date on the nascent plurilateral talks, a number of genuine reservations may be advanced, both procedural and substantive in nature, that the Agreement being devised could easily or anytime soon be incorporated into the WTO architecture and coexist alongside the GATS (let alone replace it). That there is no precedent for such coexistence in the GATT-WTO history should already be a cause for concern to TISA protagonists.

The world economy as a whole and every WTO Member for that matter, regardless of income level, stand to gain from greater, more transparent and progressively more liberal trade and investment conditions in services markets. Services are central to all that an economy produces, exports, and invests in, such that an inefficient service sector represents a perverse tax on economy-wide efficiency. The growing acceptance of this central economic reality has fueled unprecedented autonomous liberalization in services markets around the globe in recent decades.[16] Trade agreements, and especially the GATS, have not yet proven adept at locking in such autonomous policy virtue. In the case of the GATS, broader negotiating dynamics in the Doha Round may well have exerted the largest inhibiting influence.

Progress in *negotiated* market opening in services markets has been significantly greater in PTAs to date, if far from complete and still uneven across sectors. Table 11.3 below documents the implicit preference margins that hold across service sectors. It does so by comparing the Uruguay Round commitments of WTO Members, their latest Doha Round offer as well as the most liberal treatment on offer in such members' latest PTAs.[17]

The advent of TISA represents a genuine opportunity to further advance the cause of preferential liberalization in services markets among a coalition of countries representing close to seven-tenths of the global market. While this remains significantly less than that which was achieved in recent plurilateral agreements brokered at the WTO, it is far from trivial in potential market access terms.

Moreover, the TISA talks have rekindled marked interest on the part of private operators and industry associations in championing negotiated market opening, recalling at times the early feverish days of the Uruguay Round.[18] Failure to respond to such renewed private sector engagement would represent an unfortunate missed opportunity. Yet, in pursuing TISA, greater attention needs to be paid to the negotiating atmospherics and concrete steps taken to promote far greater inclusiveness, including

[16] See Schott and Muir (2012) and Ghani and Kharas (2010).

[17] For a fuller discussion, see Marchetti and Roy (2009), Mattoo and Sauvé (2011) and Sauvé and Shingal (2011).

[18] See World Trade Report (2013).

Table 11.3 Implicit margins of preference in services trade: comparing the level of services trade liberalization across sectors

Sectors	GATS	DDA Offers (0 to 100)	PTAs	GATS/ PTAs (%)	DDA/ PTAs (%)	Preference Margin
Professional	30	39	67	45	58	42–55
Computer	55	74	93	59	80	20–41
Postal/Courier	14	20	53	26	38	62–74
Telecoms	51	58	80	64	73	28–36
Audio-visual	17	20	50	34	40	60–66
Construction	40	46	75	53	61	39–47
Distribution	32	41	76	42	54	46–58
Education	18	25	57	32	44	56–68
Environmental	20	30	62	32	48	52–68
Financial	36	40	53	68	75	25–32
Health	8	11	34	24	32	68–76
Tourism	51	61	83	61	73	27–39
Maritime	12	23	57	21	40	60–79
Rail	14	20	52	27	38	62–73
Road	16	18	56	29	32	68–71
Aux. Transport	21	24	58	36	41	59–64

Source: Sauvé and Shingal, Chapter 10 in this volume.

on the part of the WTO secretariat in an observer capacity, than has been the case so far.

At a critical juncture for the WTO and the DDA, one may legitimately ponder the systemic implications of the proposed TISA and question the incentives its completion would entail for the DDA's services talks should agreement be reached among the RGFS grouping.

This chapter has suggested a number of relatively simple corrective gestures that could be taken to ensure that the negotiating process is more genuinely inclusive and transparent and does not needlessly pit developing countries against the predominantly OECD-centric RGFS grouping in a manner that could prove inimical to the confidence, goodwill and cooperation that will need to be supplied in vastly greater quantities for the DDA to be completed and for the WTO's credibility as a liberalizing legislature to be restored. TISA participants could furthermore adopt approaches to liberalization and rule-making with a view to facilitating, rather than hindering, the process of eventual anchoring in the WTO. This chapter has advanced a few practical ideas to this end.

Looking ahead, plurilateralism and variable geometry approaches to rule-making and market opening are likely to prove important ways of keeping the WTO relevant, of sustaining the multilateral bicycle's forward journey, while also acknowledging the increasing diversity of collective preferences – and concomitant interests and abilities – among a membership made up overwhelmingly today of developing countries whose primary export interests may not always lie in services (even as their infrastructural import needs should prompt greater engagement in services talks).

Whenever possible, WTO Members should explore and pursue, under one common roof, the scope that exists for flexible approaches to rule-making and market opening commanding adequate critical mass. Pursuing plurilateral outcomes in an open setting that allows for economies of scale and learning is not the same thing as negotiating behind closed doors. History has not been kind to the latter initiatives.

An important final question, not addressed in this chapter but germane in the context of the ongoing discussion on a trade in services waiver for least developed countries (LDCs), is whether TISA outcomes should be extended automatically and unconditionally to LDCs on a non-reciprocal basis.

REFERENCES

European Commission (2013), "Negotiations for a Plurilateral Agreement on Trade in Services", Europa Communiqués de Presse, Memo/13/107, Brussels: European Commission (15 February 2013). Available at http://europa.eu/rapid/press-release_MEMO-13–107_en.htm.

Ghani, E. and H. Kharas (2010), "The Services Revolution", *Economic Premise*, No. 14, Washington, DC: the World Bank. Available at http://siteresources.worldbank.org/INTPREMNET/Resources/EP14.pdf.

Harbinson, Stuart and Bart de Meester (2012), "A 21st Century Work Program for the Multilateral Trading System", Washington, DC: National Foreign Trade Council. Available at http://www.nftc.org/default/trade/WTO/NFTC21stCenturyTradeAgenda2012.pdf.

Horn, H., P. Mavroidis and A. Sapir (2008), *Beyond the WTO? An Anatomy of EU and US Preferential Trade Agreements*, Bruegel Blueprint Series, Volume VII, Brussels: Bruegel.

Hufbauer, G.C., J. Bradford Jensen and S. Stephenson (2012), "Framework for the International Services Agreement", *Policy Brief*, Number 10–12 (April), Washington, DC: Peterson Institute for International Economics.

Marchetti, J. and M. Roy (2009), *Opening Markets for Trade in Services: Countries and Sectors in Bilateral and WTO Negotiations*, Cambridge: Cambridge University Press.

Marchetti, J. and M. Roy (2013), "The TISA Initiative: An Overview of

Market Access Issues", *WTO Discussion Paper*, Geneva: World Trade Organization.
Mattoo, A. and P. Sauvé (2011), "Services", in Chauffour, J.-P. and J.-C. Maur, eds., *Preferential Trade Agreement Policies for Development: A Handbook*, Washington, DC: The World Bank, pp. 235–74.
Sauvé, P. and A. Shingal (2011), "Reflections on the Preferential Liberalization of Services Trade", *Journal of World Trade*, 45(5), 953–63.
Sauvé, P. and N. Ward (2009), "The EC-CARIFORUM Economic Partnership Agreement: Assessing the Progress on Services and Investment", ECIPE Paper, Brussels: European Centre for International Political Economy, (January). Available at http://www.ecipe.org/publications/ecipe-working-papers/the-ec-cariform-economic- partnership-agreement-assessing-the-outcome-on-services-and-investment.
Schott, J. and J. Muir (2012), "Prospects for Services Trade Negotiations", Peterson Institute for International Economics Working Paper 12–17 (October), Washington, DC: Peterson Institute for International Economics.
World Trade Organization (2013), *International Trade Statistics 2012*, Geneva: World Trade Organization. Available online at: http://www.wto.org/english/res_e/statis_e/its2012_e/its12_toc_e.htm.
World Trade Report (2013), "USTR Receives Comments on Proposed International Services Agreement", Washington, DC: World Trade Report, 29(8) (4 March).

APPENDIX: ARTICLE V OF THE GATS (ECONOMIC INTEGRATION)

Article V Economic Integration

1. This Agreement shall not prevent any of its Members from being a party to or entering into an agreement liberalizing trade in services between or among the parties to such an agreement, provided that such an agreement:
   (a) has substantial sectoral coverage,[19] and
   (b) provides for the absence or elimination of substantially all discrimination, in the sense of Article XVII, between or among the parties, in the sectors covered under subparagraph (a), through:
      (i) elimination of existing discriminatory measures, and/or
      (ii) prohibition of new or more discriminatory measures, either at the entry into force of that agreement or on the basis of a reasonable time-frame, except for measures permitted under Articles XI, XII, XIV and XIV bis.

2. In evaluating whether the conditions under paragraph 1(b) are met, consideration may be given to the relationship of the agreement to a wider process of economic integration or trade liberalization among the countries concerned.
3. (a) Where developing countries are parties to an agreement of the type referred to in paragraph 1, flexibility shall be provided for regarding the conditions set out in paragraph 1, particularly with reference to subparagraph (b) thereof, in accordance with the level of development of the countries concerned, both overall and in individual sectors and subsectors.
   (b) Notwithstanding paragraph 6, in the case of an agreement of the type referred to in paragraph 1 involving only developing countries, more favorable treatment may be granted to juridical persons owned or controlled by natural persons of the parties to such an agreement.
4. Any agreement referred to in paragraph 1 shall be designed to facilitate trade between the parties to the agreement and shall not in respect of any Member outside the agreement raise the overall level of barriers to trade in services within the respective sectors or subsectors compared to the level applicable prior to such an agreement.
5. If, in the conclusion, enlargement or any significant modification of any agreement under paragraph 1, a Member intends to withdraw or modify a specific commitment inconsistently with the terms and conditions set out in its Schedule, it shall provide at least 90 days advance notice of such modification or withdrawal and the procedure set forth in paragraphs 2, 3 and 4 of Article XXI shall apply.

---

19 This condition is understood in terms of number of sectors, volume of trade affected and modes of supply. In order to meet this condition, agreements should not provide for the a priori exclusion of any mode of supply.

6. A service supplier of any other Member that is a juridical person constituted under the laws of a party to an agreement referred to in paragraph 1 shall be entitled to treatment granted under such agreement, provided that it engages in substantive business operations in the territory of the parties to such agreement.
7. (a) Members which are parties to any agreement referred to in paragraph 1 shall promptly notify any such agreement and any enlargement or any significant modification of that agreement to the Council for Trade in Services. They shall also make available to the Council such relevant information as may be requested by it. The Council may establish a working party to examine such an agreement or enlargement or modification of that agreement and to report to the Council on its consistency with this Article.
   (b) Members which are parties to any agreement referred to in paragraph 1 which is implemented on the basis of a time-frame shall report periodically to the Council for Trade in Services on its implementation. The Council may establish a working party to examine such reports if it deems such a working party necessary.
   (c) Based on the reports of the working parties referred to in subparagraphs (a) and (b), the Council may make recommendations to the parties as it deems appropriate.
8. A Member which is a party to any agreement referred to in paragraph 1 may not seek compensation for trade benefits that may accrue to any other Member from such agreement.

Index